Cracking the
SAT
Subject Test™
in World History

2nd Edition

The Staff of The Princeton Review

PrincetonReview.com

The Princeton Review
555 W. 18th Street
New York, NY 10011
E-mail: editorialsupport@review.com

Published in the United States by
Penguin Random House LLC, New York,
and in Canada by Random House of Canada,
a division of Penguin Random House Ltd., Toronto.

ISBN: 978-1-5247-1084-2
eBook ISBN: 978-1-5247-1099-6
ISSN: 2374-2771

SAT Subject Test is a trademark of the College
Board, which is not affiliated with
The Princeton Review.

The Princeton Review is not affiliated with Princeton
University.

Editor: Colleen Day
Production Editors: Lee Elder and Liz Rutzel
Production Artist: Bob McKeehen

Printed in the United States of America on partially
recycled paper.

10 9 8 7 6 5 4 3 2 1

2nd Edition

Editorial
Rob Franek, Editor-in-Chief
Casey Cornelius, VP Content Development
Mary Beth Garrick, Director of Production
Selena Coppock, Managing Editor
Meave Shelton, Senior Editor
Colleen Day, Editor
Sarah Litt, Editor
Aaron Riccio, Editor
Orion McBean, Associate Editor

Penguin Random House Publishing Team
Tom Russell, VP, Publisher
Alison Stoltzfus, Publishing Director
Jake Eldred, Associate Managing Editor
Ellen Reed, Production Manager
Suzanne Lee, Designer

Acknowledgments

Special thanks to Adam Robinson, who conceived of and perfected the Joe Bloggs approach to standardized tests and many of the other successful techniques used by The Princeton Review.

The Princeton Review would like to extend special thanks to Brooks Barber and Kevin Kelly for their contributions to this edition, as well as Jonathan Chiu for his expert guidance. Thank you also to Bob McKeehen, Lee Elder, and Liz Rutzel for their time and attention to each page.

Contents

Get More (Free) Content viii

Part I: Orientation 1

1   Knowing the Basics 3

2   Learning the Techniques 11

3   Cracking the Test 19

Part II: Practice Test 1 33

    Practice Test 1 35

    Practice Test 1: Answers and Explanations 53

Part III: Content Review for the SAT Subject Test in World History 75

4   The Rise of Human Civilization 77

    Humanity's Prehistory: A Brief Review 78

    Ancient Mesopotamia 81

    Ancient Egypt 87

    Ancient Africa 91

    Ancient India 93

    Ancient China 97

    The Outsiders: The Americas 101

    Major Civilizations: Mesoamerica 102

    Civilization: A Human Characteristic 104

    Chapter 4 Key Terms, People, and Events 106

    Summary 107

    Chapter 4 Drill 108

5   From Civilizations to Empires 111

    How Do We Know an Empire When We See It? 112

    Persia: The First Great Empire? 114

    Greece: From Polis to Empire 118

    Rome in a Few Brief Pages? Can't Be Done! 127

    Byzantium: The Eastern Empire 132

    China: Empire, the Chinese Way 133

    India: Empires of the Subcontinent 137

    The Americas: Hello? Anyone There? 139

    Learning from the Rise and Fall of Empires 140

    Chapter 5 Key Terms, People, and Events 141

    Summary 142

    Chapter 5 Drill 143

6   The Age of World Religions 145

Why Study Religion? 146

The Importance of Religion to World History 146

Judaism 147

Early Christianity 152

Islam 156

Inter- and Intrareligious Conflicts 159

Eastern Religions 162

Hinduism 162

Buddhism 164

Shinto 166

Eastern vs. Western Religions 167

Chapter 6 Key Terms, People, and Events 168

Summary 169

Chapter 6 Drill 170

7   World Civilizations in Transition: 1000 to 1500 173

1000–1500: An Age of Transition 174

Europe: From Rome to Renaissance 174

The Renaissance: Europe Rekindles Its Greek and Roman Heritage ... 182

The Transformation of Trade and Society 185

Islamic Empires from East to West: Caliphate Life 190

Toward the Far East 192

The Americas 195

Chapter 7 Key Terms, People, and Events 198

Summary 199

Chapter 7 Drill 200

8   The Modern World Emerges: 1500 to 1900 203

Why the Emphasis on Europe? 204

Europe in the Age of Revolutions 205

The Middle East: The Europeans Are Coming! 222

The Far East: Asia Slowly Opens Its Doors 222

The Americas: Independence in the 19th Century 228

Africa: The Short End of the Colonial Stick 228

Chapter 8 Key Terms, People, and Events 230

Summary 232

Chapter 8 Drill 234

9   War and Peace: 1900 to Present 237

    The 20th Century: The Progress Paradox 238

    Europe: War, Recovery, and Reconciliation 240

    Another War to End All Wars 245

    Postwar Europe, 1945 to 1990 250

    Middle East: An Empire Falls, Nations Emerge 253

    China: The Path from Communism to Capitalism 255

    Japan: From Empire to Capitalism 257

    Korea and Vietnam: Cold War Battlegrounds 258

    India: Independence, Partition, Industrialization 261

    The Americas 263

    Africa's Long Colonial Ailment: Corruption, Chaos, and Conflict 265

    The 20th Century: Continuity and Change 267

    Chapter 9 Key Terms, People, and Events 268

    Summary 270

    Chapter 9 Drill 271

Part IV: Chapter Drill Answers and Explanations 273

    Chapter 4 Drill Answers and Explanations 275

    Chapter 5 Drill Answers and Explanations 278

    Chapter 6 Drill Answers and Explanations 280

    Chapter 7 Drill Answers and Explanations 282

    Chapter 8 Drill Answers and Explanations 284

    Chapter 9 Drill Answers and Explanations 287

Part V: Practice Test 2 289

    Practice Test 2 291

    Practice Test 2: Answers and Explanations 311

Get More (Free) Content

1 Go to **PrincetonReview.com/cracking.**

2 Enter the following ISBN for your book: 9781524710842.

3 Answer a few simple questions to set up an exclusive Princeton Review account. (If you already have one, you can just log in.)

4 Click the "Student Tools" button, also found under "My Account" from the top toolbar. You're all set to access your bonus content!

Need to report a potential **content** issue?

Contact **EditorialSupport@review.com.**
Include:

- full title of the book
- ISBN number
- page number

Need to report a **technical** issue?

Contact **TPRStudentTech@review.com**
and provide:

- your full name
- email address used to register the book
- full book title and ISBN
- computer OS (Mac/PC) and browser (Firefox, Safari, etc.)

The **Princeton Review**®

Once you've registered, you can...

- Take a full-length practice SAT and/or ACT

- Get valuable advice about the college application process, including tips for writing a great essay and where to apply for financial aid

- If you're still choosing between colleges, use our searchable rankings of *The Best 382 Colleges* to find out more information about your dream school.

- Access comprehensive study guides and a variety of printable resources, including additional bubble sheets, end-of-chapter Key Terms lists, and more

- Check to see if there have been any corrections or updates to this edition

- Get our take on any recent or pending updates to the SAT Subject Test in World History

Look For These Icons Throughout The Book

 ONLINE ARTICLES

 PROVEN TECHNIQUES

 APPLIED STRATEGIES

 COLLEGE ADVISOR APP

 MORE GREAT BOOKS

Part I
Orientation

1   Knowing the Basics
2   Learning the Techniques
3   Cracking the Test

Chapter 1
Knowing the Basics

The SAT Subject Tests are a series of one-hour exams that are part of the SAT Program of the College Board. Unlike the SAT, the SAT Subject Tests are designed to measure knowledge in specific subjects such as biology, history, French, and math. They are scored separately on a 200–800 scale.

How Are SAT Subject Tests Used by College Admissions?

Because the tests are given in specific areas, colleges use them as another piece of admissions information and, in some cases, to decide whether applicants can be exempted from college requirements. For example, a certain score may excuse you from a basic English class or a foreign language requirement.

Should I Take the SAT Subject Tests?

Schools have varying policies when it comes to Subject Tests; they may be required or recommended for admission or certain majors and programs of study. Your first order of business is to start reading those college catalogs and websites. College guidebooks, admission offices, and school counselors should have the information you need to keep up with the changes.

As to which tests you should take, the answer is simple. Take the SAT Subject Tests

- on which you will do well
- that may be required by the colleges to which you are applying

The best possible situation, of course, is when you can achieve both goals with the same Subject Test.

Some colleges have specific requirements; others do not. **Again, start asking questions before you start taking tests.** Once you find out which tests, if any, are required or recommended, determine which will showcase your particular strengths. Colleges that require specific tests generally recommend that you take two subject tests from the following five groups: laboratory science, history, foreign language, math, and English.

When Should I Take Them?

SAT Subject Tests are generally offered in October, November, December, May, June, and August at test sites across the country. Not all subjects are offered at each administration, so check the dates carefully. You can take up to three Subject Tests per test date.

The ideal time to take an SAT Subject Test is when the material is freshest in your mind. So, in the case of World History, take the Subject Test while you're taking a world history course in school, or soon after the course ends. Don't postpone the test until the following year.

Check out The Princeton Review's entire series of review books for the SAT Subject Tests.

How Do I Register for These Tests?

Most students choose to register for Subject Tests on the College Board website at www.collegeboard.org. If you do not have access to the Internet, you can pick up a copy of the registration form (usually available in your school counselor's office) and register by regular mail.

What's a Good Score?

A good score is a score that fits within the range of scores your colleges of choice usually look for or accept. However, if your score falls below the normal range for Podunk University, that doesn't necessarily mean you won't get in or won't exempt from a core course. Schools are often fairly flexible in what they are willing to look at as a "good" score for a certain student. Why? Each student brings a different set of qualities that schools are interested in. The more qualities/extracurriculars/recommendations/hobbies/world conquest plans you have that a college desires, the more lenient that school will be in evaluating your SAT Subject Test in World History.

What Is Score Choice™?

Score Choice allows you to choose which SAT Subject Test scores you want colleges to see, at no additional cost. This is great news! For one thing, if you take more than one SAT Subject Test on a given date, you'll be able to choose which tests from that date you'd like to submit to colleges. For example, if you take the World History test followed by the French test, but you don't think that the French test went very well, you can simply opt out of having that French scores sent to your schools.

This score-reporting policy is optional for students. This means that you aren't required to opt in and actively choose which specific scores you would like sent to colleges. If you decide not to use Score Choice, then all of the scores on file will automatically be sent when you request score reports.

For more information about this score-reporting policy, visit the College Board website at https://collegereadiness.collegeboard.org/sat/scores.

Why Read This Book?

You could certainly take the SAT Subject Test in World History today and get some of the questions right. But you'd probably miss a good portion of the questions you could have gotten right if you understood test taking a little better.

You could also review all of your old World History assignments, hoping they'd be less boring this time around. Unfortunately, no: They're still boring. You could even try one of those gargantuan study guides, crammed with ten thousand little

The best way to improve your score is to learn *how* to take the SAT Subject Test in World History.

Visit the College Board's website, collegeboard.org, for more information and practice questions.

snippets of information. But you'd still miss a good portion of the questions you could have gotten right if you just understood how to take the test.

You may be sensing a pattern: The ONLY way to beat a standardized test is to develop a system or a strategy that allows you to answer the questions correctly and get a higher score. Don't be haphazard in your approach to the test: The secret is to learn to work and study methodically. Knowledge of world history will, of course, help you out. But to answer the questions, it isn't so much what you know as *how you apply* your knowledge.

The SAT Subject Test in World History is not just about knowing history. In other words, getting a good score in this test depends upon more than just the depth of your history knowledge or scholastic abilities. Scoring high on this test, or frankly any other standardized test, comes down to the sharpness of your test-taking abilities. But don't be intimidated—this is actually absurdly good news. Why? Because the simple skills of test-taking, which you can master quickly, will put YOU—not the College Board—in the captain's seat!

This is where The Princeton Review comes in. As your flight instructors, our mission is to understand, analyze, and simulate standardized tests so we can help students beat those tests and make their scores soar. We may base our flight plan on the College Board's maneuvers, but you, the student, have always been our co-pilot. This book, and The Princeton Review in general, is a blend of our own knowledge of all things test prep and your feedback. Each revision to this book over the years is a direct result of OUR own research into the SAT Subject Test in World History and YOUR comments as to what you'd like to see more or less of in each iteration. With this in mind, over the next few pages we'll explain our core beliefs on the SAT Subject Test in World History and how you can use this book to crack the exam.

The Test Balances Facts with Concepts

Mastering the SAT Subject Test in World History requires a combination of both factual knowledge and a basic understanding of historical concepts and general themes. Some questions are very straightforward, asking you simply to identify people, places, documents, or events. Other questions require you to reason your way to an answer using a combination of factual and conceptual knowledge. Therefore, it isn't enough to know who Aung San Suu Kyi was; you should also be sure to be able to identify why she was important. Context is key!

However, there is one more very important part to doing well on the test: you need to understand how the test writers construct the test, the questions, and especially the answers so you can avoid traps and use Process of Elimination (POE) to find answers. Remember, no one is born a good or bad test taker. A good test taker realizes the importance of both what to expect from a test and how to deal with the information.

The Test Is a Treasure Hunt and This Book Is the Map

Picture a good SAT Subject Test in World History book as a treasure map. If the map is too vague, you may get a general sense of where the treasure is, but you will not have enough specific information to reach the exact spot of the treasure. On the other hand, if the map is covered top to bottom with ultra-specific details and an over-abundance of little factoids, you may not be able to follow the general route to get the treasure.

This book aims to strike a balance: enough content to make the sharp lefts and rights when you need to, but with a broad enough view to make sure you always know the general direction you should be headed.

If you learn

- that the test is predictable
- that you need to balance factoids with concepts
- how the test writers write the test

...then you will negotiate every turn on your treasure hunt with both the knowledge and techniques necessary, and earn your reward (a much higher score)!

How to Use This Book

The last piece of your orientation to *Cracking the SAT Subject Test in World History* is an overview of what's to come, and how to use it to ensure your highest possible score. While you can view the contents of this book in any order, it is highly recommended you follow this book in the order listed below. Each major part of this book has some direct relevance to the next piece. In other words, it is unlikely you will get the most out of each section without having read the previous section.

Step 1: Learn How to Take and Crack the Test

The next two chapters in Part I deal with learning the basics of the World History exam itself and then cracking the questions that appear on the exam. No matter what you intend to use this book for or your current level of history knowledge, it is crucial you complete Part I before going anywhere else—this is where you will learn our test-taking techniques.

Step 2: Take and Score Practice Test 1

In Part II you'll find Practice Test 1, along with its answers and explanations and a scoring guide. We encourage you to use this test as a diagnostic and take it before diving into the content review chapters in Part III. This way, you can assess your strengths and weaknesses and determine what areas you need to focus on as you review. Time yourself for one uninterrupted hour, and then review the answers and explanations. Score the exam per the instructions in the scoring guide to figure out how close you came to your target score (the range accepted by your school or schools.) If you exceeded it, fantastic! If you met it, great! If you didn't, don't worry! No matter what happened, your goal should be to improve on the second test.

Step 3: Review the History, Practice the Questions, and Learn the Fact Lists

Part III is a fairly comprehensive review of world history. In those chapters, we include a wealth of information, including some of the more relevant factoids that are likely to appear on the exam. The chapters are divided into time periods that reflect similar changes in civilizations throughout the world, which will be important for a concept we call "Era-Based Thinking" later on. Remember that we need to balance facts with concepts so knowing how a religion affected multiple cultures can be just as or more important than knowing the who, what, when, and where concerning that religion.

At the conclusion of each chapter, you'll find a drill directly related to the content in that chapter. All drill questions have explanations, which you may check in Part IV. These questions are great indicators of both your mastery of the content and of our techniques. View each chapter as a single "assignment," so to speak. Ideally, you should attempt the drill as soon as possible after reading the chapter to assess what you've retained and what you still need to review.

Finally, there are boxes throughout each chapter highlighting important people, places, events, and dates. The purpose of these fact lists is to build your understanding of era-based concepts and to compare and contrast ideas and information like major world religions. Studying the fact lists within each chapter will help you see the information in context—this way, the next part of the book will make even more sense.

Step 4: Take and Score Practice Test 2

After reading the content review chapters, taking the end-of-chapter drills, and studying the key terms, summaries, and fact lists, take Practice Test 2 in Part V. Score your exam using the scoring guide, and compare your results to that of Practice Test 1. Note the areas where you improved as well as any topics where you continue to struggle.

Step 5: Review the Necessary Content

Go back and review any material you are still having trouble with. Preparing for a test is a process, and there's a lot to remember when it comes to world history, so don't be discouraged if it takes some time for facts to stick. Just keep reviewing Part III, studying our test-taking techniques, and quizzing yourself with the end-of-chapter drills. You may even want to take a second stab at one or both of the practice tests. Review in whatever way works best for you—just keep practicing.

Our Job and Your Job

This book is designed to help you raise your SAT Subject Test in World History score. It's written, it's published, and you're holding it in your hands. That means our job is done. Your job is to read it, study it, tackle the questions and practice tests, and learn what it has to teach. We had fun doing our job, and believe it or not, you'll have fun doing yours. So let the fun begin!

Want to know which colleges are best for you? Check out The Princeton Review's College Advisor app to build your ideal college list and find your perfect college fit! Available for free in the iOS App Store and Google Play Store.

Chapter 2
Learning the Techniques

To beat the SAT Subject Test in World History, it's important to understand era-based thinking, pacing, and guessing.

Break the continuum of history into easily digestible chunks!

THINK "ERA" FOR ERROR-FREE THINKING

History is a long continuum of time consisting of many overlapping events and people, some of which had a greater impact than others. It is easy to be intimidated by all of the stuff you have to know or THINK you have to know. But you don't have to remember all of this information as one historically jumbled mess.

The easiest way to think about the thousands of years of world history is to break the continuum into bite-sized chunks. This book will refer to each period, each chunk of history, as an era. You can organize all the facts you know into eras, or historical time slots. Just keep all the tidbits of information in a particular time period under one heading in your mind (and in your notes). The heading should be some name—a person, an event, a war—that reminds you of the era. When you have the vast and varied information organized into only a few important eras, you will find it easier to recall the material on the test.

The content review chapters in Part III of this book are organized into eras and designed to give you the information you need to know about each time period. From now on, whenever you learn anything about a certain time period, file it away in your brain vault under the title of its era. In fact, you probably already do this for some time periods.

Think of the Indian Independence Movement

What comes to mind? Maybe it's Mahatma Gandhi, Queen Victoria, nonviolent civil disobedience, or the Hindustan Socialist Republican Association. Or perhaps you're thinking of Bengal and Punjab, the Quit India Act, the Salt March and those Christmas Island and Royal Indian Navy mutinies. Whatever you remember is helpful; the specifics don't really matter. The point is when you think of the Indian Independence Movement, you should automatically recall some key events and people connected to that time.

Now answer this question.

This question may seem specific, but you need to know only the important details to answer it.

1. Which of the following was immediately responsible for precipitating India's independence from British control?

    (A) Gandhi's campaign of targeted destruction of British facilities
    (B) A campaign of nonviolent protest against Britain during World War II
    (C) The partition of the Indian territory into India and Paskistan
    (D) The chaos following the assassination of Mahatma Ghandi
    (E) Anticolonial terms imposed on the Allies by the Treaty of Paris

The era in this question is early- to middle-20th century, and it concerns India's independence. You should be looking for the key themes in this era: societal upheaval, World War II, nationalism, and specific to India, Gandhi's nonviolent civil disobedience and its contrast to the violent protests of groups like the HSRA. With that in mind, (A) should be eliminated because if we know one thing about Gandhi, he never endorsed a "campaign of targeted destruction of British facilities." Choice (E) should also be eliminated, because who won World War II, exactly? Right, the Allies—so it's pretty unlikely they'd allow "anticolonial terms" to be imposed on them at the Treaty of Paris—hardly seems like a smart call.

That leaves us with (B), (C), and (D). All three of them seem like something that has to do with India or its independence. The question, however, contains a very important word: precipitating, which means causing or bringing about. So, the question isn't looking for something that happened after India's independence. Gandhi was assassinated a year *after* India was independent, so his death couldn't have brought about independence. There goes (D). As for the partitioning, you may remember it officially occurred after India's independence. A geographic partition was in place beforehand, but this didn't bring about India's independence—the partition existed to separate multiple groups who had already participated in escalating violence. There goes (C). Choice (B) is the best answer, as it matches what we were already pretty sure about—Gandhi championed nonviolent protest and was the biggest name in the Indian independence movement.

The example sounds like a specific question, but you really didn't have to know too many details about the Indian independence movement in order to answer it. You had to only think about the key figures and themes from that time, and then choosing the best answer to fit the era.

PACING YOURSELF

Any standardized test is an endurance test, the academic equivalent of running a two-mile race over hurdles. The SAT Subject Test in World History contains 95 multiple-choice questions to be completed in 60 minutes. That leaves you with about 40 seconds per question. The fact is, you may run out of time and not be able to finish all of the questions.

Don't worry. It's okay to run out of time, but you must *pace yourself*. Pacing means balancing speed with accuracy. You need to get to as many questions as you can, but not so many that you get them all wrong because you are working too quickly. Use the Two-Pass System to choose which questions to answer and which questions to skip for the time being. Pacing may also mean that you spend a few extra seconds on a question you think you can get right. Basically, it means choosing questions according to your own strengths and weaknesses, not according to how SAT Subject Test writers arrange them on the exam.

Use the Two-Pass System
Answering 95 questions in 60 minutes—are they kidding? Give yourself a break; approach the test with the Two-Pass System. On your first pass through the questions, skip any questions along the way that you can't answer or that you think will take some time. Then, take a second pass through the test to do the remaining questions. The Two-Pass System will keep you from getting bogged down and losing time!

You certainly want to finish the test, but you want to do so on your own terms. To get you started, we've provided you with a pacing chart for the exam. Be careful: when the pacing chart suggests that you leave up to 10 questions blank, those 10 should not necessarily be the *last* 10 on the test. There could be several easy questions among the last 10, so be sure to get to them. Of those hypothetical 10 questions, you want to leave blank only those questions that have you completely stumped. For each of the other questions, if you can safely eliminate even one answer choice, you should guess; we'll explain why in the section on scoring a little later. Maybe you'll skip five questions in the first 80–85 problems, and then quickly decide which of the five or so out of the last 10 questions to come back to is there is some time left.

The pacing chart shows you how many questions you need to get right and how many you can afford to miss in order to achieve your target score. Tailor these charts to your own test-taking style as much as possible. When you take the practice tests in this book, pay attention to your strengths and weaknesses.

- **Do you start out great and then lag in the middle of the test?** You may be losing focus. Practicing the endurance aspect of the exam by taking our practice tests to condition yourself for 95 questions in 60 minutes is a good way to address this issue.
- **Do you tend to get stuck on a question and then spend too much time on it?** Be more aware of when you do this so you can make a quick decision to guess on that question if you've eliminated at least one answer, or skip it if you've eliminated none. Either way, move on!
- **Did you misread the question?** You may have been moving too quickly. You want to balance accuracy and speed—You want to get questions right slowly rather than wrong quickly, even if it means you have to aggressively guess on some to buy yourself that time.
- **Did you pick a choice that didn't make sense within the era of that question?** You may need to review that era. Be sure to say to yourself, "What era *should* this piece of information have been filed under?"

After you take each practice test, be sure to spend some time analyzing what questions you missed and asking yourself, "Why?" This way you can concentrate on NOT making the same mistakes on the real exam.

It is in your best interest to "eyeball" every question in the test. How else will you know if you should try it?

Test Tip

It's crucial to keep track of any questions you skip so you don't make errors filling in your answer sheet. To practice, use the bubble sheets provided at the end of this book, or download and print out as many copies as you like——you can find a blank bubble sheet in your online Student Tools when you register your book! Follow the steps on the "Get More (Free) Content"page at the front of this book to access this form as well as more bonus content.

The chart will help you target the score you want on the test you are taking. But remember, it is only a guide. Even if the chart says that you can safely skip 10 questions, it is to your advantage to guess smartly on as many questions as possible.

Pacing Chart for the World History Subject Test										
		Questions 1–35			Questions 36–70			Questions 71–95		
Score on Practice Test	Shooting for	Time spent	Must answer	Guess or skip	Time spent	Must answer	Guess or skip	Time spent	Must answer	Guess or skip
200–340	450	35 min	25	10	25 min	20	15	0 min	0	0
350–440	520	30 min	25	10	20 min	20	15	10 min	10	15
450–540	600	25 min	30	5	20 min	28	7	15 min	15	10
550–600	660	25 min	32	3	20 min	30	5	15 min	18	7
610–700	750	20 min	34	1	20 min	33	2	20 min	22	3
710–800		20 min	35	0	20 min	35	0	20 min	25	0

Time Is of the Essence

In order to pace yourself correctly, you must be aware of the time and where you are in the test at any given point. It's easy to do. In your mind, separate the total number of questions roughly into thirds. For the first third give yourself 20 to 25 minutes. The middle third should take you about 20 to 25 minutes. Finally, for the last third (actually a bit less), target about 15 minutes. A little more time per question is allowed in the first and second thirds of the test. This is because you are likely to be more alert at the start of the exam, so it pays to spend time on these questions. In the last third, you may be a little more tired, stressed, or even panicky. Your goal in the last third is to read the questions so that you can make quick, educated guesses, even if you only have 10 minutes left. If you have been pacing yourself well, and happen to have 15 to 20 minutes left for the last third, you will be able to maintain your pace and answer the questions with the relative speed you used in the previous sections.

To accurately keep track of the time, you may want to jot a time frame down at the top of your answer sheet near your name. For example, if the test starts at 11:20 A.M., jot down 11:40, 12:05, and 12:20. Then you can refer to these times to quickly see that you must complete the first third by approximately 11:40, the middle third by 12:05, and the rest by 12:20. (Be sure to either erase your notes or write only in a designated area, like where you put your name. Stray marks elsewhere can cause the College Board computers to malfunction.)

Questions	Minutes per Section	Total Time into Test
1–35	20–25	20–25 minutes
36–70	20–25	40–50 minutes
71–95	10–20	60 minutes (exam ends)

Use these time guidelines in conjunction with the pacing chart for your specific Subject Test.

SCORING: WILD GUESSES VERSUS SMART GUESSES

The SAT Subject Tests are scored on a scale of 200 to 800. This score, the one that is reported to you and to colleges, represents a translation of the raw score you actually acquire in taking the test. The raw score is tabulated by adding one point for each question you answer correctly and subtracting a quarter of a point for each question you answer incorrectly. Each blank gives you zero: no points either way. Think about this mathematically: one correct guess balances four incorrect guesses.

Now that you know about the guessing penalty, you can safely ignore it. Why? Using era-based thinking, you will always be able to make educated guesses, and every educated guess wipes out the negative effect of the penalty. If you can safely eliminate one answer choice out of five, and then guess on the remaining four, you have a one-in-four chance of getting the question right. At first sight, one-in-four odds may not sound so great, but over the whole test, these numbers are significant. If you pace yourself and follow the era technique carefully and thoughtfully, you are likely to guess correctly.

By using Process of Elimination (POE) and guessing smartly, you place the guessing odds in your favor. When you eliminate choices, there is no guessing penalty—only a reward!

A TALE OF THREE STUDENTS

Let's look at how three hypothetical students approached their SAT Subject Test in World History. Nervous Nina is a good student but a bad test taker; she took the test slowly and carefully, correctly answering most of the questions that she tried, but she ran out of time around question 80. Guessing Gary is an okay student, a great tester, and an aggressive guesser; he finished the test by working carefully on the questions he knew and quickly guessing on the harder questions. And finally, Average Andy is an average student and an average test taker; he took the test as he would any other, without any real concern about pacing; he guessed on a handful, and he ran out of time at the end.

In looking at the following chart, remember that correct answers receive 1 raw score point and incorrect answers result in a loss of $\frac{1}{4}$ raw score point. Blanks result in 0.

	Nervous Nina	Guessing Gary	Average Andy
Answered Correctly	60 (+60)	50 (+50)	50 (+50)
Answered Incorrectly	20 (–5)	15 (–3.75)	15 (–3.75)
Guessed Right	0 (0)	15 (+15)	5 (+15)
Guessed Wrong	0 (0)	15 (–3.75)	15 (–3.75)
Left Blank	15 (0)	0 (0)	10 (0)
Total Raw Score	55	57.5 = 58	46.5 = 47
Final Score	**620**	**640**	**570**

On this chart, "Answered Correctly" means that they knew the answer with their own history knowledge and got the question right. "Answered Incorrectly" means that they thought they knew the answer but got the question wrong. "Guesses" mean that they didn't know the answer and they knew they were guessing.

It doesn't seem quite fair that Gary got a better score than Nina even though Nina knew more. Too bad she didn't get to finish the test. And compare Gary to Andy; they both "knew" the right answer to 50 questions, and they both answered wrong on 30 questions—yet their scores differ by 70 points! Why? Because Gary was a better guesser—he guessed right 15 times, while Andy guessed right only five times.

The key, therefore, is in the guessing. Gary was simply a better guesser—more aggressive and better able to narrow down the choices when guessing. Using POE can make all the difference!

POE is your friend. Eliminate any answer choice you *know* is wrong and then guess from among the remaining choices.

REVIEW: ERA-BASED THINKING AND GUESSING

1. Think of history not just as a collection of a billion tiny facts, or factoids, such as exact date and names, but also as a series of eras: the dawn of World Religions, the Renaissance, the World Wars, and so on.

2. For any question you do not absolutely know the correct answer to, start by defining in your own mind what era that question refers to. Sometimes the wording of the question will actually state the era, although often it will not.

3. Read all of the answer choices and determine which ones clearly do not relate to the era. Eliminate those choices.

4. Of the remaining choices, choose which one most closely relates to the era.

5. If you can't eliminate down to just one answer choice, eliminate what you can and then guess from the choices you have left. In the long run, you'll gain more points than you lose.

Chapter 3
Cracking the Test

WHAT THIS BOOK CAN DO FOR YOU

This book is not intended to teach you all the history you would ever need to know to ace the SAT Subject Test in World History—after all, there's a *reason* that your school textbooks are a thousand pages long! We hope that the history classes you've taken in school have given you a good head start in that department. Instead, this book is intended to help you review for the test in three ways. First, we offer you effective approaches to taking the test. Second, the historical summaries in the coming chapters provide both facts and historical concepts to help you brush up on the "big picture" ideas of history. Third, the tests and explanations provide not only a measure of how well you know the material, but also a more detailed review of the history you need to know. The explanations in particular are chock-full of useful details, so be sure to review them for those questions you get wrong.

THE TEST

The breakdown of the SAT Subject Test in World History is as follows:

Time	60 minutes
Questions	95 multiple choice
Scoring Range	200–800
Scoring Details	+1 point for correct answer
	0 points for questions left blank
	$-\frac{1}{4}$ for incorrect answers

Remember, you do not have to answer the questions in order. Answer the questions you know first.

Time Periods Covered

Prehistory and civilizations to 500 C.E.	25%
500–1500 C.E.	20%
1500–1900 C.E.	25%
Post-1900 C.E.	20%
Cross-chronological	10%

Regions Covered

Europe	25%
Africa	10%
Southwest Asia	10%
South & Southeast Asia	10%
East Asia	10%
The Americas (excluding the U.S.)	10%
Global or comparative	25%

THE SYSTEM

The idea of studying for a test on roughly 6,000 years of world history can be a little daunting. The best way to study this vast period and subsequently remember some of the important facts about it on the SAT Subject Test in World History is to look at history in a systematic way. Despite the thousands of years that have passed and billions of people who have lived and events that have occurred, only a few incidents and people are deemed worthy enough for you to study as high school students. This may seem unfair and biased, but consider yourself lucky; would you really want to be responsible for all that history on this test?

Like other SAT Subject Tests, the World History test is long, and you need to understand pacing to do your best. So, if you skipped Chapter 2, which covers pacing, go back and read it now. Also, if you happen to be studying for both the U.S. History test and the World History test, you may notice some overlap in the techniques. Feel free to skip over similar sections, but remember, the Subject Test in World History does have some significantly different types of questions, so look out for these types as you read this section.

Need help prepping for the SAT? *Cracking the SAT Premium* has all the content review, strategy, and practice you need to help you get a top score.

History as Eras, Not Isolated Facts

Most questions on the test are very specific, but nearly every question is connected to an era and a country. As we review world history, we'll find that there are only a few events within each period that have remained noteworthy over the passage of time. Thus, if you can recognize the general period (the era) and the place (the country) of the question, you will have greatly narrowed your choices for the correct answer. Often, you only need a vague knowledge of what the question is specifically asking in order to answer it correctly. Let's look at an example:

1. The political power of such monarchies as the Tudors in the late fifteenth century was maintained by

   (A) the military strength of the monarch and his ability to keep order
   (B) the removal of all church powers from state control
   (C) the continental leadership of the Roman Catholic Church
   (D) the growth of an international trading network
   (E) the decentralization caused by the feudal system

Even though you might not know who the Tudors were, you can still answer this question with general knowledge of the 15th century. Think about the period right near the end of the Middle Ages and what would have kept a strong monarch in power. We can get rid of (B), (C), (D), and (E) because they would all have weakened a monarch in the 15th century. Only (A) would help keep a strong monarch in power. Therefore, (A) is the correct answer.

1. Read—Connect to Era and Country

There are four steps to this era-based thinking strategy.

Your primary approach is to read the question and connect it to its era and country.

2. Eliminate Anti-Era or Non-Era Answer Choices

Eliminate whatever answer choices *cannot* be true, based on what you know about that time period and place. You can usually limit your options to a few "maybes" after this step. On the SAT Subject Test in World History, common sense is a great tool. Don't think that all of the answer choices are automatically good ones merely because you are staring at them on a printed piece of paper. Some of the choices are ludicrous when you consider the era and the country of the questions. Watch out for these choices and eliminate them.

2. Which of the following reforms was implemented in France following the French Revolution?

   (A) Equality for all regardless of race or gender
   (B) The right to decent and affordable housing
   (C) The establishment of a republic
   (D) Reduced powers of the military
   (E) The end of serfdom in France

Which of the answer choices can't be true?

Think of the era. The French Revolution took place in the late 18th century. What happened during the 18th century in France? Choice (A) is out because it implies that French women were granted some type of equal rights, which didn't occur until recently. Choice (B) is incorrect for similar reasons. Choice (D) is incorrect because Napoleon, the great French general, rose to power after the French Revolution. Choice (E) is incorrect because feudalism had been weakening for centuries by the time the French Revolution occurred; serfdom was abolished by Louis IX in the 13th century. So, by eliminating the anti-era choices, you find that the correct answer is (C).

3. Let the Question Be Your Guide

The SAT Subject Test in World History contains a wide variety of question types. So after you have identified the era and the region, it is best to approach each specific type of question individually. These question types are outlined in the next section.

4. Last Resort: Guess and Move On

Pacing is even more important on this test than on some of the other SAT Subject Tests. Both very long and very short questions are scattered throughout the test. Sometimes the long ones are straightforward, while the short ones are tricky. So don't assume that you should skip the long ones and only do the short ones, or the other way around. As you practice, try to find out how well you do on each question type. Note how you do on the long, quote-like questions. If you always get them right, always do them. If the short ones throw you, figure out if your mistakes are based on carelessness or if you personally find a certain type of question generally impossible. Then tailor your test taking accordingly. Never spend too much time on any one question. If you can eliminate even one answer choice, guess and move on.

Review: The System

1. Read the question and connect it to an era and a country.
2. Eliminate anti-era or non-era answer choices.
3. Let the question be your guide.
4. Last resort: guess and move on.

THE QUESTIONS

Quote Questions

As many as 10 quote questions may appear on the test, but luckily they are easy to spot and fairly straightforward. In these questions, you are given a quote or a short piece of writing and asked to identify either the speaker, the time period, or the general philosophy of the writer/speaker. These questions are general, and the answer choices tend to be very different from each other, so the era and country technique works very well. Sometimes there are two questions for one quote, which makes these questions efficient to do. Sometimes several questions refer to a group of quotes. These may be trickier and a little more time-consuming than the standard quote question.

The biggest danger is spending too much time on these questions. If, when you're confronted with a quote or short paragraph, your instinct tells you, "I should read this carefully," it's time to retrain yourself. You want to read quickly and only read as much as you need to get a general idea of who is talking about what. The question that follows the quote will always be something on the order of "Who might have said this?" "This philosophy was popular when?" or "This theory is called what?" And the answers will usually be very distinct from each other, like (A), Gandhi; (B), Franklin D. Roosevelt; or (C), Hitler.

So the most efficient way to approach these questions is to hit them running. Read the question first so you know whether you are looking for a who, a what, or a when. Then read the quote, always thinking about what you are looking for. As soon as you grasp what the quote is referring to, jump to the answer choices and find it. If, in the first sentence, you figure out the quote sounds like something a knight would say, find that answer. If your first impression is not specific enough to get you the answer, go back and finish reading the quote. All the information to make the right decision is there. Let's try an example:

Have you ever walked into a room in your house and then suddenly forgotten what you went in there for? Reading the quotes on the SAT Subject Test in World History can give you the same feeling. Until you read the question, you have no idea what you're supposed to get out of the quote. So here's a simple solution—read the question first!

Questions 1-2 refer to the following statement.

"The treaty has no provisions to aid the defeated Central empires toward becoming good neighbors, nothing to help stabilize the new European states, nothing to help reclaim Russia. It does not promote economic cooperation among the Allies nor does it encourage any type of peaceful coexistence. This agreement will undoubtedly lead to worldwide instability."

1. The treaty referred to in the statement above is most likely

   (A) the Congress of Vienna (1815)
   (B) the Treaty of Versailles (1919)
   (C) the Hitler-Stalin Pact (1936)
   (D) the Marshall Plan (1947)
   (E) the Warsaw Pact (1955)

2. The "worldwide instability" mentioned above most likely predicts

   (A) the Crimean War
   (B) World War I
   (C) World War II
   (D) the Cold War
   (E) the Thirty Years War

Looking at the questions, we see that we need to determine when this quote was written. A "quick read" of the quote shows that the war was between the central states of Europe and the Allies. In addition, the treaty is described as lacking provisions to aid stability, so it is most likely the treaty after World War I that led up to World War II. Therefore, the answer to question 1 is (B), and the answer to question 2 is (C). Even if you are unsure of the name of the World War I treaty, the date 1919 should give you a clue.

Sometimes these questions will include quotes from two or more different viewpoints. Take a moment to identify the quotes before you answer the question; it may be helpful to jot down what you think about each quote beside it. Don't write much, just one or two words to remind you of it, like "18th century" or "farmer." Try to limit your need to read anything twice; it's a big time waster. All the same, if you need to reread to make a decision, do it. Nothing wastes time like staring back and forth between two or three answer choices, when a quick glance at the quote might dispel your doubts.

Review: Quote Questions

1. Read the question first.
2. Read only as much of the quote as necessary. Think era and country.
3. Eliminate incorrect answer choices.
4. If more than one choice is left, go back and quickly finish reading the quote.

LEAST/EXCEPT/NOT Questions

EXCEPT questions are also very popular on the SAT Subject Test in World History; there may be up to 25 of these questions on the test. LEAST and NOT questions are the cousins of EXCEPT questions, so you can treat them in the same manner.

EXCEPT Questions Are True or False Questions in Disguise

The trick to dealing with an EXCEPT question is to forget about the EXCEPT part and answer it like a true/false question. Usually, it's the backward nature of the EXCEPT in the question, not the subject of the question itself, that gets people confused. So, cross out that word and your troubles will be solved. Read the question without the EXCEPT, and then answer "Yes" or "No" to each answer choice. A "Yes" will be a true statement and the "No" will be the false one, or the exception. On an EXCEPT question the right answer will always be the "No." Remember, you are looking for the exception, or the one that is not true for the question itself.

3. All of the following countries contributed to the development of Renaissance culture EXCEPT

(A)	Italy	YES.	Eliminate.
(B)	the Soviet Union	NO.	It wasn't even around.
(C)	France	YES.	Eliminate.
(D)	Spain	YES.	Eliminate.
(E)	England	YES.	Eliminate.

This is an easy example, but it clearly shows how to use the EXCEPT trick. You will find it much easier to keep track of the question you are trying to answer by using this method.

"One of These Things Is Not Like the Others"

Sometimes one answer choice on EXCEPT questions will stick out noticeably from the others. This is a good thing! The one that's not similar to the others is the exception, which in these questions is the correct answer. Combine this technique with the era and country technique and you will often find that the exception is the anti-era choice. It seems that the easiest way for the test writers to create a "false" answer is to pull something from another time period.

4. Blahblahblah eighteenth-century philosophy blahblah EXCEPT

(A) religious tolerance
(B) freedom of thought and expression
(C) thought about political and social structures
(D) the communal sharing of land
(E) value in scientific logic

Eighteenth-century philosophy would place the question in the Enlightenment period in Europe, and (D) noticeably is out of that era. The idea of communal property in Europe is from the 17th century, and it was developed among minority Christian sects in Cromwellian England. So, using your era knowledge, (D) is clearly the anti-era choice and the right answer.

Review: EXCEPT Questions

1. Cross out the EXCEPT—Answer "yes" or "no."
2. Ask, "Which one of these things is not like the others?"
3. The "no" or the anti-era/non-era choice is right.

Roman Numeral Questions

These questions can be used in two primary ways.

Learn as You Go

You approach these questions by learning as you go and using POE. If you know option I is wrong, cross out all the answer choices that contain I.

5. Which of the following states had centralized leadership?

    I. Ancient Athens
    II. Eighteenth-century England
    III. Germany in 1939

(A) I only
(B) II only
(C) I and II only
(D) II and III only
(E) I, II, and III

Start with I: Ancient Athens was a democracy and was decentralized. From this information, we can eliminate (A), (C), and (E) because these choices contain option I. Because both (B) and (D) have II, let's look at III to decide which choice is right. Germany in 1939 was ruled by Adolf Hitler under strongly centralized leadership. Therefore, if III and II both had centralized leadership, the answer must be (D).

Time Sequence

The second way that the SAT Subject Test writers use the Roman numerals format is to ask you to give an order of events, like the order of the events for the Russian Revolution. These questions are especially difficult because you must put four or five events in chronological order that you probably remember as just a single block in time. So, it's best to look toward the ends, that is, the beginning event or the final event of the sequence. If you know that III occurred first, cross out any ordering that does not have it first. If you happen to know that III was first and IV was last, the odds are that only one answer choice will match this, and you will not have to bother with the ones in the middle. Let's try one of these.

6. Beginning with the earliest, which of the following represents the correct chronological order of events around the time of the French Revolution?

    I.   Declaration of the Rights of Man
    II. The Reign of Terror
    III. The reign of Louis XVI
    IV. The rise of Napoleon

(A) I, II, III, IV
(B) III, I, II, IV
(C) II, I, III, IV
(D) IV, II, I, III
(E) III, I, IV, II

You should remember that Napoleon came after the French Revolution and that Louis XVI was in power before the Revolution. From this information, you can eliminate (A), (C), (D), and (E). Also, the Reign of Terror came shortly after the Declaration of the Rights of Man. Therefore, (B) is the correct answer.

Review: Roman Numeral Questions

1. Learn as you go by using POE.
2. If it's a time-sequence question, look to the ends. Decide what happened first and what happened last.

Charts, Pictures, and Cartoons

Expect to find about 10 questions on the SAT Subject Test in World History that refer to either a picture, chart, or political cartoon. You will also see several geography-based questions accompanied by maps. The picture questions tend to be identifications of architectural forms or art. The first rule in dealing with any of these questions is to read the question first. Many of the maps can be confusing, and there is no point in studying them if you are not yet sure what the question is. The second step is to identify the region. Often the SAT Subject Test writers use these questions to focus on the non-European parts of the world, and they are testing whether you know anything about, say, Africa or Latin America. Just as in the era and country technique, you want to place yourself in the geographical context of the picture or map of the question.

If these steps do not get you the correct answer, use common sense or the information given in the question. Ask yourself, "What are they testing with this question?" or "What do I need to know about this region that is different from other regions?" This questioning should get you down to only a couple of choices. Then guess and move on.

Do not get trapped on a chart or picture question. These questions are usually pretty easy, but if one is confusing you, move on. It's a trap to waste several minutes on one question, thinking, "I should be able to get this one!" Spending too much on any one question steals time away from other questions.

> Remember, it's foolish to waste time on any one question—keep moving.

Let's try some examples.

Roman Numeral POE Quiz

A: Roman numeral I is clearly false so we can get rid of (A), (C), and (E). Is II true?
Who cares? Roman numeral III is true, so the answer must be (D), because it is the only answer left that has III in it.

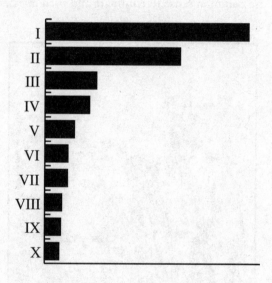

7. The graph above shows the relative populations of the ten most populous countries in the world in 1981. Which of the following is Country II ?

    (A) The People's Republic of China
    (B) India
    (C) The Soviet Union
    (D) The United States
    (E) Brazil

You may know that China has long had the largest population in the world, so it can't be Country II. Which choice is the next likely to be "highly populated"? If you pick India, (B), you are right. The former Soviet Union had the largest land mass, but its population was about the same as that of the United States.

Know Your Geography

For the SAT Subject Test in World History, it pays to know your geography. While geography obviously helps on map questions, it can also help on other questions. Often the answer to an EXCEPT question can be found with a little geographical knowledge. The EXCEPT may be a country that is geographically far from the other countries listed, or it may be the place that is landlocked while the others have seaports. In the European history review section, pay special attention to the maps in each chapter. Used with the era and country technique, geography knowledge will help your score.

Political Cartoons

You will encounter one or two political cartoons on the exam. They will be like the cartoons on the editorial page of your newspaper, although they may be in a very different style than you are used to. The more modern a cartoon is, the better you will be able to relate to its humor. On the older ones, look for historical clues, so that you can place the era or country of the cartoon. If you can connect to the era of the cartoon, the correct answer will reveal itself to you. If you are unsure of the time period, use common sense to eliminate and then guess.

"I cannot tell a lie; he did it with his little submarine."

8. The person represented in the cartoon above is most likely

   (A) Kaiser Wilhelm II in World War I
   (B) Benito Mussolini in World War II
   (C) Otto von Bismarck in the Franco-
       Prussian War
   (D) Joseph Stalin in the Cold War
   (E) Francisco Franco in the Spanish Civil War

Connect to the era of the cartoon—when was submarine warfare important? Both the Franco-Prussian War and the Spanish Civil War were fought on land (just think about them on a map), and the Cold War was a nonmilitary diplomatic conflict, so you can eliminate (C), (D), and (E). To distinguish between the remaining two answer choices, it helps to know that Germany had a powerful submarine fleet in World War I (the helmet in the cartoon also provides a clue). So, the correct choice is (A). The sinking of the *Sussex*, a French passenger ship, was an example of the aggressive submarine warfare of the Germans. When the Germans broke the Sussex Pledge and resumed unrestricted submarine warfare, the United States entered World War I.

Review: Charts, Pictures, and Cartoon Questions

1. Read the question.
2. Identify the region.
3. Use the information provided in the question, your geographical knowledge, and common sense.

Factoid Questions—The Name Game

Generally speaking, the SAT Subject Test in World History has more factoid-based questions with short answer choices than does the U.S. History test, which has longer questions and longer answer choices. For you, this has both advantages and disadvantages. The World History test questions can be done a little more quickly, and there are not as many tricks to interpreting the answer choices, but these factoid questions also tend to be based on more obscure information. If you know the factoid, you are in luck; just answer it and move on. If you are unsure about it, there is still hope.

Play Your Hunches

Don't psych yourself out. These questions are easier than you think—even if you have never heard of the question's subject matter! You see, someone has to get these questions right or the SAT Subject Test writers couldn't put them on the test. Unlike some other standardized tests, here it pays to answer by instinct on the hardest questions. Even on the toughest questions, the answer will probably not be something you've never heard of, so go for what you know. By the same token, you should…

Pop Quiz

Q: The Roman Empire in the 1st century B.C.E. and the Arab world in the 8th century C.E. extended into how many continents?

Go for the Famous Person or Thing

The answer will more likely be someone or something you've heard of, so even if you think you're stumped, choose the most famous person or thing. Now, if you are sure the most famous person is wrong, eliminate that answer. Then choose the answer with the second most famous person. This "educated" guessing takes some practice. As you take practice tests, notice the names that keep cropping up. If you have never heard of one of the correct answers, look that person or event up in an encyclopedia or history text. Check out the following examples.

9. This is about . . . who knows? who knows? who knows?

   (A) Aristotle   The famous guy.
   (B) Lucretius   Who?
   (C) Seneca   Who?
   (D) Ovid   Poet, right?
   (E) Erasmus   Who?

10. Blah something about some great Russian leader blahblahblah

   (A) Ivan the Terrible   Heard of him, but not great.
   (B) Peter the Great   Must be great, heard of him.
   (C) Alexander I   THE Alex the Great was pre-Russia; who's this guy?
   (D) Nicholas I   Who?
   (E) Nicholas II   Who?

Definitions: A Special Kind of Factoid Question

Sometimes the test will ask you to simply define a term, identify a person, or describe an event from history. Think of these as a kind of "historical vocabulary" question. We've provided lists of key terms at the end of each chapter of content review. These should help you with some of the most common and more obscure vocabulary you might see on the test.

Review: Factoid Questions

1. Play the name game.
2. Guess and move on.

Part II
Practice Test 1

- Practice Test 1
- Practice Test 1: Answers and Explanations

Practice Test 1

The Princeton Review Practice SAT Subject Test in World History

The following is the first practice Subject Test in World History. In order to get a good estimate of your score, you should take it and all other practice exams under test conditions.

- Give yourself one hour to do the test when you are not going to be bothered by anyone. Turn off your phone and don't sit near your computer or tablet.
- Clear a space to work in. You want no distractions.
- Have someone else time you. It's too easy to fudge the time when you are keeping track of it yourself.
- Tear out the answer sheet provided in the back of the book. This way, you will get the feel for filling in all those lovely ovals.
- Don't worry about the complicated instructions; just pick the correct answer.

Instructions for grading follow the answers and explanations.

GOOD LUCK!

WORLD HISTORY
TEST 1

Your responses to the Subject Test in World History questions must be filled in on the Test 1 answer sheet (at the back of the book). Marks on any other section will not be counted toward your Subject Test in World History score.

When your supervisor gives the signal, turn the page and begin the Subject Test in World History.

WORLD HISTORY TEST 1

Directions: Each of the questions or incomplete statements below is followed by five suggested answers or completions. Select one that is best in each case and then fill in the corresponding oval on the answer sheet.

Note: The SAT Subject Test in World History uses the chronological designations B.C.E. (before the Common Era) and C.E. (Common Era). These labels correspond to B.C. (before Christ) and A.D. (*anno Domini*), which are used in some world history textbooks.

1. Which of the following was the first animal domesticated in most cultures that have kept domestic animals?

    (A) The cat
    (B) The cow
    (C) The chicken
    (D) The dog
    (E) The goat

2. Aztec pyramids and Babylonian ziggurats were similar in all of the following ways EXCEPT:

    (A) Both were step-pyramids, instead of true pyramids.
    (B) Both stored food for the gods.
    (C) Both were frequently expanded by further building.
    (D) Both had powerful religious significance.
    (E) Both were built in most prominent cities.

3. Contemporary Turkey and the Ottoman Empire are similar in that

    (A) both governed peoples of many different ethnicities
    (B) neither tolerated linguistic diversity within the nation
    (C) both were ruled by a single ruling family
    (D) neither discriminated against religious minorities
    (E) both had a substantial role in facilitating East-West trade

4. What was the most important reason that Chinese citizens moved to Southeast Asia and to Indonesia during the Ming dynasty?

    (A) The offer of land for settlement
    (B) A governmental forced-emigration policy
    (C) The opportunity to escape political repression at home
    (D) Trade and business opportunities
    (E) The arrival of soldiers in conquered territories

5. Within the Ottoman Empire, people of non-Muslim religions were

    (A) allowed to practice their religion, but had restricted political rights
    (B) forcibly converted to Islam through continuous persecution
    (C) driven into neighboring lands to free up space for Muslim expansion
    (D) permitted to practice their religions on an equal basis with Muslims
    (E) granted religious freedom if they served in the military as Mamluks

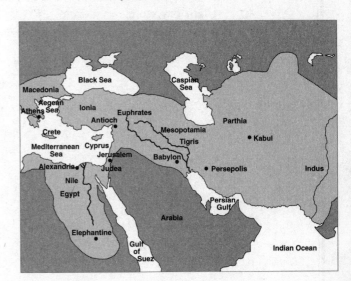

6. The map above shows the extent of which of the following?

    (A) The conquests of Alexander the Great, c. 326 B.C.E.
    (B) The Roman Empire, c. 136 C.E.
    (C) The Persian Empire, c. 500 B.C.E.
    (D) The Etruscan civilization, c. 264 B.C.E.
    (E) The conquests of Attila the Hun, c. 469 C.E.

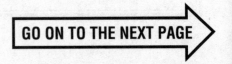

GO ON TO THE NEXT PAGE

7. "The power of population is indefinitely greater than the power in earth to produce subsistence for man. Population, when unchecked, increases in a geometrical ratio. Subsistence only increases in an arithmetical ratio."

The statement above was drawn from the writings of

(A) Friedrich Engels
(B) Adam Smith
(C) John Maynard Keynes
(D) Charles Darwin
(E) Thomas Malthus

8. Which group dominated trade along the Silk Road in 800 C.E. ?

(A) Chinese traders
(B) Portuguese sailors
(C) Italian merchants
(D) Muslim traders
(E) Mongol herdsmen

9. "Their reason for killing and destroying such an infinite number of souls is that the Christians have an ultimate aim, which is to acquire gold, and to swell themselves with riches in a very brief time and thus rise to a high estate disproportionate to their merits. It should be kept in mind that their insatiable greed and ambition, the greatest ever seen in the world, is the cause of their villainies."

The text above is a description of the Spanish conquistadors' contact with the

(A) natives of southern India
(B) peoples of Indonesia
(C) inhabitants of the New World
(D) residents of southern China
(E) indigenous population of Madagascar

10. The Native American cultures of the Mississippi Valley were able to develop sedentary civilization because

(A) imported Mexican crops, such as beans and corn, enabled the development of agriculture
(B) European demand for furs permitted the Mississippians to live off of their trading profits
(C) widespread irrigation projects permitted farming in land that had previously been infertile
(D) climate change caused a general thawing of Mississippian glaciers, making the land habitable
(E) domestication of bison provided a newly stable source of food and raw materials

11. Ghana, the Mali empire, and other West African empires became rich through trade in gold, salt, and which other main trade product?

(A) Copper
(B) Coal
(C) Silks
(D) Ivory
(E) Steel

12. All of the following were invented or first developed within China EXCEPT

(A) opium
(B) gunpowder
(C) silk
(D) the compass
(E) the printing press

13. Which of the following was the earliest method used to record numbers in most societies?

(A) Writing on paper
(B) Exchange of gifts
(C) Painting on caves
(D) The tally stick
(E) Wampum record belts

GO ON TO THE NEXT PAGE

14. Which of the following was immediately responsible for precipitating India's independence from British control?

    (A) Gandhi's campaign of targeted destruction of British facilities
    (B) A campaign of nonviolent protest against Britain during World War II
    (C) The partition of the Indian territory into India and Pakistan
    (D) The chaos following the assassination of Mahatma Gandhi
    (E) Anticolonial terms imposed on the Allies by the Treaty of Paris

15. "If the Shah is not destroyed, you shall become slaves of pagans. Foreigners shall take your womenfolk; they shall plunder all your natural wealth and put the Muslim community to eternal shame."

    The speech putting forward these ideas was delivered to help promote an Islamic revolution in

    (A) Indonesia
    (B) Turkey
    (C) Iraq
    (D) Jordan
    (E) Iran

16. Which of the following did Russia and Japan share in the sixteenth and seventeenth centuries?

    (A) A Chinese influence on art, literature, and politics due to geographical proximity
    (B) The invasion of the Mongols, which cut off access to trade with the west
    (C) Swift Westernization
    (D) Complete lack of trade with Europe and Asia
    (E) Monarchy-based forms of government with strictly centralized power

17. In 1973, OPEC nations conducted an embargo against certain Western countries

    (A) to discourage further intervention in the Iran-Iraq War
    (B) because of internal politics within the Saudi regime
    (C) as leverage to secure membership in the United Nations
    (D) because a temporary lack of supply meant there was no oil for export
    (E) to retaliate against countries that supported Israel

"We shall not flag or fail. We shall go on to the end. We shall fight in France, we shall fight on the seas and the oceans, we shall fight with growing confidence and growing strength in the air, we shall defend our island, whatever the cost may be. We shall fight on the beaches, we shall fight on the landing grounds, we shall fight in the fields and in the streets, we shall fight in the hills; we shall never surrender."

18. The quote cited above most likely comes from which of the following World War II-era leaders?

    (A) Benito Mussolini
    (B) Adolf Hitler
    (C) Winston Churchill
    (D) Franklin Roosevelt
    (E) Charles de Gaulle

19. "As soon as they had dragged him to the block ... the priest, who was to kill him, would come and strike him a blow . . . and offered the heart to the sun. The lords from the provinces who had come to observe the sacrifice were shocked and bewildered by what they had seen . . . "

    This description of human sacrifice might have been associated with

    (A) the Ottomans describing the Mongols
    (B) the French describing the Algerians
    (C) the Romans describing the Gauls
    (D) the Spanish describing the Aztecs
    (E) the Russians describing the Cossacks

GO ON TO THE NEXT PAGE

20. The shaded region of the map above indicates lands that, in 1510, were under the control of which empire?

   (A) The Aztec Empire
   (B) The Spanish Empire
   (C) The Mayan Empire
   (D) The Olmec Empire
   (E) The Inca Empire

21. The Ottoman conquest of Constantinople in 1453 coincides with which of the following events in Europe?

   (A) The Lutheran Reformation
   (B) The invention of the printing press
   (C) The creation of the League of Nations
   (D) The Muslim invasion of Spain
   (E) The fall of the Carolingian Empire

22. Which of the following crops originated in West Africa?

   (A) Wheat
   (B) Teff
   (C) Yams
   (D) Potatoes
   (E) Millet

23. Which of the following Russian leaders was most responsible for adopting Western European customs in the Russian empire?

   (A) Ivan the Terrible
   (B) Peter the Great
   (C) Catherine the Great
   (D) Nicholas II
   (E) Rasputin

24. When American President Franklin D. Roosevelt said, "Yesterday, December 7, 1941—a date which will live in infamy," he was referring to which of the following events?

   (A) The bombing of Hiroshima and Nagasaki
   (B) The liberation of the concentration camps at Auschwitz
   (C) The invasion of Czechoslovakia
   (D) The attack on Pearl Harbor
   (E) The suicide of Adolf Hitler and Eva Braun

25. England and Japan played similar roles in their respective regional economies of the fifteenth century in that

   (A) neither nation was fully integrated into the continental trading network
   (B) both nations were major suppliers of textiles
   (C) both nations were the most powerful trading nations of their regions
   (D) both nations were politically weakened as a result of the Black Death
   (E) both nations engaged in trade under the cover of paying tribute

26. The year 1868 was significant to Japanese history because it marked

   (A) the return to absolute power of the emperor
   (B) Tokugawa Ieyasu's founding of the Tokugawa shogunate
   (C) the capital's first move to Kyoto
   (D) Japan's first contact with the West in 200 years
   (E) the beginning of the Meiji period

GO ON TO THE NEXT PAGE

27. "Upon this a question arises: Whether it be better to be loved than feared or feared than loved? It may be answered that one should wish to be both, but, because it is difficult to unite them in one person, it is much safer to be feared than loved, when, of the two, either must be dispensed with. Because this is to be asserted in general of men, that they are ungrateful, fickle, false, cowardly, covetous . . . "

The remarks above from Machiavelli's political treatise *The Prince* most strongly resemble the ancient Chinese philosophy known as

(A) Confucianism
(B) Taoism
(C) Moism
(D) Legalism
(E) Jainism

28. The Nazi-Soviet Pact led to which of the following?

(A) The division of Poland and the Baltic states between Hitler and Stalin
(B) The outbreak of the Russian Revolution
(C) The Communist Party purges of the 1930s
(D) The appointment of Hitler to the office of chancellor
(E) The destruction of Stalingrad

29. Between the Middle Ages and the Renaissance, the main centers of European trade moved from

(A) central Europe to the Atlantic coast
(B) Western to Eastern Europe
(C) the Mediterranean to the Atlantic
(D) northern Europe to the Mediterranean
(E) the Atlantic coast to the Mediterranean

30. The processes of empire-building under China's Wen and Europe's Charlemagne had which of the following in common?

(A) Both allowed conquered peoples to practice their traditional religions.
(B) Both brought diverse cultures under the control of a single ruler.
(C) Neither had strong backing from the dominant religious establishment.
(D) Neither emperor resorted to violence in order to achieve his goals.
(E) Each emperor imposed his own language on the peoples he conquered.

31. Simón Bolívar, the Latin American independence leader, wanted to

(A) establish an American monarchical dynasty
(B) forge one grand American republic south of Mexico
(C) rule Gran Colombia, or Latin America, as a dictator
(D) create a federation of independent Latin American republics
(E) secede Colombia from Spain and adopt French rule

32. Which religious tradition developed directly out of Hinduism?

(A) Zoroastrianism
(B) Shintoism
(C) Judaism
(D) Buddhism
(E) Confucianism

33. All of the following were instrumental in ending the apartheid regime in South Africa in the early 1990s EXCEPT

(A) peaceful nonviolent resistance
(B) the onset of the AIDS epidemic
(C) anti-apartheid terrorist violence
(D) international protest and disapproval
(E) internal demographic change

GO ON TO THE NEXT PAGE

34. The building pictured above was most likely constructed in

    (A) ancient Greece
    (B) feudal Japan
    (C) medieval France
    (D) Renaissance Florence
    (E) postindustrial Germany

Questions 35-36 refer to the following passage.

"In conformity, therefore, to the clear doctrine of the Scripture, we assert, that by an eternal and unmistakable counsel, God has once and for all determined, both whom he would admit to salvation, and whom he would condemn to destruction."

35. The passage above exemplifies the ideas of

    (A) secular humanism
    (B) predestination
    (C) historical determinism
    (D) classical liberalism
    (E) Taoism

36. The passage above is taken from the writings of

    (A) Erasmus of Rotterdam
    (B) John Calvin
    (C) Karl Marx
    (D) John Stuart Mill
    (E) Lao Tse

37. Which of the following is most similar to the Prague Spring of 1968 in Czechoslovakia?

    (A) The Tiananmen Square democracy protests in China
    (B) The Qing dynasty Hundred Days of Reform
    (C) The Solidarity movement in Poland
    (D) The Orange Revolution in the Ukraine
    (E) The rule of the commonwealth of England

38. The reign of which of the following Roman leaders marked the transition between the Roman Republic and the Roman Empire?

    (A) Nero
    (B) Tiberius
    (C) Constantine
    (D) Caligula
    (E) Julius Caesar

39. The blanket above demonstrates designs most closely associated with the native peoples of

    (A) the American Southwest
    (B) Peru
    (C) the American Northwest
    (D) Madagascar
    (E) the American Northeast

GO ON TO THE NEXT PAGE

40. All of the following were rulers or ruling families in Europe in the 1500s EXCEPT

    (A) the Tudors of England
    (B) Peter the Great of Russia
    (C) the Hapsburgs of Austria
    (D) the Bourbon dynasty of France
    (E) King Ferdinand and Queen Isabella of Spain

41. At the height of Spanish control in North America, the territory of Mexico extended north and east to the source of which river?

    (A) The Ohio River
    (B) The Rio Grande
    (C) The Mississippi River
    (D) The Missouri River
    (E) The Pecos River

42. Which of the following types of taxes were paid by both ancient Egyptians and pre-Revolutionary French?

    (A) Taxes on the use of salt
    (B) Taxes on use of roads and waterways
    (C) Taxes in the form of forced labor
    (D) Taxes on foreign trade goods
    (E) Taxes in the form of money

43. This cartoon is most likely commenting on

    (A) the American Civil War of 1861-1865
    (B) the 1905 separation of Norway and Sweden
    (C) strained relations between Japan and Korea in the 1950s
    (D) Russia's failure to create working-class solidarity in the 1920s
    (E) Bismarck's difficulty maintaining German unification

44. Which of the following changes best supports the claim that the regional politics of the Mediterranean world changed dramatically in 284 C.E.?

    (A) The end of the Punic Wars
    (B) The split of the Roman Empire into eastern and western halves
    (C) The birth of Muhammad
    (D) The demise of the Egyptian pharaohs as regional power-brokers
    (E) The banning of Gnostic sects

45. During its isolationist period, Japan maintained contacts with all of the following countries EXCEPT

    (A) Korea
    (B) the United States
    (C) China
    (D) the Netherlands
    (E) the Ryukyu Islands

46. "The King is God's Earthly Vicar, the anointed representative of the Almighty, who once designated by God, can be recalled only by God. To deny the authority of God's Vicar is to deny the authority of God Himself, which only He, and no mortal Parliament, nor Estates-General, nor Clamoring Mob, can presume to exercise."

    The Chinese concept of the Mandate of Heaven differs from this description of the European philosophy of the divine right of kings in that

    (A) the Chinese believed that the eunuchs should share authority with the emperor
    (B) the European viewpoint does not acknowledge the king as directly descended from Heaven
    (C) the Mandate of Heaven did not imply that the emperor rules by divine favor
    (D) a Chinese emperor could lose the Mandate of Heaven through poor rulership
    (E) the Chinese clergy played a greater role in determining the Mandate of Heaven

GO ON TO THE NEXT PAGE

47. Which of the following was a leader of Marxist revolutions in Latin America?

    (A) Simón Bolívar
    (B) Che Guevara
    (C) Pancho Villa
    (D) Miguel Hidalgo
    (E) Samuel Houston

48. Through most of human history, women have been

    (A) politically dominant decision-makers in most societies
    (B) given an equal degree of economic freedom as men
    (C) assigned a different, but equally important, role from men
    (D) treated as subservient to, and possibly property of, men
    (E) responsible for making key domestic policy decisions

49. The painting above is characteristic of the

    (A) Tang dynasty in China
    (B) Ottoman Empire in Turkey
    (C) Safavid Empire in Persia
    (D) Tokugawa period in Japan
    (E) Byzantine Empire in Greece

50. Which religion had the greatest impact on West African culture?

    (A) Buddhism
    (B) Islam
    (C) Zoroastrianism
    (D) Christianity
    (E) Judaism

Questions 51-52 refer to the statement below.

"Without the shedding of any blood I returned from Munich bearing peace with honor."

51. The statement above was made by

    (A) Winston Churchill
    (B) Woodrow Wilson
    (C) Adolf Hitler
    (D) Neville Chamberlain
    (E) Franklin D. Roosevelt

52. The policy exemplified by the statement above is called

    (A) appeasement
    (B) pacifism
    (C) isolationism
    (D) interventionism
    (E) gunboat diplomacy

"Nothing which implies contradiction falls under the omnipotence of God."

53. From which work is this quote taken?

    (A) Principles of Philosophy, René Descartes
    (B) A Treatise of Human Nature, David Hume
    (C) Summa Theologica, Thomas Aquinas
    (D) Meditations Sacrae, Sir Francis Bacon
    (E) Utopia, Sir Thomas More

54. Which is the best characterization of native Australian technology before the arrival of Europeans?

    (A) Paleolithic
    (B) Neolithic
    (C) Copper tools
    (D) Bronze tools
    (E) Iron tools

GO ON TO THE NEXT PAGE

55. In Islamic doctrine, the term "Greater Jihad" refers to a struggle

    (A) against impurities in one's own soul and practice
    (B) to spread Islam by discussion and debate
    (C) to achieve a unified Islamic state in the Middle East
    (D) against unorthodox practice of Islam
    (E) for conversion of non-Muslims by any means

56. Widespread military conflicts between which two religious groups took place in Palestine beginning in the 11th century C.E.?

    (A) Jews and Muslims
    (B) Jews and Christians
    (C) Christians and Muslims
    (D) Muslims and Hindus
    (E) Hindus and Buddhists

57. "If there ever was in the history of humanity an enemy who was truly universal, an enemy whose acts and moves trouble the entire world, threaten the entire world, attack the entire world in any way or another, that real and really universal enemy is precisely Yankee imperialism."

    This comment reflects the expressed ideas of

    (A) Augusto Pinochet
    (B) Ferdinand Marcos
    (C) Manuel Noriega
    (D) Vladimir Lenin
    (E) Fidel Castro

58. Which of the following events precipitated the outbreak of World War II ?

    (A) Germany's annexation of the Sudetenland
    (B) Japan's bombing of Pearl Harbor
    (C) Germany's invasion of Poland
    (D) Germany's "blitzkrieg" bombing of London
    (E) Italy's alliance with Germany and Japan

59. Under which dynasty did China first establish its civil service program?

    (A) The Han
    (B) The Qin
    (C) The Tang
    (D) The Zhou
    (E) The Sui

60. The Boer Wars of 1899-1902 led to the formation of

    (A) the Transvaal Republic and the Orange Free State
    (B) Lesotho, Botswana, and Swaziland
    (C) an egalitarian British colony in South Africa
    (D) an independent state dominated by former colonists
    (E) the Organization of African Unity

61. The Ottoman Empire and the Safavid Empire were similar in all of the following ways EXCEPT:

    (A) Both ruled over substantial parts of Mesopotamia.
    (B) Both were opposed by large European alliances.
    (C) Both linked peoples of Europe with East Asia.
    (D) Both empires were officially Muslim.
    (E) Both ruled over a diverse group of cultures.

62. The departure of Chiang Kai-shek from mainland China in 1949 led to

    (A) the establishment of two contending Chinese states
    (B) a relaxation of Cold War tensions
    (C) Soviet withdrawal from mainland China
    (D) the end of communist rule in China
    (E) the unconditional surrender of Japan to the Allies

GO ON TO THE NEXT PAGE

63. All of the following were Spanish explorers EXCEPT

   (A) Vasco de Gama
   (B) Francisco Pizarro
   (C) Hernán Cortés
   (D) Ponce de Leon
   (E) Ferdinand Magellan

64. Beginning with the earliest, which of the following most accurately describes the chronology in which the following developments occurred?

   I. The writing of Hammurabi's code
   II. The building of the Great Pyramids of Giza
   III. The Persian conquest of Mesopotamia
   IV. The conquests of Alexander the Great

   (A) I, IV, II, III
   (B) IV, I, III, II
   (C) I, II, III, IV
   (D) II, I, III, IV
   (E) III, I, IV, II

SELECTED COUNTRIES IN 1978

Ethiopia	120
Haiti	260
Egypt	390
Taiwan	1,400
Israel	3,500
Saudi Arabia	7,690

65. The numbers in the table above represent

   (A) population in thousands
   (B) net exports in millions of U.S. dollars
   (C) per capita income in U.S. dollars
   (D) national debt in millions of U.S. dollars
   (E) arable land in square kilometers

Source: "The Crossroads of Asia. Transformation in Image and symbol," 1992.

66. This very early image of the Buddha most likely entered China through

   (A) British opium traders from India
   (B) Portuguese traders through the Spice Islands
   (C) central Asian trade over the Silk Road
   (D) cultural exchanges with Japanese monks
   (E) Thai mercenaries fighting for the Han dynasty

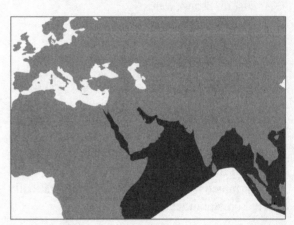

67. Which of the following groups controlled trade in the shaded region of the map above in 1400 and in 1550, respectively?

   (A) Islamic merchants and Italian traders
   (B) Islamic merchants and Portuguese sailors
   (C) Portuguese sailors and Italian traders
   (D) Italian traders and Islamic merchants
   (E) Portuguese sailors and Islamic merchants

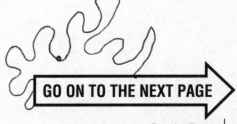

GO ON TO THE NEXT PAGE

68. The Five Pillars of Islam include all of the following EXCEPT

    (A) evangelism
    (B) charity
    (C) faith
    (D) fasting
    (E) pilgrimage

69. Ancient peoples used domesticated dogs for all of the following reasons EXCEPT

    (A) tracking down criminals
    (B) help while hunting
    (C) as draft animals
    (D) as a food source
    (E) protection from other animals

70. The earliest form of Chinese writing has been found

    (A) cast on bronzeware
    (B) written on silk in ink
    (C) etched on clay tablets
    (D) carved into bamboo slats
    (E) carved into tortoise shells

71. "I reiterate our call for . . . the immediate ending of the state of emergency and the freeing of all— and not only some—political prisoners . . . . It is our belief that the future of our country can only be determined by a body which is democratically elected on a nonracial basis."

    Who delivered this speech when released from prison in 1990 ?

    (A) Anwar al-Sadat
    (B) Benjamin Netanyahu
    (C) Mohammad Suharto
    (D) Mahatma Gandhi
    (E) Nelson Mandela

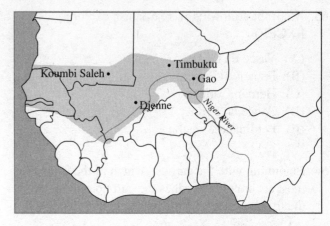

72. What is represented by the shaded area in the map above?

    (A) The largest extent of the Mali Empire
    (B) The area comprising the Kingdom of Axum
    (C) The area claimed by the Babylonian Empire
    (D) The extent of the sixth-century Byzantine Empire
    (E) Twentieth-century Portuguese colonies in Africa

73. "If you are neutral in situations of injustice, you have chosen the side of the oppressor. If an elephant has its foot on the tail of a mouse and you say that you are neutral, the mouse will not appreciate your neutrality."

    When Desmond Tutu, first black South African Anglican Archbishop of Cape Town, made the statement above, he was referring to his activism regarding which major problem in his nation?

    (A) The slave trade
    (B) Communism
    (C) Widespread poverty
    (D) Apartheid
    (E) Domestic violence

GO ON TO THE NEXT PAGE

74. The ancient Egyptians built the pyramids for which of the following reasons?

    (A) As storage facilities for grain
    (B) As tombs for the pharaohs and their queens
    (C) As monuments to military victories
    (D) As tools to map astrological phenomena
    (E) As locations for ritual sacrifice

75. All of the following societies used stringed instruments in the fifteenth century EXCEPT

    (A) Western Europeans
    (B) the Iroquois
    (C) the Chinese
    (D) the Ottomans
    (E) Eastern Europeans

Questions 76-77 are based on the pictures below.

Source (right): Jean-Pol Grandmont

76. What pair of human societies first used these animals?

    (A) Andean peoples (left) and the Chinese (right)
    (B) Western Europeans (left) and South Africans (right)
    (C) Andean peoples (left) and Eastern Europeans (right)
    (D) Central Europeans (left) and Pacific Islanders (right)
    (E) South Asians (left) and North Americans (right)

77. By 1450 C.E., both of these animals were commonly used to accomplish which of the following?

    (A) Carrying loads
    (B) Pulling plows
    (C) Mounted combat
    (D) Pulling wagons
    (E) Providing meat

GO ON TO THE NEXT PAGE

78. The painting above would most likely be found in

    (A) a Gothic cathedral
    (B) a Buddhist monastery
    (C) an Egyptian temple
    (D) a Renaissance palazzo
    (E) an English colonial meetinghouse

79. The quest to achieve liberation from the cycle of rebirth and desire by living rightly and breaking worldly attachments is characteristic of

    (A) Taoism
    (B) Hinduism
    (C) Islam
    (D) the Baha'i faith
    (E) Buddhism

80. Before the 1990s, Hong Kong and Macau were controlled by which two European powers?

    (A) Britain and France
    (B) Spain and Portugal
    (C) Britain and Portugal
    (D) Britain and Spain
    (E) France and the Netherlands

81. Women in Qing China and Renaissance Europe had similar roles because

    (A) in both societies, they could have substantial independence once they were widows
    (B) in neither society did they have a role in the production of trade goods
    (C) in both societies, they had substantial influence in choosing their husbands
    (D) in neither society could they own property under any circumstances
    (E) in both societies, they were frequently involved in their husbands' business ventures

82. Which of the following was a large temple complex built by the Maya?

    (A) Machu Picchu
    (B) Chichen Itza
    (C) Choqa Zanbil Ziggurat
    (D) Huayna Capac
    (E) Hagia Sophia

83. The earliest Roman society was most directly influenced by which of the following cultures?

    (A) Persian
    (B) Mayan
    (C) Mauryan
    (D) Assyrian
    (E) Etruscan

84. Which of the following societies has been strongly influenced by Confucian values?

    (A) New Guinean society
    (B) Mongolian society
    (C) Ak Koyunlu society
    (D) Korean society
    (E) Turkish society

85. Babylonian civilization was characterized by all of the following EXCEPT

    (A) a codified legal system
    (B) an understanding of arithmetic and geometry
    (C) an economy based on hunting and gathering
    (D) an ability to track the course of planets
    (E) a written language

86. "With this salt, I am shaking the foundations of the Empire."

    This statement was made during a nonviolent resistance campaign led by

    (A) Nelson Mandela
    (B) Patrick Henry
    (C) Sun Yat-sen
    (D) Mohandas K. Gandhi
    (E) Brennus of Gaul

87. Myths from ancient Mayan, Indian, Viking, and Semitic peoples all feature references to

    (A) a great flood
    (B) a thunder god
    (C) tricky snakes
    (D) sea monsters
    (E) human sacrifice

Questions 88-89 refer to the passage below.

"An accountable peasantry subject to other men; much use of the service tenement (i.e., the fief) rather than salary, which was inconceivable; the dominance of a military class; agreements concerning obedience and protection which bound man to man and, in the military class, assumed the distinctive form called vassalage, the breakdown of central authority."

88. The passage above most likely describes conditions in

    (A) imperial Rome
    (B) thirteenth-century France
    (C) fifteenth-century Florence
    (D) nineteenth-century Britain
    (E) twentieth-century Japan

89. According to the passage, the holder of a fief

    (A) must provide military service to his lord
    (B) is most likely a peasant
    (C) exercises power throughout his lord's territory
    (D) must pay rent on his land to his lord
    (E) cannot be a member of the clergy

90. Which group conquered large portions of the Iberian peninsula in the early eighth century C.E.?

    (A) The Visigoths
    (B) The Franks
    (C) The Celts
    (D) The Muslims
    (E) The Jews

GO ON TO THE NEXT PAGE

91. The structure pictured above was most likely built by the

    (A) Egyptians
    (B) Romans
    (C) Mayans
    (D) Incas
    (E) Hebrews

92. All of the following are predominantly Islamic states EXCEPT

    (A) Pakistan
    (B) India
    (C) Morocco
    (D) Yemen
    (E) Malaysia

93. "He is Shaka the unshakeable.
    Thunderer-while-sitting, son of Menzi
    He is the bird that preys on other birds,
    The battle-axe that excels over other battle-axes.
    He is the long-strided pursuer, son of Ndaba,
    Who pursued the sun and the moon.
    He is the great hubbub like the rocks of Nkandla
            Where elephants take shelter
    When the heavens frown . . . "

    This poem is describing a famous leader of a people from

    (A) West Africa
    (B) Central Africa
    (C) East Africa
    (D) North Africa
    (E) South Africa

94. In the twentieth century, both South Korea and Taiwan became industrial powers by

    (A) eliminating tariffs to establish a free market for goods, capital, and human resources
    (B) encouraging the development of foreign-owned and -invested industries within the national borders
    (C) removing centralized planning from the economy and permitting industrialists to develop independently
    (D) using tariffs to protect developing local industries funded by gift money from the United States
    (E) making all management and national investment decisions through democratic processes

95. Place the following German regimes in the proper chronological order.

    I. The Weimar Republic
    II. The Federal Republic of Germany
    III. The Third Reich

    (A) I, II, III
    (B) II, III, I
    (C) III, I, II
    (D) I, III, II
    (E) II, I, III

STOP

If you finish before time is called, you may check your work on this test only.
Do not turn to any other test in this book.

Practice Test 1: Answers and Explanations

- Practice Test 1 Answer Key
- Practice Test 1 Explanations
- How to Score Practice Test 1

PRACTICE TEST 1 ANSWER KEY

Question Number	Correct Answer	Right	Wrong	Question Number	Correct Answer	Right	Wrong	Question Number	Correct Answer	Right	Wrong
1.	D	___	___	33.	B	___	___	65.	C	___	___
2.	B	___	___	34.	C	___	___	66.	C	___	___
3.	A	___	___	35.	B	___	___	67.	B	___	___
4.	D	___	___	36.	B	___	___	68.	A	___	___
5.	A	___	___	37.	B	___	___	69.	A	___	___
6.	A	___	___	38.	E	___	___	70.	E	___	___
7.	E	___	___	39.	A	___	___	71.	E	___	___
8.	D	___	___	40.	B	___	___	72.	A	___	___
9.	C	___	___	41.	C	___	___	73.	D	___	___
10.	A	___	___	42.	C	___	___	74.	B	___	___
11.	D	___	___	43.	B	___	___	75.	B	___	___
12.	A	___	___	44.	B	___	___	76.	C	___	___
13.	D	___	___	45.	B	___	___	77.	A	___	___
14.	B	___	___	46.	D	___	___	78.	D	___	___
15.	E	___	___	47.	B	___	___	79.	E	___	___
16.	C	___	___	48.	D	___	___	80.	C	___	___
17.	E	___	___	49.	C	___	___	81.	A	___	___
18.	C	___	___	50.	B	___	___	82.	B	___	___
19.	D	___	___	51.	D	___	___	83.	E	___	___
20.	A	___	___	52.	A	___	___	84.	D	___	___
21.	B	___	___	53.	C	___	___	85.	C	___	___
22.	C	___	___	54.	B	___	___	86.	D	___	___
23.	B	___	___	55.	A	___	___	87.	A	___	___
24.	D	___	___	56.	C	___	___	88.	B	___	___
25.	A	___	___	57.	E	___	___	89.	A	___	___
26.	E	___	___	58.	C	___	___	90.	D	___	___
27.	D	___	___	59.	A	___	___	91.	C	___	___
28.	A	___	___	60.	D	___	___	92.	B	___	___
29.	A	___	___	61.	B	___	___	93.	E	___	___
30.	B	___	___	62.	A	___	___	94.	D	___	___
31.	D	___	___	63.	A	___	___	95.	D	___	___
32.	D			64.	D						

PRACTICE TEST 1 EXPLANATIONS

1. **D** Of all domesticated animals, the dog has had the longest relationship with humans; archaeological evidence shows domestication of the dog between 17,000 and 14,000 years ago, which makes (D) correct. The cat, (A), is believed to have been domesticated for only between 3,500 and 8,000 years. The cow, (B), is, after the dog, the next oldest domesticated animal; domestication began around 10,000 B.C.E. The chicken, (C), was domesticated later, only around 4,000 years ago. The goat, (E), was domesticated around 10,000 years ago.

2. **B** Both the Aztecs and the Babylonians built terraced pyramids in their largest cities as religious monuments. These buildings were frequently expanded in both cultures, but they were not used to store food for the gods specifically, so (B) is the correct answer.

3. **A** Modern-day Turkey is the country that occupies Anatolia, immediately south of the Black Sea at the eastern end of the Mediterranean across from Greece. The Ottoman Empire was centered in this area, but governed a more extensive empire between the 14th and 20th centuries. Both countries were very multiethnic, making (A) the best choice. Modern-day Turkey is a republic, so eliminate (C). Turkey also no longer has a substantial role in facilitating East-West trade as did the Ottoman Empire, so eliminate (E). Unlike modern-day Turkey, which has passed some strict laws to maintain Turkic linguistic dominance, the Ottoman Empire accepted linguistic diversity, so eliminate (B). The Ottoman Empire did, however, impose a special tax on non-Muslim residents, which eliminates (D).

4. **D** During the Ming dynasty, many ethnic Chinese moved abroad, which was unusual up to this point in Chinese history. The primary motivation for such emigration was (D), opportunities for trade and commerce. The Ming court did not offer land for settlement the way that, for instance, the American government did during the 19th century, nor did it operate a forced-emigration policy for its own citizens; eliminate (A) and (B). The idea of emigration, (C), to escape political repression was completely foreign to the mind of the average person under the Ming dynasty. Also, soldiers were settled in conquered areas sometimes, but the Ming never conquered Indonesia, so this cannot be the primary reason for ethnic-Chinese settlement there; eliminate (E).

5. **A** Under the Ottoman Empire, non-Muslims were permitted to practice, (A), but had lesser political rights; for instance, they were subject to special taxes. Non-Muslims were not persecuted into conversion, (B)—the empire maintained large Christian and Jewish populations throughout its existence—but they were also not permitted total equality regardless of religion, (D). There was no plan to forcibly remove non-Muslims for expansion purposes, (C)—the Armenian genocide was not primarily a land grab—nor were non-Muslims permitted religious equality as a result of military service, (E). Mamluks were actually kidnapped non-Muslims, usually from outside the empire proper, raised as soldiers with loyalty only to the Sultan, and often ended up converting to Islam because of their separation from their original faiths and large exposure to Islam.

6. A   The map shows the extent of the military conquests of Alexander the Great as of about 326 B.C.E., when the lands that he had overthrown stretched from the western Mediterranean regions to as far east as the Indus River Valley.

7. E   The quotation cited in this question states the main idea of *An Essay on the Principle of Population*, written by British economist Thomas Malthus, (E), in 1798. Malthus argued that populations always grow faster than the resources necessary to support them. His position conflicted with the more optimistic views of Adam Smith, (B), and other capitalist theorists. Friedrich Engels, (A), coauthored many important communist treatises with Karl Marx. John Maynard Keynes, (C), was a 20th-century economist who put forward many influential theories about the cyclical nature of economies. Unlike the men named in the other four answer choices, Charles Darwin, (D), was not an economist; he originated the theory of evolution.

8. D   Muslim traders dominated the Silk Road, especially after the Abbasid caliphs moved their capital to Baghdad in 762. Chinese traders, (A), dominated the Silk Road at an earlier period, particularly right after its beginnings in the 1st century B.C.E. Neither the Portuguese nor the Italians ever dominated the Silk Road, so eliminate (B) and (C). Finally, the Mongols did not rise to power and reestablish the Silk Road until the 13th century C.E., so eliminate (E).

9. C   Spanish conquistadors' explorations into the New World in the 15th and 16th centuries were motivated by the need to find trade routes after Muslim traders closed many European and Asian trade routes to Christians, as well to seek the wealth of the native peoples of the Americas. Spanish explorers did not come into contact with any of the populations mentioned in the other answer choices.

10. A   The natives of the Mississippi Valley were first able to develop a settled culture because of the agriculture made possible by importation of crops which originated in Mexico, (A). Their settled culture predates trade with the Europeans, (B), which was actually quite disruptive to preexisting cultural patterns, and it did not rely on widespread irrigation to permit agriculture, (C). Climate change, (D), occurred well before the settlement of this region. Bison were never domesticated, (E); the native Mississippians might have been better able to withstand European invasions if they had had such a valuable ally.

11. D   The Ghana (8th through 13th centuries) and Mali (13th through 16th centuries) empires traded in ivory as well as gold and salt. Copper, (A)—a component of bronze—was mined and traded heavily in the Roman, Egyptian, and Greek empires. Silk, (C), was traded heavily in the Far East. Coal, (B), and steel, (E), were not traded in Africa during this time period.

12. A   The drug that hastened the downfall of the Qing empire, opium, (A), was not originally from China: it was imported from India by the British. The other technological developments listed were all originally created in China.

13. **D** Most early societies recorded and ensured the accuracy of numbers by using tallies, (D), or tokens that fit together in a special way that would be difficult to duplicate. Numbers could be inscribed on these sticks or other tokens by using tick marks or other imprints, with each party getting one of the two pieces; the accuracy could be checked by sticking the pieces back together and counting. Paper, (A), was not prevalent early on in any society; and wampum record belts, (E), were characteristic only of certain native North American groups. Gift exchange, (B), was not a means of recording numbers, nor were cave paintings, (C), intended as a means of keeping records of numbers, so far as modern scientists can discern.

14. **B** Gandhi led the Quit India, (B), civil disobedience movement during World War II, in spite of British preoccupation with the war, and was criticized even by some other Indians for pursuing Indian independence with such important business afoot in Britain. However, Gandhi was a nonviolent protester; he did not target and destroy British facilities, (A). The partition of India and Pakistan, (C), and the assassination of Mahatma Gandhi, (D), took place after India was already independent. Anticolonial measures in the Treaty of Paris, (E), were not imposed specifically on the Allies; the Axis Powers were in no position to dictate terms to the Allies at this time. Instead, the major conferences happened to be a convenient forum to discuss colonial and postcolonial arrangements, as well as the peace terms.

15. **E** The Shah was active, and eventually overthrown by Islamic revolution in Iran, (E). Islamic revolutions never took place in the other states, nor were they ever ruled by a Shah.

16. **C** Russia and Japan both had limited contact with Western Europe up until the 16th and 17th centuries, at which time both experienced relatively rapid Westernization, (C). For Russia this was due to Peter the Great actively attempting to Westernize Russia, while Japan's exposure to the West occurred when the Portuguese arrived and established trade with the empire. While Chinese culture had an influence on Japanese society, it did not influence Russia, so eliminate (A). The Mongols had a strong influence on the development of Russia; the invasion of the Mongols in Russia was instrumental in cutting off Russian contact with the rest of Europe during the inception of the Renaissance; the Mongols never firmly established themselves in Japan, so eliminate (B). While neither country was ever completely free from outside influences, this point in time marked a rapid shift in their trade relations with the rest of the world, although they would progress very differently after this period of expanded contact; eliminate (D). Interestingly enough, a strictly centralized monarchy, (E), worked in diametrically opposed ways in regards to Westernization for each country—for Russia Westernization was spurred on by Peter the Great, while it was the lack of centralized authority that allowed for trade to flourish with Japan for the short window it did at this time.

17. **E** Oil has been a powerful political tool for those who have it, and a driving political consideration for countries which don't, ever since Western societies came to rely on it in the early 20th century. However, the Iran-Iraq War, (A), did not begin until the 1980s. Internal Saudi politics, (B), would not have been sufficient to convince the other OPEC (Organization of the Petroleum

Exporting Countries) nations to cut off a major source of revenue, however temporarily; and these nations were already members of the United Nations, (C). A lack of supply, (D), would not necessarily lead to an embargo; the issue was not that there was no oil to trade, but rather that those in a position to trade chose not to do so. This leaves (E) as the correct answer: the OPEC nations, which are mainly Arab nations, were furthering the economic front of the Yom Kippur War.

18. C The quote cited in the question comes from British Prime Minster Winston Churchill's speech before the House of Commons on June 4, 1940, so (C) is the correct answer. The clue in the quote that links it to Churchill is the line "we shall defend our island," which can logically only refer to England.

19. D Several societies in history have practiced human sacrifice, although the extent to which this was practiced is not always known. In this particular case of the Spanish describing the Aztecs, (D), it is difficult to tell how much is factual description and how much is blood libel; the Aztecs likely performed human sacrifices, but probably not as often as the Spanish claim. The passage describes a sacrifice organized by a central authority and watched by noble lords from the countryside, which implies a level of centralization surpassing what the Gauls of the Roman period probably had, so eliminate (C). The Ottomans and the Mongols were not contemporaries, so eliminate (A). The Algerians and the Cossacks did not practice human sacrifice (at least not at the time they were contacted by the French and Russians), which eliminates (B) and (E).

20. A This map shows a large portion of modern-day Mexico. The Aztec Empire, (A), ruled over this region until it was finally defeated by the Spanish in 1521. The Spanish Empire, (B), did not include this territory until later. The Maya, (C), were mostly in decline in the region by the time of the Europeans' arrival. The Olmecs, (D), were long gone by 1510. The Incas, (E), occupied the Andes, not Central America.

21. B The Lutheran Reformation, (A), began in 1521, which is too late to be the correct answer to this question. The League of Nations, (C), was formed in 1920, following World War I. Muslims invaded Spain, (D), in 711. The Carolingian Empire, (E), fell during the 10th century. The printing press was invented in 1450 by Johannes Gutenberg, which makes (B) the correct answer.

22. C Teff, (B), is native to northeast Africa, near present-day Ethiopia and Eritrea. Wheat, (A), originated in the Fertile Crescent in southwest Asia. Yams, (C), originated in both Asia and West Africa. The potato, (D), is native to the Andes. Millet, (E), is native to Asia. Thus, (C) is the answer.

23. B This is a difficult question, because several of the Russian leaders listed in the answer choices helped to Westernize Russia. Catherine the Great, (C), the tsarina who followed Peter the Great, continued her predecessor's lead in incorporating Western influences into Russian culture. Peter the Great, however, is the one who got the ball rolling and therefore is credited with the Westernization of modern Russia. The aptly named Ivan the Terrible, (A), ruled Russia with an iron hand

during the 16th century. Nicholas II, (D), and Rasputin, (E), were part of the ruling elite in the early 20th century, when the Russian Revolution overthrew the government and abolished the tsar.

24.   **D**   When Roosevelt made his famous speech about the "date which will live in infamy," he was referring to the Japanese attack on the American military forces at Pearl Harbor, (D), the event that catapulted the United States into World War II.

25.   **A**   In the 15th century, England was a supplier of woolens to the markets of continental Europe, particularly Flanders, but did not handle much trade through its own borders because goods would not need to move through England to get anywhere else. Japan during the Sengoku, or Warring States, period was mostly isolated from the major trade networks of the Asian mainland, which revolved around Ming China. Some trade took place, but Japan was far from the land-based focus of Asian trade at the time. As a result, both countries were not fully integrated into their respective continental trade networks, (A): they were not isolated per se, but they were at the edge. Only England was a major supplier of textiles in this period and could be claimed as the most powerful trading nation in its region (although the Netherlands and the Hanseatic League would be better candidates for this title). Eliminate (B) and (C). The Black Death, or bubonic plague affected continental Europe, not Asia, at this time, which eliminates (D). Only Japan engaged in trade under the auspices of paying tribute to China, so get rid of (E).

26.   **E**   In 1868 the Meiji emperor returned to power in Japan, marking the beginning of the Meiji period, (E), which was characterized by intensive efforts at modernization and Westernization, including significant political reforms. These reforms included democratization and a constitutional form of government, as opposed to absolute rule by any emperor, so (A) is incorrect. The Meiji period marked the end, not the beginning of the Tokugawa shogunate and marked the capital's move to Tokyo, not Kyoto, so (B) and (C) are incorrect. Japan had been in contact with the West continuously, even during the isolationist period (via contact with the Dutch), which makes (D) incorrect.

27.   **D**   Legalism, (D), was based on the writings of Han Feizi, a follower of Confucius who believed that human beings were essentially bad and that human nature had to be restricted for the good of the society. Confucianism, (A), took a more positive view of human nature. Taoism, (B), is more neutral: human beings find their own path, which is not innately good or bad. Moism, (C), also envisions human nature as neither good nor bad. Jainism, (E), is primarily an Indian religion with many similarities to Buddhism.

28.   **A**   The German-Soviet Nonaggression Pact (aka the Nazi-Soviet Pact or the Hitler-Stalin Pact) made official each nation's promise not to attack the other. It also included a secret provision outlining the manner in which Germany and the Soviet Union planned to take control of Eastern and Central Europe. The pact detailed which portions of these regions would belong to each country. The conclusion of the pact allowed Hitler to invade Poland without fear of Soviet reprisal; in fact, the Soviet Union invaded Poland around the same time, and the two nations divided Poland as they had previously agreed. Relations between the two nations soon grew troubled—a totalitarian led

each country, after all, and that's not exactly a great formula for stable long-term relations—and the pact was finally nullified in 1941, when Germany invaded the Soviet Union.

29. A   During the Middle Ages, European traders traveled overland to reach Asia. The route passed through central Europe, which became a financial center. Advances in seafaring, however, allowed traders to travel east more quickly by sea. As a result, trading centers quickly sprung up on Europe's Atlantic coast, the point of departure for most trading ships.

30. B   Three of the (incorrect) answer choices for this question describe situations that would have been extremely uncommon—practically impossible, in fact—in the ancient world: a conquering nation allowing the conquered people to continue practicing their faith, (A); massive conquest, (C), without the support of the dominant religion (in fact, Charlemagne was crowned emperor of Rome by the Pope); and conquest without violence, (D). That leaves just (B) and (E) as possible answers. Of the two, (E) would be far more difficult to achieve and can therefore be eliminated. Charlemagne united most of western and central Europe under his rule; King Wen, founder of the Zhou dynasty, united much of western China.

31. D   Simón Bolívar (1783–1830) was the father of South American Spanish-speaking colonies' independence movements. Starting around 1808, he led military independence movements and funded them with his family's personal wealth. Although he was briefly attached to Napoleon, he did not want to see French rule in South America, and he began his resistance after Napoleon's brother was made the king of Spain and its colonies; eliminate (E). Bolívar had no descendants and was motivated by sincere beliefs; he did not intend to establish a monarchy, so (A) is incorrect. He was president, not dictator, of Gran Colombia, a confederation of the states which he had helped liberate; get rid of (C). He was also a liberator of the Spanish colonies only; he had no intentions toward Portuguese Brazil, so eliminate (B). Bolívar intended for the South American states he liberated to function in a federal arrangement like the early model of the United States, which shows (D) to be the correct answer.

32. D   The Buddhist religious tradition, (D), developed directly out of Hinduism after the birth of Siddhartha Gautama around 563 B.C.E. The two religions have a lot in common, including a belief in reincarnation and enlightenment. One major difference is that Hindus have priests and elaborate rituals, while Buddhists do not.

33. B   Between 1948 and 1981, the official racial segregation policy known as apartheid divided South Africa into four groups: white, black, Indian, and colored (mixed-race and some San people). Predictably, areas set aside for nonwhite inhabitants had vastly inferior facilities, and the system divided families and citizens from each other. But through a combination of peaceful and violent resistance, international support for the African native peoples, and the progressive shrinkage of the white population, the white-dominated government was convinced to repeal the laws establishing apartheid. The AIDS epidemic led to increased suffering under apartheid, not to a repeal of the policies. Therefore, you can eliminate (A), (C), (D), and (E) and choose (B).

34. C The cathedral in the picture exhibits many of the characteristics of Gothic architecture: pointed arches and vaults, delicately decorated windows, and elaborate exterior stonework. Its height and curved arches rule out architecture predating the Gothic period (which began in the 1100s and ended with the Renaissance). Although this building could have been built during the Renaissance or the postindustrial era—after all, the technology was available—the building is most typical of Gothic architecture and was most likely built during that period. Therefore, (C) is the answer.

35. B Predestination holds that God is omniscient. It follows, then, that God knows whether a person will enter heaven even before that person is born, and, therefore, that person can do nothing to alter his or her cosmic fate. John Calvin and Jonathan Edwards are among history's most prominent proponents of predestination, (B). Secular humanism, (A), and classical liberalism, (D), both stress the possibilities rather than the limits of the human experience. Historical determinism, (C), takes the hard-line view of cause and effect; it holds that all history could be explained scientifically, if only one could fully reveal all the factors contributing to a result. It is similar to predestination in that it considers certain results to occur unavoidably from certain effects, but its focus is historical, not religious. Taoism, (E), is a mystical Chinese philosophy of the 3rd century b.c.e. Taoists believe that individuals have the power to affect their own enlightenment through a spiritual quest known as "the way" ("the Tao" in Chinese).

36. B See the explanation for question 35.

37. B The Prague Spring was a period of liberalization and essentially democratic reform from January through August 1968 in what was then Czechoslovakia. It is most similar to the Qing dynasty's Hundred Days of Reform, (B), which was a movement dedicated to modernizing China after the loss in the Sino-Japanese War. Reformers aimed to create sweeping social, military, and political change but were ultimately removed from power by conservative forces within the Chinese government. The Orange Revolution in the Ukraine, (D), was a 2004–2005 protest against alleged electoral fraud that led to the election of an opposition president. As a successful political protest, it differs from a top-down social movement like the Prague Spring. The Tiananmen Square protests, (A), were an attempt by Chinese students and workers in Beijing to force democratization of the government; they were turned away with considerable violence, and the protest failed. Polish Solidarity, (C), was a very widespread union movement in Poland that eventually forced the communist government out of office. The commonwealth of England, (E), was the military dictatorship of Oliver Cromwell following the English Civil War of 1642–1651; it was not a model of liberalization and progress.

38. E In 49 b.c.e. the military commander Julius Caesar emerged as the sole leader of Rome and declared himself a dictator. This action upset many in the Roman political establishment, and a few years later Caesar was assassinated, precipitating the demise of the Republic and ushering in a new age for the empire. Nero, (A), was emperor between 37 and 68 c.e. Tiberius, (B), was emperor form 14 to 37 c.e. Constantine, (C), was emperor form 306–337 c.e. Caligula, (D), was emperor between 37 and 41 c.e.

39.   A   These kinds of geometric figure designs are most closely associated with peoples of the American Southwest, (A), with this particular blanket being from the Navajo culture. Native Peruvian art, (B), tended to use more curves and depict animals, unlike this image of a buffalo-headed man. The native peoples of the American Northwest, (C), are more commonly associated with totem poles, especially involving bright paint and hooked beaks. The native peoples of Madagascar, (D), and the American Northeast, (E), would also be unlikely to depict a buffalo on their blankets.

40.   B   Peter the Great of Russia, (B), who ruled from 1696 to 1725, is best known for his attempts to modernize Russia. He launched many initiatives to improve the country's infrastructure and to bring Western knowledge of the arts and of specialized crafts to his country.

41.   C   Mexico, as New Spain under the Spanish, extended all the way northeast to the source of the Mississippi River, (C). The Ohio River, (A), began east of the border of New Spain. The Rio Grande, (B), like the Pecos, (E), is in the modern American Southwest, well within the borders of New Spain. The Missouri River, (D), also began within the borders of New Spain.

42.   C   Taxes in the form of forced labor were commonly used in the ancient world, including Egypt. Prerevolutionary French citizens were also subject to the *corvée*, or forced-labor tax, (C). Foreign goods, (D), are not known to have been a special tax category in ancient Egypt. The *gabelle*, or salt tax, (A), as well as taxes on the use of roads, (B), and excessive cash taxes, (E), were major sources of discontent for the French people under the monarchy, but were not common in ancient Egypt.

43.   B   The dog and cat in the cartoon are labeled *Sverge* and *Norge* respectively. The cat looks angry. The connection between them is burning, and a man tries to put out the flames. What does this image tell us? If you recognize the names for Norway and Sweden, (B) is the clear answer. After ending up on the losing side of the Napoleonic Wars, Norway was ceded to Sweden. The union was dissolved in 1905 thanks to a combination of Norwegian dissatisfaction with their nonsovereign situation and the rise of Norwegian nationalist sentiments.

44.   B   In 284 C.E., the Roman Emperor Diocletian split the Empire into two halves, the western and eastern. This event marked major political changes in the Empire as there were often multiple leaders ruling simultaneously and fighting one another for power and influence. The Punic Wars, (A), fought between Rome and Carthage, ended in the 2nd century B.C.E. The birth of Muhammad, (C), the founder of Islam, occurred in the late 6th century C.E. The pharaohs in Egypt, (D), ceased to wield political power after about 30 B.C.E. The Gnostics, (E), were a group of early Christians whose writings and teachings were viewed with suspicion by mainstream church authorities. Most of their books were banned by the mid-4th century C.E.

45.   B   Japan's isolationist period, the Sakoku, or Country-in-Chains, policy, began with the expulsion of most Europeans in 1650 and ended with the arrival of American Commodore Matthew Perry in 1853, so (B) is correct. During this period, trade was allowed only within certain narrowly defined geographic areas and with specific groups of people, the majority of whom were from neighboring

countries, such as Korea, (A); China, (C); and the Ryukyu Islands, (E), which were still independent at the time. The only European group excepted from the exclusion laws was the Dutch, (D), who were still allowed to trade in Nagasaki.

46.   **D**   The European philosophy of the divine right of kings was used to justify royal absolutism and to consolidate the power of smaller localities into large kingdoms that became France and England. It held that the king should have sole authority over the nation, as he was appointed by God, so his word was not to be questioned. The Chinese idea of the Mandate of Heaven stated that emperors ruled with the consent of the supernatural world and that they should be obeyed, but only so long as they maintained divine favor. Thus, (D) is the correct answer: an emperor who ruled poorly could be deemed to have lost the mandate, in which case it would be justified to overthrow him (although this was obviously a difficult belief to put into practice). Shared authority between eunuchs and the emperor was never an official Chinese belief, nor was there a unified Chinese clergy dedicated to discerning the mandate, so eliminate (A) and (E). The mandate expressly indicated that the emperor ruled by divine favor, but neither the Europeans nor the Chinese believed that the king was directly descended genetically from God; eliminate (C) and (B).

47.   **B**   Che Guevara, (B), was a Latin American revolutionary leader; he was born in Argentina but later traveled extensively, becoming involved in revolutions in Guatemala and Cuba and in attempts to foment revolutions in the Congo and in Bolivia, where he was captured and summarily executed. Simón Bolívar, (A), the father of Latin American independence, died while Marx was still a teenager. Pancho Villa, (C), had a limited coherent social plan; although he was involved in the Mexican Revolution, he was not a socialist. Miguel Hidalgo, (D), inspired the Mexican-Spanish war of independence, but he died before Marx was born. Sam Houston, (E), was involved in taking Texas from Spanish control and bringing it, through stages, to the United States; his activities began while Marx was still composing his analysis of economic relations.

48.   **D**   Society's treatment of women has historically been very unequal, (D). While women have at times been assigned a role equal to that of men, that has not been the general pattern throughout history, so (C) is incorrect. Women have never been politically dominant in most societies, so (A) is incorrect. More recently, women have been given economic freedom equal to that of men, but again, this has not been the rule in much of history; eliminate (B). Although the word *domestic* means "of the home," and women have often been relegated to a domestic role, they were not usually in charge of domestic policy; plus, the term domestic policy refers to a government's approach to governing its own citizens, not management of a household. Eliminate (E).

49.   **C**   This image of an idealized young male scholar and his older instructor is typical of painting styles prominent in the Safavid Empire in Persia, (C). Notice the Arabic calligraphy on the left-hand side. Because Arabic was never the dominant language in Tang China, (A); Tokugawa Japan, (D); or Byzantine Greece, (E), these answers can be eliminated. The Ottoman Empire, (B), was better known for calligraphy and miniatures than paintings of this type, which is characteristically Persian rather than Turkish or Greek.

50. **B** Islam originated in the Arabian peninsula, but spread farther west and south across Africa and east into Central and South Asia within the first century of its founding. Buddhism, (A), originated in India and is prevalent mainly in Asia, particularly in China. Zoroastrianism, (C), is prevalent in Central Asia in the area of Iran. Christianity, (D), spread around the area of the Mediterranean Sea in all four directions. Judaism, (E), did not spread into Africa.

51. **D** In the years leading up to World War II, many in Europe refused to believe that Germany was gearing up for a war of aggression against its neighbors. Europe had still not recovered from its previous war, and the desire for peace was so strong that many simply ignored the evidence of impending crisis: primarily, the German military buildup and the increase in German nationalism. In 1938, Germany, Italy, France, and Britain met to negotiate the Munich Pact. Germany was demanding possession of the Sudetenland, a region located in Czechoslovakia but inhabited primarily by German-speaking people. Neville Chamberlain, (D), the British prime minister who represented his nation at the meeting, pursued a policy of appeasement and led the campaign to grant Germany's wish. The strategy, however, backfired: the Munich Pact taught Hitler that Europe would back down in the face of war. Soon after, he marched into Czechoslovakia and took control of most of the country (not just the Sudetenland portion). Again, no European nation rose to stop him. Emboldened, Hitler invaded Poland in September 1939. This time, however, Europe had gotten the message. As soon as the invasion of Poland began, England and France declared war on Germany, and World War II began.

52. **A** See the explanation for question 51.

53. **C** Thomas Aquinas (1225–1247) was an Italian Dominican Friar and a prominent theologian in the philosophy of *scholasticism*. This is an approach to learning that strongly emphasized dialectical reasoning and the resolution of contradiction, primarily for the purpose of defending religious dogma against an increasingly pluralist context. René Descartes, David Hume, and Sir Francis Bacon were all philosophers of Empiricism, which was dedicated to the acquirement of knowledge through observation or the sensory experience; eliminate (A), (B), and (D). Thomas More, (E), was a social philosopher dedicated to the Humanist movement that took place during the European Renaissance.

54. **B** Before the arrival of Europeans, native Australians used primarily high-quality Neolithic stone tools, (B), with polished and purpose-shaped edges. Although they were not a principally farming people, primarily because of the unpredictability of the Australian climate, their tools were more refined and purposed than would be characteristic of Paleolithic technology, (A). Metals were not used in native Australian craft before the arrival of Europeans, which eliminates (C), (D), and (E).

55. **A** The idea of *jihad*, or struggle, is an important part of Islam. However, despite its portrayal in the Western imagination since the Crusades, jihad is not substantially about warfare as a means of increasing territory. Instead, the "Greater jihad" is the struggle within one's own soul, (A), to make oneself better able to submit to the will of God. The struggle to spread Islam peacefully, (B), and to prevent unorthodox heresies, (D), are other forms of jihad, as is military conflict in some cases;

but conversion of non-Muslims by any means, (E), is not the highest priority. A unified state in the Middle East, (C), is not part of the doctrine of jihad, although some Middle Eastern Muslims might desire it.

56. **C** The 11th century C.E. saw the beginning the Crusades, widespread military conflicts in the "Holy Land." Christian rulers in Europe sent armies east to Palestine, ostensibly with the goal of "recapturing" Jerusalem away from the Muslims, (C).

57. **E** This quote is critical of Yankee (that is, American) imperialism. Which leader in the answer choices had the worst relationship with the United States? Cuba was a Spanish colony and then heavily influenced by American interests until the revolution led by Fidel Castro, (D). Castro, the long-time Communist leader of Cuba, is a strong critic of American foreign policy and the author of this quote. Choices (A), (B), and (C) were anti-Communist military dictators who generally enjoyed good relations with the United States, although Noriega ran afoul of Washington toward the end of his reign. Vladimir Lenin, (D), was more focused on bringing down capitalism and the tsarist rulers of Russia and, therefore, is not as likely to have made such a pronouncement.

58. **C** See the explanation for question 51.

59. **A** Heavily influenced by Confucian thought, the Han, (A), established an early form of the civil service program in the first or 2nd century B.C.E. While this program was not fully developed until later, under the Tang dynasty, (C), it was under the Han that the Chinese began to use merit examinations in order to select people for employment in the state bureaucracy.

60. **D** The Boer Wars pitted British colonists against Dutch-descended Afrikaners in the Transvaal Republic and the Orange Free State, (A), both established in the mid-1800s. British victory brought both areas into the British Empire, although soon after the entire region was united as the Union of South Africa and was granted autonomy, (C). Afrikaners went on to control the Union of South Africa (formed in 1910), imposing segregation of the races through apartheid until 1994. Lesotho, Botswana, and Swaziland, (B), all existed long before the Boer Wars. The Organization of African Unity, (E), was formed in 1953.

61. **B** The Safavid Empire ruled over Iran and surrounding territory from 1501 to 1735, and established Shi'a Islam as the official religion of Iran. The population of the empire was quite varied and included parts of and people from neighboring Central Asian states. Shah Abbas I sponsored trade along the Silk Road routes, which had been revived in the 16th century. Of the answers, only (B) is not true of the Safavids—there was no large-scale "opposition" to the Safavids during their existence.

62. **A** When, in 1949, it became apparent that the communists would soon take over mainland China, republican Chinese leader Chiang Kai-shek fled to Taiwan and established a government-in-exile there. Taiwan, with substantial assistance (at the time) from the United States, established itself as a republican stronghold and has continued to maintain its claim to being the only legitimate government of China, while the mainland communists assert the same about their own government.

In 1971, the communist Chinese assumed the position on the UN Security Council previously held by the nationalists, and today an overwhelming majority of nations (including the United States) do not recognize Taiwan's claims. Choice (A) is the correct answer.

63. **A** Vasco de Gama, (A), was a Portuguese explorer; he was the first European to reach India by sailing around the Cape of Good Hope on the southern tip of Africa. The other explorers listed were Spanish. Francisco Pizarro, (B), made several expeditions to South America and was instrumental in the Spanish conquest of the Inca Empire. Hernán Cortés, (C), conquered the Aztecs for Spain, Ponce de Leon, (D), landed in Florida while searching for gold, and Ferdinand Magellan completed the first voyage around the world and claimed the Philippines for Spain.

64. **D** The building of the pyramids at Giza, (Egypt) took place over a span of several decades around 2500 B.C.E. Hammurabi's Code was written in the 18th century B.C.E. The Persian conquest of Mesopotamia occurred in the 7th century B.C.E. The conquests of Alexander the Great occurred in the 4th century B.C.E.

65. **C** You have to use POE to answer this question correctly. As you read each answer choice, look for evidence that the answer cannot be correct. When you find it, eliminate the answer. With luck, there will be only one answer choice left when you are done. For (A) to be correct, the population of Egypt would have to be 390,000. That's how many people live in a mid-size city! More than seven million people live in Cairo (the capital of Egypt) alone. Get rid of this answer. For (B) to be correct, Haiti would have to export 260 million dollars' worth of goods more than it imports: That's way too high a figure. In fact, total Haitian exports added up to about $90 million as late as 1996. Choice (C) makes sense: the chart lists these countries in order of the strength of their economies. Saudi per capita income is relatively high because the country is a leading oil exporter. Keep this answer choice. For the same reason, (D) cannot be correct: because of its strength as an oil producer, Saudi Arabia carries little or no debt. Finally, these dimensions of arable land don't match the size and geography of the countries listed, (E). So (C) is the only choice that works.

66. **C** Beginning in at least the 1st century C.E., Buddhism entered China through the Silk Road, which was a main conduit for the spread of other religions and cultures, as well as a trade route from India through China and eventually to the West. Buddhism did not come from the West, so (A) and (B) can be eliminated. Buddhism also did not originate in Japan, so get rid of (D) as well. Last, eliminate (E): not only is it unlikely for mercenaries to spread religion, the Thai did not adopt Buddhism until 1360 under King Ramathibodi, much later than the Han dynasty, which itself was a Confucian state.

67. **B** Around 1400, Islamic merchants from the Ottoman Empire monopolized trade around the Persian Gulf and in the Indian Ocean. Among Europeans, only the Portuguese were eventually able to compete, because they had exclusive access to the routes around Africa; they came to dominate Indian Ocean trade themselves for a time. Thus, (B) is the correct answer. Italians had a dominant

trading position in the Mediterranean, but they themselves did not travel for trade in the Indian Ocean; eliminate (A), (C), and (D). Choice (E) mixes up the order of the two groups' dominance in the region.

68. **A** The Five Pillars of Islam are the five essential responsibilities of all Muslims. They include prayer, almsgiving, faith, fasting during the month of Ramadan, and pilgrimage to Mecca. Evangelism, (A), the practice of attempting to recruit converts, has played a major role in Islamic history, but it is not fundamental to the religion. Rather, its practice is the result of the zealousness of individuals, such as Arab traders and other itinerants.

69. **A** The domestication of the dog was historically one of the most powerful assets of early humans, because dogs are immensely useful: they are called "man's best friend" not because of the current relationship, but because of the services rendered throughout human history. Early domesticated wolves were great help hunting game, (B), and protecting humans, (E), particularly by keeping night watch over a band of humans. The Native Americans used dogs to pull sleds, (C), and many peoples, especially those who had few other sources of animal protein, have used dogs for food, (D). However, the idea of using dogs to track criminals, (A), is a modern one; in ancient times, this would not have been an issue the way it is today, as criminals would have had many fewer places to hide in a small band of hunter-gatherers (and running away from the group would have been as bad as the punishment for the crime itself).

70. **E** The earliest Chinese writing is found on oracle bones, which were tortoise shells, (E), and ox bones that were heated to produce cracks and used to make predictions about the future. Although characters were cast on bronze, (A), occasionally during the Shang dynasty and frequently during the Zhou, this was much later than the earliest Chinese writings, which predate the Shang proper. Chinese writing was never etched on clay, (C)—the Sumerians were the ones who wrote in this manner—nor was Chinese carved on bamboo, (D); instead, bamboo slits were used as a writing surface with ink and brush. Chinese was also written in ink on silk, (B), but all surviving evidence of this practice comes much later than the oracle bones, coming considerably later than the time of Confucius.

71. **E** Nelson Mandela, head of the African National Congress, was imprisoned in 1964 by the South African government as a result of his anti-apartheid activism, including armed resistance. After 27 years in prison, Mandela was freed thanks to international pressure on the South African government to do so, making (E) the correct answer. Gandhi was imprisoned for a time, but he died in 1948, which eliminates (D). None of the remaining figures were ever imprisoned.

72. **A** This map indicates the largest extent of the Mali Empire, (A), a West African empire that became powerful because of its trade in gold, salt, and ivory. Several empires have arisen in this area over history, but the Kingdom of Axum, (B), is not one of them: it was located in East Africa. The Babylonian Empire, (C), was present in southwestern Asia in the Mesopotamian region, not in West

Africa. Similarly, the Byzantine Empire, (D), was located in the eastern Mediterranean. By the 20th century, Portuguese colonies in Africa, (E), were limited primarily to Mozambique in East Africa and to scattered territories on the African coast; they would not have stretched so far inland as this map suggests.

73. **D** Along with Nelson Mandela, Desmond Tutu was the spiritual leader of black South African resistance to apartheid, (D). Although widespread poverty, (C), one result of apartheid, and domestic violence, (E), are very serious problems, Reverend Tutu is not famous for his opposition to them directly. Using this language to oppose communism, (B), would be hyperbolic. Plus, communism was not a major motivating force in South African racial politics. The slave trade, (A), was primarily West African when it officially existed; it is not legally carried out during contemporary times.

74. **B** The ancient Egyptians built the pyramids as tombs for the pharaohs and their queens, (B). Because the Egyptians had a strong belief in the afterlife and because they venerated their leaders as gods, it was of utmost importance that the pharaohs and their queens be buried in grand fashion according to their status.

75. **B** Stringed instruments of some form are to be found in every culture connected to the Mediterranean and Eurasian trade networks, dating back at least as far as the lyre in ancient Greece. Every group on this list was part of that trading and cultural exchange network except the Iroquois, (B), as Native Americans did not make contact with Europeans before the end of the 15th century. The other cultures mentioned all had some variety of stringed instrument.

76. **C** The llama was originally domesticated in the Andes. Domestication of the horse first took place somewhere in Eastern Europe, perhaps in present day Hungary or Ukraine, and spread to include all of Europe and large parts of Asia and Africa. Thus, (C) is the correct answer. The Chinese were not the first people to domesticate horses, so eliminate (A). South Africans and Pacific Islanders did not independently domesticate any large animal species, which eliminates (B) and (D). The horse was not present in North America before the arrival of Europeans and the Columbian Exchange, eliminating (E).

77. **A** Both the llama and the horse were often used to carry loads, (A). Plow-pulling, (B), was most commonly performed by cattle in most societies where they were available, and plows were not used in the Andes, where the llama originated. Llamas also are not suitable for riding, eliminating their use for mounted combat, (C). Andes peoples did not use wheeled transport, so llamas were not used for pulling wagons, (D). And Europeans did not commonly eat horses, (E), because they were too useful as draft and war animals, making them prohibitively expensive as a food source. Good knowledge of the technologies and animals involved in the Columbian Exchange will guide you through this question.

78. **D** POE should help you find the correct answer to this question. The realistic style evident in the paintings should help you get rid of (A), (B), and (C), all of which refer to art styles that are unrealistic and highly stylized. Choice (E), an English colonial meetinghouse, would never have been so

ornate as to include such paintings as the ones shown in the picture. These artworks are clearly the possession of a culture with great riches and considerable leisure time; thus, (D) is the best answer.

79. E   The religion whose goal is to escape the cycle of rebirth and suffering by breaking worldly attachments through proper living is Buddhism, (E). Taoism, (A), as a religion, involves the worship of a large number of gods through elaborate rituals; Hinduism, (B), is also a polytheistic religious belief system that entails its own code of conduct, while Islam, (C), is a monotheistic religion that also involves the belief of submission to the will of God. The Baha'i faith, (D), is a syncretic, though independent, belief system emphasizing the oneness of gods and of religions and advocating, among other things, the importance of social justice.

80. C   Hong Kong and Macau were controlled by Britain and Portugal, respectively, before the 1990s. You should be familiar with the fact that Hong Kong was ruled by the British until 1997, which eliminates (B) and (E). France, (A), had a fairly minor role in China; its Asian colonies were located in Vietnam, farther south. Spain's colonial presence, (D), was focused mainly in the New World; Spain's colonization had a westerly focus ever since the Treaty of Tordesillas of 1506.

81. A   Throughout much of human history, women have been controlled to various degrees by men. In many societies, the only women who could truly have a measure of independence were those who outlived their husbands and were able to control their own economic resources. In both Qing China and Renaissance Europe, widows could, in fact, have a measure of independence. In both these societies, women were involved in producing goods for trade and could own property under the right circumstances, eliminating (B) and (D). In Europe they were also officially involved in running the family business, eliminating (E). In both societies, women (especially of the upper class) had little choice over whom they would marry, eliminating (C).

82. B   Chichen Itza is today a major archeological site in Yucatan, Mexico, a remnant of the Maya civilization that peaked there circa 600 C.E. Machu Picchu, (A), was a major Incan city high in the Andes mountains of Peru and was inhabited until the Spanish conquest in 1532. Choqa Zanbil, (C), was built in 1250 B.C.E. in what is now Iran, and remains one of the few ziggurats found outside of Mesopotamia. Huayna Capac, (D), was an Incan emperor who lived from 1493 to 1527. Built in the 6th century C.E., the Hagia Sophia (the Church of Holy Wisdom), (E), is located in Istanbul and is one of the greatest architectural achievements of the Byzantine Empire.

83. E   According to legend, the city of Rome and Roman civilization more generally were founded when the brothers Romulus and Remus settled in the western part of the Italian Peninsula. An older civilization, the Etruscans, (E), already lived in the area and the Romans adopted many aspects of Etruscan culture. The other answers are incorrect for geographical and chronological reasons.

84. D   Confucian values spread outward extensively from China, growing to influence most of the rest of East Asia, most especially Japan and Korea, (D). There was little cultural influence, however, between the Chinese and the New Guineans, (A), or the Turks, (E). The Ak Koyunlu, (C), were a Turkish tribal confederation (known as the "White Sheep"), and they were also not substantially

influenced by Confucianism. The Mongols, (B), ruled over China for 100 years, but they were one of the few groups to do so without substantially assimilating Chinese culture, including Confucian values.

85. **C** Hunting and gathering societies do *not* make great scientific and cultural advances. They're too busy hunting and gathering. Choice (C) has to be the correct answer: if Babylonia had been a hunter-gatherer society, it never could have developed a codified legal system, (A); advanced arithmetic and geometry, (B); astronomy, (D); or a written language, (E).

86. **D** The British Empire's salt monopoly was challenged by Mohandas K. Gandhi, (D), more commonly known as Mahatma Gandhi, at the conclusion of his Salt Satyagraha, the 1930 march to the seashore to make salt in defiance of the British salt monopoly. Nelson Mandela, (A), was never opposed to a particular empire, but instead the racist apartheid policies of the South African government. American revolutionary Patrick Henry, (B), would have been more concerned with tea than salt. Dr. Sun Yat-sen, (C), considered the father of modern China, also opposed an empire, but had no special interest in salt. Brennus of Gaul, (E), sacked Rome, but did not use salt to do it.

87. **A** Mayan, Indian, Viking, and Semitic mythology all make mention of a deluge or great flood, (A), sent to destroy humanity. Semitic mythology does not recognize a thunder god, (B), while tricky snakes, (C), do not appear in Viking mythology, and sea monsters, (D), are not prominent in many of the mythological systems mentioned. Human sacrifice, (E), is not widely mentioned in Indian mythological traditions.

88. **B** There are a lot of details in the quotation, but you can answer this question by ignoring most of them if you pick up on one key fact: the social structure described is feudal. The mention of fiefs, peasants, and vassalage is your tip-off. Rome, Italy, Britain, and Japan were not feudal during the eras indicated in the answer choices.

89. **A** This is a tricky one, because the passage is not written all that clearly. Still, you can answer this if you remember a few things about feudalism and use POE to get rid of incorrect answer choices. Fiefs were grants of land and workers from the lord; holders of fiefs received these from their lord and, of course, owed their lord something in return. Choice (A), then, makes sense. Peasants did not own land under feudalism, so eliminate (B). Only the lord or a king could exercise power throughout a lord's territory, so eliminate (C). Under feudalism, the church and the clergy were very powerful; no law would have prevented clergymen from holding fiefs, so eliminate (E). Choice (D) is more difficult to eliminate. To get rid of it, in fact, you have to understand the reference to vassalage, a system under which lesser lords bound themselves into military service in return for land and other favors from their lord.

90. **D** Muslim armies, (D), under the Umayyad caliphate invaded and conquered much of the Iberian Peninsula (modern-day Spain and Portugal) in the early 8th century c.e. This military campaign was part of the broader Muslim expansion across the Middle East, North Africa, Asia, and Europe that followed the death of Muhammad.

91. **C** Mayan pyramids are distinguished by their flat tops, which the Maya used as observatories from which to study the stars. Stairways leading to the top also distinguish Mayan pyramids from those built in Egypt, (A). Egyptian pyramids usually have pointed tops and smooth walls that are scalable only with difficulty. The Romans, (B); Incas, (D); and Hebrews, (E), did not build pyramids.

92. **B** More than 80 percent of Indians are Hindus. Islam is India's second-largest faith, accounting for about 12 percent of the population.

93. **E** This poem sings the praises of Shaka of the Zulu. The Zulu were a Bantu-speaking ethnic group in South Africa, (E), a powerful influence in the 12th century and most powerful under Shaka and his successors from around 1800 through the Anglo-Zulu War in 1878–1879. The names beginning with N-consonant clusters in the poem are typical of Bantu languages. East Africa, (C), would include Ethiopia and Eritrea and possibly Sudan, which is not the correct area; North Africa, (D), suggests Egypt, the Middle East, and perhaps the Berber lands stretching west toward the Atlantic, which is also incorrect. West Africa, (A), would most likely refer to the Sahel, which is more usually associated with Mansa Kankan Musa and the Malinese Empire. Central Africa, (B), includes the modern-day Republic of Congo and Democratic Republic of Congo, among other states; although this is a Bantu-speaking region, it is not an area that would have been under the leadership of Shaka.

94. **D** Both South Korea and Taiwan became developed, industrialized nations thanks to protectionism, (D), and ready access to American capital. In the South Korean case, this extended to the government giving negative-interest loans to some industrialists in order to encourage development of production capacity. Choices (A) and (B) have not led to successful industrialization in any country, despite orthodox economic theories which claim they should, and completely democratic economic policy, (E), has never been tried. Choice (C) is not accurate; both South Korea and Taiwan organized industrial development through a certain measure of central planning, although it did not nearly resemble the Chinese and Soviet communist governments.

95. **D** Here are the pertinent dates: Weimar Republic (1919–1933); the Third Reich (1933–1945); the Federal Republic of Germany (1949–present). Between the end of World War II and 1949, Germany was an occupied country.

HOW TO SCORE PRACTICE TEST 1

When you take the real exam, the proctors will collect your test booklet and bubble sheet and send your answer sheet to the processing center where a computer looks at the pattern of filled-in ovals on your answer sheet and gives you a score. We couldn't include even a small computer with this book, so we are providing this more primitive way of scoring your exam.

Determining Your Score

STEP 1 Using the Answer Key at the beginning of this chapter, determine how many questions you got right and how many you got wrong on the test. Remember, questions that you do not answer don't count as either right answers or wrong answers.

STEP 2 List the number of right answers (A) here.

(A) _____

STEP 3 List the number of wrong answers (B) here and divide that number by 4. (Use a calculator if you're feeling particularly lazy.)

(B) _____ ÷ 4 = _____

STEP 4 Subtract the number of wrong answers divided by 4 from the number of correct answers. Round this score to the nearest whole number. This is your raw score.

(A) _____ – (B) _____ = (C) _____

STEP 5 To determine your real score, take (C) your raw score from Step 4 above and look it up in the left column of the Score Conversion Table on the next page; the corresponding score on the right is your score on the exam.

Practice Test 1 Score Conversion Table

Raw Score	Scaled Score	Raw Score	Scaled Score	Raw Score	Scaled Score
95	800	55	680	15	440
94	800	54	670	14	430
93	800	53	670	13	430
92	800	52	660	12	420
91	800	51	660	11	420
90	800	50	650	10	410
89	800	49	640	9	400
88	800	48	640	8	400
87	800	47	630	7	390
86	800	46	630	6	390
85	800	45	620	5	380
84	800	44	610	4	370
83	800	43	610	3	370
82	800	42	600	2	360
81	800	41	600	1	360
80	800	40	590	0	350
79	800	39	580	−1	340
78	800	38	580	−2	340
77	800	37	570	−3	330
76	800	36	570	−4	330
75	800	35	560	−5	320
74	790	34	550	−6	320
73	790	33	550	−7	310
72	780	32	540	−8	300
71	770	31	540	−9	300
70	770	30	530	−10	290
69	760	29	520	−11	290
68	760	28	520	−12	280
67	750	27	510	−13	270
66	740	26	510	−14	270
65	740	25	500	−15	260
64	730	24	490	−16	260
63	730	23	490	−17	250
62	720	22	480	−18	240
61	720	21	480	−19	240
60	710	20	470	−20	230
59	700	19	460	−21	230
58	700	18	460	−22	220
57	690	17	450	−23	210
56	690	16	450	−24	210

Part III
Content Review for the SAT Subject Test in World History

4   The Rise of Human Civilization
5   From Civilizations to Empires
6   The Age of World Religions
7   World Civilizations in Transition: 1000 to 1500
8   The Modern World Emerges: 1500 to 1900
9   War and Peace: 1900 to Present

Chapter 4
The Rise of Human Civilization

The period from the earliest known prehistory to 500 C.E. is a pretty wide swath of time, but therein lie the origins of most of civilization as we know it.

In this chapter, we'll start with a brief (very brief) review of prehistory. Then, we'll move on to a discussion of the defining characteristics of human civilization, and look at how and why civilization differs from humans' prior way of life. Once we've defined civilization, we'll move on to a survey of ancient cultures around the world and look at how these civilizations developed—the advancements they made and the challenges they faced. The chapter will close with a discussion of common themes and important differences. We begin not just with the history of ancient cultures, but the history of all of humanity—*your* history. Enjoy!

HUMANITY'S PREHISTORY: A BRIEF REVIEW

Prehistory...

...describes the period of human history before the advent of the written word.

The term **prehistory** is used to describe the earliest times of human society, when communities existed, but no written records were left. When historians talk about human **culture**, they are interested in how humans behave, interact with each other, and express themselves. Culture is a broad category that encompasses belief systems, intellectual pursuits, artistic endeavors, religion, language, values, customs, and the ways in which people create and use symbols. When describing societies from the past, historians typically distinguish between the physical remnants of a society—also known as **material culture**—and everything else.

What we know about the prehistoric period is informed by other fields of study such as anthropology and archeology, which rely heavily on **fossil remains** and **artifacts**—pottery, jewelry, weaponry, buildings, and many other human-made items—to tell the story of ancient peoples. Human beings, of course, evolved over a period of several million years. As a species, we have our origins in Africa, but at some point our ancestors migrated to Asia and Europe as well.

The earliest time period about which historians have reliable evidence is commonly known as the **Paleolithic period**, or "Old Stone Age." The term Stone Age is a little misleading, but historians use it because it was during that time period, around 2.5 to 2 million years ago, that humans began to use tools made of chipped stone. These early humans made tools of other materials as well, most notably bone, wood, and antlers, but those material artifacts have not survived as well throughout the millennia.

At the end of Chapters 4 through 9, we've provided a list of key terms, people, and events along with a definition for each. You can also find printable versions of these lists in your Student Tools when you register your book! See the "Get More (Free) Content" page at the beginning of this book for step-by-step instructions.

So what can fossils and artifacts tell us? In sum, early humans were primarily **nomadic hunter-gatherers**, traveling seasonally to find food and to live in the most hospitable conditions. The markings found on prehistoric animal bones suggest that early humans used weapons and other tools to kill and butcher meat. This does not, however, mean that our ancestors were eating meat all of the time. While we often picture "cavemen" hunting meat every day, anthropologists now believe that the majority of early people's nutrition came from gathering food such as nuts and berries (with meat probably reserved for special occasions and feasts). The problem with reconstructing what exactly it was that Paleolithic people ate is that organic matter decomposes quickly so there are no remains from which to paint a clear picture.

The earliest hunter-gatherers probably lived in small groups or bands, dividing responsibilities among men and women. Because they moved frequently to take advantage of migrating animals and more favorable settings for foraging, these humans did not erect permanent structures. Instead, they sheltered in caves or built huts from tree branches, rocks, and other materials. Animal skins and furs tied together with rope or rawhide would have probably been the primary type of clothing worn during this early time period.

The Paleolithic period was when humans began to develop language, science, religion, and other aspects of culture. As hunter-gatherers, our ancestors would have needed to know a lot about the natural world—which types of plants were safe to eat, the migration patterns of animals, etc. Early humans would have needed to develop ways of making clothing and tools and to communicate effectively with each other in order to survive in groups.

Paleolithic humans may have developed music and dance, but there is no way to know for sure. On the other hand, historians do have a fair amount of information about **prehistoric art**, such as the **Lascaux cave paintings** in France, which give some description of the rituals and spirituality of early human culture in addition to information about food-gathering methods. These paintings, estimated to be about 17,000 years old, were discovered in 1940 by a group of teenagers! Many of the images depict animals, some of which were hunted for food (cattle, bison, deer) and some of which were not (rhinoceros, panther, hyena). Other images depict humans dressed in animal-skin clothing and smeared with paint.

The Lascaux cave paintings, along with those of another site in France (Chauvet), also contain stenciled human hands and abstract symbols. Historians don't agree about the exact purpose of all these prehistoric paintings—were they intended to educate the young? Do they incorporate prehistoric star charts and astronomical knowledge? Were the paintings used in religious rituals? Could they have been records of or memorials to past hunting successes? We may never know for sure, but undoubtedly these artworks are an invaluable part of the story of human history.

The Neolithic Revolution

The **Neolithic** (New Stone Age) period of prehistory, which lasted from roughly 8500 to 3500 B.C.E., is important because it marks the real change from primitive social organizations to something much more. This was the period when, according to archeological evidence, humans began to settle down to farm the land and, most important, domesticate plants and animals for both food and labor. Humans still engaged in hunting and foraging, of course, but the shift to agriculture and animal husbandry in many parts of the world transformed the ways in which our ancestors lived.

Agricultural processes probably developed over many years. Some of the earliest evidence comes from Mesopotamia, where people figured out how to take the most productive strains of wild grasses and cultivate them into the plants that we now know as wheat and barley. These farming methods spread to parts of the Mediterranean world and to Europe.

Because of differences in climate and rainfall, Saharan and Sub-Saharan Africa developed separately. Instead of wheat and barley, early Africans cultivated such crops as sorghum, millet, groundnuts, and gourds. In the Indian subcontinent and parts of East and Southeast Asia, rice was widely cultivated, while in the Americas people were busy growing maize, manioc, potatoes, and quinoa.

During the Neolithic period humans began to domesticate animals in addition to developing farming techniques. The first domesticated animal was the dog, probably because it was useful in tracking and hunting game, herding other animals, and protecting settlements. Other types of domesticated animals were used for meat, milk, and transportation. The types of animals domesticated by Neolithic peoples varied quite a bit according to geographical differences: sheep, goats, cows, and pigs in the Middle East and Europe; donkeys in North Africa; camels in the deserts of Arabia; water buffalo in Asia; and llamas in South America (just to name a few).

Apart from their usefulness for food, milk, skins, wool, and leather, animals pulled plows and their dung was used for fertilizer. In some parts of the world, notably Africa and Central Asia, humans practiced **pastoralism**, a form of agriculture in which the tending of animals was central and often involved moving from place to place in order to provide the herds with the best available water and pasture land.

The cumulative effects of these changes were that due to agriculture and animal husbandry, larger groups of people were able to survive together and settle permanently rather than having to move from place to place, following the seasons and migrating animals to find and hunt food (the pastoralists were mobile, but relied upon the use of domesticated animals rather than hunting wild ones).

Historians don't have all the answers about why the Neolithic revolution occurred, but in addition to the obvious stability of agriculture and animal husbandry, global climate change (warming) may have facilitated these shifts in the way most people lived. It is important to note that there were major exceptions to this model: in Australia, for example, people relied upon hunting and foraging until quite recently; in other places, such as the Pacific Northwest and the Gulf of Mexico, fishing was the primary source of food.

The Neolithic period was important in many respects beyond the transformation in food production. More stable settlements led to more lasting architecture, more complex social constructs (including more formal leadership structures), and more possibility for creative developments such as decorative (rather than just functional) art and other aesthetic endeavors. The fact that these early civilizations built permanent homes and other structures makes it possible to find evidence of their presence thousands of years later, even if we don't know all the details of exactly how or why people settled as they did.

The bottom line is this: prehistory is important because it lays the foundation for the development of **civilization**, which, for our purposes, is best understood as distinct groups of people living as a settled unit: people living together with a shared set of laws and supported by agriculture.

Next Stop: Civilization

Civilization did not arise instantaneously once people settled down and planted things. People did not even start to form societies in only one place. Civilization arose in a number of places—not all at the exact same time, but with some common characteristics and patterns of development. Among these patterns are: settled agriculture; some type of formal political organization; a shared religious/philosophical code; the development of writing; the creation of more diverse labor and social class divisions; advancements in metallurgy and architecture; and the pursuit of knowledge and artistic creativity.

The most vital of these characteristics was settled agriculture, as it provided the food stocks necessary for the building of cities—the breeding grounds for human creativity. Not surprisingly, then, ancient history was dominated by civilizations that arose in fertile river valleys on different continents. Despite their extremely intermittent contact, these ancient societies—in India, China, Africa, Egypt, and Mesopotamia—share most of the characteristics of civilization. Only one group of major ancient civilizations—those of Central America—developed according to a different pattern. Although less well-known, civilizations of North America, South America, and New Guinea tended to develop separately from the river-valley pattern.

Let's take a look at each civilization, up close and personal.

ANCIENT MESOPOTAMIA

c. 3500 B.C.E.	Rise of Sumerian culture in southern Mesopotamia
c. 3300 B.C.E.	Cuneiform writing is developed; ziggurats are built; wheel is invented; bronze metallurgy becomes common.
c. 2350 B.C.E.	Sargon, ruler of the Semitic-speaking Akkadians, begins conquering the Sumerian city-states; the Akkadians rule for around 200 years.
c. 1790–1750 B.C.E.	Rule of King Hammurabi; development of Hammurabi's Code
c. 1000 B.C.E.	Hebrew scriptures are written down.
c. 900–600 B.C.E.	Assyrians come to dominate Mesopotamia.
c. 500 B.C.E.	Persian Empire conquers Mesopotamia.

Ancient **Mesopotamia**, nestled between the Tigris and Euphrates rivers, is often called the cradle of human civilization. Mesopotamia, which literally means "the land between the rivers," is a great case study for us to see how the earliest human societies developed into outright civilizations. The **Sumerians**, who settled southern Mesopotamia sometime around 3500 B.C.E., were the first people of the **Fertile Crescent** to be considered a civilization. We know from personal names recorded on inscriptions dating back to around 3000 B.C.E. that the Sumerians spoke an early form of **Semitic**, a language group that also includes Hebrew, Aramaic, and Arabic. From around 2000 B.C.E. the Akkadian language (also Semitic) became the dominant language of Mesopotamia.

Alphabet Soup
Here is a quick guide to commonly used abbreviations:

B.C.E.	"Before the Common Era"—refers to the same time period as B.C., "before Christ"
C.E.	"Common Era"—refers to the same time period as A.D., "anno Domini"
c.	"circa" Latin for "around"—used to denote an approximate date

The Sumerians had many firsts: they developed the first written language; they invented the wheel; they invented the way we tell time; they may have written the first novel; and they probably invented beer. Perhaps the Sumerians' greatest achievement, however, and the one that led to these other inventions, was the development of **settled agriculture**. How, exactly, did these Mesopotamian peoples accomplish such a feat? Irrigation. By building complex networks of canals, drainage ditches, dikes, and dams, they were able to move water from the large rivers and their tributaries to the surrounding countryside.

Settled agriculture resulted in a vastly greater population, which in turn energized the development and organization of political structures, a defining characteristic of civilization. Settled agriculture required people to work together in large groups, both for building irrigation networks and for harvesting crops, shearing animals, and other tasks. Population sizes larger than in any previous human experience required new ways for people to relate to one another, so that strangers without family ties would live peacefully instead of trying to kill one another on sight. In most societies, this mutual tolerance first developed under a powerful chieftain or strongman, who was able to intimidate others into behaving peaceably.

While the earliest years of the Sumerian civilization were probably characterized by small village settlements, as these villages grew larger they would have morphed into larger communities (**city-states**) with leadership structures that developed out of the village council model. In Sumeria, these early leaders eventually became powerful kings who first ruled individual city-states and then came to rule over many city-states. Although these early kings were powerful, they shared their power with the temple priests, who together ruled on behalf of their city-state's patron god.

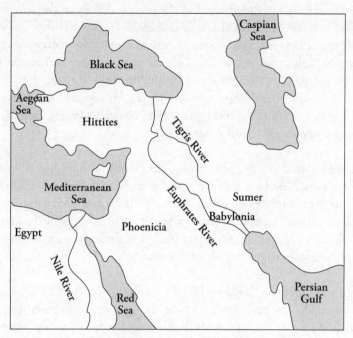

Early Civilizations in the Middle East

The stable food source supplied by settled agriculture made the first cities possible. Although not large by today's standards, the largest Sumerian cities reached as many as 100,000 residents (however, the norm of the time was cities of only a few thousand residents). Cities this large could not be supported without a constant, stable food supply. Fortunately, the Sumerians were able to grow more food than the farmers themselves needed.

The ability to create a food surplus freed around 10 percent of the population to pursue other interests such as governing, writing, reading, building, buying, and selling. Such large groups of people living together also meant reaching a critical mass of human creativity for the development and spread of new ideas. This stability, together with the freedom to do something other than spend all day in the fields, made cities and civilization possible.

How Big Is a City of 100,000?
Pretty big! Here are the populations of a few modern cities to give you a sense of scale:
- Santa Fe, New Mexico: 62,200
- Trenton, New Jersey: 82,000
- Berkeley, California: 102,000
- Tucson, Arizona: 525,000
- Charlotte, North Carolina: 670,000

Cities were not only the centers of power and religion, but also centers for the trading of goods and ideas. At the center of Sumerian cities were the great **ziggurats**, large, sloping step-pyramid temples that symbolized the power of the kings, the priests, and the gods. Each city-state probably had at least one temple complex dedicated to a single deity or multiple deities that were thought to preside over the wellbeing of the community. As such, the priests in charge of these temples wielded enormous power: the temples owned land, so the priests were powerful in economics and politics as well as religion.

In addition to the ziggurat (dedicated to the principal deity of the temple), Sumerian temple complexes contained minor chapels dedicated to other deities, courtyards and plazas, housing and dining facilities, shops and storerooms, and were surrounded by high protective walls. Since the temples were considered the gods' residence on earth, there was an enormous amount of ceremony and ritual that took place in these vast and important complexes. Historians believe that some of the larger temples, such as the one dedicated to the god Marduk in Babylon, may have employed several thousand priests!

It is not clear to what extent the common people would have had access to these temple complexes. The best archaeological evidence for Sumerian peoples' private religious lives comes from **amulets**, small objects intended to protect against evil and the demonic forces believed to affect daily life. Many of the amulets that have been found in Mesopotamia depict images of demons and contain spells that would have been used to combat those demons.

Knowledge and creativity flourished in the Sumerian cities of Uruk, Lagash, Ur, Nippur, and Eridu. Sumerian society was the first to develop writing, possibly as early as 3300 B.C.E. Starting with pictograms (a type of writing that conveys meaning through the images' resemblance to physical objects), the Sumerians eventually developed the **cuneiform** script, which became the standard alphabet across much of the region as Sumerian culture spread as a result of trade and conquest. It is important to note that cuneiform is not a language, but rather a writing style that was used by people who spoke Sumerian, Akkadian, Hittite, and Persian, among other languages.

The cuneiform writing style, inscribed upon wet clay tablets using sharp tools, consists of wedge-shaped markings that represented whole words or syllables. Unlike the modern English alphabet, which contains merely 26 letters, cuneiform writing required a person to master hundreds of different combinations of wedges and probably took several years to learn.

While only a small percentage of the population would have been able to read and write, the development of cuneiform writing served to create entirely new categories of workers: scribes, teachers, and students. Writing allowed leaders to document laws, merchants to record their sales, and poets to transcribe the stories that had been passed down through the generations. The oldest known examples of cuneiform writing document economic transactions, but the Sumerians wrote other types of texts as well. Some of the many pieces of writing that archaeologists have found concern politics, religion, philosophy, and science.

Beyond their agricultural and literary achievements, the ancient Mesopotamian civilizations developed other important technologies. There is evidence to indicate that they used wheeled carts and sleds (pulled by animals), and some pretty sophisticated engineering must have been involved in building the great ziggurats. In warfare, horse-drawn chariots were widely used, and Mesopotamian armies used siege machinery to encircle and attack their enemies' fortified cities.

The Sumerians were skilled in astronomy and math as well. Have you ever wondered why we use units of 60 to count time? This system comes from ancient Mesopotamia, where mathematicians used a base-60 number system to account for fractions and percentages (as opposed to the base-10 number system that we use for most things today).

Cycle of Conquest

On the political front, however, the Sumerians did not live happily every after. In fact, they were merely the first in a succession of peoples that came to dominate what is today Iraq. Around 2350 B.C.E., the Sumerians were conquered by the **Akkadians**, a Semitic-speaking people who lived further up the Tigris and Euphrates rivers, around the modern-day city of Baghdad (the ruins of the most important city of this time period, Babylon, could be seen from Saddam Hussein's summer palace near Baghdad). The leader of the Akkadians, **Sargon**, called himself the "king of Sumer and Akkad," indicating his rule over both his people and the Sumerians. Although the Sumerians were conquered by Sargon, much of Sumerian culture was adopted by the invading Akkadians. They integrated Sumerian cuneiform and parts of the Sumerian religion into their own culture.

Sargon's dynasty had lasted only 200 years when the Sumerians regained control of southern Mesopotamia under the **Third Dynasty of Ur** (c. 2115–2000 B.C.E.). However, the Sumerians soon succumbed to the rule of the Amorites, also known as the Old Babylonians. The most famous of the Old Babylonian rulers was **Hammurabi** (c. 1790–1750 B.C.E.). He, too, came to rule over Sumer and Akkad. And, of course, Hammurabi is best known for the infamous **Hammurabi's Code**.

Hammurabi's Code is the best surviving example of the legal codes that existed in ancient Mesopotamia. The stele of Hammurabi, the large stone sculpture that has preserved Hammurabi's Code, contains not only the 282 individual codes of law, but also depicts in bas-relief the sun god Shamash passing the tablet of laws over to Hammurabi, not unlike the way in which the Hebrew God is said to have passed the Ten Commandments to Moses.

Hammurabi's Code is very important in the history of law, in part because it provided judges with principles by which to decide cases as well as specific examples that judges could use as precedents (something that is common in modern legal systems). The Code also tells us a lot about how ancient Mesopotamian society was structured, since different legal frameworks and punishments applied to people of different classes (and genders). The types of issues dealt with in the Code are quite broad ranging, including contracts, trade, property, inheritance, divorce, military service, and sexual behavior. Many crimes were met with harsh punishment, often corporal in nature, and the death penalty was widely used.

The Epic of Gilgamesh
Indeed, it is because of cuneiform script that today we know the tale of the *Epic of Gilgamesh*, which is considered one of the first examples of literature in the world. An epic poem, *Gilgamesh* describes the relationship between a king and his companion, who is sent by the gods. Apart from its importance as one of the earliest known works of world literature, *Gilgamesh* is notable because of its numerous literary and thematic parallels with parts of the Hebrew Bible (garden of paradise, flood, etc.) and its influence upon later writers.:

Semitic...

...in this context is a *linguistic* term. Semitic languages include Akkadian, Amharic, Aramaic, and Arabic, as well as Hebrew.

Bas-Relief

A *bas-relief* is a type of sculpture created by carving out a flat piece of wood or stone, so that the image is raised. It is the opposite of *sunken relief*, in which the image is carved into the surface with the resulting image being recessed.

After the Akkadians, the cycle of conquest in ancient Mesopotamia continued with the fall of Hammurabi's dynasty as the **Hittites** and **Kassites** briefly controlled the formerly Babylonian lands. Then, in 900 B.C.E., the **Assyrians** came to dominate greater Mesopotamia. The Assyrians were not particularly nice to the people they conquered. They had a bad habit of torturing and exiling the peoples of the land they invaded, and are perhaps best known for conquering the lost tribes of ancient Israel. In fact, the Assyrian Empire was the largest of its time, stretching from the Black Sea area in the north to North Africa in the south, and from the eastern part of the Mediterranean in the west to Persia (modern-day Iran) in the east.

But for all of their adventures in war, the Assyrians had an intellectual side as well. The Assyrian king Ashurbanipal constructed the largest library of the ancient world around 650 B.C.E. in the city of **Nineveh**, the Assyrian capital city (near the modern day city of Mosul, Iraq). It was in Nineveh that the first complete text of the *Epic of Gilgamesh* was kept (the collection found at Nineveh is now housed in the British Museum in London).

The rule of the Assyrians was also short-lived as the Chaldeans, also known as the Neo-Babylonians, conquered and destroyed Nineveh in 610 B.C.E. But the Chaldeans themselves were conquered soon after by the great Persian Empire in 539 B.C.E. Not to be outdone, **Alexander the Great**, the infamous Macedonian king, conquered Babylon, the heart of Mesopotamia, in 331 B.C.E. The point of all this background detail (look out for more on the ancient Middle East in the next couple of chapters) is that ancient Mesopotamia was never controlled by one people for any great length of time, historically speaking. Each ruling civilization, however, left its mark on the land between the rivers. And at the very least we can thank the Sumerians for the 60-second minute, the Babylonians for the idea of a written code of law, and the Assyrians for preserving one of the oldest stories of humankind, the *Epic of Gilgamesh*.

ANCIENT EGYPT

c. 3100 B.C.E.	Upper and Lower Egypt are unified under the control of a single king; hieroglyphic writing develops.
c. 2500 B.C.E.	The pyramid of Pharaoh Khufu, the largest of the Great Pyramids of Giza, is constructed over the course of decades during the Old Kingdom.
c. 2150 B.C.E.	The Old Kingdom is brought to an end by decades of drought and famine.
c. 1900 B.C.E.	New Kingdom Pharaohs begin to trade with other cultures of the Mediterranean and conquer Nubian lands to the south.
c. 1600 B.C.E.	Lower Egypt is invaded by the Hyksos, who occupy the delta region for decades.
c. 1500 B.C.E.	The "age of the great pharaohs" begins and sees Egypt at its most powerful.
c. 1200 B.C.E.	The death of Ramses the Great marks the end of the "age of great pharaohs" as Egypt's civilization begins a slow decline.

Geography as Destiny

We cannot review ancient Egypt without talking about the importance of the Nile River to the development of Egyptian civilization. Unlike the unpredictable nature of the Tigris and Euphrates rivers, the Nile flooded regularly every year, providing natural irrigation and vital silt for the nourishment of crops. In this sense at least, settled agriculture was easier in Egypt than in ancient Mesopotamia. The Nile was also an oasis of civilization surrounded by natural geographic barriers. To the west and east, vast and inhospitable deserts bordered the Nile Valley.

To the south, a series of cataracts, or large waterfalls, prevented any invaders from readily sailing down the Nile into Egyptian territory. And finally to the north, Egypt was bordered by the Mediterranean Sea, a natural barrier in the infancy of ocean travel. Although Egypt was relatively close to ancient Mesopotamia, its culture developed rather independently, and somewhat differently, because of the natural barriers of water and desert.

In ancient times, Egyptians referred to the "black land," which was the inhabitable area near the river (so-called because of the dark color of the soil), and the "red land," which was the uninhabitable desert. There were a couple of oasis settlements in the desert to the west of the Nile, but for the most part the river was the key to life until very recently in Egyptian history.

The Nile also provided ancient Egyptians with one of their most widely used crops, the papyrus plant. Papyrus was used for making paper, of course, but could also be used to make rope and sails. The Nile was important not only because of its role in agriculture, but also because it was the main avenue for travel, communication, and trade. In fact, even in modern-day Egypt, the vast majority of the population lives very close to the river.

Rise…and Decline. Rise…and Decline. Rise…Okay, You Get the Idea

Historians have identified roughly thirty dynasties in **early Egyptian civilization**, so the details can get a bit overwhelming. We'll focus on just a few of the most important political developments. The Nile flows from south to north, so the northern delta region is lower in elevation than the southern region. The study of ancient Egypt generally begins with the unification of Upper (southern) and Lower (delta region) Egypt, possibly under the rule of a king named Narmer, or Menes, around 3100 B.C.E. This time period is often referred to as the **Early Dynastic period**.

After this era, the history of ancient Egypt is divided into three "kingdoms"— Old, Middle, and New—with three intermediate periods of instability falling in between. Egypt's unification likely occurred over a period of decades, if not centuries, as leaders of local *nomes* (local units of administration) consolidated their power over more and more towns and cropland up and down the Nile.

Hieroglyphic writing, too, developed during this same general time period. Unlike Sumerian cuneiform writing, hieroglyphs were pictures that resembled physical objects or animals but symbolized words or syllables. During its early stages, hieroglyphic writing was primarily used by the priestly class. The kings of the Early Dynastic period became increasingly responsible for maintaining political and religious order throughout the Nile valley. This focus on order, or *ma'at*, was inspired by the stability that the Nile River brought to Egyptian life.

Rise…

The **Old Kingdom** (2700–2200 B.C.E.) is one of the most famous time periods of ancient Egyptian history, primarily because of the incredible building that took place. It was during this time period that the Egyptian leaders became viewed as divine god-kings, or **Pharaohs**. And not surprisingly, the powers of the temple priests increased greatly during this time as well, as the priests were needed to maintain the religious rites involving the Pharaoh.

During the Old Kingdom, the way in which the Egyptian language was written changed. While hieroglyphs continued to be used on temples and other monuments, a cursive script developed concurrently as an easier way to perform recordkeeping and other administrative tasks. Of course, the Egyptians also wrote poetry, magical spells, and other types of texts.

The great power of the Pharaohs during this time is best symbolized by the building of the **Great Pyramids of Giza**, constructed during the fourth dynasty. The Great Pyramid of Khufu, the largest of the three Great Pyramids and built around 2500 B.C.E., remained the tallest human-built structure in the world for nearly 4,500 years until the construction of the Eiffel Tower in 1889 C.E. Until relatively recently, historians believed that only slaves could have built the Great Pyramids, yet recent excavations of worker villages near the site have suggested that the pyramid builders were not only working voluntarily, but were also quite well cared for. Only a king, and only a government of great power and influence, could have assembled the tens of thousands of workers needed to build the Great Pyramids. After the fall of the Old Kingdom, no pyramids approaching the size of the Giza Pyramids were ever built again.

So why did the Egyptians expend so much energy constructing the pyramids? They believed that there existed a cosmic order characterized by renewal (a mirror of the natural world and the consistent patterns of the Nile's rise and fall). Because the Pharaohs were associated with this cycle of renewal and because they were thought to be so vital to the proper functioning of the world, the Egyptians went to great length to make sure that their leaders' bodies and spirits were prepared for the afterlife. The famous **Book of the Dead**, which archaeologists have found in many royal tombs, contains magical spells and ritual instructions that were intended to guide the spirit in the afterlife.

Egyptians also took great care to preserve the physical bodies of the deceased, and not just for royals. The wealthy were able to have their bodies preserved using the most advanced techniques of **mummification**, in which the vital organs were removed from the cadaver and preserved in stone jars. The body was then desiccated (dried out) using salts and chemicals, and wrapped in linen before being placed in coffins and buried inside tombs. The pyramids, the most recognizable burial places, were the tombs for the Pharaohs and their wives, but other wealthy people had less elaborate tombs constructed for their burials as well. Common people did what they could afford to preserve their bodies for the afterlife, but often had to make do with simpler mud brick tombs or pit graves.

...And Decline

Around 2150 B.C.E., the dynasties of the Old Kingdom collapsed under what many historians now believe was a decades-long famine caused by drought and the failure of the usually dependable Nile to flood and nourish the land. When the central government under the Pharaoh collapsed, ambitious local warlords took over the day-to-day running of Egyptian life. This period of government collapse and general chaos is referred to as the **First Intermediate period**. It is not particularly historically significant except that it offers a good example of what happens when a powerful central authority loses power and control, for whatever reason.

Rise (Again)...

The **Middle Kingdom** arose around 2000 B.C.E., when the leaders of the eleventh dynasty united Egypt again under a central government and a single leader. The Pharaohs of the Middle Kingdom placed less emphasis on their own burial tombs (like massive pyramids) and focused more on city buildings that could be used by the general public. By authorizing more municipal building, the Pharaohs of the Middle Kingdom were acting more like modern leaders—providing for the people as a way to project power. The Middle Kingdom also saw Egypt begin to expand beyond its naturally protected borders. Egypt conquered and occupied Nubia (modern-day Sudan) to the south in order to secure a steady stream of valuable natural resources, including timber and gold. The Pharaohs of this time also dispatched trade expeditions to the eastern Mediterranean along the shores of modern-day Syria and Israel-Palestine. Egypt was beginning to feel its own power.

...And Decline (Again)

With the Pharaohs on the verge of becoming a regional power, their authority collapsed as a series of power struggles and poor leaders crippled the central government. Not surprisingly, as the central government collapsed around 1700 B.C.E., regional warlords once again tried to take advantage of the situation, and civil war broke out. This period of decline and unrest is called the **Second Intermediate period**. During this decline, Egypt was invaded by a Semitic tribe known as the Hyksos, who were thought to have been driven from their homelands by other invaders. The Hyksos conquered and occupied portions of Lower Egypt, while multiple Egyptian warlords retained control over southern parts of Egypt.

Rise (One More Time)...

A powerful noble family from Thebes, the historical capital of Egypt, battled to push the Hyksos out of the delta region, ushering in the time period known as the **New Kingdom** (1570–1070 B.C.E.). Ahmose, avenging the death of his father and older brother, led the Egyptians in battle with the Hyksos, defeating them and becoming the first Pharaoh of the New Kingdom. He followed this victory by reconquering Nubia, which had been lost during the Second Intermediate period. The leaders who followed Ahmose began an imperialistic foreign policy designed to prevent any further invasions from foreign conquerors—a policy of preemptive strike, if you will. Despite his achievements, Ahmose is one of the least famous of the New Kingdom pharaohs. Considered the era of the great pharaohs, the New Kingdom saw the reigns of Amenhotep III, Akhenaten, Tutankhamen, and Ramses the Great. It was under the reigns of these rulers that ancient Egypt reached its pinnacle of power and imperial reach.

It was also during the New Kingdom that Egypt engaged thoroughly in political propaganda. Have you ever wondered why Ramses II is called Ramses the Great? He wasn't a particularly great warrior, but he made sure he littered Egyptian cities with mammoth-sized statues of himself, and he embellished a bit when he depicted temple carvings of himself winning great battles. We know so much of Ramses today because of all the time, effort, and money (none of it his) that he put into building anything he could put his name on. But even though Ramses may have exaggerated his conquests, he is still considered the last of Egypt's great pharaohs. Following Ramses the Great's reign, Egypt once again fell in a period of political instability and turmoil.

...And Fall (This Time For Good)

The **Third Intermediate period**, beginning as early as 1200 B.C.E., was a period of decline from which the ancient Egyptians would not climb back. Beginning in 800 B.C.E., Egypt was ruled by a succession of foreign leaders—the defeat they had so desperately tried to avoid. At first it was Egypt's former rival to the south, Nubia, which ruled Egypt for a time. Then the Persians briefly made Egypt a part of their growing empire. And then Alexander the Great conquered Egypt in 332 B.C.E. on his way to conquering the rest of the known world. Over the thousand years after Alexander's conquest, nearly all aspects of Egypt's ancient culture—its religion, language, architecture, and art—disappeared into history.

The story of ancient Egypt is another example of the emergence of civilization—of how humans developed government, language, and shared religious philosophy, and built timeless works of art and architecture. Because of the way Egyptians practiced mummification, they developed a fairly advanced knowledge of anatomy. The pyramids and other monumental structures required expertise in engineering and construction techniques. In other realms, the Egyptians made advances in mathematics and astronomy.

Like all ancient civilizations, Egyptian society came to an end under the pressures of time and outside domination. Although its culture died out nearly 2,000 years ago, one example of how Egypt's culture still influences our modern time is the Washington Monument in the American capital—it's an Egyptian obelisk.

ANCIENT AFRICA

c. 3000–1000 B.C.E.	Agriculture spreads in sub-Saharan Africa.
c. 1500 B.C.E.	Bantu migrations begin.
c. 1000 B.C.E.	Kush create their own autonomous kingdom.
c. 750–666 B.C.E.	Kush kings rule Egypt.

The Bantu Migrations

Unlike that of the Near East, much of Africa's very early history is unknown to us due to a lack of archeological evidence (we will learn a lot more about some of the major African civilizations in later chapters). However, there are a few important events and civilizations from Africa's earliest period of human society that we do know. The **Bantu migrations**—most likely spurred by growing population and the development of inhospitable agricultural conditions thanks to the slow southward spread of the Sahara Desert—began around 1500 B.C.E. and continued until around 500 C.E.

The Bantu, a group of peoples originally from the area of the Niger River in West Africa, gradually began to abandon their nomadic ways and farm instead. As they migrated, they spread their knowledge of iron (picked up around 500 B.C.E., most likely from the Near East) and agriculture, as well as their language family, across much of eastern and southern Africa. Indeed, the linguistic commonalities in many parts of Africa provide the best evidence that these migrations occurred (today, there are about 250 Bantu-based languages, the most widely spoken of which is Swahili). The Bantu migrations didn't completely wipe out all other modes of life, but they did bring more settled societies to wide expanses of the African continent.

No Bronze Age for You!
African civilizations were unusual in their technological development in that they mostly skipped the "Bronze Age" that most other civilizations went through, going straight from using stone tools to smelting iron, which they learned from their Near Eastern neighbors.

Jenne-Jeno

Although many civilizations that arose in Africa did so with the help of contacts with other, more developed societies, not all did. The settlement of **Jenne-Jeno** in the Niger River Valley, in the West African region also known as the Sahel, was established around 250 B.C.E. Jenne-Jeno seems to have developed to a rather significant size (more than 7,000 inhabitants) without contact with other more advanced societies.

Unfortunately, we do not know nearly as much about these early African civilizations as we could, because they did not develop writing as early as did their peers elsewhere in the world. By comparison we know far more about Mesopotamia and Egypt because of extensive written records left behind. Without writing, we are left to reconstruct these cultures based on art and artifacts alone.

The Kush

Around 1000 B.C.E., we see the rise of the **Kush** civilization, which was heavily influenced by its neighbors, the Egyptians (the area controlled by the Kush includes parts of what is today southern Egypt and northern Sudan). As Egypt declined, the Kush rose to power in the area, even ruling Egypt for a bit after that civilization fell. The Kush spread their empire south and traded heavily across Africa, but there is no record that the Kush were influential elsewhere. They were heavily influenced by Egyptian culture and social structures, but we have no surviving evidence of a distinct Kush culture. Their greatest period of strength was from 250 B.C.E. to around 50 C.E.

ANCIENT INDIA

Now for a change of location—let's give a warm welcome to... ancient South Asian civilizations!

c. 3000 B.C.E.	Harappan civilization
c. 1600–1000 B.C.E.	Aryans move into the Indus Valley
c. 1500–500 B.C.E.	Vedas, the sacred texts of Hinduism, gradually set down in writing
c. 1000–750 B.C.E.	Aryans move into the Ganges Valley
c. 563 B.C.E.	Birth of Siddhartha Gautama (Buddha)
c. 320 B.C.E.	Invasion of India by Alexander the Great

The first major civilization on the Indian subcontinent arose in the Indus River Valley around 3000 B.C.E. The two great cities of **Harappa** and **Mohenjo Daro** (these are modern names—the ancient names are unknown) were walled cities built on a grid structure. Why is this significant? Because that kind of planning is a sign of organization on a large scale; the sophisticated technology and massive manpower needed to build this kind of city required a highly organized and powerful ruling class. Harappa may have had a population as large as 35,000 people, while Mohenjo Daro was even larger. In both cities, archeological studies show signs of centralized leadership, extensive wealth, and structures serving religious and other ceremonial purposes. The cities had sewage systems and drainage structures to transport waste away from the urban areas, which was a crucial component of any large-scale human habitation.

Although Harappa and Mohenjo Daro have been thoroughly excavated by archaeologists and are thus the most well known sites from the Indus Valley, most of the population probably lived in smaller settlements that were similarly structured. The same types of physical artifacts and construction techniques have been found at minor sites throughout the Indus Valley region, suggesting that these societies enjoyed a certain level of standardization.

Advanced agriculture was also in evidence in the Indus Valley, demonstrating that the Harappan civilization was able to control the power and resources of the river through irrigation. A lot of metal artifacts have been found in the area, indicating that the Indus Valley peoples may have had more advanced metallurgical skills than did their counterparts in Mesopotamia and Egypt. Moreover, the metal goods found in the Indus Valley consist primarily of tools, whereas those found in Mesopotamia and Egypt are mostly jewelry and other decorative items (suggesting that metal goods were more widely available to common people in the Indus Valley).

Both Harappa and Mohenjo Daro were major trading centers, with most goods going from the cities to the hinterlands; boats from the coastal region, however, transported goods as far as Mesopotamia! As in Egypt, the rivers were the easiest way to move things around. Archaeologists believe that these civilizations had trading contacts with their immediate neighbors in eastern Persia and Afghanistan as well as with people further afield.

The social structure was controlled by a powerful priestly class, which in turn was supported by an administrative class. Although a system of writing has been discovered in the ancient Indus Valley, historians have yet to decipher its code (some linguists doubt that the "texts" really constitute a system of writing language at all—most of the inscriptions that have been found are extremely short and may therefore represent a type of non-linguistic symbol system). Even so, the societies of the Indus displayed the hallmark characteristics of human civilization.

The Harappan civilization declined over a period of time, although it is unclear exactly why. Its decline may have been the result of a succession of natural disasters (flooding, earthquakes, etc.). However, many migrants moved into the region as the civilization prospered, which may have led to social instability and economic hardship. Many of the newcomers were herders, who may have neglected the existing infrastructure and altered the economy of the region: more herding, less agriculture.

Next Up: The Aryans

The **Aryan people** gradually moved into the area formerly controlled by the Harappan civilization. Originally nomadic herders from Central Asia, the Aryans moved into the Indus Valley in the western part of the Indian subcontinent in 1600–1000 B.C.E. and into the Ganges Valley in the east in 1000–750 B.C.E. The Aryan legacy is with us today; this empire hosted the development of the two major religions of the area, Hinduism and Buddhism.

The term Aryan defines the language spoken by these people. No relation to the so-called Aryans of 19th- and 20th-century Europe.

The Aryans eventually converted to agriculture, taking the same advantage of the fertile land in the river valleys that the preceding peoples did. At first their society consisted mainly of priests (known as **Brahmins**), warrior nobility, and peasants, plus slaves of various ethnicities—the Aryans subjugated other peoples in and around their territory. Eventually, as the society became more agricultural, its structure became more varied: Merchants, traders, and artisans were added to the mix, yet another characteristic of civilization. It was during the Aryan period when the foundation was laid for India's rigid caste system.

The Origins of the Caste Structure

During the Aryan period, economic wealth through increased production and trade led to the rise of powerful merchant and artisan classes that also exercised power in the society. India's society became more stratified, with **varnas** (broad social categories such as Brahmins, merchants, and warriors, the top three castes in the power structure) and **castes** within the varnas. Below the top three were peasants and artisans, followed lastly by the untouchables. The rigid hierarchical structure meant that people were born, lived, and died members of the same caste as their families—they could marry with people of the same caste only. Rules against **miscegenation** (marriage between two people of different ethnic groups or castes) existed to keep the classes separate from one another.

This **caste system**, one of the strictest in early societies, was bolstered by certain Hindu beliefs regarding the soul. One's caste determined one's **dharma**, or life path, and thus delimited what kind of role one would play in society throughout one's life. According to this belief system, one's soul lives on after death and moves on to another body—the soul is **reincarnated**. All of the good and bad one does in life is carried on by the soul in the form of **karma**, a sort of point system for goodness. Earn enough good karma and your soul moves up a notch in the caste system and will be reborn better off in the next life than today. Earn enough bad karma and you move down. Defying the rules of your caste means that you are violating your dharma and mucking up your karma. But if you accept your lot in life, no matter how bad it is, you earn good karma and a chance at a better life next time.

The Aryans ruled most of this area of India until **Alexander the Great** and his armies encroached into Indian territory in 327 B.C.E. Alexander's successful forays into India were important because direct contact between the West and India had been rare. As a result of Alexander's appearance, trade was heightened, as were cultural connections. Greek mathematics and astronomy influenced the Indians, while Indian philosophy influenced Greek thought. However, Alexander's soldiers were tired after many years of war, and they retreated from India in 324 B.C.E. The vacuum left behind by Alexander was filled by the next great Indian ruler, Chandragupta Maurya. (We will learn more about Alexander and the Maurya Empire in the next chapter).

Brahmins Know Best

The Vedic priests—the Brahmin caste—of the Aryan empire had enormous power. They educated the elite and held many administrative posts in addition to fulfilling their strictly religious duties advising rulers, forecasting the future, and placating the gods through ritual sacrifice. They had the monopoly on understanding the sacred religious texts known as the Vedas, which, between 1500 and 500 B.C.E., they wrote down for posterity. The Vedas formed the basis of what is now called Hinduism, and for a long time only Brahmins were able to read them. This exclusive insight into and access to the sacred texts, as well as Brahmins' control over public and private ritual, formed the basis of Brahmin power in Aryan society.

In learning about native Asian religions, such as Hinduism, it is important to remember that we live in a much more cosmopolitan age than our ancient forebears. People in ancient India did not believe in Hinduism as a particular distinct religion that a person chooses to follow; instead, Hinduism was considered a description of the spiritual realities of the world. The gods undeniably existed; reincarnation was a fact; karma was self-evident. These beliefs were taken for granted by other religious movements, such as Jainism and Buddhism, and were expressed in many different ways within Hinduism through the years, from traditional upper-class Brahmanic rituals, to other expressions of belief among lower classes, to specific cults dedicated to one god of the pantheon in bhakti, or devotional Hinduism. For instance, some Hindu practitioners (mostly noble or Brahmin) rejected their traditional dharmas and became monks dedicated to an extreme ascetic spiritual life, hoping to become one with the World Spirit, Brahman. It is from this latter group that a new religion arose in the 6th century B.C.E.

Buddhism Versus the Brahmin System

Timeline of Major Religions, Oldest to Youngest
Judaism—c. 1750 B.C.E.
Hinduism—1500 B.C.E.
Buddhism—6th century B.C.E..
Christianity—1st century C.E.
Islam —7th century C.E.

Buddha (born c. 563 B.C.E. as Siddhartha Gautama) was originally a prince, a member of the class that ruled India, and was raised with every luxury imaginable. But upon encountering death and disease as a young man, he became unable to enjoy his material well-being. Instead, he left home to become an ascetic within the Hindu tradition. This variety of Hinduism turned away from Vedic Hinduism's focus on ceremony, ritual, and ordinary dharma and focused instead on personal spiritual development. However, Buddha found the extreme asceticism (including ritual starvation) of the Hindu mystics to be distracting to his spiritual advancement, so he rejected their austerities and instead decided to live as a monk practicing moderation.

It was shortly after this time that, while meditating, he realized the **Four Noble Truths**, which are the basis of Buddhist beliefs: That all life is suffering; that suffering is the result of cravings for permanence in an ephemeral world; that craving may be stopped, thus stopping the cycle of death, karma, and rebirth; and that the way to stop cravings is by following a code of personal and mental conduct known as the **Eightfold Path**. The end of the cycle of rebirth and suffering known as nirvana is the result of attaining **enlightenment** about the true nature of existence. Buddha championed the idea that through meditation, self-study, the rejection of material wants, and right living, any person regardless of caste or place in life could attain enlightenment on his or her own. In keeping with these beliefs, this also meant that he rejected the caste system and welcomed those of all castes and (to some extent) genders, providing an alternative to the intricate ritual practices of Brahmanic religion from which the Brahmins derived their influence over worldly leaders. Buddhism eventually became enormously influential not just in India, but also in most other South and East Asian cultures.

Speaking of Asian cultures, let's take a closer look at India's northeastern neighbors.

ANCIENT CHINA

c. 5000–3500 B.C.E.	Yangshao and Longshan Neolithic cultures
c. 2200–1700 B.C.E.	The (probably mythological) Xia dynasty
c. 1700–1100 B.C.E.	The Shang dynasty
c. 1100–256 B.C.E.	The Zhou dynasty
c. 604–517 B.C.E.	The life of Lao Tzu, the founder of Taoism
c. 551–479 B.C.E.	The life of Confucius

The culture that would dominate ancient Chinese civilization was born in the **Yellow River** (Huang He) Valley in northern China, which boasted extremely fertile soil typical of this kind of geographical area. Much of eastern Asia is mountainous, so the river valleys were a logical place for humans to settle down. Periodic flooding deposited nutrient-rich soil from the river onto the surrounding countryside, making the land capable of sustaining prolonged, widespread agriculture. Although the river could be deadly to those caught in its floods, and its changes in course could mean enormous trouble for settled farmers, the riches it provided were too significant to ignore.

Neolithic China saw a number of significant settlements develop in the prehistoric period in the Yellow River region, among them the Yangshao (c. 5000 B.C.E.) and Longshan (c. 3500 B.C.E.) cultures. These cultures farmed land, domesticated animals, created pottery, defended their territory against invaders, and in the case of the Longshan, developed rituals of ancestor worship and buried their dead. What separates these settlements from the dynasties that follow is a gradually more complete historical record. Civilization in China began with the Yangshao and the Longshan, but flourished with the next three dynasties.

The Three Dynasties: The Xia, Shang, and Zhou

The Xia Dynasty

The first of the traditional three ancient Chinese dynasties was the **Xia** (c. 2200–1700 B.C.E.). Archeological records have not conclusively established that this dynasty ever existed, at least as a dynasty. Given the low levels of centralization, even into the Shang dynasty, it is possible that the Xia "dynasty" was an anachronistic description given by the Shang to the previous culture. We know that there was a collection of clans, each with its own ruler, and that the kings were also religious figures considered to have divine rights and powers. They built walled cities, raised armies, and traded extensively. They may have even had rudimentary writing, but this claim is disputed among historians.

The Shang Dynasty

The first real urban kingdom in China—and the first to have a real written record—is the **Shang dynasty**, whose people rose to prominence around 1750–1500 B.C.E. We know more about the Shang than we do the Xia thanks to artifacts like oracle bones, animal bones inscribed and used in rituals by those entrusted with telling the future. These bones are valuable because they allow historians to know the names and approximate ruling periods of various rulers.

The Shang period also saw the development of a Chinese pictographic writing system, which helped create a sense of distinct identity among those who used it and which eventually became the ideographic Chinese writing system we know today. The earliest known oracle bones date to around 1300 B.C.E., but historians believe that the Shang were using these written texts much earlier. The writing itself consisted of hundreds of monosyllabic characters, each of which represented an object or an idea. As in Mesopotamia and Egypt, this writing system was very complex and was likely known and used only by a small number of the elite.

Like the Aryans in India, the Shang were nomad-warriors. Also like the Aryans, the Shang were ruled by kings. The Shang were more urban than their predecessors, building not one but multiple capital cities over the course of their rule. Archeological evidence shows that theirs was a tiered social structure: the king, aristocrats, warriors, merchants, artisans, peasants, and slaves each lived in different parts of the urban areas, demonstrating clear class distinctions. Wealthier individuals probably lived inside the center of the cities, whereas commoners largely lived in the surrounding agricultural areas.

As was the case in India, Chinese religious figures (shamans, priests, and the like) had a certain amount of power because of their purported abilities to speak to the gods and make offerings to assure the safety and prosperity of the society. Unlike in India, the king himself was seen as having a similar ritual duty to communicate with the gods, acting as an intermediary between Heaven and the people.

The Zhou Dynasty

After the Shang came the **Zhou**, c. 1100 B.C.E. The Zhou conquered the Shang, whom the Zhou claimed had lost the **Mandate of Heaven**, or divine support for their rule. According to the theory of the Mandate of Heaven, the power to rule came from the gods and was not an inherent right belonging to a man. So whenever a ruler was deemed to have lost the Mandate of Heaven by ruling in an unjust manner, it was acceptable (even necessary) to overthrow him and put someone else in charge (although as you can imagine, this was not always so easy in practice). The proof for a ruler's possession of the Mandate of Heaven was the prosperity and order of society at large.

We know about the Zhou thanks to extensive written records, which reveal much more about this dynasty than is known about the earlier dynasties. The two most important such records are the so-called *Book of Documents* (containing governmental orders, letters, and historical records) and the *Book of Songs* (containing poems and ballads recounting and celebrating the lives of Zhou rulers).

The Zhou period saw a number of innovations in political and bureaucratic structure. For example, to boost their power base, the Zhou practiced a **feudal system**, permitting local leaders or nobility to become vassals of the emperor. The vassals served and were loyal to their masters in exchange for **fiefs** of land from which they could collect revenue. In other words, a feudal system was created.

The Zhou also built enormous cities that required a new level of organization. These cities, like those of the Indus Valley, were laid out according to a grid plan and were aligned with astronomical features, embodying the ancient Chinese notion of **feng shui** (the idea that human-built structures should be harmoniously aligned with the forces of the natural world).

Because of these political and social complexities, it is no surprise that the lesser nobles of the Zhou dynasty expanded the role and power of their courts, just as the imperial court expanded. Although these individuals were mainly concerned with the household maintenance of the feudal lord and with representing him on diplomatic missions, this led to the development of an administrative class that would play important roles in later dynasties as well as in the development of important schools of political thought.

The Zhou dynasty continued until around 400 B.C.E., when it began to lose power over its vassals. The empire gradually disintegrated, breaking into smaller fiefdoms ruled by local warlords, none of which rose to power above all others. The **Warring States** period (481–221 B.C.E.) was an era of near constant struggle for dominance among the many rulers in China. Indeed, the Shang and Zhou periods were both rife with warfare. One of the most famous Chinese texts of this time period is Sun Tzu's *Art of War*, which is a sort of military handbook that provides chesslike instructions for deceiving and dominating the enemy. The Zhou dynasty finally ended in 256 B.C.E. Twenty-five years later a new dynasty arose: the **Qin**, considered the first true Chinese empire. We'll cover the Qin in a later chapter, so before we move on, let's take a look at some of the most important cultural movements spawned in the Zhou period.

All Hail the Big Heads: The Philosophers of the Zhou Era

The two most important intellectual developments of this time period in China were **Confucianism** and **Taoism** (sometimes spelled Daoism). The philosopher Confucius (551–479 B.C.E.) was a poor *shi*, a landless noble of the warrior class.

He was disappointed in the ruling classes, and traveled the empire teaching a system of ethics and leadership based on order, harmony, and loyalty rather than war, and led by educated, wise men rather than barbaric warlords. One of the key texts for understanding Confucianism is the *Analects*, which was not really written by Confucius himself but by his disciples who wrote down his teachings after they had been handed down orally over an unknown period of time.

Confucius' ideas were not religious as much as they were ethical and social. He believed that the family was the most important part of society, and that the best rulers would be those who demonstrated their superior leadership rather than those born into the ruling elite. He also believed that rulers should govern with propriety and put common interests of the public over personal ones. He believed that a superior gentleman (*junzi*) was educated, courageous, rational, and properly observant of the rituals and laws of society. Most important, he believed such men were made, not born.

Building on the notion that the family unit was supreme, Confucius taught the concept of "filial piety," which held that children had the obligation to be respectful and obedient to their parents. In the same way, subjects had the obligation to be respectful and obedient to their rulers, who in turn were expected to govern humanely (like just and loving fathers). This hierarchy applied to the sexes as well—wives were expected to act toward their husbands in the same way that children acted toward their parents (although the Chinese concept of **yin/yang** theoretically represented the male/female complementarity in the natural world, in practice women held an inferior position in ancient Chinese society).

Confucius's teachings did not have a broad impact in China until the **Han dynasty**, around 200 B.C.E.; the Confucian school of government was one of dozens during the intellectual ferment of the Warring States period. After his death, others influenced by his teachings began their own schools of thought, diverging in many ways but still influential. The philosopher Mencius believed people to be essentially good, while the thinker Han Feizi assumed people were basically bad. Han Feizi's beliefs were more influential, informing a field of thought known as **Legalism**, a form of strict authoritarian rule designed to keep those wicked people under control. Legalism would come to dominate later dynastic political structures, particularly that of the Qin dynasty.

Confucian Facts—Get 'Em While They're Hot!
The Analects—a collection of Confucian sayings considered basic reading in China until the Communist era.

Central Ideas of Confucianism
- Rulers must be moral and educated *junzi* ("gentlemen").
- One must focus on one's behavior in the present.
- One must respect elders and revere the past.
- One must have filial piety, as embodied in the five cardinal relationships: father and son, ruler and subject, husband and wife, elder brother to younger brother, friend to friend.

At this point in the chapter, you should have come across all of the defining characteristics of human civilization in the development of ancient Chinese culture. Far from Mesopotamia and Egypt, China developed settled agriculture, a formal ruling structure, a system of writing, diverse working and social classes, and a shared religious philosophy. By all accounts, ancient China was as advanced as the cultures of the ancient Near East.

Last, there was **Laozi** (also called Lao Tzu, c. 604–517 B.C.E.) who was less interested in ways to structure governments and more interested in how to lead a good (or happy) life. Taoism was a naturalistic school of thought. By following the **Tao**, or natural order, and the natural changes of situation and fate, one could live harmoniously and happily in spite of adversity, most especially by remaining humble and small. In contrast to Confucianism, which advocated engagement with society, Taoism emphasized the importance of removing oneself to some degree from the complexities of society.

THE OUTSIDERS: THE AMERICAS

c. 1200–500 B.C.E.   Olmec civilization

c. 300 B.C.E.–700 C.E.   Teotihuacán civilization

c. 200 B.C.E.–600 C.E.   Anasazi and Hopewell cultures

c. 300–900 C.E.   Peak of the Mayan civilization

Last—but not least—we come to the outsiders in the **Americas**. Why do we describe them as outsiders? Because **early American civilizations** evolved completely isolated from the developments in (and natural environments of) Asia, Africa, and Europe, they apparently followed a different rulebook. For one thing, they did NOT develop in river valleys, unlike other ancient civilizations. The fact that ancient American civilizations evolved as they did makes it clear that there is more than one way for a major civilization to grow and prosper.

Settled agriculture came later to **Mesoamerica** (from northern Mexico down to modern-day Nicaragua in Central America) than it did to the other places we've discussed so far. For example, permanent villages based on settled agricultural practices, the first step to larger societies, developed in Mesoamerica at the same time that the Shang dynasty ruled China—a pretty big difference in developmental calendars! Mesoamerica started to see pottery in 2000 B.C.E., whereas the Japanese (the first people worldwide to develop the art) were making pottery as early as 10,000 B.C.E., a very substantial difference.

However, this is not to say the achievements of ancient Mesoamerican civilizations were not impressive in their own right.

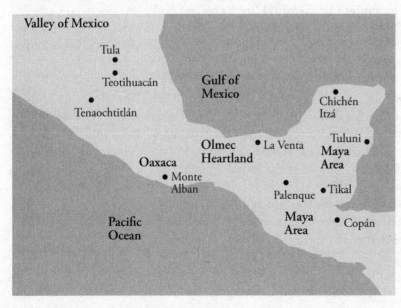

MAJOR CIVILIZATIONS: MESOAMERICA

The **Olmec civilization** is often called the "mother civilization of Mesoamerica." Existing around 1200–500 B.C.E. on the southeast coast of present-day Mexico, the Olmec civilization shows all of the signs of advanced development. Indigenous populations took advantage of the rich jungle environment in which they found themselves and learned to cultivate local plants as well as process minerals such as jade and quartz. Fishing was a major food source, but archaeological evidence reveals the presence of irrigation systems and settled agriculture as well. Planned urban areas, organized religion, the beginning of calendar and writing systems, and impressively monumental architecture (enormous stone heads are their trademark) were also present during the Olmec civilization's era.

There were several major population centers in the Olmec world, all known by their modern Spanish names (San Lorenzo, Las Ventas, and Tres Zapotes). Historians do not know whether these cities were rivals of each other or whether they developed independently. Archaeologists have discovered large earthen platforms that were probably used for political or religious rituals. The Olmec buildings that have survived contain decorative stonework and sculpture, so there is evidence of a fairly skilled artisan class. In contrast to the elites, who lived in finely built houses, the commoners made do with simple mud and stick buildings.

Not much is known about Olmec political life, but the colossal stone heads that are characteristic of Olmec culture are each individually carved and probably represent specific kings or other rulers. A polytheistic culture, the Olmec believed in deities with both male and female characteristics with a combination of human and animal features. As we would expect, religious leaders played a prominent role in Olmec society.

In short, the Olmec had a sophisticated social structure and mastered technology that enabled them to cut and move the huge stones used to build pyramids and other huge structures (did you think the Egyptians had a monopoly on pyramid-building?). We don't know why their civilization declined, but it is generally accepted that their knowledge and culture was dispersed throughout other Mesoamerican peoples.

The **Teotihuacán** culture of Central Mexico also reached an impressive level of complexity by the 1st century C.E. The name Teotihuacán means "the Place Where Men Become Gods," and it is clear from the structures left behind that religious ritual was central to the Teotihuacán culture. It boasted large urban areas, huge temple complexes to various gods, including everyone's favorite feathered snake deity, Quetzalcoatl. The Pyramid of the Sun, in fact, was the highest structure in Mexico until well into the modern age. The Teotihuacán culture also influenced other civilizations in Mesoamerica, but eventually this powerful society fell to outside invaders in the 7th century, dissolving completely by the 8th century C.E.

Last, there is the **Mayan** civilization, which reached its peak between 300 and 900 C.E. in southern Mexico and Central America. It is considered the high point of Mesoamerican civilization, cultural achievement, and sophistication. The Maya had it all: agriculture to sustain thousands of people, a highly organized urban society, complex religion and elaborate ritual systems, sophisticated arts and culture, and of course, monumental architecture. The Maya also developed complex writing (a logographic system with both phonetic and semantic elements), made significant innovations in the fields of mathematics, and calculated astronomical distances with astonishing accuracy. Their calendar, based on the solar year, was 365 days long—sound familiar?

The Mayan civilization collapsed suddenly for reasons not completely known. Their agricultural system—a combination of slash-and-burn agriculture and exploitation of local wetlands—was probably unable to support such a large population. Warfare between rival chiefs and kings and widespread disease are also possibilities, although the fall of the Maya could have come about as the result of all three (and crop failure would certainly have led to the latter two). We will learn more about the Teotihuacán, the Aztecs, and the Mayan civilization in future chapters.

Commonalities

All of the major Mesoamerica civilizations had one great weakness: they lacked a major river around which to grow. Without a river, Mesoamericans were more vulnerable to sustained drought and other natural disasters that interfered with agricultural growing seasons. Whether the lack of a river is the cause of all these societies' declines is not known for certain, but it certainly did pose unique challenges to these societies as compared to those in the Near East, Asia, India, and Africa.

Mesoamerican civilizations also kept alive their predecessors' cultural legacies and perpetuated them to the next—from the Olmecs to the Teotihuacán, Maya, Toltecs (c. 900–1100 C.E.), and Aztecs (c. 1100–1521 C.E.) and beyond.

Our Friends to the North and South

South America, especially Peru, also had its share of impressive early civilizations. The Chavín of Peru (c. 900 B.C.E.) were the progenitors of future Peruvian civilizations and were the first in the Americas to enter the Bronze Age. Located high in the Andean mountains, the Chavín dominated a huge geographical area and traded with other societies in the coastal regions of South America. The llama was an enormously important animal in this world, since it could be used for meat, clothing, and transportation across difficult mountain terrain.

Code Breaking
For many years, the rise and fall of Mayan civilization was one of the great archaeological mysteries. No one could read the Mayan script, the key to truly understanding any great culture. To learn more about how archaeologists and linguists finally unlocked the secret of the last great undeciphered writing system, check out the book *Breaking the Maya Code* by Dr. Michael D. Coe.

Systems of Writing
Logographic A single character represents a complete unit of meaning, often a complete grammatical word. Chinese, as well as Japanese and Korean (when written with Chinese characters), are examples of logographic systems.

Alphabetic A single letter represents a sound, or part of a syllable. English is included here, as are the other European languages.

Syllabic A single character represents a syllable or group of sounds. Cuneiform and the writing systems of many Native American languages are syllabic. Japanese and Korean also both have syllabic alphabets (called "syllabaries"), *hiragana* and *katakana*, and *hangul*, respectively.

The cities of Chavín contained vast complexes of terraced mounds and platforms, many of which contain elaborate carvings of animals such as jaguars. Many impressive artifacts have been found at these sites, including gold and silver ornaments that indicate an advanced understanding of metalwork and other technologies. More about Chavín and the Inca civilization will be discussed in another chapter.

North America saw a number of major civilizations that developed around waterways, although nothing on the scale of Mesoamerica. The **Anasazi** culture arose between 200 B.C.E. and 700 C.E. in what today is Utah, Arizona, Colorado, and New Mexico. The Anasazi built stone and brick dwellings not unlike those of many other prehistoric cultures, but later moved into the cliffs and canyons to protect themselves from invaders. Archaeological evidence shows that the Anasazi traded with Mesoamerican civilizations to the south, a significant distance in prehistoric times (especially without wheels or pack animals!). Much like the Maya, the Anasazi culture declined for reasons not completely known to us, but most likely it was the result of a number of contributing factors.

Like their Mesoamerican brethren, the North American civilizations disappeared over time but absorbed the cultures of other surrounding societies while passing along their own. The **Hopewell** (200–500 C.E. in northeast and midwest North America) and **Mississippian** (800–1300 C.E.) cultures shared many traits, the most distinctive being mound-building and significant artistic sophistication. Mounds have been built for various reasons worldwide—defense, burial, ceremonial or religious temples—and are still visible today. However, these cultures did not create the kind of monumental stone architecture that the Mesoamericans did and did not support the massive urban populations seen farther south.

The ancient civilizations of the Americas shared many important characteristics of other civilizations, even though the American exemplars arose later than did those in other places. Some, like the Maya, built urban societies to rival many in Asia in terms of size, complexity, and strength. Others were less advanced technologically and, therefore, left far fewer traces behind for future researchers to uncover.

CIVILIZATION: A HUMAN CHARACTERISTIC

The development of human civilization is remarkably similar across the varied geographies of the ancient world. Whether we are looking at the ancient Mesopotamians, Egyptians, Africans, Indians, Chinese, or natives of the Americas, their progress of development is often more similar than dissimilar to one another. This shouldn't be surprising: They were all human!

There are many examples of such similarities. Most early societies used rivers to promote settled agriculture. An ocean away, the ancient Mesoamericans built structures remarkably similar to Egyptian pyramids and Sumerian ziggurats. The earliest ancestor of the cuneiform writing developed by the Sumerians looks remarkably similar to early Chinese writing—the difference being that the Chinese continue to use a system much like their ancient script. From what we know, all ancient societies had detailed religious and philosophical histories. The ancient Maya developed the most accurate calendar of the ancient world. And finally, all ancient societies developed some form of systematic, organized leadership, be it kings, councils, or priests.

Humans formed ancient civilizations across the globe in many of the same ways and during much of the same time, with each contributing collectively and uniquely to the shared cultural memory of humanity. The development of urban populations led to numerous societal changes, not all of them positive. Along with cities came vast differences in wealth and increasing social stratification. Slavery was prevalent in most ancient civilizations, although it was often not racially based as was the case in the United States prior to the Civil War. (Slaves in the ancient world were often taken captive during warfare or were forced into servitude after going into unmanageable debt.)

The role of women changed when societies became more urbanized as well. Many anthropologists think that during humanity's prehistory, women played a prominent part in locating and gathering food. Men's participation in formalized agriculture was more prominent because the tasks involved required more brute physical strength. Additionally, since cities had more abundant and reliable sources of food, women were able to have more children and the home became the main province of women's activities.

Change and Continuity

Nearly all of these ancient civilizations have been lost to the modern world. Although we pay homage to these ancient societies by maintaining bits and pieces of their cultural contributions in our time, their languages, their religions, their customs, and their governments are all but gone and live on only in history books. The age-old cycle of conquest has left behind the Sumerians, the Egyptians, the Bantu, the Harappans, the Olmec, and the Maya. The glaring exception, however, is the Chinese. Prehistoric North Chinese cultures, even when conquered, were still conquered by elements of their own civilization, and each subsequent regime built upon and reinforced previous cultural achievements rather than destroying them. Many of these elements exist in Chinese society today, in some modified form. On the other hand, the ancient Egyptian language exists only in the minds and mouths of a select few academics. Continuity and change is a theme that will persist throughout human history as well as throughout the coming chapters.

Civilization's Firsts

Pottery Japan, around 10,000 B.C.E.

The wheel Mesopotamia, 5th century B.C.E.

Bronze Began around 3500 B.C.E. in the Near East. Arrived at different times in different cultures: China c. 2100 B.C.E., central Europe around 1800 B.C.E., South America (the Chavín of Peru) around 900 B.C.E.

Iron In the Near East, began in late Bronze Age, around 1200 B.C.E. Other times: 1100 B.C.E. in India; between 800 and 600 B.C.E. in Europe; first signs in Egypt and Sumer in 4000 B.C.E., but really began to be produced in 1400 B.C.E.; 6th century B.C.E. in China.

Potter's wheel Not exactly known—anywhere between 6000 and 2400 B.C.E., could be Mesopotamia, Egypt, or China (or a combination thereof).

CHAPTER 4 KEY TERMS, PEOPLE, AND EVENTS

Paleolithic period
Earliest time period (to c. 8500 B.C.E.) about which historians have reliable evidence; also called the "Old Stone Age" because human beings used tools made of stone

Nomadic hunter-gatherers
Early humans who moved around seasonally in search of food and hospitable conditions

Neolithic Revolution
Period from c. 8500 to c. 3500 B.C.E. during which humans began to settle down and domesticate plants and animals

Mesopotamia
Also called the "Fertile Crescent"; one of the first regions in which humans developed full-scale civilization.

Epic of Gilgamesh
An epic poem and one of the earliest known examples of literature; has many parallels with parts of the Hebrew Bible, such as the garden of paradise and the great flood

Hammurabi's Code
The best surviving example of the legal codes of ancient Mesopotamia. Hammurabi's Code explains legal principles as well as cases of precedence to which judges could refer.

Early Egyptian civilization
The period of Egyptian history (c. 3100 to c. 1200 B.C.E.) marked by the repeated rise and fall of many dynasties

Bantu migrations
The Bantu people began to settle into an agricultural lifestyle around 1500 B.C.E., spreading their knowledge to eastern and southern parts of Africa.

Aryan people
Originally nomadic people who moved into the Indian subcontinent between 1600 and 1000 B.C.E. and developed an agricultural civilization in the Ganges River Valley

Caste system
A system of socioeconomic organization unique to Indian culture. It had multiple levels: priests, warriors, merchants, peasants, and the untouchables. This caste system was rooted in Hindu beliefs and was maintained through rules against mixing with members of the other levels.

Four Noble Truths
(1) All life is suffering; (2) suffering is the result of cravings for permanence in an ephemeral world; (3) that craving may be stopped; (4) the way to stop cravings is by following a code of conduct called the Eightfold Path, which leads to enlightenment

Mandate of Heaven
A Chinese belief in the divine support for political rulers. Any ruler who lost the Mandate of Heaven had lost the power to rule, which usually meant they had been defeated militarily.

Confucius (551–479 B.C.E.)
Founder of one of the most important systems of thought in China. It was primarily ethical in nature, rooted in the development of specific leadership and personal qualities for the purpose of creating good government.

Taoism
A naturalistic religious system founded by Lao-Tzu (or Laozi) that teaches that people can live in harmony with the natural order.

Early American civilizations
Varied in nature but different from the other early civilizations in that they did not develop around river valleys. They are completely detached from the developments in Asia, Africa, and Europe.

Summary

o   Around 8000 B.C.E. human civilizations around the globe begin the transition toward civilization.

o   Civilization is characterized by
*   settled agriculture
*   some type of formal political organization
*   a shared religious/philosophical code
*   the development of writing
*   the creation of more diverse labor and social class divisions
*   advancements in metallurgy and architecture
*   the pursuit of knowledge and artistic creativity

o   Mesopotamian civilization was launched by the Sumerians. Although they were followed by a cycle of conquest in the region, they live on through their timeless cultural contributions.

o   Egyptian culture began much like that of Mesopotamia, yet persisted for thousands of years through a series of declines to build the greatest structures of the ancient world (i.e., Great Pyramids).

o   Indian civilization gave birth to two of the world's major religions, Buddhism and Hinduism. This early cultural legacy lived on, even though politically these civilizations did not recentralize until the 13th century C.E.

o   Chinese civilization began with the Three Dynasties of the Xia, Shang, and Zhou, and is home to some of the most famous of early philosophers such as Lao-Tzu and Confucius. The continuity of Chinese culture over the span of thousands of years was made possible by a well-developed writing system and local geographic factors.

o   African civilizations did not reach the high point that Asian and Near Eastern cultures did in this early period, but they did benefit from contact with their neighbors to the east.

o   Mesoamerican and other civilizations of the Americas reached, in some cases, grand heights of sophistication, urbanization, and technological development, even if those developments came later to those peoples than comparable developments did in the Near East and Asia.

Chapter 4 Drill

Answers and explanations can be found in Part IV.

1. Each of the following ancient civilizations developed according to the river valley pattern EXCEPT

   (A) the Egyptian
   (B) the Harappan
   (C) the Sumerian
   (D) the Babylonian
   (E) the Maya

When Meng I Tzu asked what filial duty meant, the Master answered, "It is not being disobedient." Afterwards when Fan Ch'ih' was driving him, the Master told him told him, saying: "Meng Sung asked me what filial piety meant, and I replied: 'Not being disobedient'" Fan Ch'ih thereupon asked, "What did you mean?" The Master answered: "While parents live, serve them with decorum; when they are dead, bury them with decorum and sacrifice to them with decorum."

2. The quotation above most likely comes from which of the following sources?

   (A) The *Art of War*, by Sun Tzu
   (B) The *Avesta*
   (C) The *Tao Te Ching*, by Lao Tzu
   (D) The *Bhagavad Gita*
   (E) The *Analects of Confucius*

3. Which of the following ancient texts is generally acknowledged to be one of the earliest works of world literature?

   (A) The *Epic of Gilgamesh*
   (B) The *New Testament*
   (C) The *Iliad*
   (D) The *Book of the Dead*
   (E) Aesop's *Fables*

4. Which of the following best describes the primary reason that historians know less about the early civilizations of sub-Saharan Africa than they do about those of Egypt, Mesopotamia, Asia, and Mesoamerica?

   (A) A plague decimated the Bantu population around 1000 B.C.E.
   (B) The early sub-Saharan African civilizations did not develop a system of writing.
   (C) The destruction that followed a series of barbarian invasions wiped out most of the historical record of the Kush empire.
   (D) The sub-Saharan African climate is not conducive to the preservation of historical artifacts.
   (E) Linguists have not been able to decipher the system of writing used during sub-Saharan Africa's early history.

5. Which of the following was the highest class within the hierarchical caste system of early Hinduism?

   (A) Warriors
   (B) Peasants
   (C) Priests
   (D) Merchants
   (E) Artisans

6. The colossal stone head pictured above most likely comes from which of the following civilizations?

   (A) Hittite
   (B) Egyptian
   (C) Chinese
   (D) Olmec
   (E) Aztec

7. Which of the following best describes the historical importance of Hammurabi's Code?

   (A) It is a record of the funerary practices of the ancient Egyptians.
   (B) It is the oldest known example of Persian mythological literature.
   (C) It contains the most reliable contemporary account of the Punic Wars.
   (D) It is notable for its depiction of everyday life in ancient Israel.
   (E) It illustrates the legal system of ancient Mesopotamia.

8. Each of the following is associated with early Buddhist belief EXCEPT

   (A) the Four Noble Truths
   (B) the Eightfold Path
   (C) the Mandate of Heaven
   (D) Nirvana
   (E) rebirth

9. Which of the following best describes the prominent characteristics of the Maya civilization?

   (A) Monumental architecture, complex religious ritual, widespread agriculture, and highly organized urban society
   (B) Pastoral society, nomadic population, complex religious ritual, and highly developed artisans
   (C) Extensive written texts, widespread agriculture, pastoral society, and caste system
   (D) River valley settlement, no written records, polytheistic religion, monumental architecture
   (E) Slash-and-burn agriculture, extensive written texts, pastoral society, and textile manufacturing

10. Which of the following is commonly acknowledged as the first urban dynasty in ancient China?

    (A) The Zhou
    (B) The Shang
    (C) The Qin
    (D) The Tang
    (E) The Xia

Chapter 5
From Civilizations to Empires

If "civilization" is the first major stage of recorded history, then "empire" could be considered the next step in human development. Empires develop as civilizations and their leaders move beyond their traditional homelands to conquer the lands of others. So how do we know an empire when we see it? That's what we're going to cover in this chapter.

HOW DO WE KNOW AN EMPIRE WHEN WE SEE IT?

The Akkadians, whom we discussed in the previous chapter, are often considered the first empire in history (although some historians also point to earlier Sumerian groups). In this chapter, we will learn about a number of other empires that made an enormous impact on human history. Some of them, such as the empire of Alexander the Great, will be familiar (from movies, at the very least), while others are not as well known.

Just as the earliest ancient civilizations shared a variety of common characteristics, so too did the empires of antiquity. Identifying the common traits of empires allows us to determine whether a civilization is, in fact, an empire. This is important because empires, for better or worse, were motivators of human progress. Managing an expansive empire was far more complex than ruling over one's own people. It required something greater than what had been accomplished before.

Conquest over Great Distances

For many of us, the word "empire" gives off a bad vibe, something reminiscent of the bad guys in science fiction films who always seem to want to take over the universe. Just like in the movies, the empires of history begin with conquest. The conquest of one civilization over another may happen for a variety of reasons, including the need or desire for natural resources or the ambitions of a ruler.

For whatever motivating reason, conquest always ends with one people replacing the political leadership of another people with its own. To be considered an empire, the amount of land that is conquered must be geographically significant and contain a unique cultural identity. Connecticut couldn't call itself an empire by conquering Rhode Island. Likewise, Rome didn't become an empire by conquering the Italian peninsula; Rome became an empire by conquering the entire Mediterranean region.

Ambitious, Charismatic Leaders

Another defining characteristic of an empire is its leaders. Civilizations often became empires because of the ambitions of a single ruler. Whether Caesar, Genghis Khan, or Alexander, we usually come to know empires by their rulers. Great imperial leaders such as these men were often experienced military generals who led their troops in conquest. Furthermore, great leaders were often just as important in maintaining the stability of the empire after the conquest. Some empires disintegrated soon after losing their leaders, as did the empire of Alexander the Great. In this chapter you will also learn about imperial leaders who may be less familiar, from China, India, and other regions.

Military Prowess

Conquest, obviously, implies a certain degree of military prowess. To conquer lands and peoples requires a large, semiprofessional, technologically advanced military. Of course, these terms meant something different in the ancient world than they do today. Even so, having the better army often meant the difference between victory and defeat in the ancient world. But conquering foreign lands was sometimes the easy part; maintaining an empire was more difficult, requiring victorious military forces to occupy foreign lands for an indefinite period of time—just ask the Romans! Most of the empires that we will cover in this chapter became empires because of the success of their militaries in battle.

Governing Diverse Peoples

As human civilizations conquer one another, they are suddenly larger, and more culturally and linguistically diverse than before. Governing diverse peoples requires a more complex governmental bureaucracy that can effectively manage, not to mention control, the needs of a great number of people across great distances. In creating ways to manage and control a large empire effectively, imperial leaders developed systems of government that more closely resemble modern governments than the early chiefdoms and kingdoms.

Comparing Empires

Of course not all of the empires that we will cover in this chapter will neatly display all of these characteristics. However, you will notice a great deal of similarities among the various empires of antiquity, be they from different parts of the world or from different periods of time. Yet there will also be some notable differences among these great empires. Be sure to take note of these similarities and differences as you review the following great empires.

Advances in Government

How did empires control such huge swaths of territory and so many different peoples? A few things helped:

Shared local-central government
One way to assert control was to send government authorities to govern a particular province or locale. Another was to add the previous local leadership to the imperial payroll.

Concept of citizenship
Conquering powers differentiated their own people (citizens) from the conquered (noncitizens). Empires could use the promise of citizenship and its added privileges to control conquered peoples.

Managing an "international" economy
If different people use different currencies, it's next to impossible to determine the real value of goods. To avoid this problem, many early empires established common currencies, which allowed the diverse peoples of the empire, both conquering and conquered alike, to engage in trade and commerce with relative ease.

Uniform legal and tax codes
Managing diverse peoples also required the further development of legal and tax codes. The easiest way to do this was for the central imperial authority to apply its own system of laws and taxation across the entire empire, although an empire that wanted to endure would always leave some room for local custom.

Advancements in engineering
Finally, a large empire required not only the conquering of peoples, but also the transport of things from here to there. This need led to extensive networks of roads, some of which were so well built they survive to this day.

PERSIA: THE FIRST GREAT EMPIRE?

c. 3200 B.C.E.	Several small kingdoms unite to form the powerful Elamite dynasty in the Iranian plateau.
c. 2000–1000 B.C.E.	Huge numbers of Aryans migrate westward from the Indian subcontinent.
c. 1737 B.C.E.	Zarathustra, one of the first prophets of monotheism upon whose teachings the Zoroastrian religion was built, is born.
c. 728 B.C.E.	Deioces became the ruler of the vast Median Kingdom.
c. 693 B.C.E.	The armies of the Assyrian ruler Ashurbanipal destroy the great Iranian city of Susa, marking the end of the Elamite dynasty.
c. 560 B.C.E.	Cyrus the Great defeats the Median king Astyages and unites the Medians and the Persians, creating the vast and powerful Achaemenid Persian Empire.
c. 529 B.C.E.	Cyrus the Great is killed in battle and his son, Cambyses II, takes the throne.
c. 521 B.C.E.	After Cambyses' death, Darius I ("Darius the Great") becomes king.
c. 490–479 B.C.E.	The Greeks and Persians battle for territory.
c. 485 B.C.E.	Darius I dies and Xerxes I becomes king.
c. 465 B.C.E.	After his father's assassination, Artaxerxes becomes king.
c. 404–359 B.C.E.	Artaxerxes II becomes king and rules over the Persian Empire for longer than any previous leaders.
c. 359 B.C.E.	Artaxerxes III becomes king during a turbulent time of wars with Egypt and Greece.
c. 336–330 B.C.E.	Darius III fights Alexander the Great of Greece.
c. 330 B.C.E.	Darius III is murdered and the Persian Empire is effectively over.

Ancient Iran, otherwise known as Persia, presents an early example of empire. Because of its geographical position, Iran has always been the middle ground between western Asia (the Middle East) and southern and eastern Asia. In fact, some historians trace the so-called "clash of civilizations" between east and west to the wars between the Greeks and the Persians.

The traditional Iranian homeland is bounded by mountain ranges on most sides, with the Persian Gulf in the south. To the northeast, however, ancient Iran was somewhat vulnerable to attacks from nomadic groups originating in the central Asian plateau. Throughout their long history, the Persians engaged in numerous wars with surrounding civilizations, but their geographic advantage enabled them to conquer a vast swath of land.

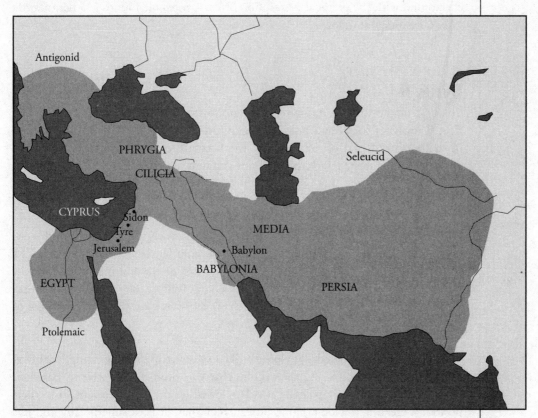

The Height of the Achaemenid Persian Empire, c. 500 b.c.e.

At its height, the Persian Empire was much larger than that of the Assyrians, stretching from the Black Sea region in the west to the Indus Valley in the east. Persian kings developed significant networks of roads across these vast geographical areas and also established an efficient system of communication that enabled them to run a complex administrative bureaucracy that lasted for hundreds of years.

As was the case in other parts of the world, the development of irrigation techniques and other agricultural innovations allowed the ancient Iranians to live and farm in the plains regions. Because the climate of the area was (and is) extremely hot, the Persians created intricate systems of underground irrigation that involved technologically sophisticated vertical shafts.

In many ways the Persians were the inheritors of the cultural and technological achievements of the civilizations of Mesopotamia, discussed in the previous chapter. Unfortunately for historians, there is very little textual evidence from the Persian world, so much of our information about Persian society comes from archaeology and the writings of various Greek historians (who hated the Persians and whose opinions are thus to be taken with a grain of salt).

There is significant artistic evidence about Persian society from its great ancient cities, such as Persepolis. On buildings and tombs, Darius and others commissioned ornate stone reliefs and sculptures depicting everyday life, battles, and the royal family. The people depicted in these artistic works have a distinctive look; hairstyles, beards, clothing, and pointed footwear identified them as Persian and correspond with the physical description of Persian people found in other (mainly Greek) historical sources.

Cyrus II

The first of the various Iranian people groups to develop advanced and sophisticated forms of social and political organization were the Medians, who settled in the northwest part of the country. The Persians, called Achaemenids after an ancestral leader, united with the Medians through marriage. The first major leader to come of this union was Cyrus II, who was the son of a Persian chieftain and a Median princess.

When Cyrus II (Cyrus the Great) rose to power in central Asia in the 6th century B.C.E., he laid the groundwork for an empire that would at its height spread from as far west as Macedonia to as far east as beyond the Indus River in India. Cyrus conquered the kingdom of Lydia as well as the entire Anatolian region (modern Turkey), including some Greek city-states on the eastern fringes of the Greek world.

When Cyrus II conquered Babylon, he did so respectfully, recognizing local customs and beliefs and freeing the peoples that had been held captive in Babylon, most notably the Jewish exiles. Cyrus II allowed local officials to remain in their positions, creating a wide-ranging bureaucracy that, at least superficially, did not disrupt or oppress conquered peoples. (Cyrus was a skilled propagandist.)

Cyrus II died while battling nomadic Iranian tribes in the northeast, but during his lifetime he was extraordinarily successful as a military and political ruler. Cyrus II's son Cambyses II was less successful a leader than his father, but he led the Persians to numerous military victories in Egypt and even sent troops far south down the Nile to explore Nubia and southern Libya. Greek historians portray Cambyses II as a crazed murderer, but Egyptian sources indicate that he was probably a pragmatist like his father, respecting the local customs and administrative policies of the lands that he conquered.

Darius I

It took another relative of Cyrus II—**Darius I**—to rule the Persian Empire to its peak. A talented military leader as well as a skilled administrator, Darius I ruled this enormous multilingual, multicultural empire for 35 years. It was under his leadership that long-lasting contributions to Persian civilization were introduced, including the first written Persian language, codified legal and tax codes, standardized currency, a huge system of roads, a canal linking the Nile River to the Red Sea, and the spread of irrigation and agricultural practices and technologies across the empire.

Darius I ruthlessly crushed all resistance to his rule and expanded Persian-controlled territory to include parts of northern Greece, modern-day Pakistan, and southern Russia. In addition to land routes, Darius made use of Persian shipbuilding knowledge and navigational skill and explored the oceans and rivers by boat (even constructing a canal connecting the Nile and the Red Sea).

In order to rule over this vast territory, Darius divided Persian lands into twenty administrative provinces, each of which was headed by a **satrap**, or provincial governor. The satrap was typically ethnically Persian, often related by blood to the royal family, but lived in the province that he governed and therefore became knowledgeable about local customs and developed relationships with local elites. The satraps' duties included collecting **tributes** of money or resources and sending those tributes back to the king.

In a similar vein as the peoples of the Indian subcontinent discussed in the previous chapter, the Persians organized their society along class and occupational lines. At the top of the hierarchy were the warriors, an aristocratic group of people who owned land as well as participated in military activities. The king, of course, was the highest-ranked member of this warrior class.

Beneath the warrior class were the priests, who had responsibility over religious rituals, including sacrifice. At the bottom of the hierarchy were the peasants, farmers, and shepherds, who primarily lived in rural parts of the Persian Empire. Persian elites were often polygamous, with the king in particular marrying multiple wives. Women of the lower classes did not have much power, but aristocratic women wielded some significant influence in matters of family life and politics.

Zoroastrianism

As was the case in all ancient societies, religious ritual played an important role in the Persian Empire. Unlike their Egyptian and Greek counterparts, however, the Persians were largely monotheists. The great god of **Zoroastrianism** was called Ahuramazda, but unfortunately the origins of this belief system are unknown. The religious texts of Zoroastrianism include the hymns attributed to Zarathustra (a.k.a. Zoroaster), who lived some time in the late 2nd or 1st century B.C.E.

A central feature of Zoroastrianism is the struggle between good and evil, in particular the constant battle against demonic forces believed to influence human life on earth. According to Zoroastrian belief, good is destined to prevail in this cosmic struggle. In life, Zoroastrianism encouraged people to live justly, and taught that actions would have consequences in the afterlife. Other important features of Zoroastrianism included an emphasis on truth telling and veneration for the natural world, especially fire.

While it is not very widely known today, Zoroastrianism was an extremely important religion in the ancient world and influenced Judaism, Christianity, and Islam (all of which we will discuss in greater detail in the next chapter). Many thematic elements of the "big three" monotheistic religions, in fact, have similarities to Zoroastrianism. The concepts of heaven and hell, God and the devil, salvation, reward and punishment in the afterlife, and the end of time can all be found in Zoroastrianism. The rise of Islam meant the end of widespread Zoroastrianism in Iran; today only a very small number of Zoroastrians remain, mainly in eastern Iran and India.

GREECE: FROM POLIS TO EMPIRE

c. 2500 B.C.E.	Greek speakers present on mainland Greece
c. 1450 B.C.E.	The development of Linear B writing
c. 1400–1200 B.C.E.	The height of Mycenaean civilization
c. 1250 B.C.E.	The Trojan War
c. 1200–750 B.C.E.	The Greek "Dark Ages"
776 B.C.E.	The first Olympic games
c. 750 B.C.E.	The development of the Greek alphabet
c. 750–730 B.C.E.	The *Iliad* and the *Odyssey* composed
c. 569 B.C.E.	Birth of the mathematician Pythagoras
c. 497–479 B.C.E.	Wars with the Persians
490 B.C.E.	Greeks defeat Persians at the battle of Marathon; democracy flourishes in Athens.
431–404 B.C.E.	Peloponnesian War
c. 399 B.C.E.	Trial and execution of Socrates
c. 380 B.C.E.	The Athens academy established by Plato
336–323 B.C.E.	Reign of Alexander the Great
146 B.C.E.	Roman invasion and conquest of Greece

Greece—The Early Years

Civilization flourished on the shores of the Aegean Sea as early as 3500 B.C.E., but we know very little about the earliest cultures of the Greeks and their island neighbors to the south, the Minoans of Crete, because we have yet to decipher their writing. What we do know about these early Aegean civilizations is primarily based on the archaeological ruins of the Minoan city of Knossos and the Greek city of Mycenae.

The great palace remains at Knossos suggest a highly advanced society. In sum, the art and artifacts from Knossos, including a painting of a man leaping over a bull, suggest a carefree culture with few, if any, enemies. The remains at Mycenae, however, suggest a much more militaristic culture. Rather than an open and expansive palace complex like Knossos, Mycenae was focused around a citadel built atop a large hill, surrounded by 20-foot-thick walls. A limestone relief of two lions, a warning to all who might want to conquer the city, topped the entrance to the fortified city.

Mycenae is important to Greek history because in Greek mythology Mycenae was the home of Agamemnon, the king who conquered Troy in the Trojan War. But both Mycenae and Knossos disappear from the history of the Aegean sometime around 1200 B.C.E., marking the beginning of the Greek "Dark Ages" (so-called because there is very little archaeological evidence or other information about life and culture).

From Dark Age to Golden Age

We know even less about the Greek Dark Ages than we do about the early years of Greek civilization. During this time period, the population seems to have dropped significantly and historians sometimes explain the drop as resulting from a lack of access to food and other resources. What we do know, however, is that during the time between c. 1200 and 750 B.C.E., the Greeks lost, and then regained, their knowledge of writing. At the fall of the Mycenaean civilization, the Greeks were using a script known as **Linear B**.

Greece's poverty and isolation began to change around 800 B.C.E., when Phoenician ships from the eastern Mediterranean began to reach the Greek mainland and trade began to flourish. By the time they emerged from the dark ages, the Greeks had not only adopted a new alphabet (the modern Greek alphabet), but they also had gained a cultural history in the form of the military and individual epics such as the *Iliad* and *Odyssey*, traditionally attributed to Homer (these epics were originally oral and were passed down through the generations, only to be written much later than their original compositions). From this shared history the Greeks expanded their power and influence across the Mediterranean.

Whereas Linear B was written using pictograms, the development of the Greek alphabet as we know it today was a major advancement in human writing systems because it included symbols that represented both consonants and vowels and thus

It is not entirely clear how and why Greek writing first came into existence, but it certainly had a number of practical uses for merchants and others. In the years after its early development, Greek writing was used for all manner of texts, ranging from literature and philosophy to scientific and mathematical texts to law codes to history to inscriptions.

could be used to accurately represent the full range of sounds and syllables contained in the Greek language (cuneiform and hieroglyphs, discussed in the previous chapter, as well as other pictograms, represent words or ideas but not sounds). The use of an alphabet with only twenty-two letters also meant that Greek was relatively easy to learn and could be mastered by people other than the scribal or priestly classes (and thus reading and writing became more democratic).

The Polis

The early Greek societies were not good candidates for imperial glory. Their cities were rather small compared to those in ancient Mesopotamia because of the lack of major river systems and arable land suitable for large-scale agriculture. Therefore, the character of early Greek society was the city-state, or **polis**. As the population of Greece grew, the *poleis* (plural of *polis*) didn't get much larger; the Greeks merely built more and more cities, eventually moving beyond the Greek mainland to colonize the shores of western Anatolia (modern-day Turkey) as well as the coasts of eastern Italy and Sicily.

Most of the Greek city-states consisted of only a few thousand inhabitants; a few, such as Athens, were larger, ranging into the tens or hundreds of thousands. Many had common characteristics, such as a hilltop **acropolis** (literally, "top of the city") with temples and administrative buildings, an **agora** (gathering place for trade and other activities), and fortified walls surrounding the center of the urban area. People lived outside the city walls as well, but came inside for protection when necessary.

The city-states of ancient Greece were relatively independent and fought each other frequently. Instead of relying upon a professional standing army, the Greeks practiced a type of warfare that involved farmer-warriors who were called up or conscripted during times of conflict but otherwise lived and worked with their families. Because so many of the warriors had responsibilities to take care of on their lands, military campaigns often took place during times of the year when there were fewer agricultural tasks to attend to.

One might assume that these geographically diverse city-states would become culturally diverse as well. However, this did not happen. The Greek city-states remained culturally unified by the Greek language and by shared events such as the Olympic games, as well as by their shared history as written by Homer. The Greek city-states did, however, differ greatly from one another politically, which allowed for a great variety of political structures, from good old-fashioned kingship to the purest form of democracy the world has ever seen.

Kings, Tyrants, And Democrats . . . Oh, My!

Athens itself went through this great variety in political structures. As Greece emerged from the dark ages, Athens was ruled by a series of kings, many of whom were considered tyrants (*tyrant* comes from the Greek *turannos*, meaning "one absolute ruler"), including the ruler **Draco** (c. 621 B.C.E.), whose laws were particularly, well, *draconian*, meaning "exceedingly harsh."

The move toward less autocratic rule began under the reign of Solon, who ruled beginning c. 590 B.C.E. His greatest achievement was writing a constitution, which created the **Council of Four Hundred**, allowed all free men to vote and canceled all public and private debts (sounds nice, doesn't it?). However, after Solon left Athens for travels around the Mediterranean, Athens again succumbed to tyrannical rule. Things had deteriorated so badly in Athens that by 510 B.C.E., a group of Athenians called upon **Sparta**, considered by many in Greece at the time as the unofficial military of Peloponnesus (the large, southernmost peninsula in Greece), to come in and restore order.

After the Spartans restored order in Athens, a reformer in the mold of Solon, named Cleisthenes, came to power. By 508 B.C.E., he had established citizenship based on geography, rather than on social rank or nobility, and he subsequently created ten voting districts throughout the Athens and its countryside, from each of which fifty citizens were selected by lottery to the new **Council of Five Hundred** for one-year terms. All free male citizens (the poor were still excluded) of Athens were expected to participate in a popular **assembly** on almost a weekly basis. Six thousand Athenians were needed to achieve a quorum (minimum number for conducting business) during the assembly meetings. Although the Council guided the discussions of the assembly meetings, the power resided with the people, and, thus, **demokratia** (*demos*, people; *kratos*, power), or *democracy*, was born.

It is important to note that while Greece was indeed the birthplace of democracy, it hardly resembled the democracies of the modern era. Only free adult males of pure Athenian lineage were eligible to participate in this "people power," and since that eligibility excluded women, children, slaves, and foreigners, probably only about 10% of the Athenian population could actually participate in assembly meetings.

It is impossible for historians to know the exact numbers, but it has been estimated that approximately one third of the Greek population in classical antiquity were slaves. Unlike slavery in the United States prior to the Civil War, slavery in ancient Greece was not racially based. Most slaves were foreigners (i.e., foreign to the city-state in which they were enslaved), but were not necessarily ethnically different from their masters. Slaves participated in all sorts of activities, but most of them worked in households performing menial tasks.

The status of women in ancient Greece varied widely. In Sparta, for example, it seems that women were more independent than elsewhere in Greece (indeed, Sparta was criticized by Athenian men for allowing its women to participate in public activities to a degree unheard of in Athens). Generally speaking, Greek women were expected first and foremost to be wives and mothers, and to run the household with the assistance of their domestic slaves. Slave women, on the other hand, had no rights, and could be used sexually by their masters (as could male slaves).

You're Outta Here!
Ostracism had a special meaning in ancient Athens. Athenian citizens would occasionally hold popular votes to banish individuals deemed dangerous to the state by writing those individuals' names on pottery shards (or *ostraka*).

War with Persia

The war with the Persian Empire and the rise of Athens as the central power of Greece go hand in hand. Athens was a young, budding, democratic city on the rise when the Persians came knocking. By 500 B.C.E., Persia had conquered Anatolia, including the Greek city-states along the western coast, a colonized region the Greeks called Ionia. Although the Persians allowed the city-states to rule themselves, in typical Persian hands-off fashion, the Ionian city-states were still required to pay taxes to the royal treasury in Persepolis. Some of these Greek city-states revolted against Persian rule (this is known as the **Ionian Revolt**) and pleaded to mainland Greece, particularly Athens, for help. Athens obliged and provided ships as well as soldiers.

Infuriated by Athenian interference, the Persian king, Darius, decided to invade Greece and rid himself of the Greek problem. In 490 B.C.E., Darius landed nearly 50,000 troops on the plains of **Marathon**. He had every reason to expect victory as Persia had conquered Babylon only fifty years prior. The Athenian forces met the Persians at Marathon with only around 10,000 hoplites.

Hop to It!

Hoplites were the citizen-soldiers of ancient Greece. Battles consisted of hoplites in tight formations known as phalanxes working together as a group. It might sound democratic in theory, but to be effective, a unit like this had to have incredibly strict discipline; there was little room for independent thought, debate, or discussion on the battlefield.

Even though the Persians enjoyed a five-to-one advantage, the discipline and training of the hoplites resulted in a Greek victory. Knowing the Persians would continue their assault, the winning Greek general dispatched his fastest runner, Pheidippides, to Athens (26 miles from Marathon—hence the name of the popular road race) to notify his countrymen of the Athenian victory and the impending second battle.

Ten years after Marathon, Darius's son, **Xerxes**, mounted a second invasion of the Greek mainland in attempt to avenge his father's defeat and to end the Greek threat to his empire. Again, the Greeks faced incredible odds against a Persian force estimated at about 250,000 or more. And again, the Greeks handed the Persians defeat after defeat.

The first was at Thermopylae in 480 B.C.E., when 7,000 Greeks were led by 300 elite Spartan hoplites (yes, like the movie), who sacrificed themselves to allow Athens enough time to evacuate. The Athenians, having fled to their naval fleet of 300 ships, trapped and defeated an overconfident Xerxes, who had a fleet of nearly 1,000 ships. The final battles of the Persian War were fought in 479 B.C.E., as the Athenians and the Spartans again teamed up to defeat Persian land and sea forces. This willingness of the Athenians and the Spartans, who were traditional adversaries, to cooperate against the Persians, is most likely the reason that the small Greek city-states were able to defeat the great Persian Empire.

Grecian-Style Temple

Photo by Julian Ham

The Golden Age of Athens

The period between the end of the Persian War in 479 B.C.E. and 430 B.C.E. is known as the **Golden Age**, or Classical Age, of Athens. After the defeat of the Persians, Athens decided to assert its dominance over its fellow Greek city-states. In 477 B.C.E., Athens led the formation of a new military alliance, called the Delian League, to protect against any future invasions by the Persians or other enemies.

The Spartans were notably absent from this new alliance. Soon after the formation of the alliance Athens became heavy-handed, not allowing other city-states to leave the league, going so far as attacking them to keep them in the league. Furthermore, in 454 B.C.E., Athens decided to move the treasury of the Delian League from Delios to (where else?) Athens itself.

The Athenians took advantage of having the Delian League treasury. They started a massive project to rebuild the acropolis, which had been sacked by the invading Persians. The centerpiece of this new project was the Parthenon, a great temple built in honor of Athens's patron goddess, Athena. Athens's leader during this time was **Pericles**, who not only led Athens into its golden age, but also into the Peloponnesian War and to its downfall.

War Between Athens and Sparta

Sparta began to worry that Athens's domineering control over its Delian allies would soon threaten Sparta's own alliance, the Peloponnesian League. Fearing loss of its own power and influence, and fearing the extremely powerful Athenian navy, Sparta preemptively attacked Athens in 432 B.C.E., sparking the **Peloponnesian War**. Knowing they couldn't defeat the Spartans on land, the Athenians barricaded themselves behind their city walls as the Spartans pillaged the countryside.

The Athenians counterattacked by invading Sparta's allies by sea. Ultimately, this ended up being a losing strategy for Athens, whose leader Pericles died early in the conflict, in 429 B.C.E. Athens, however, stubbornly resisted takeover until 404 B.C.E., when Sparta, funded by the Persians (go figure), finally sacked the city. Although Sparta won the final battle of the war, the decades-long conflict was economically and culturally devastating, and ultimately a loss for both sides and for Greece as a whole. A true Greek empire would have to wait for Alexander.

The Empire of Alexander the Great

Spartan Culture: Truly Spartan

Although Sparta defeated Athens in the Peloponnesian War, Sparta did not leave behind much of a cultural legacy. Most of the Ancient Greek culture that influenced Western civilization came from Athens and Macedon. Sparta placed such an emphasis on military life that its people had little time for art, philosophy, or literature. One exception: We now use the adjective *spartan*, meaning "austere, simple, and self-disciplined."

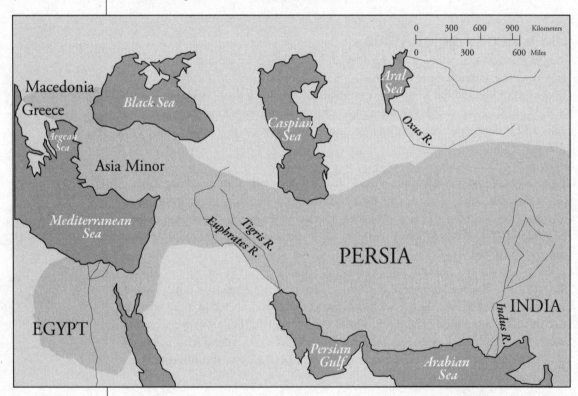

The Height of Alexander the Great's Empire, 4th Century B.C.E.

The rise of **Alexander the Great** begins with the conquests of his father, **Philip of Macedon**, ruler of a region just north and east of Greece proper. From the time he was appointed king in 359 B.C.E., Philip conquered much of the Balkan Peninsula and dozens of Greek city-states, including Athens in 338 B.C.E. Philip's goal in conquering Greek city-states was to unite Greece and Macedonia in alliance to fight Persia. His war with Persia, however, would be fought by his son, Alexander, as Philip was assassinated in 336 B.C.E.

Alexander was 20 years old when he succeeded the throne of his father. He wasted little time beginning a military campaign against the Persians. And again, just as they had been during the wars of the previous century, the Greek forces were almost always outnumbered by the Persians. Alexander's troops were incredibly well trained and disciplined, battle-hardened by years of conquest under Philip. Alexander won key battles against the Persians in 334, 333, and 331 B.C.E. throughout Anatolia, Syria and Mesopotamia. In 332 B.C.E., he conquered Egypt.

Alexander also conquered Babylon, and even Persepolis, the Persian capital. These victories, however, were not enough for him. There was another half of the Persian Empire to conquer, the half that stretched from modern-day Afghanistan to the Indus River valley. His desire to conquer the world exhausted his army and led to a near mutiny. After agreeing to return home to Greece, Alexander died in Babylon in 323 B.C.E. He was just 33 years old.

Although short-lived, Alexander's empire had lasting consequences for the spread of Greek culture throughout the ancient Middle East. Because of the extensive travel and colonization that took place during this time period, the Greeks interacted with other societies and influenced them as well as learned from them. Greek influence continued, during what is called the **Hellenistic Age**, even through the break-up of Alexander's empire.

Greek language, art, and architecture became commonplace throughout the lands of Anatolia, Egypt, and Mesopotamia (and at the same time, the cultures of these regions influenced Greece as well). Greek-style cities sprouted up all over the place, and one could find cities all over the Mediterranean region with Greek temples, public baths, and amphitheaters. Hellenistic culture dominated the western Mediterranean until the rise of the Roman Empire, and continued to be dominant throughout Syria and Mesopotamia until the rise of Islam in the 7th century C.E.

Greek Religion and Philosophy

The Greeks were polytheistic people whose deities were both male and female. Some of these deities were associated with nature, such as Poseidon (lord of the sea), while others were idealized versions of heroic humans (such as Apollo). Religious ritual in ancient Greece was an important part of private family life as well as public ceremonial life. The temples, which were thought to be the residences of the gods on earth, were the primary location in which religious rituals took place. Chief among these rituals was sacrifice, ranging from simple gifts of wine or bread to more elaborate (and bloody) slaughtering of animals.

Finally, we cannot move on to the Romans without saying a brief word about **Greek philosophy** and intellectual tradition. *Philosophy*, literally "love of wisdom," has long been associated with ancient Greece. The **Sophists** were among the earliest teachers of wisdom; wise men who often traveled itinerantly and taught public speaking and logic in the agoras, the Sophists helped to develop the nascent Greek discipline of rhetoric (persuasive speaking that has applications in philosophy, politics, and law).

In addition to the religious activities of the temples, the Greeks sought advice and prophecies from **oracles**, which were sacred places at which the gods were believed to communicate directly with humans. The most famous of these is the **Oracle at Delphi**, where, according to myth, Zeus declared the center of the earth was located. At the Temple of Apollo at Delphi, the Greeks kept an eternal flame burning continuously. So important was the oracle that Greek rulers almost always consulted it before undertaking wars, founding new city-states or colonies, and other major endeavors.

It was during the golden age of Athens that philosophers such as Socrates, Plato, and Aristotle made their greatest impact. **Socrates**, who lived approximately 470 to 399 B.C.E., was an innovator in the sense that he shifted philosophical inquiry from the natural world to questions of ethics. As a teacher, Socrates had a number of young disciples with whom he would converse and debate. Unfortunately, Socrates was critical of the status quo and angered quite a few Athenian elites, who eventually put him on trial for "corrupting the youth" and had him executed.

One of Socrates' students, **Plato**, founded a philosophical academy outside of Athens in which young men could come to receive the ancient equivalent of a college education. Plato wrote all sorts of treatises, most of which take the form of "dialogues" between Socrates and others (some of which may have been imagined and some of which may have been based on oral traditions).

Another important classical philosopher was **Aristotle**, who lived approximately 384 to 322 B.C.E. A former student at Plato's academy, Aristotle founded his own philosophical school (called the Lyceum) and lectured and wrote on a huge number of topics, ranging from politics and law to ethics to physics and astronomy. Aristotle, in fact, was so well regarded that Philip of Macedon hired him to be the private tutor to his son, Alexander the Great!

ROME IN A FEW BRIEF PAGES? CAN'T BE DONE!

753 B.C.E.	According to myth, Rome is founded on the Tiber River by the brothers Romulus and Remus. Rome is subsequently ruled by seven kings.
509 B.C.E.	The last of the seven kings is driven from power. The Roman Republic is established, instituting a multi-branched, representative government.
390 B.C.E.	Rome is sacked by the Gauls (from modern-day France).
264–146 B.C.E.	Rome battles Carthage (north Africa) in the Punic Wars. Roman victory establishes Italian dominance over the Mediterranean.
44 B.C.E.	Julius Caesar is killed on the Ides of March, two years after declaring himself "dictator for life."
117 C.E.	The Roman Empire is at its largest under Emperor Trajan.
284 C.E.	Emperor Diocletian splits the Empire in half, with one ruler in Rome and one in Byzantium.
312 C.E.	Constantine the Great becomes the sole ruler of the Empire.
313 C.E.	Edict of Milan grants Christians the right to worship without the threat of government persecution.
330 C.E.	Constantinople becomes the capital of the eastern part of the Empire.
379 C.E.	Emperor Theodosius makes Christianity the official religion of the Empire.
402 C.E.	Ravenna becomes the capital of the western part of the Empire.
410 C.E.	Rome is sacked by the Visigoths (from modern-day Germany).
455 C.E.	Rome is sacked by the Vandals (from modern-day Poland).
476 C.E.	The last Roman emperor, Romulus Augustulus, is deposed.

This marks the end of the Roman Empire in the western Mediterranean. The former eastern part of the Roman Empire develops into the Byzantine Empire.

A Mythical Founding

The ancient Romans traced their mythological history all the way back to **Aeneas**, one of the few survivors of the Trojan War. Aeneas is said to have escaped the Greek siege of Troy with a band of survivors who then sailed across the Mediterranean to land on the Italian peninsula. Through some creative mythology, including help from Mars, the god of war, the bloodline of Aeneas was passed down to two brothers, **Romulus** and **Remus**. Can you figure out which one is said to have founded the city of Rome in 753 B.C.E.?

According to Roman legend, the rule of Romulus was followed by six kings, many of whom are believed to be **Etruscan**, a people who lived along the western coast of Italy north of Rome. It is likely the early Romans incorporated much of Etruscan culture into their own, including language (Latin), mythology, art, and architecture. The last of the Etruscan kings, Tarquinius Superbus, was a tyrant who was expelled from the city in a Roman rebellion. After the expulsion of the last Etruscan king, Romans vowed never to allow Rome to be ruled by a tyrant again.

The Republic Is Established

After the expulsion of Tarquinius Superbus, the Romans established a republican form of government in 509 B.C.E. in order to limit the possibility that any one man could become supreme ruler. They divided the power of the state among different branches of government, most notably the Senate, run by the patrician upper classes, and the popular assemblies, run by the plebian common classes (the upper classes, it must be noted, wielded most of the power in this arrangement). The Romans also instituted yearly term limits and dual office holders as further checks on personal power. The highest of these office holders were the consuls, all of whom held the highest civil and military authority of the government. The Senate, however, remained the primary legislative and deliberative body of the Roman government, as it was dominated by the wealthiest and most notable of Roman families.

Expansion Across the Mediterranean

Rome, however, would be nothing without its armies. Although the republic would provide for stable government, Rome's armies would provide the conquests for the fledgling power of the Mediterranean. Over the 250 years following the formation of the republic, Rome conquered the entire Italian peninsula using a generous helping of "big stick" diplomacy. Basically, the young republic's neighbors knew they were little match for Rome's increasingly powerful armies, and many simply formed alliances with Rome without offering a fight. By 264 B.C.E., Rome dominated the entire Italian peninsula and increasingly threatened its neighbors across the Mediterranean.

The peoples most threatened by this Roman show of force were the Carthaginians. By the time Rome took control of the Italian peninsula, **Carthage** was already the dominant trading power of the Mediterranean, controlling most of North Africa, the southern coasts of Spain, and even the islands of Sardinia and Sicily.

Competition between Carthage and Rome led to the **Punic Wars** (Punic comes from Phoenician, the language of the Carthaginians), which were fought over the next hundred years.

The Second Punic War, fought between 218 and 201 B.C.E., is best remembered because of Carthaginian general **Hannibal**'s famous alpine crossing with elephants to invade Italy. Although initially devastated by Hannibal's invasions, Rome not only recovered to destroy Carthage, but by 146 B.C.E. had also conquered the once mighty Greeks. Rome was now the boss of the Mediterranean.

When You Win, You Lose
The phrase *pyrrhic victory* comes from King Pyrrhus, a king of ancient Greece. Although he won battles against the Romans, his forces were devastated by the massive losses of life and resources. So a pyrrhic victory is one that comes at great cost to the victor.

All Hail Caesar! Nah, Let's Kill Him Instead

Although Rome looked unbeatable after defeating Carthage and subduing Greece, all was not well on the home front. Centuries of war had placed an unbearable burden upon the common people, whose farms were nearly ruined while Rome's citizen-soldiers were off fighting. This "agrarian crisis" sparked a political clash that ended in the assassinations of high-level magistrates in the government. The Roman republic was trading debate for violence and murder, and by 100 B.C.E., the once stable state was now in full-fledged crisis.

As the republic weakened, a series of military generals began to assert their power in Roman politics. The most famous of these generals was **Julius Caesar**, who made a name for himself by conquering Gaul (modern-day France), and adding to the Roman Empire's possessions, as well as by invading Britain. Upon returning to Italy from his conquests in 49 B.C.E., Caesar refused to give up authority over his army (which was customary for a returning general) and decided instead on civil war.

By 45 B.C.E., Caesar was victorious and declared himself dictator for life. His leadership, however, was short-lived; a group of senators led by Brutus and Cassius killed him on the Ides (15th) of March in 44 B.C.E. The senators who killed Caesar believed they were fulfilling the vow made by their ancestors never to allow a tyrant to rule over Rome.

Augustus and the *Pax Romana*

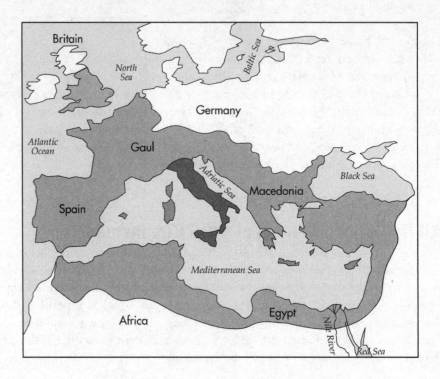

The Extent of the Roman Empire c. 100 C.E.

Caesar's death destabilized the republic even more, leading it back into civil war for the next 13 years. The planners of Caesar's assassination were not particularly prepared for Caesar's adopted son, Octavian, to avenge his father's death. Octavian and his allies pursued his political rivals Mark Antony and Brutus, defeating Brutus in battle and driving Antony to suicide.

Octavian, however, was an unlikely candidate to bring stability back to Rome. He was adopted, had plenty of potential enemies, was an inexperienced general, and by all accounts, not a particularly healthy man. But he was a political genius. Rather than claim for himself the position of dictator for life, as did Caesar, he called himself *princeps*, "first citizen," meaning first among equals. This gesture signified to Romans, especially those who made up the Senate, that Octavian was more interested in healing Rome than claiming power for himself. In return, in 38 B.C.E., the Senate granted Octavian the honorific title of *imperator*, or emperor, and in 27 B.C.E. they added the title Augustus as a mark of their respect. Augustus, as he was henceforth known, created a new government, replacing the republic of old with an imperial government that placed the emperor and the elite Senate as the seats of power.

Although far less representative than the republic, this system of government provided enough stability to launch Rome into its greatest era of peace and prosperity, the *Pax Romana* (Roman peace); this period lasted from the ascendancy of Augustus in 27 B.C.E. to the death of Marcus Aurelius in 180 C.E.

The Empire Declines, Christianity Rises

The empire reached its zenith during the *Pax Romana* in 138 C.E. under the reign of **Hadrian**, whose wall in Britain (near the border between England and Scotland) marked the northernmost reach of the empire. But following the death of Marcus Aurelius in 180 C.E., Rome once again fell into an era of civil unrest and instability. In order to overcome a century of instability, the emperor Diocletian, who came to power in 284 C.E., created the tetrarchy, or "rule of four." In doing so Diocletian broke the empire into two pieces—the Roman-dominated west and the Greek-dominated east—with each piece to be ruled by an emperor and a second-in-command. If the emperor, or Augustus, of either the east or the west were to die, the second-in-command, or Caesar, would step in. Diocletian thought the empire's division and planned succession would make it easier to manage a large empire, but it may have actually hastened its fall.

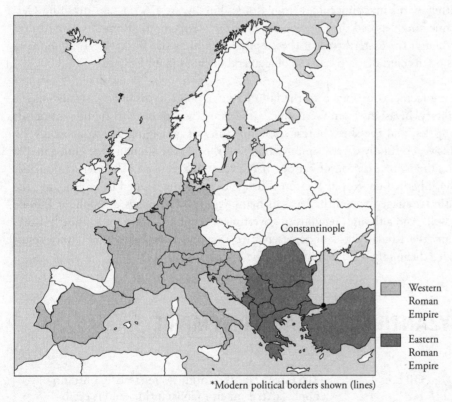

Constantinople

Western Roman Empire

Eastern Roman Empire

*Modern political borders shown (lines)

The Division of the Roman Empire

Constantine, Diocletian's successor, instituted even more dramatic changes to the empire. Unlike Diocletian, who actively persecuted Christians, Constantine passed the **Edict of Milan** in 313 C.E., granting official toleration to Christians throughout the empire. Furthermore, Constantine, a Christian convert himself, promoted Christianity above all other religions by funding church-building programs throughout Rome, Jerusalem, and his new capital city, **Constantinople**. Constantinople (modern-day Istanbul), built upon the old city of Byzantium, continued a shift of political power and influence toward the eastern, Greek-dominated portion of the Roman Empire.

Although ruled politically by Rome, the eastern empire was dominated by Greek language and culture. Yet Christianity came to dominate both the eastern and western part of the empire. In 300 C.E., Christianity could be found only in the major metropolitan areas of the empire. By 600 C.E., however, Christianity was dominant throughout the entire lands of the empire including Spain, North Africa, Egypt, and even Mesopotamia.

The Fall

As Christianity's power and influence was rising throughout the empire, the power of the Roman state and of the Roman emperors was waning. In 380 C.E., emperor Theodosius required that all Romans believe as the archbishop of Rome, or the Pope, believed. The power of the Christian church became evident in 452 C.E. when it was Pope Leo I, not the emperor, who convinced Attila the Hun to withdraw his invading forces from Rome. Finally, in 476 C.E., an invading Germanic king deposed the last emperor of the western empire, Romulus Augustulus. Although the eastern part of the empire lived on as the Byzantine Empire, most historians consider 476 C.E. the official end of the Roman Empire.

Many factors contributed to the fall of Rome: political instability, strains on the military, invasions from Germanic barbarians, the rise of Christianity, economic struggles, and the sheer bureaucratic difficulty of managing a geographically expansive, culturally diverse empire. But even though the Roman state ended in 476 C.E., the Romanization of Europe had already taken place. The Germanic tribes who inherited control of Western Europe from Rome wanted to be Roman. The Latin language formed the basis of many regional languages throughout Europe as well. And although republican government remained dormant for nearly 1,800 years, the Roman ideas of representative rule and balance of power were resurrected during the Enlightenment of the 18th century.

Blah Blah
The word *barbarian* comes from the ancient Greek word *barbaros,* meaning a "non-Greek," or one who speaks a language one doesn't understand. The word is onomatopoeic: "Bar-bar" is the sound that people speaking unintelligibly make, similar to "blah-blah" in English.

BYZANTIUM: THE EASTERN EMPIRE

330 C.E.	The Greek city Byzantium is renamed Constantinople (after Emperor Constantine) and is established as the eastern capital of the Roman Empire.
527 C.E.	Emperor Justinian's reign begins.
529–534 C.E.	Rome's civil law is codified into the Justinian Code.
532–537 C.E.	The Hagia Sophia is constructed in Constantinople.
568 C.E.	Byzantine Empire loses many battles and lands in Italy and North Africa.
693 C.E.	Muslim armies attack Constantinople.
726 C.E.	Iconoclastic controversy begins over the use of religious images in the Christian church.

Although scholars don't agree on exactly when the **Byzantine Empire** was born, many look to the establishment of Constantinople as the eastern capital of the Roman Empire in 330 C.E. as its beginning. What is known is the unique tapestry that was Byzantium: a Roman state that was religiously Christian and culturally Greek. The Byzantine Empire stood for 1,000 years, coming to an end in 1453 C.E. when Constantinople fell after a Turkish invasion.

The Byzantine Empire left a rich legacy. Emperor Justinian, who ruled from 527 to 565 C.E., codified Roman civil law into a compendium known as the **Justinian Code**, which is the basis for much of Europe's legal traditions. Justinian was also responsible for construction of **Hagia Sophia**, the Church of Holy Wisdom in Constantinople, which remains one of the architectural treasures of the modern world. Although built as a Christian church, it was converted to a mosque in the 15th century after the Ottomans took over the city.

Byzantium was a site of many religious struggles. The 7th century brought constant pressure on the empire from the rising Islamic powers to the east and south. Constantinople feuded with Rome over religious doctrine (particularly over the proper use of icons, or religious images believed to have sacred power, in the 8th century) and fell victim to crusaders in 1204. Never able to fully recover from the ravages of the crusaders, the empire weakened over time until its final fall in 1453.

> **Why Did Rome Fall but Byzantium Remain Standing?**
> Byzantium outlasted its western Roman counterpart for a number of reasons. First and foremost, the Byzantine Empire was supported by an efficient, well-run administrative structure, which maintained stability in the empire for centuries. Second, Byzantium was not as widespread territorially as was Rome, which made it easier to maintain its borders. Third, the Byzantine Empire had a number of large urban centers, which created more cultural stability and made it easier to defend. Rome, on the other hand, pushed its borders far beyond where its forces could defend themselves against its enemies, and was pressed to use more mercenaries (especially Germanic peoples) in the distant lands. Last, the Byzantines had better relations between social classes than did the Romans.
>
> In general, the Roman Empire—both the western and eastern wings—left an enormous cultural, political, and religious legacy that inspired the imperial powers of later centuries.

CHINA: EMPIRE, THE CHINESE WAY

221–206 B.C.E.	Qin dynasty (founded by Qin Shi Huang)
206 B.C.E.–220 C.E.	Han dynasty (founded by Liu Bang)
220-589 C.E.	The "Six Dynasties" period
581–618 C.E.	Sui dynasty
618–907 C.E.	Tang dynasty

When we last left China, the Zhou dynasty had slowly disintegrated, and China found itself in the Warring States period. This period of decentralized and diffused authority would eventually come to an end, though, and real imperial China would soon begin.

All for One And He's Not You: The Qin Unify China

The **Qin** dynasty was founded in 221 B.C.E. under Qin Shi Huang. The Qin had an astonishingly brief run as the ruling power of a unified China—the dynasty ruled for less than 20 years, outlasting its founder by a scant four years—but its legacy is undeniable. By far the most important Qin legacy far outlived the dynasty itself: The Qin ushered in the Chinese Empire, which existed more or less continuously from the founding of the Qin dynasty to the 20th century, when communism replaced imperial rule.

Centralization 101: How the Qin Unified China

Unification of China happened at several levels. Qin Shi Huang (also sometimes referred to as Shi Huangdi; both names mean "first emperor") unified China politically by conquering the other states that had emerged at the breakdown of the Zhou dynasty (the Warring States period). Upon gaining power, Qin Shi Huang replaced the pesky local feudal lords (who were hard to control) with civilian and military administrators who worked for the dynasty, who could be (and usually were) transferred or fired at will, and whose authority was not hereditary.

These administrators created a system of standardized practices to run the state and legal systems—a bureaucracy. They also standardized currency, a writing system (the basis of the writing system used today), and weights and measures. But the Qin weren't strengthened only by bureaucracy: Empires need armies, so Qin Shi Huang built huge armies with the peasants he had freed from their feudal bonds. These peasants, therefore, came to serve the empire rather than local lords, diluting the power of local warlords to resist the power of central authority.

An empire needs infrastructure to protect and ease the movement of goods and people. To that end, Qin Shi Huang built roads and standardized axle widths to ensure that carts could run in the ruts of the new roads. And even when he was the ruler of only one state, Qin Shi Huang also embraced Legalism (see the previous chapter), and persecuted Confucianists, who criticized such harsh imperial rule.

To keep his subjects in check and quell criticism of his rule, the Qin ruler went so far as to promote wide-scale burning of any book other than those on Legalism, medicine, agriculture, and a few other subjects. As with most book burners, Qin Shi Huang did not stop at books: he also executed non-Legalist scholars. These actions together resulted in the loss of most of the culture and thought of earlier China, a period at least as rich and broad as the Greek classical era.

The Qin period is distinctive for building as well. Qin Shi Huang had a lavish tomb built for himself in the capital Xianyang (today known as Xi'an) and also commissioned the creation of a **terra cotta army** of more than 8,000 life-sized figures of men, chariots, and horses that would protect him after his death. He also built the precursor to the modern **Great Wall of China** by linking together existing walls built along the northern edge of the empire by local rulers during earlier, more fractious times.

Ironically, the Qin dynasty fell thanks to the efforts of the same class that helped build it: the peasantry. Fueled by anger over taxes and the constant need for labor to bring to fruition the ruler's huge building projects, a peasant revolt brought down the Qin in 206 B.C.E. The Qin were in power less than a century, but their legacy was long lasting. China was unified. It had a written language. The infrastructure built by Qin Shi Huang made it easier to keep such a huge area under control, and the precedent for a strong administrative class would continue through the rest of the imperial period. The age of empire in China had begun.

Bring on the Han

Liu Bang, a peasant turned bandit, became China's next emperor after the fall of the Qin. In doing so, Liu Bang founded the **Han** dynasty, which would rule China for the next 400 years. The Han dynasty kept the aristocracy in check by limiting the size of their fiefdoms. Liu Bang ended Legalism's monopoly as the state philosophy, although it remained influential at the administrative level. Although Liu Bang himself was partial to the Taoist philosophy, it was the **Confucian** school of thought and ethics that came into ascendancy and became the basis for Chinese rule for the next 2,000 years.

Under Confucianism, China developed the first civil service, open to anyone who could pass the exams. Though privileged families had a clear edge, people could theoretically move into the ranks of state administrators through hard work and ability, not just by birth. Confucianism revived the writing and study of history, as well as the codification of a case-based legal system (one based on prior rulings) that continued to be used in China for centuries.

The Han also expanded the size of the empire considerably through a mix of diplomacy and sheer military might, taking over modern-day Guangdong and southern China as well as areas of present-day Korea and Vietnam. The expansion of the empire meant more markets to fuel the Chinese economy. Thanks to the Han's territorial conquests, Chinese trade grew. The **Silk Road**, trade routes along which silk and other luxury goods flowed to the West, enriched the economy significantly.

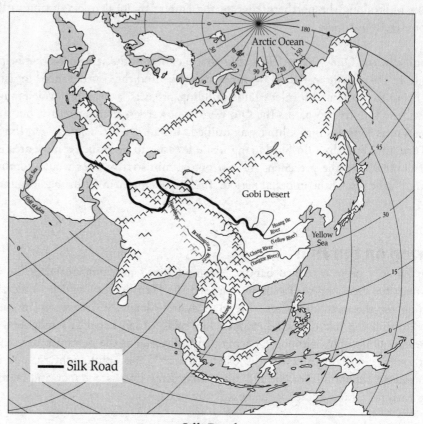

Silk Road

A short period of instability between 9 and 23 C.E. saw the fall of Han and the rise of Wang Mang, who fell from power quickly after managing to alienate every level of Chinese society, from the aristocracy to the peasantry. The Han dynasty was soon restored and would rule for another 200 years, although it had been substantially weakened by the time it officially ended in 220 C.E.

After the fall of the Han, China fell into disarray and would not be unified politically again until 581 C.E. However, even though China was politically decentralized, the common bonds of Chinese culture held the territory of the empire mostly together during the periods when no single ruler controlled the state.

The Sui Dynasty: Picking Up the Pieces

China's imperial history was revived in 581 C.E. with the rise of the **Sui** dynasty, founded by Emperor Wen. The Sui dynasty was short-lived but accomplished much in the 37 years it controlled China. It conquered and reunified central China, endeared itself to the common people through a judicious combination of Taoist, Confucian, and Buddhist principles, and completed the **Grand Canal**, a link between the Yangzi and Yellow rivers which made it possible to expand agriculture and urbanization to larger areas of China. Unfortunately for the Sui, between military losses and the extreme amount of both economic and human sacrifice involved in building the canal, the people rebelled, and the Sui were overthrown by a general in the imperial army, who established the next dynasty—the Tang.

The Tang: The Flourishing of an Empire

The **Tang** dynasty ruled China from 618 to 907 C.E., expanding the empire beyond Chinese territory into the surrounding territories of Mongolia and central Asia as far as Afghanistan. The Tang dynasty also held sway over Tibet and parts of Korea, Vietnam, and Japan. Many people in those areas overtaken by the Chinese assimilated to Chinese language and culture, intermarried with Chinese, and generally became part of Chinese society.

The Tang period saw a number of important inventions that would be influential far beyond the borders of the empire. Among the most important, the **block printing** system allowed for the faster and more efficient creation of books and other written material.

Additionally, trade flourished along the Silk Road, spreading Chinese culture far beyond the borders of China proper. In particular, the Buddhist belief system spread into Tibet, central Asia, and other surrounding areas. The presence of Buddhist monuments such as the giant Buddhas of Bamiyan in Afghanistan demonstrate how far Buddhism's influence spread beyond the borders of China and India.

Let's now move southwest into the Indian subcontinent. What empires arose here, and what are their legacies? As we will see, the major Indian empires came and went, but their cultural legacies—much like those of the Chinese—played a significant role in the continued unity of this territory, even in the absence of a strong centralized government.

INDIA: EMPIRES OF THE SUBCONTINENT

324–185 B.C.E.	Mauryan Empire
c. 266 B.C.E.	Emperor Asoka conquers and unites most of southern Asia.
c. 260 B.C.E.	Emperor Asoka converts to Buddhism and subsequently promotes animal rights, equality, and nonviolence.
c. 230 B.C.E.	Emperor Simuka declares independence from the Mauryan Empire and establishes the Satavahana dynasty.
c. 184 B.C.E.	Mauryan Empire declines and Pusyamitra Sunga establishes the Sunga dynasty.
c. 240–540 C.E.	Gupta Empire

Let's now move southwest into the Indian subcontinent. What empires arose here, and what are their legacies? As we will see, the major Indian empires came and went, but their cultural legacies—much like those of the Chinese—played a significant role in the continued unity of this territory, even in the absence of a strong centralized government.

When we last left our discussion of ancient Indian civilizations, India was invaded by Alexander the Great in 327 B.C.E., bringing to an end the Aryan dynasty and leaving behind a civilization in disarray. A number of warlords battled one another for control of the now leaderless territory, but only one came out victorious: **Chandragupta Maurya**. Maurya founded (no surprise here) the Mauryan Empire, which ruled in the Ganges River area (the eastern, less strongly Aryan part of India) from 324 B.C.E., expanding westward as Alexander's armies and influence retreated, until the empire finally fell in 185 B.C.E.

Meet the Mauryan Empire

The **Mauryan Empire** installed a number of institutions that truly made it an empire. Most important, a state structure that existed above the simple hereditary lineage of the ruling family was created. This state created rules for the conduct of its citizens as well as principles for overseeing state behavior, the caste structure, religious practice, and the economy. This kind of oversight into all aspects of Indian life required a well-run administrative arm.

Chandragupta Maurya's son Bindusara and grandson **Asoka** (also spelled Ashoka) expanded the empire, but it was Asoka's reign that also expanded Buddhism beyond India into surrounding empires, leaving a lasting legacy.

Buddhism in India was given a tremendous boost when, after defeating a neighboring kingdom in 260 B.C.E. but feeling overcome with remorse at the devastation he brought, Emperor Asoka converted to Buddhism and made it the state religion. Doing so greatly weakened the influence of the Hindu priests (the Brahmins) who had risen to great heights of power under the previous Aryan dynasties, and brought peace to the kingdom for many years. Under Asoka's reign, Buddhist shrines were built throughout the empire, and Buddhism spread into Central Asia and China (more on the spread of Buddhism in China a bit later), aided in particular by the heavy trade of goods and ideas along the Silk Road.

Another way in which Asoka aided the spread of Buddhism as well as his laws throughout his kingdom was the construction of numerous gigantic stone pillars across the Indian subcontinent. Originally built in the mid-to-late 3rd century B.C.E., these pillars contained inscriptions as well as sculptures of animals. Many of these pillars were located at Buddhist monasteries and pilgrimage sites, but unfortunately only a few remain (due in part to the fact that Muslim armies destroyed them as part of a broad campaign of iconoclasm).

What Goes Up Must Come Down: The Fall of the Mauryans

The Mauryan Empire began to disintegrate soon after Asoka's death in 232 B.C.E. Unfortunately, the Mauryans were not successful in creating an administrative system of governance that could survive beyond their lineage. The Brahmins eventually came back into power in the absence of a single unifying dynasty as the cultural force uniting many petty kingdoms.

India would not see another imperial dynasty until 320 C.E., when Chandra Gupta seized power in northern India. Although other dynastic families filled the gap between the end of the Mauryans and the rise of the Guptas, none were able to unify the area to the level embodied in the term *empire*. However, trade continued to flourish, even in absence of a centralized authority.

The Gupta Empire: India's Golden Age of Culture

The **Gupta Empire** embraced the Brahmins and Hinduism, leading to a renaissance of Hindu culture and a decline of Buddhism in India. It was during the Gupta dynasty that **Sanskrit** became used not only as a religious language but also as a means of official communication, literature, and philosophy.

The Guptas didn't control such a broad expanse of India as the Mauryans had, but they did oversee several centuries of relative peace and prosperity, leaving local rule to local rulers. Gupta rule came to an end in 5th century C.E. at the hands of invading Huns (who were simultaneously invading the Roman territories in the west).

The Huns' encroachment into the Gupta Empire destabilized the state and disrupted the crucial trade routes that fed the wealth of the empire. The center crumbled, local rulers claimed their stakes, and Buddhist culture suffered nearly fatal blows. However, Indian culture survived and flourished outside of India and is evident in present-day Cambodia, Java, and Sumatra. The Hindu temple complex of Angkor Wat in Cambodia (c. 12th century C.E.) and the Buddhist center at Borobudur in Java (c. 8th century C.E.) testify to the continuing influences of India's great religions.

THE AMERICAS: HELLO? ANYONE THERE?

We don't have much to say about the Americas in this chapter on empires. Why? Because the Americas simply developed according to a different schedule than did Asia, the Near East, and Europe. Whereas the previous empires described earlier in this chapter fit roughly into the period from 500 B.C.E. to 1000 C.E., those of the Americas arose well after this period. But never fear! We will discuss the peoples and societies of the Americas in a later chapter.

LEARNING FROM THE RISE AND FALL OF EMPIRES

It appears that all empires eventually fall. The Mediterranean, Mesopotamia, and South Asia all saw their share of empires rise and fall, but what about China? Although Chinese dynasties came and went just as other empires covered in this chapter, Chinese culture and language as well as Confucian philosophy remained dominant throughout these dynastic transitions and have even carried through to modern-day China. No doubt China is the exception rather than the rule when it comes to empires.

The fates of Greece, Rome, Persia, and India are the norms of human history. All of these empires were forced to govern a vast array of culturally diverse peoples over great geographic expanses. Trying to govern such geographically and culturally diverse areas placed great strains on the governments, the armies, and the economies of these empires. Such strain left them vulnerable to "barbarian" invasions, enabled foreign religions and philosophies to flourish, and allowed for political and social revolts from within.

In the end, China did a better job than other empires of assimilating its invaders and conquered people, maintaining a common, dominant moral philosophy, and preserving its language and culture. To this day, the state remains the highest level of authority in China. Other parts of the world, however, witnessed the increasing dominance of religion. We'll cover the rise of these world religions in the next chapter.

CHAPTER 5 KEY TERMS, PEOPLE, AND EVENTS

Darius I

The greatest leader of the Persian Empire, ruling from 521 to 485 B.C.E. During his reign, the Persian Empire stretched from modern-day Greece to Pakistan, and many of the political and cultural markers of the Persian Empire developed.

Zoroastrianism

An extremely important religion in the ancient world, which believed in the duality of the world, a struggle between good and evil at the center of which is the human being. Zoroastrianism influenced Judaism, Christianity, and Islam significantly.

Iliad **and** ***Odyssey***

Greek epics originally told as oral histories and eventually written down and attributed to Homer

Polis

The ancient Greek city-state and the center of Greek culture. Some of the most prominent examples are Athens and Sparta.

Golden Age

The period of Ancient Greek history between the end of the Persian War in 479 B.C.E. and 430 B.C.E. During this time Athens founded the Delian League and asserted itself over the other Greek city-states, with the exception of Sparta.

Alexander the Great

Infamous Macedonian king who conquered Babylon, in the heart of Mesopotamia, in 331 B.C.E. His conquest is only an example of all the various wars and rulers that plagued ancient Mesopotamia for thousands of years.

Hellenistic Age

Time period during which Greek culture and thought continued to influence large parts of the world, even after Alexander's empire dissolved

Greek philosophy

Many of the greatest early philosophers were Greek, and there are many famous Greek schools of thought. Examples are the Sophists, Socrates, and Plato.

Pax Romana

A long period of peace in the Roman Empire, beginning with the installation of Augustus Caesar in 27 B.C.E. and ending in 180 C.E. with the death of Marcus Aurelius

Edict of Milan (313 C.E.)

Passed by Constantine, this declaration granted official toleration to Christianity in the Roman Empire.

Justinian Code

Rule of law that has had significant impact on Europe's legal traditions. Created by the Emperor Justinian, who ruled the Byzantine Empire between 527 and 565 C.E.

Summary

o The great empires of antiquity are often characterized by conquests over great distances; a charismatic, ambitious leader; military prowess; and governing diverse peoples.

o The Persian Empire was a model of a "good" empire, because it was often respectful of the diverse peoples it conquered, even allowing the local leaderships to remain in power. The Persian Empire, at its largest extent, spanned from the Balkan peninsula in the west to the Indus River Valley in the east.

o The Greeks started down their road to empire as small, independent city-states that were united by Greek language and mythology. The Greeks grew in strength to such a degree that they were able to defeat Persian invasions in the 5th century B.C.E. Toward the end of the 4th century, Alexander the Great created a Greek Empire by, in part, conquering the Persians. After the death of Alexander, Greek culture carried on throughout the Mediterranean for centuries.

o Rome's mythical history emphasized both its militaristic and republican heritage. Rome used both its great armies and stable government to gain control of the entire Mediterranean, Western Europe, Egypt, and Mesopotamia by 180 B.C.E. Over the following 200 years, however, the Roman Empire declined as a result of geographic and militaristic overextension, political instability, the rise of Christianity, invasions, and economic distress.

o The Byzantine Empire, beginning after the fall of Rome, was a bit of a hybrid. The empire combined Roman political and legal structure, Greek language and culture, and a heavy dose of Christianity. Although Byzantine power waned in its final centuries, it lasted until the Ottoman conquest in 1453 C.E. Many historians credit the Byzantine Empire for preserving "western culture" through the dark ages of Europe, though the darkness of those ages has been greatly exaggerated.

o China's empire was unique in that it never truly fell. Dynasties changed hands as new political rulers conquered others, but Chinese language and culture remained dominant throughout these dynastic changes, and remains dominant even to this day. China's cultural hegemony throughout antiquity stands in contrast to the other empires in this chapter. Where only bits and pieces of the other empires survived over the last 2,000 years, China's culture has remained fairly intact.

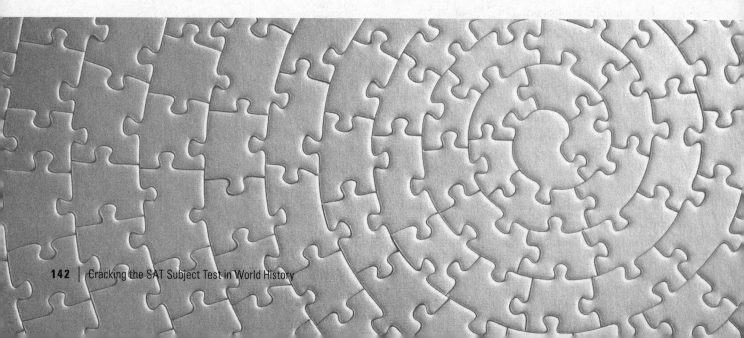

Chapter 5 Drill

Answers and explanations can be found in Part IV.

1. Which of the following dynasties was responsible for unifying China and ushering in an age of empire in the third century B.C.E.?

    (A) The Han
    (B) The Qin
    (C) The Gupta
    (D) The Tang
    (E) The Zhou

2. Which of the following was a major legal achievement of the Byzantine Empire?

    (A) Hammurabi's Code
    (B) The Draconian Constitution
    (C) The Twelve Tables
    (D) The Code of the Assura
    (E) Justinian's Code

3. Which of the following presents these four events associated with Roman civilization in the correct chronological order?

    (A) Constantinople becomes the capital of the eastern Empire; foundation of the Republic; Punic Wars; death of Julius Caesar
    (B) Death of Julius Caesar; Constantinople becomes the capital of the eastern Empire; Punic Wars; foundation of the Republic
    (C) Foundation of the Republic; death of Julius Caesar; Punic Wars; Constantinople becomes the capital of the eastern Empire
    (D) Foundation of the Republic; Punic Wars; death of Julius Caesar; Constantinople becomes the capital of the eastern Empire
    (E) Punic Wars; death of Julius Caesar; Constantinople becomes the capital of the eastern Empire; foundation of the Republic

4. Each of the following is a major characteristic of ancient empires EXCEPT

    (A) military prowess
    (B) conquest over great distances
    (C) use of a single language
    (D) governing diverse people groups
    (E) ambitious, charismatic leaders

"He who upholds Truth with all the might of his power,

He who upholds Truth the utmost in his word and deed,

He, indeed, is Thy most valued helper, O Ahuramazda!"

5. The hymn quoted above most likely comes from which of the following religious texts?

    (A) The *Hymns of Zarathustra*
    (B) The *Hebrew Bible*
    (C) The *Upanishads*
    (D) The *Oxyrhynchus Hymn*
    (E) The *Ramayana*

6. The image above most likely depicts which of the following?

   (A) The Pyramids of Giza, Egypt
   (B) The Church of Hagia Sophia, Constantinople/Istanbul, Turkey
   (C) The Acropolis of Athens, Greece
   (D) The Royal Treasury, Petra, Jordan
   (E) The Temple of Borobudur, Indonesia

7. Why did Buddhism in India receive a significant boost around 260 B.C.E.?

   (A) The Emperor Asoka made Buddhism the official religion of the Mauryan Empire.
   (B) Buddhist monks from Tibet enacted an effective campaign of missionary work.
   (C) The population had become disenchanted with the Hindu caste system.
   (D) Invading armies from the north forcible converted the entire population.
   (E) A charismatic new prophet attracted thousands of followers as he traveled around the countryside.

8. Which of the following was NOT a characteristic of the Roman Republic?

   (A) Division of political power
   (B) Term limits on political leaders
   (C) Military conflict with Carthage
   (D) A mythical founding
   (E) Equitable political representation across class boundaries

9. Who controlled Egypt in 300 B.C.E.?

   (A) The Romans
   (B) The Arabs
   (C) The Greeks
   (D) The Persians
   (E) The Assyrians

10. Which of the following was a characteristic of the Han dynasty in China?

    (A) The creation of a terra cotta army
    (B) The standardization of state currency
    (C) The completion of the Grand Canal linking the Yangzi and Yellow rivers
    (D) The development of a civil service open to anyone who could pass the requisite examinations
    (E) The invention of the block printing system

Chapter 6
The Age of
World Religions

The time period between 1500 B.C.E. and 720 C.E. witnessed the rise of great religions that endure to this day. Other religions have simply come and gone from world history. Still others remain but have few adherents. In this chapter we will focus on the great religions of the world, the religions that have had, and continue to have, great effects on the course of world history. We have already learned a little bit about some of the eastern religions, notably Hinduism and Buddhism, but in this chapter we will explore the belief systems and practices of these and other major religions in more depth.

WHY STUDY RELIGION?

Whether you are a religious person or not, understanding the history and characteristics of religion around the world is a crucial part of the study of human cultures and civilizations. Religions seek to answer some of the most difficult and profound questions of human existence, such as why we are here and how we should think and behave, and as such they are inherently worthy of study.

Some historians believe that religions in the ancient world developed as pre-scientific ways in which our ancestors sought to understand the world around them, whereas others believe that religions enable people to make sense of their lives and live in community with others. The scholarly study of religion does not espouse any particular belief system, nor does it pass judgment on whether any particular religion is correct or incorrect. Rather, when historians discuss religion, they seek to understand the many ways in which humans use stories and symbols in order to convey big ideas about who we are and how we are connected to the world around us.

THE IMPORTANCE OF RELIGION TO WORLD HISTORY

What Makes a Religion "Great"?

For the purpose of this chapter, the great religions we will cover are defined by three criteria. First, these religions are considered great because they continue to be practiced around the globe, while many other religions have simply died out or have too few adherents in our modern age to have a major impact on world events (such as Zoroastrianism, which we encountered in the previous chapter). Second, the religions covered in this chapter (with the notable exception of Judaism) have hundreds of millions of adherents worldwide. They have not only endured over the centuries, but also spread considerably.

Finally, and perhaps most important, these religions are considered great because of their lasting effects on human history. For the most part, the emergence of all of these religions fundamentally changed the societies in which they emerged as well as the societies to which they ultimately spread. These effects influenced not only prior beliefs and customs, but also politics, social relations, the nature of conquest, as well as the pursuit of knowledge, art, and architecture. These effects are not limited to history; they remain with us to this day.

The Three Great Monotheistic Religions

The three great monotheistic religions of the world are Judaism, Christianity, and Islam. These three are typically grouped together because they are bound by two broadly unifying themes. First, they promote the worship of a single god—the same god, in fact; second, all three can trace their theological histories back to the **patriarch** (meaning "father") **Abraham**. Although they share some of the same traits, the histories of these great religions differ tremendously. In the next few sections we'll look at a very brief history of Judaism, Christianity, and Islam from their births through around the 12th century C.E.

JUDAISM

c. 2000–1500 B.C.E.	Abraham and the other patriarchs active
c. 1800 B.C.E.	Migration of Abraham from Mesopotamia to Canaan
c. 1500–1200 B.C.E.	Life of Moses; exodus from Egypt and wandering of the Hebrews in the desert; the Twelve Tribes
c. 1020 B.C.E.	Anointing of King Saul by the Prophet Samuel, inaugurating the period of the monarchy
c. 1000 B.C.E.	Jews united and kingdoms expanded by King David; Jerusalem established as the Israelite capital
c. 960 B.C.E.	First Temple in Jerusalem built by King Solomon
c. 920 B.C.E.	Division into two kingdoms: Israel and Judah
722 B.C.E.	Israel (northern kingdom) conquered by Assyrian armies
586 B.C.E.	Judah (southern kingdom) conquered by Babylonian King Nebuchadnezzar, who also destroys the Temple in Jerusalem; beginning of "Babylonian Captivity"
516 B.C.E.	Consecration of the Second Temple; exiled Jews return from Babylon
c. 500–400 B.C.E.	Compilation of many of the books in the Hebrew Bible ("Old Testament" to Christians)
333 B.C.E.	Jewish lands conquered by Alexander the Great on his way east
c. 300–250 B.C.E.	Formation of the Septuagint (Greek translation of the Hebrew Bible)
167–165 B.C.E.	Maccabean Revolt against Greek rule (a.k.a. the Hasmonean Revolt)
63 B.C.E.	Judea becomes a client kingdom of the Roman Republic
c. 30 C.E.	Beginning of the Jesus movement
66–73 C.E.	First Jewish-Roman War (a.k.a. the Great Revolt)
70 C.E.	The Second Temple destroyed by Romans under Titus
c. 100 C.E.	Canonization of the Hebrew Bible mostly complete
115–117 C.E.	Second Jewish-Roman War (a.k.a. the Kitos War)
132–135 C.E.	Third Jewish-Roman War (a.k.a. the Bar Kokhba rebellion)
c. 200–500 C.E.	Major Jewish texts such as the Mishnah and the Talmud are compiled and codified

From Abraham to Solomon

The earliest years of Judaism remain somewhat obscure to historians. Theologically, of course, Jews trace their ancestry back to the mythical Adam and Eve, but the oldest texts that we know about date to around 1200 B.C.E. As was the case in many ancient societies, the Jews transmitted stories about their own history and traditions orally over a period of several hundred years before formally writing anything down, and as such it is somewhat difficult to use texts such as the Hebrew Bible to reconstruct the exact history of any given time period. Linguists believe that the form of the Hebrew language used in the biblical texts (which is quite different from modern Hebrew) died out around 500 B.C.E., after which point Aramaic was the main language of the Jews in Israel.

The world from which Judaism and the ancient Hebrew people emerged was a decidedly polytheistic one. According to Jewish scripture, Abraham traces his roots to ancient Mesopotamia, whose peoples would have worshiped many Sumerian and Babylonian gods during the age of Abraham (c. 2000-1800 B.C.E.). The story shifts from Mesopotamia to **Canaan** (basically modern-day Israel, Palestine, and Lebanon), where Abraham moved and where Judaism developed. Geographically, Israel would seem to be a pretty insignificant place, but in fact it was the cradle of some of the most influential events in world history (the modern country Israel was founded in 1948; in this book, when we discuss ancient Israel, we are referring to the tiny swath of land between the eastern edge of the Mediterranean Sea and the Jordan River).

The uniqueness of Abraham's story was his claim that the Hebrew God, declaring himself the one and only God, creator of the earth, revealed himself directly to Abraham. Scholars disagree about the exact timeline of events, so while some consider Judaism the first monotheistic religion, others think Zoroastrianism claims the title. In any event, Abraham's declaration of monotheistic faith had the effect of asserting that everyone else's gods were false gods, which certainly didn't win him many friends. In addition to Abraham's importance in the history of monotheism, his life marked the formation of a holy covenant, or agreement, between God and the ancient Jews. According to the Torah, the Jewish holy book, Abraham agrees that he and his descendants will dutifully worship God, and God in return will give the land of Canaan to Abraham's people.

Abraham and his descendants were itinerant pastoralists. According to the Hebrew Bible, Abraham's son Isaac and later his grandson Jacob were the leaders of these pastoral Israelites. Unfortunately there is not much archaeological or textual evidence to confirm the story, but according to Jewish tradition the Israelites ended up in Egypt. The famous story of Moses describes the Israelites' "exodus" from Egypt and subsequent wandering in the Sinai desert. Because the biblical account contains a number of embellishments and folkloric themes, it is impossible for historians to be sure about the details, but in any event the Israelites ended up back in the land of Canaan, probably sometime in the 13th century B.C.E.

Once back in Canaan, the Hebrews (who called themselves "children of Israel") divided themselves into twelve tribes that were assigned to specific geographical regions and were led by tribal chieftains. These groups continued to tell stories about their common ancestry and part of their collective identity centered on the **Ark of the Covenant**, in which they believed the sacred law tables given by God to Moses were held.

After this tribal period there is a little more historical information because the story of the Jews coincides with the stories of other ancient Near Eastern peoples, such as the **Philistines**. During the period between roughly 1200 B.C.E. and 1000 B.C.E., the Philistines and the Israelites were in a near-constant state of war. In part because of this ongoing conflict, the Israelites thought that they needed a strong central leader, and the Jewish Prophet Samuel anointed a man named Saul the first king of Israel in approximately 1020 B.C.E. Saul died while fighting the Philistines, and his son-in-law **David** then took over the throne.

According to the biblical account, **King David** successfully united the Jews and moved his administrative capital to **Jerusalem**, where remains of his building achievements can still be seen today. Legend holds that David brought the Ark of the Covenant to Jerusalem and thus the city became extremely important both politically and religiously in the history of Judaism. Indeed, it was David's son, King **Solomon**, who commissioned the building of the **First Temple** in Jerusalem around 960 B.C.E. During Solomon's time, Israel actively traded with its neighbors and its leaders amassed a fair amount of wealth.

During this early First Temple period, the temple priests gained significant power and authority. As the central site of worship and sacrifice for all the Jews, Jerusalem itself began to take shape as a central part of the historical consciousness of the Jewish people, as it remains today (a common expression of hope and prayer in contemporary Judaism includes the line, "Next year in Jerusalem!"). The increasingly hierarchical nature of the priesthood and religious leadership during this time period mirrored what was happening in ancient Jewish society more broadly. The expansion of Jerusalem led to a broader class divide between rich and poor than had existed in Israel up to that point, and the numerous protests and rebellions against the ruling aristocracy testify to a certain pervasiveness of discontent.

When King Solomon died sometime around 920 B.C.E., the once-unified kingdom was split into two. The northern half, called Israel, had its capital at **Samaria**, while the southern half, called Judah, had its capital at Jerusalem. Over the next several hundred years, these divided kingdoms sometimes lived at peace and other times fought one another. While monotheism had largely taken hold among the people, it is during this time period that a number of Israelites were apparently attracted to "foreign" gods such as Ba'al and Asherah (we know this because the prophets of the Hebrew Bible often inveighed against these foreign gods threatened punishment for anyone who strayed from belief in the "one true God," Yahweh.

It Wasn't Easy Being Jewish in the Ancient World

Nearly all of what we know about the ancient Jewish peoples comes from Hebrew scripture with little other historical corroboration. But what we do learn from historical evidence is that the ancient Jews, like most Mesopotamian peoples, were conquered many times over. Ancient Assyrian records from Nineveh confirm some stories of the Old Testament, including the Assyrian destruction of ancient **Israel** (one of two ancient Jewish kingdoms, the other being Judah) and siege of **Jerusalem** in 722 B.C.E.

The Babylonian king Nebuchadnezzar conquered Judah, the kingdom that survived the Assyrian onslaught, in 586 B.C.E. Nebuchadnezzar destroyed the temple of Jerusalem, the center of Jewish worship, and exiled the Jewish ruling classes, taking them back to Babylon. This period of exile is known as the **Babylonian Captivity** and marks the beginning of the Jewish "Diaspora," meaning "scattering" or "spreading out."

Many historians believe that it was during this period of Jewish history that the Hebrew scriptures (Old Testament) were written down for the first time in order to preserve Jewish tradition during a time of imprisonment away from their homeland. Other changes occurred as a result of the Babylonian Captivity as well: since the Jews could not physically go to Jerusalem to conduct their religious rituals, they began to meet in **synagogues**, gathering places in which the community could worship and participate in educational activities. Other markers of Jewish communal identity were strengthened and developed during this time period, including the importance of the **Sabbath** (day of rest), dietary guidelines, and the concept of ritual purity.

The Babylonian captivity lasted less than fifty years, because the Jews were released from their long-distance imprisonment when the Persian Empire conquered the Babylonians in 539 B.C.E. After being freed by the Persians, most of the exiled Jews returned to Jerusalem and gradually rebuilt their temple and the kingdom, naming their new kingdom Judea. Alexander the Great disrupted Independent Jewish rule yet again in 333 B.C.E., when his army rolled through Judea to claim it as a part of Alexander's great empire.

After about 250 years of Hellenistic rule, a Jewish revolt briefly regained Hebrew rule over Judea. The leaders of this revolt were the **Maccabees**, military rulers of the **Hasmonean dynasty**. This victory in 165 B.C.E. is celebrated today as the Jewish holiday of **Hannukah**. In addition to reducing the influence of Hellenistic culture among the Jews, the Hasmoneans expanded the boundaries of Judea by conquering neighboring provinces. After a hundred years, however, Judea lost its independence (yes, again) as it was brought under the control of Rome in 63 B.C.E. The Romans ruled over the Jews through a series of governors, whom the Jews considered merely puppet-kings. Roman appointee **Herod** (37 to 4 B.C.E.), however, took advantage of his Roman piggy bank to lavishly rebuild the temple of Jerusalem and to build **Masada**, a fortress in the hills of Judea. The remains of Herod's temple and Masada still stand in Israel today.

Women and Early Judaism

Early Judaism was strongly patriarchal, so as you might expect, women were subordinate socially. Their main occupation was tending to their families. However, early Jewish history includes important women such as Abraham's wife Sarah; Esther, wife of a Persian king who helped save Persia's Jews; and Ruth, an ancestor of King David.

The Romans initially tolerated the Jews and gave them a somewhat special status because of their "ancient" religion (the Romans loved things that were old!); they didn't require the Jews to worship Roman gods. This special status, of course, was contingent on good behavior. Growing tired of Roman rule, the Jews attempted the First Revolt, from 66 to 73 C.E. The result was disastrous for the Jews. The Romans reacted, well, in true Roman fashion by laying siege to Jerusalem, destroying the temple, and overtaking the last Jewish holdouts in the Masada fortress (many of whom committed mass suicide rather than surrender).

The Romans then exiled many Jews from Judea and turned it into a true Roman colony ruled by Romans, who worshiped the Roman pantheon of gods. Even after this defeat, the Jewish peoples attempted another fight to gain independence in Judea by launching a Second Revolt from 115-117 C.E. The Second Revolt ended in failure just as the First Revolt had; the Romans destroyed Jerusalem and banished Jews from returning to their homeland. From 132-135 C.E. there was a Third Revolt, sometimes known as the **Bar Kokhba Rebellion** after one of its leaders, but this too was a failure. Following these revolts, more Jews lived outside ancient Palestine than within. This Jewish diaspora spread across the Mediterranean and the Near East, forming close-knit Jewish communities throughout the lands of the Roman Empire and beyond.

The Life of a Dispersed People

Living outside of their homeland was a challenge for the Jewish people of the diaspora. However, the discrimination and persecution they faced from the communities to which they moved helped the Jews maintain their cultural and religious identity. Often unwilling to assimilate Jews into their own cultures and forcing them to live in separate communities, their new homelands encouraged the Jews to rely upon themselves for their success and survival. This "otherness" felt by the Jews throughout history contributed to the **Zionist**, or return to the homeland, movement of the late 19th century.

The irony of the history of the Jewish people is their impact relative to the size of their population. What defines Judaism as a great religion is not its number of followers, which is quite small compared to Christianity or Islam, but its subsequent influence on these two religions. The introduction of monotheism to the ancient world changed the course of history. Christianity, also a monotheistic religion, itself began as a Jewish sect. And even Islam traces its history to the Jewish patriarch Abraham. Without Judaism, would either Christianity or Islam have begun?

The influence of Jewish peoples on history also manifests itself in history's reaction to the Jews. Anti-Semitism, or anti-Jewish discrimination, traces its roots all the way back to the diaspora. As Jews were forced from their homeland—first by the Assyrians, then the Babylonians, and finally by the Romans—they became foreigners in the lands of others, differentiated by their unwillingness to accept Ba'al, Jesus, or Allah, as well as by their customs and traditions. Anti-Semitism has unfortunately remained a constant of world history, contributing to such tragedies as the World War II Holocaust as well as influencing the Jewish resettlement of Palestine, sparking the continued conflict between Israelis and Palestinians.

EARLY CHRISTIANITY

27 B.C.E.–14 C.E.	Reign of the Roman Emperor Augustus, who was worshipped as a son of god and whose birth was proclaimed as "gospel" ("good news")
c. 4 B.C.E.	Birth of Jesus and death of Herod the Great, the Roman client-king of Judea, Samaria, and Galilee
4 B.C.E.–6 C.E.	The lands of Herod the Great are divided by the Romans among his three sons (known as the "Herodian Tetrarchy")
14–37 C.E.	Reign of the Roman Emperor Tiberius
c. 26–30 C.E.	John the Baptist's ministry
c. 27 C.E.	Beginning of Jesus's ministry
c. 30 C.E.	Jesus crucified by the Romans; his followers settle in Jerusalem
c. 35 C.E.	Conversion of Saul of Tarsus, who later becomes known as the Apostle Paul and writes about half of the New Testament
c. 60 C.E.	Imprisonment and execution of Apostle Paul
64 C.E.	Great fire in Rome; Emperor Nero blames Christians and executes many
c. 70–90 C.E.	New Testament Gospels of Matthew, Mark, and Luke written
c. 100–120 C.E.	New Testament Gospel of John written
249–251 C.E.	First major persecution of Christians under Emperor Decius
c. 251–356 C.E.	Antony the Great, "Father of Christian Monasticism," lives as an ascetic in the Egyptian wilderness and inspires countless followers across the Christian world
303 C.E.	Persecution of Christians under Emperor Diocletian
312 C.E.	Emperor Constantine claims Jesus as his patron after defeating his enemy Maxentius at the Battle of the Milvian Bridge and becoming the sole ruler of the western Empire

Christianity (continued)

313 C.E.	Edict of Milan issued by Emperor Constantine, restoring confiscated Christian lands and goods and promising freedom of worship.
324 C.E.	Emperor Constantine defeats rival Licinius and becomes ruler of entire Roman Empire
325 C.E.	First Council of Nicaea convened by Constantine (an attempt to achieve theological and political consensus in the Christian church)
351–363 C.E.	Paganism reintroduced by Emperor Julian
391 C.E.	Christianity established as the official religion of the Roman Empire by Emperor Theodosius
405 C.E.	Jerome completes the Vulgate (Latin Bible); extremely influential in western culture and literature

Christianity, the Early Years

Christianity adopted the Hebrew Bible as its own Old Testament and therefore shares the same religious history as Judaism, including a lineage from the Hebrew patriarch, Abraham. In fact, in the early years of the Jesus movement, it is somewhat difficult to distinguish Judaism from Christianity. Jesus's disciples and most of the earliest believers in Jesus were Jewish, and it was not until some years after Jesus's death that the religion began to spread among the Gentiles (non-Jews).

Christianity begins, of course, with Jesus, who was born around 4 B.C.E. in the town of Bethlehem (near Jerusalem) and grew up in the town of Nazareth in Galilee (northern Israel). We know very little about the historical Jesus, just as we know little about early Judaism. In fact, all of what we know about him comes from Christian scripture, particularly the four gospels of the **New Testament**, which were written decades after Jesus's death in c. 30 C.E. So what does scripture tell us about early Christianity? Although born a Jew, Jesus's teachings differed from the Jewish norms of the times. He rejected both Jewish dietary laws and the dominant role of the Jewish priesthood.

Jesus, along with a core group of followers, traveled ancient Palestine, primarily preaching to the poor and less fortunate. Some of Jesus's followers considered him the son of God and the Jewish Messiah, or anointed one (*Christos* in Greek). Historians of early Christianity disagree about the core nature of Jesus's teachings. Some believe that he was a type of apocalyptic prophet whose primary mission was to warn people about the imminent end of time; others view him more as a traditional Jewish **rabbi** (teacher) whose main concern was to reform the Judaism of his day; a somewhat less popular, but still widespread, view is that Jesus was a revolutionary whose goal was to address societal injustice. Whether one or all of these theories are true is impossible to say, but what is clear is that Jesus got himself into trouble with the authorities.

Most in the Jewish community, particularly those in the elite Jewish priesthood, did not recognize Jesus as Messiah. But as Jesus continued his teachings, both he and his followers left behind a growing rank of converts and a fledging organizational structure that would eventually turn into the Christian church. While the Jesus movement did not attract too much notice during Jesus's own lifetime, it eventually spread throughout the Mediterranean region and beyond.

As Jesus's message and congregation spread, both Jewish leaders and the Romans became increasingly suspicious of his growing influence. According to Christian scripture, the authorities seized Jesus, held a mock trial under the Roman prefect **Pontius Pilate** and executed Jesus by crucifixion. Christianity, like many Jewish sects of the day, could have ended with Jesus' death (as we learned earlier in the chapter, there were many revolts and rebellions during this time period that did not develop into full-fledged global movements). But it was with Jesus's death that Christianity began to evolve from an obscure sect into a religion that would come to dominate the Roman Empire and beyond. Jesus's followers believed he rose from the dead three days after his crucifixion and spent forty days on earth before ascending to heaven. This theological belief in Jesus's resurrection and ascension to heaven play as significant a role in Christianity as do Jesus's teachings.

Many of the foundational teachings of Christianity come from the writings of Saul of Tarsus (a city in modern-day Turkey), later known as the **Apostle Paul**. According to Paul's own account, he originally was a persecutor of the early Christians but experienced a mystical conversion and subsequently traveled around the Mediterranean world preaching and teaching about Jesus to any who would listen. It was Paul who really transformed Christianity from a Jewish movement to something more broad-based, as he used his Roman citizenship to facilitate travel and expound Christianity to non-Jews in a way that they would understand.

How Did Christianity Succeed Where Others Failed?

Even by 100 C.E., Christianity was not guaranteed any measure of future success. Christians were regularly persecuted throughout the Roman Empire during the 300 years following the death of Jesus. There are complex reasons for this persecution, but at least in part it was due to the Christians' refusal to worship the emperors as the Roman imperial cult required. It is important to note, however, that despite the many literary accounts of martyrdom in early Christianity, most persecutions were short-lasting and localized.

The reality of persecution certainly played a huge role in the development of Christian communal identity and brought Christians closer together. In one well-known event, the Emperor **Nero** infamously scapegoated Christians in 64 C.E. for a great fire in Rome by burning them at the stake and using them as fodder for the lions in sporting events (allegedly, anyway). Although not every Roman emperor chose to persecute Christians as vehemently as did Nero, for a while Christians were regular targets of the Roman political leadership.

Despite this hostility, Christianity took root among the common people of the empire. Rome's native religion, largely borrowed from the Greeks, was primarily the domain of the Roman elite, and only the wealthiest of Romans participated in major religious rituals of the state religion. Therefore, most commoners felt rather distanced from the complex Roman pantheon of gods and goddesses. For the common folk left out of Roman religion, Christianity presented a welcoming and desirable message. Many of the earliest Christians, furthermore, were slaves and women, who may have found Christianity's emphasis on the equality of all believers somewhat liberating.

Christianity offered a belief in a single, benevolent God and an eternal afterlife. The stories of Jesus gave ordinary Romans a personality with whom they could make an emotional connection. Furthermore, the teachings of Christianity required a stricter moral code than that of Roman traditional religion, which was enticing to those living in the turbulent provinces of the Roman Empire. In sum, Christianity offered what Roman religion did not: a better way of living during this life and the next.

It's Official: Christianity Is Welcomed Into, and Comes to Rule, the Empire

Even though Christianity won many converts among the common people, would it have survived without official sanction from the Roman state? Persecutions of Christians continued through the reign of Emperor Diocletian, who stepped down in 305 C.E. However, one of Diocletian's successors, Constantine, himself adopted Jesus as his patron out of gratitude for a military victory (this event is often referred to as the "conversion" of Constantine, but it is not clear whether Constantine maintained exclusive allegiance to Christianity or simply favored Christianity for expedient political reasons).

Constantine passed the Edict of Milan in 313 C.E., which granted official imperial toleration to Christians throughout the empire. In addition, Constantine was influential in helping to shape Christian theology. In 325 C.E., he called the Council of Nicaea, a meeting of Christian bishops, to resolve theological differences between different Christian groups. It is during the Council of Nicaea the nature of the Trinity and the Nicene Creed became official parts of Christian theology.

Women and the Christian Church
According to a strict interpretation of Christian doctrine, particularly the writings of Paul, women are to be subordinate to men at home and in the church. Although on a spiritual level men and women are considered equal in the eyes of God (both men and women can get into heaven), a few modern believers still hold that women should be socially subordinate to men.

Although Constantine often gets the credit for Roman adoption of Christianity (insofar as he prohibited construction and maintenance of Roman polytheistic temples), Christianity did not become the official religion of the empire until later. Emperor Theodosius required all Romans to believe as did the Pope, the head bishop of Rome. In 391 C.E. Theodosius outlawed pagan sacrifice and temple activity, essentially making Christianity the state religion (although the extent to which he accomplished his goal is debatable). The power of the Pope continued to rise in the empire throughout the 4th and 5th centuries. Attila the Hun invaded the Italian peninsula in 452 C.E. It wasn't the Roman emperor who repelled Attila's advance, but the Pope who convinced Attila to leave Rome untouched. Finally, after the fall of the western empire, Pope Gelasius declared his authority over any kings in the realm of the former empire.

ISLAM

c. 570 C.E.	Muhammad is born in Mecca (modern-day Saudi Arabia).
c. 610 C.E.	Muhammad starts teaching publicly and is persecuted.
c. 622 C.E.	Muhammad and his followers move to Medina in an event later known as the hijrah.
c. 630 C.E.	Muhammad returns to Mecca with a huge number of followers.
c. 632 C.E.	Muhammad dies and his father-in-law Abu Bakr is chosen as his successor (the first caliph).
c. 633–661 C.E.	Rashidun Caliphate
c. 638–711 C.E.	Muslims leave the Arabian Peninsula and conquer land from the Iberian Peninsula (modern-day Spain and Portugal) in the west to India in the east.
c. 650 C.E.	The Qur'an is compiled and transcribed.
c. 661–750 C.E.	Umayyad Caliphate
c. 750–1258 C.E.	Abbasid Caliphate (center of power shifts to Baghdad)
c. 800 C.E.	Compilation of the Hadith
909–969 C.E.	Fatimids conquer North Africa and Egypt.
c. 1000–1200 C.E.	Islam spreads to West Africa and Southeast Asia.
c. 1206–1526 C.E.	Delhi Sultanate rules India.
1299–1923 C.E.	Ottoman Empire

Islam, the Early Years

Prior to the rise of Islam, the Arabs lived primarily on the Arabian Peninsula and in the surrounding deserts. As we would expect in a desert land, many of these peoples were nomadic herders who moved from oasis to oasis and traded their goods both near and far. Not all Arabs were pastoralists, of course; archaeologists have found ample evidence of inland farming villages as well as communities that thrived on fishing and commerce in the coastal areas. The town of Mecca, so important in the history of Islam, was originally a prosperous market center where traders would gather to buy and sell goods.

The origins of the Islamic faith are traced back to the life of Muhammad (570–632 c.e.), an Arab merchant. Muhammad was evidently born in Mecca, was married to several wives, and had numerous children. According to Islamic teachings, in 610, Muhammad was meditating in a cave in the mountains outside of Mecca when he heard the voice of the angel Gabriel commanding him to recite and memorize the word of God. This was the first of many such visitations during which Gabriel recited the word of God to Muhammad, who subsequently related these revelations to his close friends and family orally and later dictated what he had learned to scribes who wrote it down in Arabic (which is why Muslims believe that Arabic is the "language of God").

After his death, Muhammad's followers gathered all the known writings and transcriptions of these visitations to create the **Qur'an** ("recitations"). Muslims consider the Qur'an (sometimes spelled "Koran") the word of God; the words of the Qur'an in their original Arabic are thus themselves considered sacred. The word Islam means "submission," and Muslims are "those who submit" to the word of God as embodied in the text of the Qur'an. Among other beliefs, one core tenet of Islam is that Muhammad was the final messenger from God to the people of earth (although Muslims also believe in many of the Jewish and Christian prophets, including Jesus, who is discussed in many sections of the Qur'an). Another distinguishing characteristic of Islam is the belief that Muslims are descended not from Abraham's son Isaac (whose mother was Sarah), as were the Jews, but from Ishmael, Abraham's other son (whose mother was Sarah's handmaiden Hagar).

The Qur'an and the **hadith** (accounts of Muhammad's saying and actions) are the basis of Islamic Law, the shari'a, which is practiced by *qadis*, Islamic judges. In early Islam, the governing and religious leaders worked more closely together, but over time the scope of power of the political rulers and religious leaders became more separate and a true Islamic Empire was born.

Five Pillars

The **Five Pillars of Islam** are the five basic tenets of the faith, combining individual spiritual responsibility, social justice, and worship of one God (monotheism). First is the belief that "There is no god but God, and Muhammad is his Prophet." Second, Muslims are required to pray five times a day in the direction of Mecca and, if possible, also in a group service at midday on Friday. Third, believers must

Women and Islam
The shari'a defines the place of women to be subordinate to that of men, but also defines a man's obligations to care for his wife and female members of his family. A man could have more than one wife, but only if he were wealthy enough to care for each of them sufficiently.

care for those less fortunate in their communities in the form of charity to the poor, orphans, or others who are in need. Fourth, believers must fast during daylight throughout the month of Ramadan. Finally, Muslims should complete the *hajj*, the pilgrimage to Mecca, at least once during their lifetime if they are physically and financially capable of doing so.

In its early period, Islam shared many concepts and rituals—prayer, monotheistic belief, ritual sacrifice, charity—with Judaism and Christianity, but also emphasized the need to convert others to accept Islam, including Jews and Christians. It is this proselytizing spirit of Islam that brought it into conflict with other belief systems as it grew in power and influence (the same can be said of Christianity, of course).

Development of a Faith

After his first visitations, Muhammad did not find many other followers outside his close family circle: His first wife Khadija, a wealthy widow, and his cousin Ali were among his first followers. Unpopular in Mecca, Muhammad fled to **Medina**, an agricultural center several hundred miles north of Mecca, in 622. This decamping to Medina is known as the *hijra*, the "migration" or "flight." Muhammad's removal to Medina marks the beginning of the Muslim calendar; therefore, Year 1 in the Muslim calendar corresponds to 622 in the Christian calendar. In Medina, Muhammad built up a community of believers, or *umma*. This marked a major shift for the Arabs, who traditionally defined community around kinship rather than faith. In Medina, Muhammad became a leader and saw some of his teachings made into law. In their efforts to spread the faith, followers of Islam clashed with surrounding tribes and those of other faiths. Eventually Muhammad and his followers took over the town of Mecca, site of the Ka'aba, an ancient site of religious worship. The Ka'aba was stripped of its idols and was converted to a Muslim shrine, and remains a major site of pilgrimage today. The Ka'aba, now considered the house of God on earth, became the focal point of Muslim religious devotion, and it is in the direction of Mecca that Muslims face when they pray.

Islam Spreads

Muhammad died in 632. Leadership of the umma was given over to Abu Bakr, Muhammad's father-in-law by his second wife, Aisha. Abu Bakr became caliph, ruler of the Muslim community (*khalifah* in Arabic means "successor"). Under Abu Bakr, Islam spread via warfare across the Arab peninsula. Islamic armies fought and defeated Byzantine and Persian Sassanid troops, spreading further until they reached beyond the Arab peninsula into Asia Minor and North Africa, but they didn't yet get past the Byzantines holding their ground at the Anatolian peninsula. Islamic forces saw many victories: Damascus, Jerusalem, and the Persian Sassanid Empire's capital at Ctesiphon all fell to Muslim invaders.

In short, Islam spread rapidly and widely, stretching from the Indus River in the east to the northwest coast of Africa by the late 8th century.

INTER- AND INTRARELIGIOUS CONFLICTS

451 C.E.	Eastern and Western churches split over theological fine points after the Council of Chalcedon.
614 C.E.	Persians capture Jerusalem and damage the Church of the Holy Sepulcher; Byzantine Emperor Heraclius forbids the practice of Judaism.
635 C.E.	Muslims capture Damascus (Syria) from the Byzantines.
639–642 C.E.	Muslims conquer Egypt.
732 C.E.	Frankish-Carolingian ruler Charles Martel defeats invading Muslim armies in France.
1054 C.E.	The Church splits into eastern and western churches (the Great Schism).
c. 1095–1270 C.E.	Christian Crusades in Muslim lands.
c. 1000–1400 C.E.	Muslims invade India.
1265–1479 C.E.	Byzantine-Ottoman wars are fought.
1453 C.E.	Ottoman Muslims capture Constantinople and change its name to Istanbul.

Islam, Meet Christianity; Christianity, Meet Islam

By 700 C.E., only 70 years after the death of Muhammad, Islam, under the Umayyad dynasty, had spread to North Africa and much of the eastern Mediterranean, completely isolating Christian Europe from Asia and the Near East. Furthermore, Islam had even penetrated into Europe itself through the Iberian Peninsula (modern-day Spain and Portugal), moving well into modern-day France.

The Muslim invaders were stopped, however, by the Frankish-Carolingian ruler, **Charles Martel** ("The Hammer"), who defeated them in western central France at the Battle of Tours in 732 C.E. Over the next 700 years, Spanish Christians fought to drive the Muslims from the Iberian Peninsula and from Europe, a struggle known as the **reconquista**. Furthermore, **Charlemagne**, Martel's grandson, fought to solidify Christian orthodoxy (along Frankish lines) over much of Western Europe.

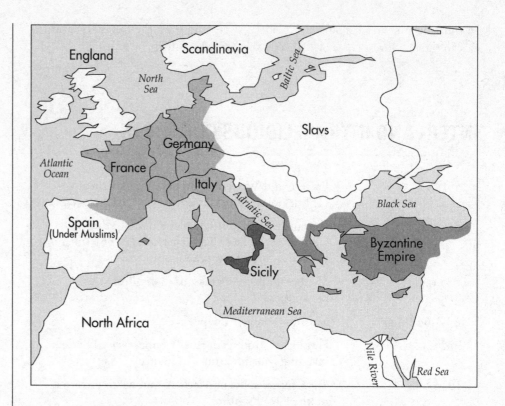

Charlemagne's Empire and Other Medieval Regions c. 800 c.e.

By 1071 c.e., Muslim Turk forces had also conquered much of the Byzantine Empire, the guardians of the old Roman East, including most of modern-day Turkey. Even though the eastern and western Christian churches had split in the **Great Schism of 1054** over doctrinal disputes, they were on good enough terms that the Byzantine emperor asked the western Catholic Pope, Urban II, for help against the invaders.

This appeal for help launched the **First Crusade** to recapture the holy land from the Muslims. Pope Urban II also saw it as an opportunity to reestablish Roman control over the Eastern Orthodox Church, which had been weakened by Muslim invasion. In an impassioned speech at the **Council of Claremont**, Urban II encouraged French knights to retake the holy land so that Christian pilgrims would remain safe in their journeys to Jerusalem—this meant taking Jerusalem from the Muslims. In 1099, the Christian crusaders did just that, slaughtering tens of thousands of innocent Muslim civilians in the process. Jerusalem was, for the moment, theirs.

From a Christian perspective the First Crusade was a major success. Crusading forces provided an entirely Christian-controlled path to the holy land for pilgrims to take. From a European perspective, the First Crusade was proof that Western Europe was starting to wake up from its post-Rome coma. In uniting to fight the Muslims and champion Christianity, Europe was laying the groundwork for the growth and turmoil it would see over the next 100 years.

The Development of Islamic Sects

Different sects developed among Muslims, mainly as a result of problems with the succession of caliphs. The third caliph Uthman was assassinated, and Ali, son-in-law of Muhammad, became the fourth caliph, although he was not the popular choice of the *umma*. Backers of Ali—the *Shi'at Ali*, or **Shi'ites**—felt that caliphs must be of Muhammad's family. On the other hand, those who supported the first three caliphs (the "Rightly Guided Caliphs") became known as **Sunni**, who believed that he who the *umma* named caliph is rightfully its leader.

In the early development of Islam, Shi'ites were more concerned with spiritual purity of the faith than were the Sunnis, and fought to have their **imams**, or religious leaders, become caliphs. All eleven of the eventual Shi'ite imams died, and the twelfth (and last) disappeared, taking the bloodline of Muhammad with him.

The ancient split between Sunni and Shi'ite Muslims over the caliphate still exists today, although this rivalry is now often about how the umma should be ruled and the place of the imams in governance. The majority of Muslims in the world today are Sunni Muslims, although Shi'ite Muslims are a majority in Iraq, Iran, and Azerbaijan.

Muslim Power: Islamic Empire

The Umayyad Empire (661–750 c.e.) is responsible for many of the most well-known monuments to Islam, including early 8th-century mosques in Medina, Damascus (the Umayyad capital), and Jerusalem, notably the Dome of the Rock (built on the ruins of the Jewish Second Temple). The Umayyads were also responsible for the spread of Islam into northern Africa and Spain and its encroachment into France (where they were stopped by Charles Martel at the Battle of Tours in 732).

As with many empires, the Umayyads overextended their reach in their quest for territorial dominance, and lost important battles in France, Armenia, Anatolia, and North Africa. One important win: the Battle of Talas River in 751 over the Chinese, which opened up the Silk Road trade routes to Muslim traders and Islamic religious and cultural influence.

After the Umayyads came the Abbasid caliphs, who took over in 750 and moved the capital of the empire to Baghdad. The Abbasid caliphs continued in the quest to unify the umma of believers and to convert non-Muslims to the faith. They were better administrators than the Umayyads had been, but problems with succession, the administration of an ever-larger empire, clashes between the center and local rule, and widespread corruption weakened the caliphate from within.

The Islamic Empire broke up into a number of independent states in the mid-to-late 9th century. The Abbasid caliphate was taken over by the Seljuk Turks, who conquered Central Asia and Baghdad in the 11th century and ruled for a bit, although they kept to the secular side of things. Muslim rule continued to spread in Southeast Asia, Africa, and India. In India, the five Muslim dynasties that constituted the **Delhi Sultanate** ruled most of that country from 1211 to 1526.

In the 12th century, the Mongols rolled into Islamic lands, bringing the caliphate to an abrupt end in 1258 with the execution of the caliph in Baghdad. But the Islamic faith continued to spread despite the lack of an Islamic head of state or Islamic Empire. In fact, more than half of the modern Muslim population of the world exists in areas never actually under rule of the Islamic Empire.

Cultural Advancements

Islamic culture flourished over time, giving birth to a number of important innovations in thought and science. Important to Western culture were Arabic translations of Greek scientific and philosophical writings, which kept alive Greek thought and tradition that otherwise may have been lost. The writings of Aristotle, for example, are known to us today through their Arabic translations, as are countless treatises on astronomy, math, medicine, and other schools of study.

Muslims scholars also fed on the learning of Indian philosophers and thinkers, further expanding the world's knowledge of medicine, astronomy, and mathematics. And of course, Muslim scholars were not merely transmitters of other cultures; they built upon all this learning as well.

EASTERN RELIGIONS

As we move on to the major religions of the East, we should make note of some important differences in the religious worldviews of the East and West. Perhaps the most important are the differences in how various religions conceive of the relationship between the world of humans and that of deities. In Christianity and Islam, there is one God who is not of this world, so there is a clear delineation between the world one lives in and the "next" world. However, in most Eastern religions, the view of humanity's relation to God is more unified and less bifurcated.

HINDUISM

c. 1500–500 B.C.E.	Composition of the Vedic Hymns (a.k.a. Vedas)
c. 800–600 B.C.E.	Composition of the *Upanishads*
c. 500–200 B.C.E.	Composition of the *Bhagavad Gita*

An Earlier Scientific Revolution

Some scientific advancements pioneered by Islamic scholars long before the European Scientific Revolution were:
1) the scientific method
2) decimal point notation
3) algebra
4) the mathematical proof
5) analytic geometry
6) integral calculus
7) theories of optics
8) chemical distillation
9) the concept of zero
10) Arabic numerals—the numbers used in this list!

If at First You Don't Succeed, Try Again Next Karmic Cycle

Unlike Western religions, which can trace their beginnings to a single person or event in time, Hinduism developed gradually out of various prehistoric belief systems and was eventually written down around 1500 B.C.E. by its followers in **Sanskrit**, one of the languages of the Aryan people. By its very nature, Hinduism is polytheistic, a coming together of many deities venerated by the various peoples who settled in India in ancient times. The variety of gods in the Hindu pantheon mirrors the variety of peoples who settled in India.

Central Beliefs

Hinduism is embodied in its sacred texts, the **Vedas**, collections of hymns and poetry ("divine knowledge") of which the Rigveda is the oldest. The Vedas tell the history of the Aryan invasions in the Indus River Valley and the subsequent development of Aryan society. The Vedas invoke the various deities and describe how to worship them properly, be it through music, rituals, prayer, or sacrifice.

The Rigveda is also the source of Hinduism's caste system, which is introduced in a passage telling how the mythical creature Purusha was sacrificed and cut into four pieces: the mouth (priests), the arms (warriors), the legs (merchants and farmers), and the feet (the working class). The jury is still out on exactly why the caste system became so rigid, but it is enough to know that caste was hereditary and that many other aspects of Hindu life were structured around this system, including separate living quarters, dietary restrictions, laws, and educations for members of different castes.

Upanishads and Other Classic Writings

A second group of writings known as the Upanishads described the rituals to be carried out by Hindu priests as well as the basic concepts of the religion. **Brahman** is the universal spirit, and each person has a soul (*atman*) that will, after a full cycle of reincarnation (*samsara*), be freed from the physical plane and be reunited with the universal Brahman spirit from which it originated. Throughout life, one must follow one's *dharma*, a set of ethical rules appropriate to one's class and caste.

The Many Faces of Hinduism

Hinduism is distinctive among the great religions for its relatively large number of deities. Here are just a few:

Vishnu The Preserver. A four-armed, blue-skinned major deity who took three steps, thereby creating man, the earth, and heaven

Ganesha The elephant-headed god who brings good luck

Shiva The Destroyer. A positive deity despite the name, Shiva symbolizes the cycle of life and death, destruction and creation.

Krishna An incarnation of Vishnu as a shepherd boy who appears in the Bhagavad Gita as the Supreme Person, the root of all other gods

Brahma The Creator God. His origins lie in a god from the same Indo-Aryan tradition that gave us the Norse, Greek, and Roman gods.

Brahman Not to be confused with the similarly named priest class or creator god. Brahman is the World Soul, the transcendent spirit of all things.

All actions in life either do or do not happen in accordance to one's dharma; those that do result in good karma, while those that don't result in bad karma. The more good karma one creates, the closer the atman comes to freeing itself from the physical plane and becoming one with the Brahman, a process called moksha. (If this sounds awfully like certain parts of Buddhism to you, don't be surprised: Remember, Buddha was a Hindu before becoming enlightened). Neither the Upanishads nor the Vedas tell a Hindu exactly how to lead his or her life—it is up to each individual to find his or her own path.

India's two great epic poems, the Ramayana and Mahabharata, also contain many of the basic rules that govern life in Hindu society. Within the Mahabharata is the Bhagavad-Gita ("Song of God"), which lays out in the form of mythical stories the basic tenets of Hinduism, such as fulfilling one's dharma and continuing one's devotion to the divine. Other pieces of literature include the Puranas, ancient stories featuring many of the gods of the Hindu pantheon.

Hinduism and Politics: Yes, Religion and the State!

Religious power and political power are often found together in India as in many other civilizations. In the case of India, the priest class held a great deal of power thanks to its monopoly on the sacred texts of Hinduism, which described the rituals required to appease various gods, and on the performance of those rituals. This is rather reminiscent of the role of the priesthood in medieval European society, but to a greater extent.

Those who wished to curry the favor of the gods (i.e., the ruling class) commissioned the building of temples, each more lavish than the last, to show their devotion to the gods. These temples were often not only places of veneration and worship, but also places of learning and the hearts of local communities. We can see the spread of Hinduism across Southeast Asia in the form of Hindu temples, which arose wherever the religion gained ascendancy.

BUDDHISM

It's nearly impossible to discuss the development of Buddhism without first introducing Hinduism, because Buddhism grew out of at least one man's alteration of Hindu mystic practice, although many of its basic tenets are rather different from those of Hinduism.

The Buddha himself was born **Siddhartha Gautama** around 563 B.C.E. As a young man, Siddhartha pondered the questions of life, death, and suffering. Hindu belief instructed people simply to accept suffering as part of their dharma: If your lot in life was not to your liking, you still needed to fulfill the obligations of your social class and hope that the next life would be better.

Siddhartha sought a path to free humans from a different kind of suffering, one seemingly inherent to living in this world: the desire for permanence in a world that constantly changes. A husband and father, he left his family to wander the world to find that path. He became an ascetic, shunning all material comfort, but he turned aside from the most extreme austerities to form his own practice, eventually reaching—through meditation and following a particular set of ethical principles—a state of enlightenment called **nirvana**. It was at this point that he became the Buddha ("He Who Has Awakened").

The Buddha rejected the idea of the caste system that bred so much suffering, as well as the priestly caste that perpetuated and justified the suffering of so many average people. Not unlike Jesus' preaching during Roman times, this kind of message endeared him to many common people but won him enemies among high-ranking Hindus who held their status thanks to the caste system Buddhism undermined. His followers also chose to use Pali, the common spoken language, rather than Sanskrit, so that his teachings would be more accessible to the common people. After the Buddha's death, his followers continued his teachings, codifying them into scripture and establishing shrines and monasteries to venerate the Buddha and perpetuate his teachings.

As usually happens after the death of an influential religious figure, different branches of Buddhism eventually developed. Theraveda Buddhism is the oldest and most traditional, viewing the Buddha as a person who achieved enlightenment via a path others can and should emulate.

Other branches of Buddhism such as Mahayana Buddhism soon challenged Theraveda belief, introducing the concepts of *bodhisattvas* (wise and compassionate individuals who vowed to forgo nirvana and continue to be reborn and suffer in order to help guide others), multiple Buddhas, and heavenly father-figure Buddhas in multiple heavens.

Sacred Buddhist Writings

Among the most important Buddhist texts are:

The Pali Canon The scriptures of Theraveda Buddhism, written in the Pali language spoken by the Buddha. They include the code of ethics for followers of Buddha, accounts of Buddha's life and teachings, and the philosophical underpinnings of Buddhism. Also known as the *tripitaka*, the "Three Baskets."

The Four Noble Truths Not necessarily a text, but the most fundamental Buddhist truths: (1) Suffering is a part of life; (2) Desire, particularly for permanence, is the source of suffering; (3) Release from desire—nirvana—brings about a release from suffering; and (4) the Noble Eightfold Path leads to nirvana.

It was Mahayana Buddhism that grew in strength enough to challenge Hinduism within India, at least until the fall of the Gupta Empire in the 6th century C.E. Eventually, though, Hinduism regained its privileged standing in India for a few reasons. First, as both religions developed, they became more alike. Hinduism adopted some of the principles that had made Buddhism so appealing to the common people, even adding Buddha to its pantheon of deities. Second, Hinduism was more deeply rooted in Indian culture and government than was Buddhism. Lastly, when Muslim invaders appeared in India between 1000 and 1200 C.E., Buddhism was attacked by the Muslims who felt it to be more of an active competitor for the hearts and minds of locals, whom the Muslims wished to convert.

Buddhism Beyond India: Where to Now?

Luckily, the story of Buddhism did not end at the Muslim invasions. Buddhists spread to surrounding areas, most notably Nepal, Tibet, and China. Buddhism, thanks to its eager followers, had already spread to China via the Silk Road even before the Muslim invasions into India, and Chinese thinkers traveled to India along the same route to study at Buddhist centers. Buddhism was able to coexist with Confucianism and Taoism during the Han dynasty (206 B.C.E.–220 C.E.) thanks to the fact that Buddhism wasn't so concerned with the intricacies of running governments, exactly the arena in which Confucianism functioned.

Buddhism flourished during most of the Tang dynasty (618–907 C.E.), breaking off into a number of different sects and continuing to grow in influence. It took a combination of Muslim incursions into parts of China in the 8th century and a late–Tang era emperor by the name of Wuzong to curb Buddhism's growth in China. A Taoist, Wuzong actively persecuted the Buddhists, confiscating lands and monasteries, destroying Buddhist temples and texts, and driving many Buddhists out of China altogether in the early to mid-9th century C.E.

Buddhism also made significant inroads in the 6th and 7th centuries into **Japan**. Buddhism in Japan continued to develop in unique ways, seen in the extreme popularity of **Zen Buddhism**, based on a Chinese form of Buddhism known as Chan Buddhism. In Japan, Buddhism also became more intertwined with politics by the 8th and 9th centuries. Buddhists in Japan were responsible for innovations in a number of important cultural areas, including the defining of the familiar aesthetic style seen in Japanese formal tea ceremonies, calligraphy, painting, and architecture, and even the modern *kana* writing system used today.

However, Buddhism wasn't the only religion existing in Japan at this time.

Philosophy, Religion, and Mixtures Thereof

Why is there no discussion of Confucianism in this chapter on religions? That's easy: Confucianism as embodied in Confucius's *Analects* is more a system of social and political philosophy governing ethical behavior than a religion. There are no supernatural elements to it, no gods to venerate that would raise it to the status of a religion. In its original formation, Taoism was also a philosophical teaching, governing a worldview and guiding the spiritual life of many people. However, in popular practice, Taoism as a spiritual philosophy soon became intermingled with traditional folk religion, creating many different highly polytheistic sects (for example, each person was believed to have a large number of gods in his or her own body alone). In later periods, many Chinese would believe that the "Three Doctrines are One." That is, that Buddhism, Confucianism, and Taoism could and should complement each other as different parts of the same spiritual path.

SHINTO

The native religion of the people of Japan, **Shinto** ("the way of the *kami*") belief centers on the forces of nature and their manifestations in the physical world as objects of veneration. Spirits (*kami*) are formless, shapeless beings that live inside plants, animals, even the earth itself, and can be either good or evil. Because *kami* have no concrete form, shrines were built so that followers have a place to worship and leave offerings, food, or prayers. Among the most important kami is the sun goddess Amaterasu, whose grandson (according to Shinto creation myth) came down to earth to become the first emperor of Japan.

With the rapid spread of Buddhism in Japan in the 6th century, one might expect Shinto to have been displaced, but this is not the case. Instead, Shinto and Buddhism existed side by side after the royal family of Japan adopted Buddhism as the state religion in the late 580s. Shinto embraced some of the concepts of Buddhism and vice versa; the kami, for example, became understood as Buddhas or bodhisattvas in their own right.

EASTERN VS. WESTERN RELIGIONS

Eastern religions create interesting contrasts with those of the West. Whereas monotheistic Western religions found it difficult to exist side by side because of mutually exclusive ideologies, Eastern religions—particularly polytheistic ones like Hinduism—were more adept at both coexisting with and adapting to other belief systems that they came in contact with or that simply were a part of their sphere of influence.

Other Religions of Note

Jainism   An ancient religion of India, which, like Buddhism, arose out of Hinduism, yet has a highly distinct belief structure and practice. Stresses spiritual independence and nonviolence; as a result requires vegetarianism of its adherents.

Sikhism   Inspired by a synthesis of Hinduism and Islam, Sikhism is a distinct religion of the Punjab region of Pakistan. Founded in 16th century. Its leaders are gurus. Baptized Sikhs must carry the Five K's, or symbols of faith, at all times.

Zoroastrianism   An ancient, yet still existent, monotheistic (or duotheistic: one benevolent god, one devil-figure) religion of Persia displaced by Islam as that religion spread eastward in the 8th century into the Sassanid Empire. Depending on whose dates you believe, Zoroastrianism may have predated Judaism as the first monotheistic religion.

Baha'i   A religion founded in 19th-century Persia as the final revelation of the Judaism/Christianity/Islam chain, Baha'i faith centers on the oneness of God, of all religions, and of all humanity.

CHAPTER 6 KEY TERMS, PEOPLE, AND EVENTS

Abraham

The patriarch who is considered the founder of the three major monotheistic faiths: Judaism, Christianity, and Islam

King David

Successfully united the Jewish people and moved the capital to Jerusalem. David and his son Solomon ruled over the united people of Israel during a Jewish golden age (c. 1020 B.C.E. to c. 920 B.C.E.)

Babylonian Captivity

After Israel was destroyed in 586 B.C.E., the Jewish people began their period of living in exile from their homeland. Many of the Hebrew Scriptures were written down during this time period.

Old and New Testaments

The two primary components of Christian Scripture. The Old Testament shares the stories of the Jewish people, and the New Testament the stories of Jesus' life and the early Christian church.

Paul the Apostle

The author of much of the New Testament and perhaps the most important of the early Christian figures. Paul opened Christianity up to the Gentiles, or non-Jews, of his time, facilitating its spread.

Great Schism of 1054

The split between the Eastern and Western Christian churches because of theological differences. The Western church was ruled from Rome, while the Eastern church was ruled from Constantinople.

Hadith

After the Qur'an, the hadith are the most important pieces of Islamic Scripture. They relate the stories of Muhammad's life and interactions with his earliest followers.

Five Pillars of Islam

The foundational practices of Islam: the profession of faith, prayer, alms-giving, fasting during Ramadan, and the pilgrimage to Mecca

Sunnis and Shi'ites

The two primary sects of Islam. The vast majority of Muslims are Sunni, meaning they follow the established succession of power from the first four Caliphs to the Umayyad dynasty. About 15 percent of Muslims are Shi'ites, who rejected the Umayyads and followed the family of Ali.

Vedas

The earliest religious texts of Hinduism, which are made up of a collection of poems and rituals

Siddhartha Gautama

The founder of Buddhism, who rejected his earthly life to pursue nirvana

Shinto

A religion native to Japan that centers on the forces of nature and how they manifest in the physical world

Summary

o Religion affects history: societies change in fundamental ways with the rise of the great religions, and religious beliefs shape politics, economics, and social structures.

o Judaism has ancient beginnings, traditionally dating from Abraham's covenant with God around 1800 B.C.E. Judaism developed as the first great monotheistic religion. Its sacred book is the Torah.

o Hinduism is among the oldest established major religions, arising in India and was first set down in writing between 1500 and 1200 B.C.E.

o Hinduism is polytheistic and is codified in the Vedas.

o Buddhism arose out of Hinduism in the 6th century B.C.E. The man born Siddhartha Gautama became the Buddha after having reached nirvana, ultimate enlightenment.

o Christianity arose out of Judaism about 2,000 years ago and formed around the teachings of Jesus of Nazareth. The Romans, who feared Jesus' power to stir up rebellion, crucified Jesus.

o Christianity is a monotheistic religion that clashed mightily with the others that it met, most notably with Judaism, and with Islam during the Crusades.

o Islam is the most recent of the great religions to develop, not arising until the 7th century C.E.

o Islam centers on the figure of Muhammad, who claims to have been visited by the angel Gabriel and given the word of God to memorize and spread to others. The Qur'an is Islam's holy book.

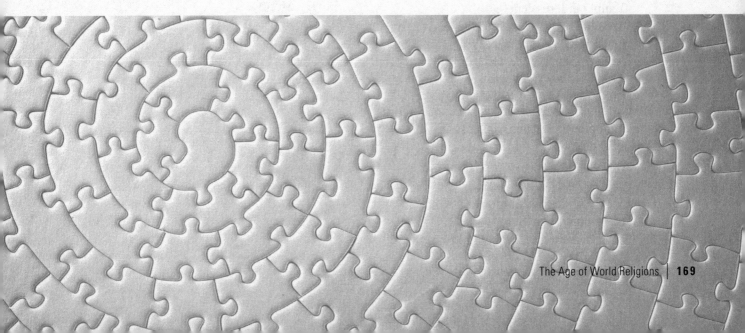

Chapter 6 Drill

Answers and explanations can be found in Part IV.

1. Which of the following presents the religious traditions listed in the correct chronological order?

   (A) Islam; Judaism; Hinduism; Buddhism; Christianity
   (B) Judaism; Hinduism; Buddhism; Christianity; Islam
   (C) Hinduism; Judaism; Islam; Buddhism; Christianity
   (D) Christianity; Judaism; Buddhism; Hinduism; Islam
   (E) Buddhism; Hinduism; Judaism; Christianity; Islam

2. In which of the following religious traditions are the forces of nature, their manifestation in the physical world, and spirits living inside plants and animals a central focus?

   (A) Christianity
   (B) Judaism
   (C) Shintoism
   (D) Jainism
   (E) Hinduism

3. Which of the following is NOT a major tenet of ancient Judaism?

   (A) The belief in one God
   (B) The belief in an ancestral lineage dating back to Abraham
   (C) The belief in the sacred importance of the Temple in Jerusalem
   (D) The belief that God granted the land of Israel to the Jews
   (E) The belief that the Messiah came to earth in the first century C.E.

4. Which of the following was the proclamation that granted religious toleration to Christians in the Roman Empire?

   (A) The Edict of Milan
   (B) The Nicene Creed
   (C) The Apostolic Constitutions
   (D) The Institutes of Gaius
   (E) The Chalcedonian Creed

5. The Maccabean or Hasmonean Revolt was a movement of Jews against which of the following occupying civilizations?

   (A) The Romans
   (B) The Greeks
   (C) The Persians
   (D) The Egyptians
   (E) The Assyrians

"Concealed in the heart of all beings is the *Atman*, the Spirit, the Self; smaller than the smallest atom, greater than the vast spaces. The man who surrenders his human will leaves sorrows behind, and beholds the glory of *Atman* by the grace of the creator."

6. The quote cited above most likely comes from which of the following major religious texts?

   (A) The *Analects* of Confucius
   (B) The Qur'an
   (C) The Gospel of John
   (D) The *Upanishads*
   (E) The Torah

7. Which of the following Islamic sects were followers of the fourth caliph, Ali?

   (A) Shi'ites
   (B) Sunnis
   (C) Gnostics
   (D) Moors
   (E) Sufis

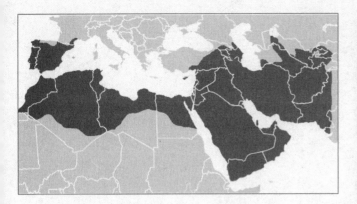

8. The map above shows the geographical extent of which of the following?

   (A) Christianity c. 200 c.e.
   (B) Judaism c. 500 b.c.e.
   (C) Hinduism c. 1500 b.c.e.
   (D) Buddhism c. 200 b.c.e.
   (E) Islam c. 750 c.e.

9. Which of the following best describes one of the major reasons that some Roman authorities persecuted the early Christians?

   (A) Their political strength was a threat to the authority of provincial leaders.
   (B) Their frequent use of military force threatened the stability of the Empire.
   (C) Their inclusion of slaves made the Romans nervous about a slave rebellion.
   (D) They refused to worship the emperor as a god.
   (E) Their vast economic success was viewed with suspicion by the Roman aristocracy.

10. The pilgrimage site depicted in the image above is most likely which of the following?

    (A) The Western Wall, Jerusalem
    (B) Lumbini, Nepal
    (C) The Ka'aba, Mecca
    (D) Holy Sepulcher, Jerusalem
    (E) Vatican City, Rome

Chapter 7
World Civilizations in Transition: 1000 to 1500

The period from 1000 to 1500 C.E. marks the real change from isolated empires to something else. To what, exactly, is difficult to say. There's no central unifying theme of this time period, as civilizations around the world experienced unique challenges in their respective geographic spheres.

But in the end it was the movement of people across borders, oceans, and mountains that put them into contact with other people that really launched this period and set the stage for the world exploration that came later: It's not too much to say that globalization began in this period.

1000–1500: AN AGE OF TRANSITION

The period from 1000 to 1500 C.E. was an age of transition for many world civilizations from Europe to the Far East. As Rome fell, Europe became a Christian continent and fell under the powerful influence of the Pope. Yet as the Church grew in power, so did the aspirations of local national rulers, touching off centuries of increasing tensions between the Church and fledgling monarchs. In this age, as in earlier ones, the focus was on the relationship of man to God (as mediated by the Church) the relationship of nations to nations, and of men to other men.

The East, meanwhile, witnessed the rise of the Mongols, an unexpected threat that conquered China, the Islamic caliphate, and Russia, contributing to periods of decline for each of those societies. On the plus side, the Mongols did reinvigorate trade between East and West along the Silk Road by providing political stability across the region for centuries.

Although somewhat limited by Mongol conquests, Islam continued to spread through North Africa in the West to India and Indonesia in the East and in doing so came to dominate the trade routes of the Mediterranean, the Middle East, and the Indian Ocean. One of the consequences of this Muslim trade dominance in the Mediterranean Sea and Indian Ocean was a Europe intent on finding trade routes to the East via other waterways (namely, the Atlantic Ocean), which eventually led to the first discoveries of new lands, including the Americas.

Unintended though it may have been, the Mongol Empire and the spread of Islam sparked a dramatic increase in contacts between peoples and cultures, either through trade or conquest. Some of these contacts were beneficial, allowing for a sharing of ideas and technology as well as goods which allowed many to prosper. For the major religions, more contact with people meant more converts. The downsides of the expanded era of cultural contact were wars and the **Black Death**, a plague that wiped out millions of people across Asia and Europe.

The Middle Ages…of What, Exactly?
The medieval period is often referred to as the Middle Ages, a period between the classical era of Greece and Rome and the modern era. The Middle Ages covers the period from the split of the Roman Empire in the 5th century to the Protestant Reformation in the 16th century and the beginnings of the Renaissance in the 14th century.

EUROPE: FROM ROME TO RENAISSANCE

It is difficult to make sense of **medieval** Europe without beginning with the **Church** (the papacy housed in Rome) and its role in the politics of this period.

The Dominance of the Medieval Church in Christian Europe

The Church during the medieval period was a supranational power that in large part replaced the political and administrative system that was lost with the fall of the Roman Empire. Local bishops filled the power vacuum and regulated life in cooperation with the local nobility; members of the elite had already moved into bishoprics early in the Church's development, filling these religious positions instead of other civil roles. Christianity was, simply put, what most Europeans had in common before the definition of modern national identities and large modern nation-states.

The kings of Europe, therefore, always had to mediate their power through two major groups: the local nobility and the Church. And when the spread of Islam threatened Christianity in Europe, it was the Roman Catholic Church that led the charge to combat Islam's spread and to recapture the birthplace of the Christian faith: Jerusalem. At the time, no single secular ruler could have amassed the forces that the Church did in launching the First Crusade in 1095.

The Rise of Papal Authority Over Europe and Resulting Tensions

The Church's intervention in the succession of kings was one place where monarchs and clergy clashed significantly. The Church considered it totally within its authority to approve succession, because all legitimate power to rule came from God to begin with. On the secular side, kings with aspirations of greater power challenged the Church by challenging the appointment of certain bishops—the fight over the replacement of the Archbishop of Canterbury in England in the 1160s (see page 176) was a good example of a king attempting to intervene in Church affairs. But who was higher on the hierarchy, kings or the Church? It depended on who was stronger or more strong-willed in the particular individual conflict, but in the early medieval period, the overall answer was the Christian Church.

> ### A Feudal Primer
>
> **Vassals** Lesser lords who provided military service, loyalty, and sometimes goods and services to their feudal lord, who protected the vassals
>
> **Feudal Monarchy** A kingdom bolstered by the feudal system; nobility served the king as his vassals
>
> **Fiefs** Lands granted to nobility in exchange for loyalty to the giver. Granting fiefs was a typical method used by kings to gain troops for war and consolidate power after the war. The nobleman who received the fief ruled it and gathered its revenues for his own coffers.
>
> **Serfs** Peasants who lived on the land of a fief. While not slaves, their social status meant they lacked many of the rights granted to free men. In particular, they were not allowed to own land, and had to pay tribute to the lord (landowner) of their fief.
>
> **Chivalry** The code of conduct for vassals (in their role as knights, or mounted armed warriors serving the king), emphasizing warrior qualities, generosity, and loyalty to one's feudal lord

The Rise of Early Nation-States

Medieval Europe saw the beginning of consolidation of ruling powers into centralized governments (monarchies), setting the stage for the development of nations and eventually nation-states. These early national entities emerged from the ashes of the Roman Empire along rough ethnic and language boundaries and were initially quite small. But over time some European nobles managed to create strong central governments through conquest as well as through shrewd political deals, consolidating small states into the larger ones we now recognize.

Let's take a quick tour around medieval Europe and review the beginnings of the European countries we know today.

France and England: A Love-Hate Relationship

Let's start in **France**, for no other reason than that French influence was so pervasive in 12th-century Europe. In fact, French language and culture was dominant in the courts of Europe and England—even the King of England spoke French! This is partly due to the fact that the formation of both countries was closely connected. In 987, King Hugh Capet ruled only a small area around Paris; for the next couple of hundred years, subsequent French kings expanded the territory. But beginning in the 12th century, England began to claim large parts of present day France. The English occupations of the French-speaking territories led to revolts and, eventually, to French statehood. The rise of the monarchy in France was the result of a slow consolidation of power.

A key method for centralizing power was to keep newly conquered lands in the hands of the royal family rather than to distribute them in the form of fiefs to the nobility (a typical way of rewarding nobles for their service to the crown). Louis IX's abolition of serfdom in the mid-13th century—hundreds of years before it was abolished elsewhere—also went far in solidifying the image of the king as protector of the people (also conveniently undercutting the economic and governing power of the lesser lords, who lost their serfs). Paris became a center for government, but also for artistic development, higher learning, and trade. After the end of the Hundred Years' War in 1453 royal power in France became more centralized. Under a series of monarchs known as the Bourbons, France was unified and became a major power on the European continent.

Church: 1, King of England: 0.5

England had different problems. In 1013 the Danish King Canute conquered England, which he ruled for 19 years (along with Denmark, Norway, and parts of Sweden). After his death in 1035 the kingdom was divided among his sons. In 1066 the English monarchy was taken over by William the Conqueror, who was the Duke of Normandy (a major territory in northern France). His descendants now faced the challenge of maintaining control over most of the British Isles as well as the family's continental holdings in France. The royal houses of England and France were connected by marriage but were constantly struggling for power among themselves. Henry II, who ruled England from 1154 to 1189, made great strides in building a government that functioned across English lands, supplanting the authority of local nobility. The royal courts were opened to almost everyone, moving judicial power to the king and out of the hands of the local nobility. Henry II also tried to extend his power over the judiciary to the clergy, who until then were not bound by secular law: At that point in time, only the clergy could pass judgment on their own members who were accused of a crime. The Church was steadfastly against any secular authority over its members. **Thomas Becket, Archbishop of Canterbury** and head of the Church in England, was Henry II's chief foe in this matter, fighting for the Church's autonomy. Becket was assassinated by the king's men, but the king was not able to bring the Church under royal judicial control.

The Gothic Style

The Gothic style of architecture was a French export that began to spread in the mid-12th century. It combined three elements—pointed arches, ribbed vaults, and flying buttresses—to create churches of massive size and unusual shapes, whose walls were able to support huge numbers of stained-glass windows that let in enormous amounts of light. Wherever French influence went, the Gothic style soon followed.

A Kingdom Divided

The three sons of Danish King Canute inherited his territories. Harold Harefoot inherited rule of England, Sweyn inherited rule of Norway, and Hardecanute inherited rule of Denmark.

Indeed, Henry II was not the first or the last monarch to clash with the Church. John, brother of Richard the Lionheart and son of Henry II, challenged the Church's power, going so far that he was excommunicated (a common fate for an ambitious monarch in those days). John wanted the power to appoint, or at least help appoint, the archbishop of Canterbury the head of the Church in England. When his own appointee was rejected by Rome, John exiled both his *and* the Church's choices for the position, leading Pope Innocent III to excommunicate the king, who then backed down. As a result, John was pressured—by the clergy as well as English nobility—to sign the **Magna Carta** in 1215, a document which proclaimed all men, even the king himself, subject to the laws of the land. This document permanently limited the powers of English kings through law (though not always in practice).

The Magna Carta established a permanent governing council that deliberated on issues important to the state. The introduction of this council, which eventually became the **Parliament**, brought together the king and the nobles, and would eventually prove to be more important than anyone at the time could have guessed; the parliamentary system and the Magna Carta became the basis for constitutional government in England and an inspiration for constitutional rule in other countries in the second half of the millennium. The drafting of the Magna Carta and the establishment of Parliament created a stable, centralized governing structure that was able to continue beyond the reign of any one king. Though lands would be gained and lost in France and the British Isles, the center remained firm and generally stable, despite heated disputes over succession such as the War of the Roses (1455–1485).

France vs. England vs. the Church: Who's Got the Power?

As was mentioned above, the formation of France and England as nation-states was not completely smooth sailing. Prior to William the Conqueror's conquest of England, no fighting had occurred between the two newly forming nations. However, the countries would engage in a series of battles and wars, fought primarily over disagreements of sovereignty and territories disputed by both nations and their rulers until the mid-14th century. These smaller acts of aggression eventually led to the series of skirmishes known as the **Hundred Years' War** (1337–1453), part of which was influenced by an unlikely candidate.

> ### The War of the Roses: Not So Rosy
> The **War of the Roses** was fought over succession to the English throne between the Houses of Lancaster and York, two branches of the ruling House of Plantagenet. Civil war at home weakened England's hold over its continental territories. The merchant classes gained in power as the nobility's influence fell, partly as a result of losses in war and partly as a result of the monarchy's plans to centralize power. The war ended with the ascension of Edward IV to the throne, but his death caused more disruption. It was **Henry Tudor** who then came to power as Henry VII of England, joining the feuding houses by marrying Elizabeth of York.

As a teenager, **Joan of Arc**, a farm girl, claimed to have heard voices that told her to liberate France from the hands of the English, who had by the early 15th century claimed the entire French territory. Remarkably, this uneducated youngster somehow managed to convince French authorities that she had been divinely inspired to lead men into battle, and they supplied her with military backing. With her army, she forced the British to retreat from Orleans, but was later captured by the French, tried by the English, and burned at the stake by the French in 1431. Nevertheless, she had a significant impact on the remainder of the war. After her death, the tide turned strongly against the English in the war, which eventually resulted in England's withdrawal from France.

In the end, the rulers of both England and (even more so) France needed to contend with the power of the Church. The Church was not unwilling to involve itself in secular politics, and the crown sovereigns of these countries could easily be threatened by contenders who gained the favor of the Church and were willing to use the Church's power to support their own plans for dominance. You should keep in mind, though, that the Church's power, and its ability to persuade lesser nobles to threaten the king's stability, lay ultimately in its support from the people rather than in military might.

Spain: No One Expects the Spanish Inquisition

Spain is a great example of a country whose rulers manipulated the power of the Church for their own ends. The monarchs of the landmass that would become Spain faced an immediate challenge: to rid Spain of the Muslim conquerors, known as the **Moors**. The fight to drive out the Muslims—the *reconquista*—began in the 11th century, when Alfonso of Castile reclaimed Toledo (with the help of a general known as El Cid) in 1085. Muslims called in reinforcements from North Africa to counter the Christians and halted the *reconquista* for several years. However, throughout the 1100s, the Christians, moving from north to south, continued to drive the Muslims out. More Muslim reinforcements were called in from North Africa, but a call from Pope Innocent III reinvigorated the *reconquista* in the early 1200s. A Castilian victory in 1212 in Las Navas de Tolosa signified the last real resistance from the Muslims.

Once the Muslim presence was under control, the Iberian Peninsula was ruled by Christians separated into several different kingdoms. Power in the Spanish-speaking region of Europe had been divided for two reasons: first, Castille was one of three independent Spanish kingdoms, and therefore no single ruler controlled the region, and second, the peasants were split along religious lines (mostly Christian and Muslim). The marriage in 1469 of Ferdinand (of Aragon) and Isabella (of Castile) laid the groundwork for unification by combining their two kingdoms, the strongest of the five major states in the Iberian Peninsula.

To strengthen their rule, Ferdinand and Isabella drove to purify Spain under the Catholic Church and thereby solidify state power. In 1490, the Grand Inquisitor arrived in Spain, ushering in the **Spanish Inquisition**, which was intended to cast out non-Christians and help the Spanish rulers to consolidate their power. By 1504, both Jews and Muslims were forced out of Spanish lands. Spain is a good example of how monarchs could use the power of the Church to gain and keep power over nobility who could challenge their sovereignty.

The Church Defends Its Lands: The Imposition of the Inquisition

Although the church had engaged in active anti-heresy activities in previous centuries, the early 13th century marked a beginning of the most widespread, and violent, campaign to be used by the Christian church against heretics and non-Christians. The Inquisition, referred to as smaller, the general push that was broken down into more localized campaigns such as the Spanish Inquisition, lasted from the early 1200s until the mid-1800s in some areas of Europe.

In 1231 Pope Gregory the IX assigned the Dominicans, an order of preachers within the Catholic Church, the responsibility to combat heresy. The Dominicans used the "inquisitorial system," a legal system in which the court or judge is an active participant in the determination of facts within the case in question. By 1252, torture was in common use when questioning or "trying" suspected heretics.

Inquisitions were practiced in several parts of Europe during this time, demonstrating the continued influence of the Church on the monarchies of individual nations in Europe. The practice continued well after the threat of non-Christian populations abated against newly converted Protestants within Europe in the early 16th century.

The Christian Church: Prelude to the Reformation

But what of developments within the Church? Why did the Church evolve as it did? When the Roman Empire under Theodosius adopted Christianity as its official religion in the 4th century, the development of the Christian Church became closely tied to the idea of empire and—after the fall of the western Roman Empire in the 5th century—continued the administrative institutions and cultural legacy of the fallen empire, albeit in a decentralized way. The **papacy**, or spiritual authority of the Bishop of Rome, was established in the 6th century, and even in this early period was a point of contention between the western Church centered in Rome and the eastern Church in Constantinople.

The **Great Schism of 1054**, which split the Church permanently into its eastern and western entities, began an era of separate development. In Western Europe, the heritage of the Roman Empire and its successors, and the rise of the Roman Catholic Church as a supranational power, muddled the development of centralized monarchies in Italy and Germany, where rulers vied for territorial power as well as Charlemagne's title of Holy Roman Emperor (which could not be claimed without official sanction from the Church). In the east, the Orthodox (Byzantine) Church clashed with the west over leadership of the Church, believing that the pope's leadership, including over the eastern Church, was largely ceremonial.

However, the western Church lacked uniformity of views as well. Rome didn't have sole claim on the papacy even among western clergy. Between 1305 and 1378, a series of French popes chose to rule from Avignon during a period known as the **Babylonian Captivity** (the name of which is derived from the 6th-century B.C.E.

imprisonment of the Jews by the Babylonians). Even though the last pope of this period, Gregory XI, returned to Rome before his death, the election of the next pope was complicated by competing factions and the desired location of the papacy in this second, or western, schism. The Council of Constance in 1414 ended the schism, reestablishing the papacy in Rome. In the end, though, the underlying theme of the medieval Church is competition with Europe's nobility for secular power, with Muslims for control of places sacred to Christianity, and with itself for spiritual and doctrinal control.

The Crusades

The Crusades were motivated partly by religion and partly by politics and exemplify the Church's competition with multiple forces in the Middle Ages. The First Crusade, launched in 1095 by Pope Urban II, was intended to recapture Jerusalem, which had fallen to the Seljuk Turks. Certainly the Byzantine emperor Alexius I welcomed the assistance from Rome, but Rome was acting with its own interests in mind. By launching the First Crusade, the pope hoped to unite Western Europe and bring the rulers of Europe under Rome's influence. He called upon Europe's faithful to serve in the name of Christianity as well as in exchange for lands in captured territories. The Crusaders were brutal, killing all Muslim residents, even though the Islamic rulers controlling the Holy Land had themselves been quite tolerant of non-Muslims.

During the Second Crusade, which took place in 1147, the crusaders marched east towards Jerusalem, but failed to accomplish any major goals, specifically a siege on Damascus. On the west side of the Mediterranean, however, a group of Crusaders took back the city of Lisbon in Portugal from Muslim rule. The Third Crusade, begun in 1189, once again was intended to recapture Jerusalem, this time from the control of Saladin, who had taken the city back from Crusaders in 1187. This crusade was weakened by internal conflicts between the kings of France and England. None of the following crusades was able to capture lands from the Muslims, and served only to weaken the crusading powers. During the Fourth Crusade, Rome attacked Constantinople (ironically one of the few cities in the region that was not actually Muslim) but lost, ruining relations between the western and eastern branches of Christianity. In the end, the Roman Catholic Church became more intolerant and repressive, as evidenced by the Spanish Inquisition and other movements to expel non-Christians or forcibly convert them to the faith. While there were eight crusades in total, which ended by the 1270s, none accomplished the tangible goals of the church. And while the Crusades led to an increase in information and dissemination of cultural knowledge through contact, it also increased the intolerance of the Catholic Church for Muslims and non-Christians in Europe.

If the Church thought its problems were over with the end of the Crusades, it was wrong: the 14th century ushered in more challenges to the Church's authority over the people of Europe, starting with the world's most famous pandemic, the Black Death.

The Black Death

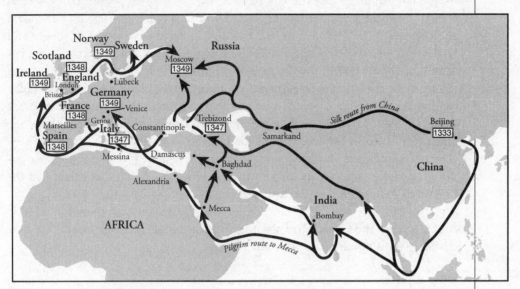

Spread of the Black Death (1333–1349 C.E.)

The Plague, or **Black Death**, began in China in the early 14th century, accompanying the Mongols into the area in the 1330s and eventually killing nearly 30 percent of the population. The disease then traveled along trade routes (on the Silk Road and by sea) to the west and south, spreading into India and the Middle East. By 1348, the Plague had reached Europe, which was already struggling to support its burgeoning populations. Traders would contract the Plague in Black Sea ports, introducing it into Italy and gradually further north. Underperforming agriculture—the result of both poor weather and a lack of technology—had already resulted in famines between 1315 and 1322. Farm wages were low, and peasants struggled to survive.

The Black Death eventually killed off around one-third of Europe's population, with higher mortality rates in urban areas. Medieval medicine at the time did not understand the causes of the Plague and was not able to treat it; embargoes and quarantines proved to be more effective in controlling the disease's spread.

The economic results of the Plague were profound. The overall population dropped, easing the problem of famine that had preceded the outbreak of the Plague. Those peasants who survived could demand higher wages because of labor shortages. Higher wages enabled them to become more self-sufficient as they were able to purchase the land they farmed. Once they became property owners, these farmers were in a better position to organize and revolt against nobles who tried to raise taxes to support war. Similarly, urban artisans and merchants fought for higher wages and a greater role in local political decision making. In the end, as a result of the Plague, there were more groups competing for power than there had been before.

Black Death

Historians and scientists believe the Black Death was most likely bubonic plague, caused by a bacterium named *Yersinia pestis*, which was spread by fleas that lived on the rats that were everywhere in the Middle Ages. By the time the first plague pandemic died out (yes, this was the first of many), it had killed as many as 75 million people worldwide!

The Church's Power Diluted

By the late Middle Ages, the Church had been somewhat weakened by several factors. First, the Crusades had exposed Europeans outside of Spain to the ideas and cultures of the Middle East, but had also changed how wars were fought and fortresses built. Major European cities were now fortified more powerfully and became bases of more centralized power of the princes and kings of Europe. Second, the Black Death's tremendous impact on Europe's population weakened people's support for the Church, which was not able to protect them from the disease's spread or help ease the pain of death. Last, the Plague decimated the ranks of the clergy, who tried to help the sick during the outbreak. As a result, a wave of new clergy filled the gaps, and these new clergymen were more prone to abuse their positions, creating much of the disgruntlement with the Church that would fuel the Protestant Reformation in the 16th century.

And just when the Church had absorbed the impact of the Black Death, the next challenge to its power arose: the Renaissance.

The Great Houses of God:
If You Build It, They Will Come (Hopefully)

Throughout the Middle Ages, the influence of the church throughout Europe could be seen not only in the political sphere but also visually in daily to life in many of the great cities of the era. A few of the major churches/cathedrals of this time include:

- Piazza del Duomo or the cathedral and tower in Pisa, Italy, begun in 1068
- Cathedral at Chartres, France, 1100–1300
- Duomo in Florence, begun in 1420
- Hagia Sophia, Constantinople, Turkey, finished 1453
- Sistine Chapel, Vatican City, restored 1477–1480

THE RENAISSANCE: EUROPE REKINDLES ITS GREEK AND ROMAN HERITAGE

The **Renaissance** is a period of flourishing artistic and intellectual developments that took place roughly between the 14th and 17th centuries. It has no defined starting point and developed in different places at different times. However, the basic ideas of the Renaissance were articulated in the writings of **Francesco Petrarch** (1304–1374), who considered the Roman Empire to be the high point of human civilization, and everything after the fall of the empire in the west to be a period of social deterioration that he termed the **Dark Ages**. Only by returning to the learning of the great Greek and Roman thinkers could humanity redeem itself. Therefore, the Renaissance was metaphysically a rebirth of European thought through the rediscovery of ancient manuscripts of the Greeks and Romans.

Access to the intellectual wealth of antiquity was made possible by Islamic scholars who had translated the teachings of ancient thinkers after the Muslims conquered the homeland of ancient Greece.

Philosophically, the Renaissance centered on the ideas of **humanism**, which placed man himself—rather than god—at the center of study and inquiry. In medieval Europe, thoughts of salvation and the afterlife so dominated personal priorities that life on Earth was, for many, something to be suffered through on the way to heaven rather than lived through as a pursuit of its own. As Europeans rediscovered ancient texts, they were struck with the degree that humanity—personal accomplishment and personal happiness—formed the central core of so much of the literature and philosophy of the ancient writers. The emphasis began to shift fulfillment in the afterlife to participating in the here-and-now. As a consequence, people began to shift their focus to life on Earth and to celebrating human achievements in the scholarly, artistic, and political realms.

Humanism, however, was not necessarily in conflict with an active spiritual life. **Desiderius Erasmus** (1466–1536) and **Sir Thomas More** (1478–1535) were just two of the notable humanist philosophers of this era, promoting ideas of equality and tolerance. Erasmus, of the Netherlands, (known as the "Prince of the Humanists"), along with being one of the most well-known learned men of the times who counseled kings and popes, was also a priest. His works focused on both ecclesiastic and humanist subjects, and he promoted religious toleration as the best pathway to truth. Sir Thomas More, of England, wrote *Utopia,* which described an ideal society, in which everyone shared the wealth, and everyone's needs were met. Erasmus and More were Christian Humanists, meaning that they expressed moral guidelines in the Christian tradition, which they believed people should follow as they pursued their own personal goals. However, not all humanist writers at this time adopted the moralistic approach in their work. The political writings of **Niccolo Machiavelli** were born from his humanist emphasis on human behavior and the nature of virtue, though they were more cynical than the Roman principles that underlay humanism. Secular education also gained prominence in the Renaissance; many of the world's greatest universities were founded in this period. Education became a means not only to be a man of God, but also to develop the skills and knowledge needed to serve the state; leaders could be made, not just born, a significant change in thought.

The great city states of Italy and mercantile centers of northern Europe hosted an enormous outpouring of artistic creation, fueled by the wealth of merchants who commissioned some of the greatest art of the era. In Italy, where powerful families in city-states such as Florence, Venice, and Milan became rich on trade, art was financed on a scale not seen since the classical civilizations of Greece and Rome. The Medici family in Florence, for example, not only ruled the great city and beyond but turned it into a showcase of architecture and beauty by acting as patron for some of the greatest artists of the time. And Renaissance art is a Who's Who of great artists: in southern Europe were **Michelangelo**, Fillipo Brunelleschi, **Leonardo Da Vinci**, Donatello, and Tommaso Masaccio; in northern Europe were Jan and Hubert van Eyck and Albrecht Durer. Unlike medieval paintings,

The Intellectual Renaissance: Europe's Oldest Universities
Bologna, Italy—1088
Paris, France—1150
Oxford, England—1167
Cambridge, England—1209
Salamanca, Spain—1218
Padua, Italy—1222
Siena, Italy—1240
Charles University, Prague, Czech Republic—1348
Jagiellonian University, Krakow, Poland—1364
Vienna, Austria—1365

which depicted humans as flat, stiff, and out of proportion with their surroundings, paintings of the Renaissance demonstrated the application of humanist ideals learned from the ancients. Careful use of light and shadow made figures appear full and real. This did not mean that art was not still being created in accordance with spirituality. The Catholic Church noticed the developments in artistic techniques and soon the greatest artists were hard at work adorning the great palaces and cathedrals of Italy. For four years, 1508 to 1512, Michelangelo painted the now-famous ceiling of the Sistine Chapel while lying on his back on scaffolding. And while highly realistic in style, most northern paintings were religiously motivated and therefore even secular paintings or portraits were filled with religiously symbolic objects and color choices that resonated with the Christian faithful.

In essence, the Renaissance (along with the university system and theology more generally) set the stage for the next great period in European history, the Reformation. It did so by encouraging the spread of secular thought as well as more critical approaches to Christian thought not mediated by the Catholic Church in Rome. The idea that the health of society rested not just on the graces of God, but also in the actions of men toward other men, shifted the paradigm of power in ways that would soon prove to be truly revolutionary.

Photo by Julian Ham

Michelangelo's *David* (one of many reproductions)

THE TRANSFORMATION OF TRADE AND SOCIETY

Now that we've taken a look at the shifting sands of religion and politics in Europe, let's take a look at one more aspect of society that begins to play a larger role as time passes: economics.

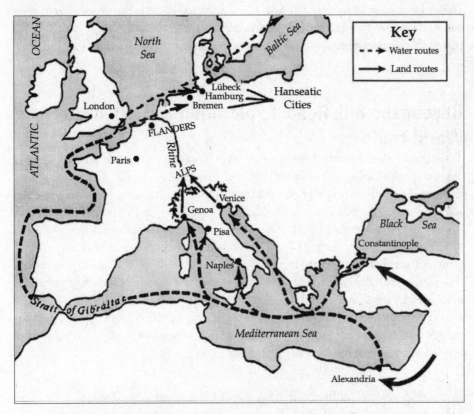

Trade Routes of the Hanseatic League (13th to 15th Centuries)

Europe: The Rise of the Middle Class

Trade is important to any society, and European societies in the medieval period were no exception. When trade routes around the Mediterranean and to the Far East became less open to European traders because of the dominance of Muslim traders, Europeans branched out in other directions into areas outside of Muslim control, shifting the centers of trade to the Atlantic Ocean and its ports.

Towns began to rise in importance as seats of nobility and as trade and production centers. The growth of towns was aided significantly by the rise of guilds. Trade guilds, which centered on particular crafts or merchandise, helped to regulate prices, wages, and the quality of goods. The guilds also were political entities that protected the interests of their members. The guild structure allowed merchants and artisans to compete with landed nobility for legal rights and privileges. The most powerful guild was the **Hanseatic League**, a collection of city-states that banded together in 1241 to establish common trade practices, fight off pirates and foreign governments, and essentially establish a trade monopoly from the region to much of the rest of the world. It worked for more than a hundred years, with more than 100 cities joining the league.

The growth of guilds and urban centers of production, trade, and commerce created a more complex class system and led to the rise of a fledgling, yet increasingly influential, *middle class* of merchants, artisans, and skilled tradesmen. The term middle class indicated a new class of society outside of the traditional three estates, or classes, of medieval life: the nobility, the clergy, and the peasantry. There had always been merchants and artisans, but until they became more organized, they couldn't capture particular rights and privileges for their class. In the coming centuries, this merchant class would slowly come to dominate international trade.

Beyond the Silk Road: Exploration and Origins of World Trade

Trade grew in the Middle Ages in more ways than one: it was not only organizing along new principles, but also striking out to seek new worlds to explore. Early explorations of the world were fueled by a mix of motivations: financial interests, scientific curiosity, and Christian missionary zeal. Getting to and from India was important to international trade, but the dominance of Muslim traders along the known trade routes leading to India motivated Christian traders to discover other routes to the Far East. Early explorers were faced with technological limitations that were eventually overcome by the invention of the astrolabe and the compass—developed by the Chinese and transmitted to the West by Muslim traders—as well as better maps, weapons, and ships capable of long ocean voyages. Once the technology was in place in the 15th century, the stage was set for European explorers to venture farther than had ever been possible.

In the mid- to late 1400s, Portuguese explorers reached the Coasts of Africa and India by sea; this voyage fueled the interest of other nations to send out their own exploratory missions. Portugal eventually claimed a number of newfound lands as their own, including Brazil, Mozambique, and Goa (a region in India). The age of colonial expansion—rather than just exploration—really took off in the 16th century and will be discussed more in the next chapter.

A Who's Who of Early European Explorers…

- **Eric the Red**—Norway/Iceland; a Viking Explorer who was the first European in Greenland
- **Leif Eriksson**—Iceland; first European to reach North America, named it Vinland; son of Eric the Red
- **Marco Polo**—Italy; one of the first Europeans to travel to China and Mongolia; famous for book The Travels of Marco Polo
- **Prince Henry the Navigator**—Portugal; claimed the Azores in the mid-Atlantic for Portugal; wanted to explore the coast of Africa and find the limits of the Muslim empire on that continent; sent Bartholomeu Diaz de Narvaez to sail around the Cape of Good Hope to the eastern coast of Africa
- **Vasco de Gama**—Portugal; the first European to reach India by sailing around the Cape of Good Hope on the southern tip of Africa
- **Christopher Columbus**—Spain; reached the Americas while trying to get to India
- **Vasco Nunez Balboa**—Spain; discovered the Pacific Ocean and the Isthmus of Panama
- **Ferdinand Magellan**—Spain; passed the southern tip of South America and reached Indonesia; completed the first voyage around the world; claimed the Philippines for Spain
- **Juan Ponce de Leon**—Spain; landed in Florida in search for gold; explored mainland America
- **Hernán Cortés**—Spain; sailed to Mexico where he came into contact with the Aztec Empire, which he conquered for Spain
- **Francisco Pizarro**—Spain; sailed to South America where he came into contact with Inca Empire, which he conquered for Spain
- **Francisco Coronado**—Spain; sailed to Mexico; explored northward to Arizona, New Mexico, and Kansas
- **John Cabot**—England; explored North America; searched for a northwest passage through the New World to the east
- **Giovanni Verrazano**—France; explored the northeastern coast of North America from the Carolinas to Nova Scotia
- **Jacques Cartier**—France; sailed up the St. Lawrence River and reached modern day Montreal
- **Sir Francis Drake**—England; circumnavigated the globe by passing through the Strait of Magellan

…And the Technology They Used

Why, all of a sudden, were so many explorers sailing around the globe? Why didn't this happen sooner? In the late 15th century, innovation was combined with a determination to apply new technologies to political and economic goals. In addition to advanced mapmaking techniques, the Age of Exploration was propelled by the following fine products:

- **The Sternpost Rudder**—Invented in China during the Han dynasty, the sternpost rudder allowed for better navigation and control of ships of increasing size. How did it end up in the hands of the Europeans? Trade, of course.
- **Lateen Sails**—These sails allowed ships to sail in any direction regardless of the wind. This was a huge improvement to ships that were dependent on the wind, especially in the Indian Ocean waters, where monsoons kept ships docked for long periods of time. Once these sails were used regularly on the Indian Ocean routes, they quickly became the standard on transatlantic voyages.
- **The Astrolabe**—Sailors used this portable navigation device to help them find their way. By measuring the distance of the sun and the stars above the horizon, the astrolabe helped determine latitude.
- **The Magnetic Compass**—Borrowed from the Chinese, through trade with Arabs, the magnetic compass allowed sailors to determine direction without staying in sight of land.
- **Three-Masted Caravels**—These large ships employed significantly larger sails and could hold provisions for longer journeys in their large cargo rooms.

To be sure, many of these inventions existed prior to the 15th century, but so much of history is about timing. In the late 15th century, these inventions had converged on one continent, a continent that was fiercely competitive about trade routes, newly wealthy and increasingly organized under strong leaders, and racing with the innovation and imagination of the Renaissance.

The Vikings: Winter Is Coming! (But It Will Be a Short One)

While we are on the subject of interconnectivity and exploration, let's take a quick look at the people who were trendsetters in that department, the **Vikings**. During the 9th and 10th centuries, Western Europe was attached by powerful invaders, most notably the Vikings from Scandinavia and the Magyars from Hungary. Although the Vikings were not the only raiders, they were perhaps the most successful. Beginning around 800, they used their highly maneuverable, multi-oared boats to raid well beyond their borders—on the open seas, up and down the north Atlantic coast, and along inland rivers.

Vikings got a bad reputation for raiding the Roman Catholic monasteries, which held much wealth and food due to the strong influence of the Catholic Church throughout Europe and England, so they were natural targets. But raiding was just one aspect of Norse economy. The Vikings were also merchants and fishermen and developed some the earliest commercial fisheries in northern Europe. They were also advanced sailors and explorers, reaching parts of the world that other Europeans would not come into contact with for another five centuries. In 1000 the Viking raider **Leif Eriksson** discovered North America, naming the site of discovery Vinland. The Vikings also had settlements as diverse as Newfoundland, Canada, around 1000, inland Russia, and northern France. The Vikings even got as far south as Constantinople, raiding it at least three times. In France, the Vikings were known as Normans (or north-men), the most famous of whom is William, who conquered Anglo-Saxon England in 1066. Vikings, in the form of the Normans, had an enormous influence on England, particularly on the English language. *Beowulf*, believed to be the oldest surviving epic poem of Old English, is set in Scandinavia and is believed to have several characters based on historical Scandinavians individuals of importance.

The Vikings weren't just raiders. They were also fishermen, merchants, sailors, and explorers.

Remarkably, however, in spite of their various victories, the Vikings, too, were converted to Christianity. This continued in a pattern of invading tribes assimilating to a common civilization in Western Europe because of religion, not political power.

Russia: Passed By

Before we leave Europe and head east, we need to return briefly to one more place: Russia. Russia holds a unique place in that it stands at the borderlands between Europe and Asia. In later centuries, Russian affairs would be part of the European sphere of influence, but during the Middle Ages, Russia was not yet a major player in Europe. Russia entered the Christian world during the reign of **Prince Vladimir of Kiev** (972–1015), who converted to Orthodox Christianity, thereby aligning Russia with the Eastern Church and Byzantium. Kievan Russia declined as Byzantium did in the 12th century, and Russia fell to Mongol conquest between 1237 and 1241. The Mongols controlled Russia's major principalities for the next two centuries until they were finally driven out of Russia by Tsar **Ivan III (Ivan the Great)** in 1480. It is significant that just when Renaissance Humanism was at its peak in Europe, Russia was cut off from these developments by Mongol rule.

ISLAMIC EMPIRES FROM EAST TO WEST: CALIPHATE LIFE

When we last left the Muslims, we saw Islam grow from a local religion of the Arabian Peninsula to the driving force of an empire stretching from Asia to Africa. However, the heyday of the Islamic Empire had come and gone, soon to be replaced by something far less centralized.

Islam Loses Ground at Home but Finds a Home Elsewhere

With the execution of the last Abbasid caliph by the Mongols in Baghdad in 1258, Islamic power in its Arab homeland was greatly weakened. That last Abbasid caliph was a caliph in name only; the Seljuks, a Turkic-speaking people, took over Iran and Afghanistan and eventually Baghdad itself in 1055. The Seljuks adopted and spread Islam throughout central Asia. They also joined the Mongols in their conquest of central Asia in the late 12th and early 13th centuries. However, the Mongol invasions did not stop the spread of Islam into non-Arab lands. Indeed, after the fall of Baghdad in 1258, Islam continued to gain ground at the borders of the former empire.

Islam had already established itself in northern India in the 10th century. Later, a Muslim general established the **Delhi Sultanate**, which existed from 1211 to 1526 and spread almost to the very southern tip of the Indian subcontinent. Islam in central and southeast Asia was also bolstered by Timur the Lame (Tamerlane), a Turkic warlord who conquered lands all the way to Delhi in the 14th century and brought Sufi mystics in tow. By the mid-16th century, aided by Islamic dominance in the area of trade, successive waves of Mongol and Turkish Muslims overtook Iran, Afghanistan, and northern India, establishing the **Mughal Empire** (1526–1707). Although Mughal rulers were Muslim, the population of most of India was still primarily Hindu. Islam eventually spread to represent about a quarter of the population.

Africa

In Africa, the story was similar: Islam spread through a combination of military victories and trade contacts. Islamic traders brought Islam to the west of Africa, including the kingdoms of Ghana, Mali, and Songhai in the 7th and 8th centuries. When the Muslim Empire spread across North Africa at this time, these African kingdoms started trading with the larger Mediterranean economy. Islamic traders penetrated the unforgiving **Sahara Desert** and reached the fertile wealthy interior of Africa, called sub-Saharan Africa, while African traders pushed northward toward Carthage and Tripoli. Previously, the desert had acted as one gigantic "don't-want-to-deal-with-it" barrier, so people typically didn't.

Increasingly, however, caravans of traders were willing to do what they had to do to get to the riches on the other side of the sand. At first, the West Africans were in search of salt, which they had little of but which existed in the Sahara. When they encountered the Islamic traders along the salt road, they started trading for a lot more than just salt. The consequence was an explosion of trade.

Why were the Islamic traders so interested in trading with West African kingdoms? Because in **Ghana** (800–1000) and **Mali** (1200–1450) there were tons, and we mean tons, of gold. A little sand in your eye was probably worth some gold in your hand. So the Islamic traders kept coming.

The constant trade brought more than just Islamic goods to Ghana and Mali; it brought Islam. For Ghana the result was devastating. The residents of the empire were subjected to a Holy War led by an Islamic group intent on converting (or else killing) them. While the Ghanaians were able to defeat the Islamic forces, their empire fell into decline. By the time the Mali came to power, the region had converted to Islam anyway, this time in a more peaceful transition.

One of the greatest Mali rulers, **Mansa Musa**, built a capital at Timbuktu and expanded the kingdom well beyond the bounds of Ghana. In 1307 Musa made a pilgrimage to Mecca (remember the five pillars of Islam?) complete with an entourage of hundreds of gold-carrying servants and camels. The journey was so extravagant and so long and so impressive to everyone who saw it, that Musa became an overnight international sensation.

But the largest empire in West Africa was formed in the mid-15th century, when Songhai ruler Sonni Ali conquered the entire region and established the **Songhai Empire**. The Songhai Empire lasted until around 1600, and during its reign, Timbuktu became a major cultural center, complete with a university that drew scholars from around the Islamic world.

Ottoman Empire: More Than Just Comfy Footstools

In 1453, the Ottoman Turks, Muslims from the east, took Constantinople, killed the emperor, and essentially brought the Byzantine Empire, which held the last vestiges of the Roman Empire, to an end. The **Ottoman Empire** came to control all of Anatolia (modern-day Turkey), Syria, Palestine, Greece, Serbia (at the Battle of Kosovo Polje in 1389), Albania, eastern Hungary, and Bulgaria, posing a potential threat to the Holy Roman Emperors farther west. The Ottoman rulers were tolerant of other religions in an age of intolerance, increasing the population of the empire by opening its doors to those who were being driven from western lands: Jews, Muslims, even Christians. However, this internal tolerance didn't mean that the Ottoman rulers were not interested in more conquest.

Under Emperor **Suleiman** (who ruled from 1520 to 1566), the Ottomans attacked farther into Hungary, even reaching Vienna's walls in Austria in 1529 and raiding the coasts of Italy and Spain by sea. The Ottoman Empire spread on the strength of three groups: the *gazis*, Islamic warriors; *Sufis*, mystics who helped convert conquered peoples to Islam; and **Janissaries**, Christian-born elite mercenaries raised from childhood to adopt Islam and fight for Islamic rulers. With the rise of the Ottomans, Islamic empires controlled all the lands from North Africa and the Mediterranean (Ottomans) to central Asia (the Safavids in Persia) to India (the Mughal Empire).

The Mysteries of Sufi Mystics

Sufism is a branch of Islam focused on the mystical, contemplative aspects of the religion. Sufi mystics were notable for their piety and their dedication to the purity of worship as well as the rapturous expression of their beliefs through dance, music, and poetry. Their piety and devotion to helping others was instrumental in spreading the message of Islam. Sufi practice continues to this day yet remains a small, controversial sect among more conservative Muslim groups.

TOWARD THE FAR EAST

Despite the presence of Islam in Asia, the history of the period from 1000 to 1500 in Asia is dominated by the rise of the Mongols and their influence on the politics and culture of the areas they conquered. Even though the Mongols were gone as a leading power by the 14th century, the effects their presence had on the development of those societies they conquered are very meaningful.

The Mongols Take Russia

The Mongols cut a long, wide swath of warfare and destruction during their heyday, spreading out and conquering peoples as far east as China and as far west as Europe. The Mongols, nomadic by nature and decentralized into tribes, did not become a force for world domination until the tribes turned from battling one another to joining together behind a single leader. Khabul Khan succeeded in uniting the Mongol tribes for a brief period in the early 12th century, under the patronage of the Jin (or Jurchen) dynasty, a nomadic people who controlled northern China at the time. But it wasn't until the rise of Khabul Khan's grandson **Chinggis (Genghis) Khan** that the Mongols became the powerful invading force that defeated nearly every major power in Asia and Eastern Europe in the 13th century.

Born Temujin around 1162, the man who would become Chinggis Khan rose to power on the basis of his military defeats of rival tribes. In 1206, a council of Mongol chieftains named him **khan**, the head ruler of all Mongol tribes. It was then he took the title Chinggis Khan. Exploiting the Mongols' extreme mobility and warrior culture, Chinggis Khan set forth to conquer surrounding territories. First stop: China. Although the various states controlling China had built fortified cities that would seem to have stopped the Mongols, who excelled at battles on open ground, the Mongols adapted quickly, mastering military technologies learned from those they conquered which enabled them to attack even fortified cities with tremendous force. The Jin (in the north) and Western Xia (in the west) fell, and the survivors were forced to pay tribute to the conquering force. Without yet conquering the Song dynasty in the south of China, the Mongols turned west and invaded as far as eastern Persia by the time Chinggis Khan died in 1227.

After Chinggis Khan's death, the Mongols split into four major khanates, but the invasions continued. The Mongols, emboldened by their victories in Central Asia, moved into Russia next. In the late 1230s, the **Golden Horde** (so named after the golden tents of the early khans) invaded Kievan Russia, which had been in decline for some time. Kiev fell, but Novgorod did not, probably because of Novgorod Prince Alexander Nevskii's willingness to negotiate with the invaders. During the Mongol occupation of Russia, the Russians paid tribute to the Mongols and grew rich from both the tribute system and increased trade. Over time the Mongols weakened, but the Russians—led by the Muscovite princes—grew in strength, and eventually the Russians joined forces to drive the Mongols out after the Battle of Kulikova in 1380.

The Mongols' strength was also unleashed on Hungary in 1240, and was poised for further incursion into the west when the Mongols disintegrated from internal conflict. Victories in Central Asia continued for a short while: Baghdad fell to the Mongols in 1258, ending the Abbasid caliphate, but the Mongol advance was stopped when they were defeated by the Mamluks of Egypt in 1260.

Song and Ming: Before and After the Mongols

Before the arrival of the Mongols into China in the 13th century, the **Song** dynasty (960–1279) created (for a while) a united China. During the Song period, China saw the decline of Buddhism and the reemergence of Confucianism, the development of iron-based industry, and the growth of the largest cities in the world at the time. Gunpowder was among those technologies developed during the Song period, although it was not used for military purposes. Despite its massive steel production and economic strength, the Song dynasty was still forced to cede large portions of its territory to non-Chinese ruling tribes, the Jin (or Jurchens) in the north and the Western Xia in the west. The coming of the Mongols would only make things worse for the Song.

The Mongols invaded Chinese territories a number of times. The Jin in northern China fell to Chinggis Khan in the early 13th century, and **Kublai Khan,** one of Chinggis Khan's grandsons, gained control over most of the rest of China under the name of the **Yuan** dynasty (1271–1368). Although Mongol control was pervasive, the Mongols tried to keep Mongol and Chinese social relations separate. Kublai Khan respected Chinese culture enough to use it to his advantage, employing Chinese bureaucrats to run the state. The Mongols allowed most other groups—Muslims, Buddhists, Taoists, Christians—to thrive, making use of their

The Upside of Mongol Conquest
Despite the ravages brought upon those kingdoms the Mongols invaded, once Mongols took control, they proved to be remarkably able and tolerant rulers. In Asia in particular, the period of Mongol rule was relatively peaceful and prosperous, and is referred to as the *Pax Mongolica*. Silk routes to the east that had been declining were revived under Mongol protection.

knowledge and skills. After Kublai Khan's death in 1294, Mongol control was weakened, as Kublai Khan's successors were not able to rule as effectively. Eventually the Yuan dynasty fell to Zhu Yuanzhang, a man of humble birth, who founded the **Ming** dynasty (1368–1644).

The Ming dynasty's first task was to purge the court and society of any traces of the Mongol presence, returning to administrative procedures that the Mongols had done away with. Zhu Yuanzhang paid special attention to land use and irrigation issues, ensuring that land would be farmed intensively and put to productive use. This helped bolster China's agricultural output, making it less vulnerable to drought and more capable of sustaining larger populations. The Ming took advantage of the wider trading contacts made under the Mongols and used them to expand economic growth on a scale unprecedented at the time. The economic prosperity of the Ming aided the growth of fine arts as well as expeditions (under admiral Zheng He) to spread the power and influence of the Ming into south and central Asia in the early 15th century. Because of internal politics, those expeditions were stopped in the mid-1400s. But in general, the Ming era was one of prosperity and growth.

Japan: A Brief History Up Until the Tokugawa Shogunate

Until now, we haven't talked much about the Japanese, who had gradually absorbed aspects of Chinese culture beginning in the 5th and 6th centuries. Because Japan consists of four main islands off the coast of mainland Asia, it was relatively isolated up until that point. While trade existed in the exchange of ideas, religions, and material goods between Japan and the rest of Asia, especially China, that rate of exchange was considerably limited. By the 7th and 8th centuries, Japan's borrowing from the Chinese became more overt and deliberate. The Taika reforms of the 640s changed the way that the Japanese court functioned, introducing Confucian bureaucracy and Buddhism as well as strict rules of court etiquette. Those who favored Chinese influence aimed to turn the Japanese monarchy into an absolutist empire and strengthen the Japanese military by forming a conscript army of peasants; however, Buddhist monks (and local lords) in Japan still held an enormous amount of power to counter these changes. Eventually, the Taika reforms proved to be only partially successful, and Japan developed its own unique culture. The Heian period in the first half of the 9th century in particular was responsible for much of the court etiquette and distinct aesthetic styles most closely associated with early Japan and described in great detail in Lady Murasaki's *The Tale of Genji*, one of the first novels (fictional narratives) ever written.

Interestingly enough, **feudalism** developed in Japan round the same time as feudalism in Western Europe, but it developed independently. In 1192 Yoritomo Minamoto was given the title of chief general, or **shogun**, by the emperor. At this time in Japan's history, the emperor was the figurehead of nation but did not hold any real power. The real power was in the hands of the shogun. Below the shogun in the pecking order were the **daimyo**, owners of large tracts of land, or the counterparts of the lords of medieval Europe. In the 11th and 12th centuries, these local rulers developed their own armies, who battled one another as well as the power of the court, giving rise to a warrior class of **samurai** who served as sort-of freelance protectors. They were part warrior, part nobility. They, in turn, divided up their lands to lesser samurai, who in turn split their land up again. Peasants and artisans worked the fields and shops to support the samurai class. Just as in European feudalism, the hierarchy was bound together in a land for loyalty exchange. The 12th century saw a rise in civil wars that would not ebb until the late 15th century. The influence of the Chinese throughout this period continued to abate; centralized power was not to be in an era of so many local warlords vying for power. Local power strengthened even more as feudalism grew and the **bakufu** (military governments) grew in number and strength, led by the shoguns.

Throughout the 14th, 15th, and 16th centuries, various shogunates rose and fell, and a pervasive influence of continued warfare threatened to decentralize the country completely. However, complete anarchy did not befall the Japanese; artistic achievements still flourished even in times of civil unrest, and eventually the country was unified and able to consolidate power under the Tokugawa shogunate (1603–1868), which ruled from Edo (now Tokyo).

THE AMERICAS

On the eve of European conquest of the Americas, Native American people had reached a level of civilization that was impressive by any standard and that also contradicted some of the principles that many associate with early societies. Unlike the great civilizations of Mesopotamia, China, and India, the great empires of the Americas did not arise in river valleys and lacked other attributes common to those other empires—proof positive that there is more than one way to build a civilization.

Mesoamerica and South America

The Aztecs: The First Mesoamerican Empire?

The **Aztecs** rose to power in central Mexico on the shores of Lake Texcoco in the 14th century C.E., founding their capital **Tenochtitlán** around 1325. Although historians don't always agree as to whether the Aztecs were a true empire, this great city-state remains one of the most powerful societies of pre-Columbian (before Columbus) Mesoamerica.

The Aztecs had an unusual social structure constructed around *calpulli*, most similar to clans. Within each *calpulli* existed additional layers of social strata, with the nobility at the top. Over time, Aztec society developed a tiered structure more like those of other societies. The state ruled over its citizens and surrounding territories through a system of tribute rather than direct rule, and also lacked the kind of wide-scale administrative system seen in other empires—two reasons that many do not consider the Aztecs to be a true empire. However, this society shared other empire-like traits:

- controlled diverse populations of people
- supported a large military
- centered around a ruler who held both religious and military power

The Aztecs are commonly known for their elaborate religious rituals involving human sacrifice, making them both hated and feared by their opponents.

The Aztecs eventually fell to the Spanish in 1521. It is unknown how long the Aztecs would have remained a power in the area had the Spanish not come along. Despite the significant size of the empire, the Aztecs had significant technological limitations. They lacked a written language, technology (such as the mill) that would have enabled them to more efficiently produce food for a huge population, metal tools such as the plow, and even domesticated livestock. However, the cultural legacy of the Aztecs remained: Mexico City was eventually built over Tenochtitlán, and the Nahuatl language of the Aztecs is still spoken by many of the native people of Mexico.

The Inca: Empire, Peruvian Style

The **Incan Empire** (1476–1534) at its most powerful covered an area of 2,000 miles from its farthest points north (near Quito in present-day Ecuador) to south (near Santiago in present-day Chile). The Incan Empire bore many of the traits already discussed as characteristic of an empire:

- covered a huge geographical area
- integrated a number of different ethic groups into its population
- had a centralized state structure, administration, and official religious practice
- entered around a god-king figure
- used a single language (Quechua) as the language of the empire

Human Sacrifice?

The Aztecs are remembered in history as one of the latest societies to practice human sacrifice. However, the number of sacrifices involved is a subject of dispute among historians. The sources that described the practice were enemies of the Aztecs (either their unwilling vassals or the Spanish), who would have had reason to exaggerate the extent of the practice—so there may be a degree of libel involved in these reports. Although the Aztecs did practice ritual religious killings, it is not truly known how frequently they did so or how many people were killed.

The empire was centered at the capital Cuzco, in present-day Peru. The ancient city of Machu Picchu high in the Andes Mountains is perhaps the most well-known city of the Incas, although it was more of a retreat than a ruling center. The Incan emperors were able to control such an enormous expanse of territory thanks to a well-built infrastructure (literally thousands of miles of roads) and a relatively stable system of control over local nobility who were integrated into the state system. Conquered peoples were brought into the armies of the Incas and given various goods in exchange for their loyalty and labor.

One of the more surprising facts about the Incas was that they managed to run such a huge empire without the aid of a writing system they could use for communication and the codification of religious or state practices and laws. They did, however, have the *quipu*, a system of knotted strings with which they kept track of numerical information and which could be used as a memory aid for ensuring that more elaborate oral records were recalled and recounted correctly. The Incan Empire came to an abrupt end with the coming of the Spanish explorers in the 1500s, the results of which we will look at in the next chapter.

CHAPTER 7 KEY TERMS, PEOPLE, AND EVENTS

Magna Carta

A document instituted in 1215 in England that limited the powers of the monarchy and made kings subject to the rule of law. This set the stage for most modern forms of governments in which there exist a separation of powers between the executive and legislative branches.

Hundred Years' War (1337–1453)

Long and constant confrontation between England and France, during which Joan of Arc played an important role

Spanish Inquisition

The process of removing all non-Christians from Spain in the late 15th century.

Babylonian Captivity

Name for the earlier Jewish exile in Babylon. During this period it refers to the moving of the Roman Catholic papacy from Rome to Avignon in France.

The Crusades

The four major crusades represent the Roman Catholic Church's desire to reclaim the Holy Land for religious and political purposes. Although temporarily successful at times, the crusades ultimately failed in the mission of taking Jerusalem from the control of Muslims.

Black Death

A massive plague that started in China and swept across the globe, eventually killing off one-third of Europe's population

Renaissance

Meaning "rebirth," the Renaissance was a period of artistic and cultural rediscovery of the Greek and Roman heritage of Europe. It is defined by humanism, and has many famous thinkers and artists including Sir Thomas More, Niccolo Machiavelli, Michelangelo, and Leonardo Da Vinci.

Hanseatic League

Representative of the rise of merchant guilds, and with them the middle class, The Hanseatic League was the most powerful of these organizations. A collection of city-states banded together to establish common practices, defend ships, and establish a trade monopoly.

Beowulf

Believed to be the oldest surviving epic poem of Old English and represent the story of historical Scandinavians

Genghis Khan

Original leader of the Mongols, who united them to conquer vast swaths of the globe. Genghis Khan and his descendants terrorized and then ruled over areas stretching from Europe to China.

Feudalism

The primary social and political structure of the early part of this period. Serfs lived on the lands of fiefs, which were ruled by vassals are feudal lords.

Shogun

Chief general in feudal Japan. The shogun was the center of power at that time, empowered by the emperor.

Tenochtitlan

Capital city of the Aztec Empire founded around 1325. This city represents the incredible architectural achievements of the Aztecs.

Incan Empire (1476–1534)

A large South American civilization centered in the capital Cuzco

Summary

o   Europe came full circle as the power of the Roman Empire was replaced by the influence of the Christian Church, which faced a multitude of challenges including internal conflict resulting in the Great Schism, the Crusades, the Black Death, the inception of early nation-states with strong national leaders, and the ideas of the Renaissance.

o   Along with challenging the church, the inception of early nation states began to give rise to a burgeoning middle class in Europe. Limited access to trade with the East by the dominance of Muslims in that area, European nation states focused instead on port-based trade along the Atlantic, giving rise to a middle class of artisans, merchants, and skilled tradesmen. Shipping and shipbuilding technology also flourished during this time.

o   Although the Abbasid dynasty was conquered by Mongols, smaller Muslim empires emerged with the Seljuk and Ottoman Turks in Central Asia and the Mughals in India. Islam spread as far as the kingdom of Mali in West Africa, all the way to the islands of Indonesia in the East.

o   The Mongols dominated this period in the East as they conquered China and headed west to conquer central Asia, the Middle East, and Russia.

o   Interaction among cultures flourished as a result of increased global trade and from the Mongol conquests, but so too does disease; the populations of China and Europe are decimated by the Plague.

o   Russia and Japan were cultures mostly cut off from the growing trade and interactions amongst other European and Asian cultures during this period. Russia was held primarily by the Mongols during this period, before which it had been aligned with the Eastern Church and Byzantium. Japan previously had limited interaction with China, in which it absorbed specific aspects of Chinese culture, but remained primarily autonomous until after the Middle Ages.

o   The Aztec and the Incan civilizations emerged as dominant cultures in the Americas on the eve of contact with European explorers.

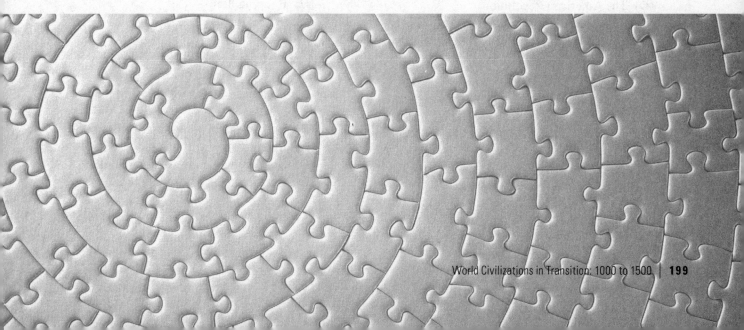

Chapter 7 Drill

Answers and explanations can be found in Part IV.

1. Which of the following was the primary result of the failed military campaigns known as The Crusades initiated by the Roman Catholic Church?

   (A) The recapturing of Jerusalem in 1088
   (B) The Great Schism of 1054
   (C) The Protestant Reformation of England, during which Kind Henry VII broke ties with the Roman Catholic Church
   (D) The commencement of The Inquisition, set into motion by Pope Gregory IX
   (E) The development of Islamic sects

2. Which of the following was NOT a result of the Black Plague's presence in Europe?

   (A) A decrease in famine
   (B) A decrease in the abuse of power by local clergy
   (C) A decrease in the population of merchants and artisans
   (D) An increase in wage demand of this burgeoning middle class
   (E) An increase in property ownership

3. Which of the following was an immediate result of the signing of the Magna Carta?

   (A) The War of the Roses
   (B) The Triple Entente of France, Britain, and Russia
   (C) The Protestant Reformation of England
   (D) The American Revolution
   (E) The assembly of Barons with power to overrule the King

4. Which of the following helped propel the development of the Renaissance?

   (A) Deism
   (B) Humanism
   (C) Copernican Theory
   (D) The social contract
   (E) Mercantilism

"All courses of action are risky, so prudence is not in avoiding danger (it's impossible), but calculating risk and acting decisively. Make mistakes of ambition and not mistakes of sloth. Develop the strength to do bold things, not the strength to suffer."

5. The quote above from Machiavelli's political treatise *The Prince* is most strongly aligned with which of the following economic approaches?

   (A) Socialism
   (B) Communism
   (C) Laissez-Faire economics
   (D) Capitalism
   (E) Utopianism

6. Which of the following cities did not develop a university during the Renaissance?

   (A) Florence, Italy
   (B) Paris, France
   (C) Prague, Czech Republic
   (D) Bologna, Italy
   (E) Padua, Italy

7. What did the Vikings and the Ottoman Turks have in common?

   (A) Both were masterful sailors of long-oared boats.
   (B) Both eventually converted to Christianity.
   (C) Both greatly expanded the reach of Islam.
   (D) Both built an empire lasting until 1922.
   (E) Both sacked Constantinople.

8. In what country did the Mongols fail to establish power?

   (A) China
   (B) India
   (C) Persia
   (D) Japan
   (E) Russia

9. All of the following were areas of disagreement for the Great Schism of 1054 between the Orthodox Christian Church and the Roman Catholic Church EXCEPT

   (A) the sacrament of communion
   (B) the immaculate conception
   (C) God as Trinity
   (D) priests' ability to marry
   (E) the use of local language in church

10. How did the Aztec Empire differ most from the Empires of Europe?

    (A) It had not developed efficient food production, such as tools and domesticated livestock.
    (B) It lacked a centralized government.
    (C) It did not have a strong military.
    (D) It had a written language.
    (E) It had no distinctive social classes.

11. During the early Ming dynasty (1368–1644), Zhu Yuanzhang paid special attention to which aspect of agriculture?

    (A) Domestication of livestock
    (B) Exchange of tea for silver
    (C) Irrigation
    (D) Feudal distribution of land for farming
    (E) Steppes

Chapter 8
The Modern World Emerges: 1500 to 1900

The time period between 1500 and 1900 C.E. witnessed the emergence of our modern world. Capitalism, industry, democracy, religious freedom, and empirical science all arose during the 400 years leading up to the 20th century. However, these achievements did not come without their fair share of conflict and war. Leading the way in both achievements and atrocities were the European powers. Beginning in this era, the history of the world is dominated by the global aspirations of European rulers and the philosophical and religious ideas of European thinkers.

This chapter will begin with the European revolutions that guided the continent's march toward global domination. The remainder of the chapter will discuss other parts of the world in the context of European contact, colonialism, and imperialism.

WHY THE EMPHASIS ON EUROPE?

Isn't this supposed to be a review of world history? Absolutely. But in studying this era of world history, the dominance of this small continent cannot be underestimated. Europe began the era in its earliest stages of global domination with colonial enterprises to the New World as well as expeditions to the East. Every civilization with whom the Europeans had contact was affected. Some fared far worse than others.

For the natives of the Americas, their lives would forever be changed. Many were killed by European diseases without ever seeing a white face. Others would see their cultures, languages, and religions slowly replaced by those of European colonialists. But the European stranglehold on the New World was eventually undermined as the continental powers lost all of their possessions to independence movements, which found their influence in European political philosophy. The most famous of these revolutions, which sparked revolutions around the world, was the American War of Independence from Great Britain.

China, unlike the Americas, desired isolation and tried to resist European culture and domination, which led to its technological stagnation for centuries. Its neighbor, Japan, also adopted an isolationist stance, but eventually adapted certain elements of Western culture and rapidly industrialized in order to successfully compete with the Western world.

The Middle East, meanwhile, by the end of the period was losing its last great Muslim empire, the Ottomans. Although the Ottoman state started the era as the most powerful world civilization, internal power struggles and external pressures from both Europe and its Muslim neighbors weakened it to such a degree that it was labeled the "sick man of Europe."

And finally, there's Africa. Two themes sum up the history of Africa during this age: slavery and colonialism. European traders found both Muslims and Africans all too willing to sell black Africans into slavery. The slave trade was vital to Europe, providing the manpower needed to support the growing cash crop economies of sugar and cotton in the New World. Unfortunately for Africans, the Europeans found the American natives far too vulnerable to disease to use as slaves. As African labor was fueling the economies of the West, Africa itself became a target of European colonialism.

There was barely a part of the world that Europeans did not affect during this era. They shared their technologies, their religion, and their ideas, often by force, with the four corners of the earth. But in turn, the Europeans could not help but be affected by the cultures with whom they came in contact. For example, the British discovered tea in India. What on earth did they drink before then? And the French were never the same after the introduction of chocolate and vanilla from the New World. These trivial examples are meant not only to amuse but particularly to highlight the power imbalance of the era. The cultural diffusion that occurred during this age was both dominated and directed by Europe. The 20th century would be no exception.

EUROPE IN THE AGE OF REVOLUTIONS

The period from 1500 to 1900 saw revolutions of every possible kind arise and change the world forever: economic, political, religious, technological, scientific, philosophical, agricultural…you name it. To trace these changes, let's take a look at Europe through the filter of revolution and visit each area in turn.

Economic Revolutions: The Rise of the *–isms*

When we last left Europe, explorers from Portugal, Spain, and other nations were just starting to embark on voyages that would change the maps of the world irrevocably. Not only would new lands be added, but existing nations would expand through colonizing new lands and peoples.

Why Colonize?

Colonies, in short, meant the promise of wealth for the colonizers. No matter how you slice it, land is valuable: It can be used to grow cash crops or timber or to mine precious metals. Europeans (both governments and individuals) had only a finite amount of land at their disposal back on their continent, so early on they looked for other lands to capture. The Spanish set off to the Americas to bring back the much-fabled gold of the Incas. The British made off with the riches of India and infiltrated China in an attempt to siphon off what they could there. The crops of the early American colonies were sent back to Europe or sold to other colonists, making the colonial powers and their regents extremely wealthy. In general, colonies were a source of income for the colonizers, enabling the governments to fund wars (religious or otherwise) at home.

> ### Mercantilism Versus Capitalism: Economic Smack-Down
>
> As world trade increased in both volume and scope in the early 1500s, different economic systems came into competition. **Mercantilism** promoted the control of trade by governments, a system that gave the European countries that adopted it a steady source of income to fund the crown, its wars, and its explorations into Asia and the Americas. **Capitalism**, on the other hand, promoted the growth of private wealth and the ownership of the means of production by individuals unfettered by church or government controls. Capitalism argued that governments should take a **laissez-faire** attitude toward trade, meaning that they should not restrict trade in any way. Capitalism received a significant boost with the rise of the Protestant Reformation, which promoted hard work, discipline, and the accumulation of wealth as signs of divine favor and moral values.

Who Colonized Whom?

In Mexico, in the lands of the Aztecs, Hernán Cortés came in and did the same in 1521. Cortes was aided by other peoples who were eager to see the Aztecs fall. As a result of the Spanish presence, smallpox and typhus decimated the native populations, making it that much easier for the Spanish to subjugate the people and destroy the native culture.

Francisco Pizarro reached the Incan Empire by 1526 and was given "permission" by the Spanish crown to conquer the area. By the 1530s, when Pizarro was in conquering mode, he met an empire already weakened by smallpox and internal struggles over succession. He had only a small force, but he had weapons and horses, which gave him a distinct advantage. The native people were brutally oppressed by the Spanish, who destroyed much of Incan culture.

The Spanish used native peoples as slave labor, but when disease decimated native populations, slaves from Africa were imported to replace them, fueling the African slave trade. Because Africa had long been integrated with the European trading networks, most Africans had built up a resistance to European diseases; Native Americans, on the other hand, did not have a chance to develop such defenses. The Spanish came to control areas in the southern part of North America, Central and South America, Mexico, and the islands of the Caribbean.

From the 16th to 19th centuries colonialism spread to nearly every corner of the globe. Any European country with a navy and a need for revenues set out to capture new lands. The **Portuguese** were the first, establishing colonies on both the west and east coasts of sub-Saharan Africa and along the east coast of South America in Brazil, where they mined gold and grew sugar. They also established a non-Mediterranean sea route to India, by sailing around the tip of Africa. The Spanish followed right on the Portuguese explorers' heels, seizing the lands in present-day Florida, Central America, and the western coast of South America formerly held by the Incas and Aztecs. The **Spanish** taxed the inhabitants via the *encomienda* system and used first native labor and then imported slave labor to mine gold and silver and work on plantations growing sugar and other cash crops. But in the end, neither Spain nor Portugal had the economic infrastructure—banks and other institutions—to enable them to grow their wealth as other colonizing powers did. The **Dutch** (in South Africa, Guiana in South America, and much of Indonesia), **French** (in eastern Canada and parts of the Caribbean), and **English** (in Indian ports and the east coast of North America) may have had fewer holdings, but they were better able to administer them and use that newfound wealth.

The Commercial Revolution: The New Economy

The trading, empire building, and conquest of the **Age of Exploration** was made possible by new financing schemes that now form the basis of our modern economies. Though many elements had to come together at once for the new economy to work, timing was on the side of the Europeans, and everything fell into place.

First, the church gave in to state interests by revising its strict ban on what are now standard business practices, like lending money and charging interest on loans. Once banking became respectable, a new business structure emerged: the **joint-stock company**, an organization created to pool the resources of many merchants, thereby distributing the costs and risks of colonization and reducing the danger for individual investors. Investors brought shares, or stock, in the company. If the company made money, each investor would receive a profit proportional to his or her initial investment. Because huge new ships were able to carry unprecedented cargoes, and because the goods were often outright stolen from their native countries, successful voyages reaped huge profits. A substantial middle class of merchants continued to develop, which in turn attracted more investors, and the modern-day concept of a stock market was well under way.

These corporations later secured royal charters for colonies, like the Jamestown colony in Virginia, and funded them for business purposes. Even when they didn't establish colonies, monarchies granted monopolies to trade routes. The **Muscovy Company** of England monopolized trade routes to Russia, for example. The **Dutch East India Company** controlled routes to the Spice Islands (modern-day Indonesia).

Increased trade led to an early theory of macroeconomics for the nations of Europe. Under the theory of **mercantilism**, a country sought to achieve trade, but tried not to import more than it exported; that is, it attempted to create a favorable balance of trade. Trade deficits forced dependencies on other countries, and therefore implied weakness. Of course, one country's surplus had to be met with another country's deficit. To resolve this dilemma, European countries were feverish to colonize.

Scientific and Philosophical Revolutions: The Power of Ideas

Economic systems may not seem to have much in common with philosophy, but changes in the way that people thought about the world, nature, and humans' place in the universe did have an effect on economics.

Prior to the **Scientific Revolution**, Europe and most of the world believed, as Aristotle asserted, that Earth was the center of the universe and that the sun, stars, and planets revolved around the earth. There certainly were numerous inconsistencies observed by scientists with regard to this theory, but most scientists continued to attempt explaining the inconsistencies rather than investigate the theory itself. During the Middle Ages, the Catholic Church and the political structure reinforced the lack of scientific investigation. The church focused everyone's attention on salvation, while the feudal system focused everyone's attention on mundane, local concerns.

But as Europe changed dramatically due to the Renaissance and the Protestant Reformation, and as the growth of universities gave structure to burgeoning questions about the world, educated Europeans began to examine the world around them with new vigor. The results were revolutionary.

The Copernican Revolution: A Revolution about Revolutions

Just as the counter-reformation was gaining momentum, **Nicolaus Copernicus** developed a mathematical theory that asserted that the earth and the other celestial bodies revolved around the sun and that the earth also rotated on its axis daily. This was pretty shocking stuff to many in the "establishment." Although most educated people had accepted the world was a sphere for centuries, even well before Columbus's voyage in 1492, the earth's position at the center of the universe was widely accepted. Copernicus's heliocentric theory of the solar system brought about much debate, and much skepticism. In 1543, Copernicus published

The Revolution of Heavenly Bodies to prove his points, but it wasn't until **Galileo Galilei**—who discovered the moons of Jupiter with his telescope—that the Copernican model really took off.

In 1632, Galileo published his *Dialogue Concerning the Two Chief Systems of the World*. He wrote the work in Italian in order to reach a wide audience and hopefully defeat the defenders of Ptolemy (the scientist who promoted the earth as the center of the universe). He showed how the rotation of the earth on its axis produced the apparent rotation of the heavens, and how the stars' great distance from the earth prevented man from being able to see their changed position as the earth moved around the sun. His proofs made it difficult to continue accepting the Ptolemaic model, which just so happened to be the model sanctioned by the Roman Catholic Church. The church put Galileo on trial before the Inquisition in Rome for heresy and he was forced to recant. His book was placed on **The Index**, a list of banned heretical works. Nevertheless, while under house arrest, Galileo continued to research and document his findings.

Astonishingly, Galileo's Dialogue remained on the list of banned heretical works until 1822!

The Scientific Method: In Search of Truth

Recall that during the High Middle Ages and the early Renaissance, the scholastic method of reasoning was deemed the most reliable means of determining scientific meaning. Scholasticism was based on Aristotelianism and therefore used reason as the chief method of determining truth. Sometimes reason led to heresies, other times reason was used to explain and complement faith, as was the case with Thomas Aquinas.

The scientific method was born out of scholastic tradition, but it took it to considerable new levels. Reason alone wasn't good enough. Under the scientific method, one had to prove what the mind concluded, document it, repeat it for others, and open it up to experimentation. At its highest stage, the scientific method required that any underlying principles be proven with mathematical precision.

Copernicus and Galileo were two fathers of the scientific method, but it took more than a century for the method to be widely used. There were many contributors. **Tycho Brahe** (1546–1601) built an observatory and recoded his observations, and **Francis Bacon** (1561–1626) published works on inductive logic. Both asserted that scientists should amass all the data possible through experimentation and observation and that the proper conclusions would come from these data. Then, **Johannes Kepler** (1571–1630) developed laws of planetary motion based on observations and mathematics. **Sir Isaac Newton** took it one step further. In *The Mathematical Principles of Natural Philosophy* (1697), he invented calculus to help prove the theories of Copernicus, Galileo, Bacon, and others. He also developed the law of gravity.

All of this led to the Industrial Revolution, which will be discussed later in this chapter. In the meantime, however, you need to understand that the Scientific Revolution led to a major rift in society. While many Christians were able to hold on to their beliefs even as they studied science, many also began to reject the church's rigid pronouncements that conflicted with scientific findings. Many of these people either became **atheists** (who believe that no god exists) or Deists (who believe that God exists but plays a passive role in life).

Deism: God as a Watchmaker

The Scientific Revolution contributed to a belief system known as **deism**, which became popular in the 1700s. The deists believed in a powerful god who created and presided over an orderly realm but who did not interfere in its workings. The deists viewed God as a watchmaker, one who set up the world, gave it natural laws by which to operate, and then let it run by itself (under natural laws that could be proved mathematically). Such a theory had little place in organized religion.

As a result of the Scientific Revolution, science became a true profession and, more important, something that governments funded rather than something undertaken by individuals only. Governments had a stake in seeing science and technology develop; scientists helped develop the navigational tools that made exploration possible, and also developed the technologies that eventually fueled the Industrial Revolution.

Revolutions in the sphere of ideas naturally extended beyond science and into belief, because science and religion both try to make sense of the world around us. It isn't any wonder, then, that revolutionary ideas would soon come knocking on the Church's door.

Religious Revolutions: It's Amazing What a Little Excommunication Can Do

The Protestant Reformation

The origins of the **Protestant Reformation** era lay in a broad dissatisfaction with the Catholic Church. Three large groups who had a bone to pick with the Church included:

1. The lower classes/**peasants**, who saw the Church as being made up of large landholders who were in cahoots with the ruling elites, who all were generally abusive to the masses. Baptists and Mennonites arose out of this class.
2. The budding **middle class**, who felt that the Church was working with the aristocrats in order to protect aristocratic privilege and economic supremacy. The middle class wanted a bigger piece of the pie, economically speaking, and felt the Church was hindering this. Calvinist (Switzerland), Puritan (England), and Huguenot (France) sects, as well as the Dutch Reformed Church, resulted from this class.

You may recognize these as the middle class plus the two medieval classes of society that were not the Church: in short, this list includes pretty much everyone.

3. **Kings** and other **nobility** who fought with the Church regarding taxes, legal jurisdiction, and political power and influence. The Middle Ages had already set the stage for a clash between secular rulers and the Church, so it isn't surprising that many rulers supported the Protestant cause as a way to curb the Church's influence in their own lands. The Anglican Church (England) and Lutherans (Germany) are two sects that had aristocratic foundations.

However, the Reformation was obviously not just about economics and power; it was a religious movement that sought to curb the excesses of the Church and correct Church doctrine. Protestants believed not only that Church leaders had become abusive and oppressive, but also that the Catholic leaders were *wrong in the way they interpreted Christian doctrine*—a hugely important issue! An error in doctrine could impede one's salvation. We are talking about eternal life here—you simply could not afford to mess this up.

Luther and Calvin: A Match Made in Heaven

Martin Luther (1438–1546) was the catalyst for the Reformation, a devout Catholic priest who at first tried to reform the Catholic Church from within. He was particularly against selling **indulgences**, a process by which a wealthy penitent could pay money to the Church in exchange for the expiation of sins. When his complaints were ignored, Luther nailed his **"Ninety-Five Theses"** to the door of the Castle Church in Wittenburg, a traditional way to open up discussion on theology at the time. The Church was extremely displeased, to put it mildly: Pope Leo X, with the support of Holy Roman Emperor Charles V, had Luther excommunicated at the Diet of Worms in 1521. But Luther soon found himself under the protection of German princes who agreed with him (and who—coincidentally, of course—opposed the authority of the Holy Roman Emperor), and he eventually produced a translation of the New Testament in German, the first step to allowing people to read the Bible for themselves.

The Power of the Press
Before the invention of the printing press and the spread of books in vernacular (spoken) languages in Europe, most people didn't know how to read. Reading material existed mostly in the form of Latin manuscripts, handwritten documents produced in monasteries, usually on religious topics. So not only was there not much to read, few knew how to read Latin.

Luther's ideas (eventually published as the Augsburg Confession) formed the core of Protestantism, a word which came to mean anyone who protested against the Catholic Church. Luther wanted to break the Church's monopoly on the interpretation of the Bible, believing that individuals needed only to learn from the Bible directly to find the path to salvation; the cycle of sin, confession, and penance—and the clergy who facilitated that cycle—was in Luther's view largely unnecessary. Luther's ideas were dangerous because he undermined the Church's justifications for its existence in a way that had never before been so fully articulated. As his ideas spread, the clergy lost their unique power over interpreting doctrine, and instead city councils and other town leaders became more central to running local churches. Revolts spread in the 1520s, as literal-minded reformers from the lower classes challenged the tax system and other rules that weren't in the Bible. These reforms went in directions Luther had not intended: He was opposed to the idea of the liberation of the peasants and of increased political rights for nonaristocrats, as were most of the princes who supported him. But although he started the changes, he was personally powerless to stop them (aside from encouraging the nobility to be brutal in putting down peasant revolts).

Luther's ideas sparked the Reformation, but soon other theologians added their own unique contributions to the mix. Few Protestant thinkers were more influential to early American history than **John Calvin** (1509–1564), who preached a more severe brand of Protestantism. Calvin believed that only certain people were born into salvation, and these "elect" had a responsibility to lead others in creating just, well-ordered societies and to accumulate wealth, a further sign of God's favor. Those who were poor were poor exactly because they were *not* among the elect. Calvin's ideas were at the heart of the Reformed (**Calvinist**) church, which first grew in influence in Geneva, Switzerland, but developed followers in the Netherlands and France as well as the new world, forming the basis of many communities in the New England colonies.

Luther and Calvin were not the only reformers active in this period. **Ulrich Zwingli**, a Swiss reformer, was a lot like Luther: He also was a member of the clergy until he left out of protest, and he claims to have come to the same conclusions as Luther did, independently. Zwingli himself was a back-to-basics reformer, eliminating music and changing the liturgy. However, some of his followers rejected the practice of baptizing infants, and actually rebaptized their adherents, gaining the name the **Anabaptists** as a result. Zwingli was not pleased with where the Anabaptists had gone with their practices and persecuted them from his post as head of the Reformed Church in Zurich. John Knox, also a former clergyman, similarly led Protestant reforms in Scotland.

Luther's Predecessors in Faith

Actually, Martin Luther was not the first person to stand up and challenge the status of the clergy in the Church. In the 1370s, an Oxford theologian named **John Wyclif** (1329–1384) criticized the corrupt clergy and the excesses of the Church, claiming that any person who could read the Bible could do what the clergy did. Wyclif inspired **Jan Hus** (c. 1370–1415), a professor and reformer from Bohemia. Hus also criticized the Church and challenged the clergy's right to claim special privileges. The fact that most of the clergy in Bohemia were foreign (Germans, to be precise) made them a prime target for Hus and his followers. Civil war erupted, and Hus was burned at the stake as a heretic. The fate of Hus made Bohemians very wary of Luther's message at first.

Luther succeeded where Wyclif and Hus failed because of the political ramifications of his beliefs: They were an excellent excuse for German princes to deemphasize their allegiances to the Holy Roman Empire and claim greater autonomy. This earned Luther a protection that Wyclif and Hus, being more involved with the university establishment, fatally lacked.

The Ramifications of Reformation

As Reformation ideas spread, Europe soon found itself divided between Catholic and Protestant beliefs. Although Holy Roman Emperor **Charles V** had issued an imperial edict that no one harbor Luther, various princes ignored the edict, using the Protestant threat as leverage against the Church to have their own complaints heard. In other places, secular leaders took advantage of the Church's weakness to seize Church land for themselves. The Church, meanwhile, was occupied not only with the proliferation of Protestants, but more importantly, with the invasions of the Turks, who had taken Constantinople in 1453 and attacked Vienna in 1529 under the leadership of **Suleiman**. Once the Turkish threat was under control, the Church could return to the Protestant claims.

Warfare between Protestant and Catholic forces worsened in the 1540s and 1550s, ending with the **Peace of Augsburg** in 1555, which proclaimed the principle of *cuius regio eius religio* (whose realm, his religion), according to which a prince could accept either the Protestant or Catholic faith according to his conscience, and the citizens of his territory would have to follow his lead. As Protestantism spread across Europe, Catholic rulers sought to stem the tide and reclaim Protestant lands for Catholicism, even though Augsburg protected the right of Protestant rulers within the Holy Roman Empire to maintain their faith. Charles V soon abdicated the Holy Roman throne, exhausted from the battles over land, politics, and faith.

English Reformation

The Reformation in England was facilitated by close trading ties with Germany as well as by one man in particular, William Tyndale, a follower of Luther's who translated the Bible into English, which helped the cause of Protestantism gain a foothold in England. **King Henry VIII** was initially suspicious of the Protestants, but used them in his fight for political power with the Catholic Church and Emperor Charles V. What really prompted Henry to split from the Catholic Church was his desire to divorce his first wife, **Catherine of Aragon**, who was not able to produce a son. Henry's advisers convinced him to take control legally of the Church in England, which allowed Henry to divorce his wife and to gain political autonomy from both Rome and the emperor. Henry seized Catholic Church lands and eventually was named head of the Church of England. During his reign, neither Protestant nor Catholic forces gained the upper hand, leaving England in an unsure position when Henry died in 1547. Henry's son Edward favored the Protestants. Under Edward's rule, the *Book of Common Prayer* was introduced in 1549, becoming the core liturgical text of England's Protestants.

Edward died in 1553, bringing Henry VIII's Catholic daughter **Mary Tudor** to the throne. Mary purged the court of Protestants and actively persecuted them throughout England, earning the nickname "Bloody Mary" in the process. She died after ruling for only five years and was succeeded by her half sister Elizabeth in 1558. **Elizabeth I** reinvigorated the Anglican Church established by her father and instituted the "**Elizabethan Settlement**," according to which the Anglican Church was dominant, and both Catholic and Protestant sects were allowed to exist.

The Reformation developed differently in different regions, each focusing on one aspect of reform more than another. In England, the Reformation instituted more political and monarchical changes and facilitated the rise of the Anglican Church. In France, Calvinists focused more on the behavior of the clergy. In Scandinavian countries, Lutheranism became the dominant religion, championed by kings who had long desired a break from Rome.

We'll See Your Reforms and Raise You: The Catholic Counter-Reformation

The Protestant Reformation motivated the Catholic Church to instigate reform within the Church itself. Catholic reformers did not believe that leaving the Church was the answer to the Church's problems; the problems had to be tackled from within by those loyal to the faith. The **Jesuit** order, founded in 1534 by Ignatius Loyola, was the Catholic Church's most effective tool in bringing Protestants back into the Catholic Church. The Jesuits functioned autonomously within the Church, reaching out to the people with their well-developed education programs.

The Catholic Church sought to bring Protestants back into the fold at the **Council of Trent**, which met three times between 1545 and 1563. However, the end result of the council was not the desired reconciliation with the Protestants; instead, the council ended by reconfirming the authority of the papacy, urging reform from within, and condemning some of the basic tenets of Protestant faith.

The Era of Religious Warfare

The potent combination of competing faiths, political and territorial claims, and economic difficulties among the common people launched mid-16th-century Europe into nearly a century of **religious warfare**. The Spanish were among the first to suffer the effects of religious schism. In 1556, when **Philip II**, son of the former Holy Roman Emperor Charles V, became king, he inherited the Netherlands as a territory of Spain from his father. Philip, who like his father was loyal to Rome, tried to maintain tight political and religious control over the domain, which angered local elites. Philip's appointment of Catholic bishops in the Netherlands and his policy of confiscating land from Protestants—even from the nobility—pushed the Netherlands into revolt. At the same time, Spain tried to go to war with England over England's tolerance of Protestants but suffered costly defeats; it was forced to give independence to its Dutch holdings, and the Netherlands became a sovereign republic in 1648. By the early 17th century, Spain was in a state of decline.

England was luckier in this era, avoiding the religious civil wars that were tearing other countries apart. Elizabeth I's long reign (1558–1603) was the source of that stability. The Catholic threat was pretty much ended when the English defeated the Spanish Armada sent by Philip. However, religious dissent still existed in England; it just didn't threaten the crown. The **Puritans**, a Protestant sect that opposed Elizabeth's position as head of the Anglican Church, were somewhat dangerous to the political status quo because some of the most powerful members of the aristocracy were Puritans, which meant that Puritanism was represented in Parliament. When Elizabeth died in 1603, the precarious stability she was able to maintain also died.

In France, civil wars took their toll as Catholic and Protestant factions fought for control over the crown. Eventually relative stability was found by Henry IV (ruled 1589 to 1610), who converted to Catholicism to keep Catholic forces (backed by the Spanish) under control—in his words, "Paris is worth a Mass." However, Henry issued the **Edict of Nantes** in 1589, which protected the Protestant minority in France (known as the Huguenots), but also allowed them to arm themselves. Eventually the Peace of Alais (1629) established a new balance, protecting Huguenots' rights to practice their faith but disarming them, meaning they were less of a threat to the crown.

Germany: Thirty Years War (1618–1648)

Fought between the Hapsburg dynasty, which ruled Austria and Spain, and the competitors for the German crown, the **Thirty Years War** (1618–1648) was, like many clashes of this era, primarily a religious conflict between Protestant and Catholic. The war didn't end the tensions in Germany; conflicts continued for several centuries after the formal end of the war. By the time the war ended, the Protestants had gained the upper hand.

The **Peace of Westphalia**, which ended the war, had a number of important consequences for the royal houses of Europe. The Holy Roman Empire was weakened, and Germany was decentralized. Spain was already weakened by the revolt in the Netherlands and the war with England. At the end of a century of religious warfare, Sweden and France were the winners, becoming the dominant powers in the coming century. Political and geographic changes also came on the heels of Westphalia; fixed borders were drawn, and the citizens living within those boundaries were subject primarily to the ruler of that land, rather than to the Church or neighboring rulers. In other words, the peace furthered the development of modern nation-states.

Russia: A Sleeping Giant Finally Wakes

Once again, before we move on to the next big section, we pay a visit to Russia. When we last left, the Russians were just casting off Mongol influence. Indeed, Russia didn't really exist as a world power until it began to modernize and reach out to the West. When Ivan III broke the "Mongol yoke" in 1480, he ushered in the growth of Muscovite princes and expansion of Muscovite power in the next two centuries. But it was **Peter the Great** (who ruled until 1725) who deliberately turned Russia toward the West, gathering information during his own travels to the West and inviting Western advisers to Russia to help him modernize nearly every aspect of Russian government, military, and society. He built St. Petersburg on the shores of the Baltic Sea to serve as a "window to the West" and to spearhead efforts to control Baltic Sea trade after defeating Sweden, Russia's most dangerous enemy, in the Great Northern War, which ended in 1721 with the Treaty of Nystad. Russia also began its aggressive expansion westward, seizing lands from Sweden and Poland. There were three exceptions to Russia's turn toward westward influence: Russia remained Orthodox, capitalism was repressed in favor of state control over the economy and trade, and the feudal system of **serfdom** continued to rule the domestic economy.

Political Revolutions: 1688 to 1789

In the late 17th and for much of the 18th century, political revolutions in Europe and its holdings continued the trends seen in previous centuries. Revolutionaries rejected the divine rights of kings and fought for increased secular power at great cost to church power. By doing so, political revolutionaries put more power in the hands of the common people (non-aristocracy) and solidified the nation-state as the form of government in ascendance.

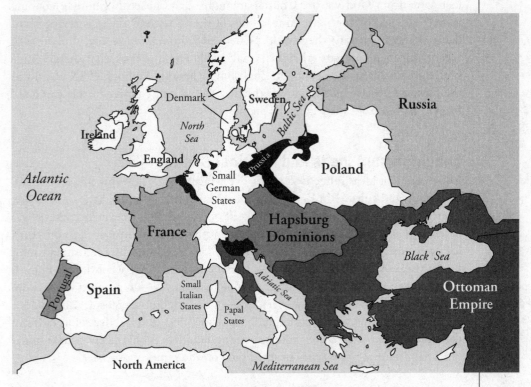

Absolute Monarchies c. 1650

Three revolutions serve as touchstones to help us trace the development of secular power in this era. First was the **Glorious Revolution** in England (1688), which confirmed the power of the Parliament over the monarch. Next, the **American Revolution** (1776)—a revolution of the elite on the fringes of colonial rule—abolished the monarchy in the colonies altogether, bringing a new, elected democratic government to power. Finally, there is the **French Revolution** (1789), a revolt against entrenched power structures in the most powerful nation in Europe. This was a revolution not of the elite, but of the poor and the middle class against all forms of privilege held by the Church and the aristocracy; the government in France eventually developed into a constitutional monarchy.

Setting the Stage: The Enlightenment

The revolutions that changed the political face of monarchic Europe didn't come out of nowhere. They were the natural progression of political, economic, and philosophical development, and were particularly influenced by the ideas of Enlightenment thinkers. The **Enlightenment** signaled a shift toward secular ideas, a trend that had begun with the Reformation. The Enlightenment continued the development of ideas that supported secular power at the expense of ecclesiastical power and the rights of the individual over those of the aristocracy. This mindset is a logical extension of the Reformation idea of individual salvation, which is the heart of Protestant belief and in agreement with the individualistic ethos of the classical world.

Authority came to mean something very different than it had previously; it didn't just come from God via the Church anymore. Laws governing human conduct weren't dictated by the spiritual teachings of the Church or the self-serving mandates of the aristocrats; they could be derived from *human reason*. This in turn meant that man had **natural rights**, unalienable and universal, that should guide both individual and state conduct. Englishman **Thomas Hobbes** (1588–1679) was the most influential spokesman for the idea that a king's power to rule came not from God, but from the will of the people.

Enlightenment Ideas and Political Change

Enlightenment ideas influenced nearly every facet of life: government, economics, education, and culture. In England, political liberalism promoted the right to life, liberty, and property most importantly. Property was significant because it was believed that citizens gave the government authority to control society in return for protection of citizens' property rights, an idea developed by Englishman **John Locke** (1632–1704). This is called the **social contract**. Also, according to English law, a citizen is defined as someone who owns property—so property ownership, especially land ownership, was very important. English liberalism also calls for minimal government intervention into the economic and social lives of its citizens; the state's power is restricted to establishing boundaries that allow people to express their natural rights without infringing on the rights of others.

"To understand political power aright, and derive from it its original, we must consider what estate all men are naturally in, and that is, a state of perfect freedom to order their actions, and dispose of their possessions and persons as they think fit, within the bounds of the law of Nature, without asking leave or depending upon the will of any other man."
—John Locke, Second Treatise of Government, 1690

In France, the birthplace of the Enlightenment, arose the *philosophes*, writers and social critics who championed the idea that human reason should be the basis for solving the problems of society and creating a social order that benefited nearly everyone. Human progress could happen only with the constant development and expansion of knowledge, a theme which encouraged the support of scientific study and the spread of education to those beyond the nobility. The greatest Enlightenment thinkers all shared this belief in the power of knowledge and the perfectibility of human society through the political application of human reason: Montesquieu, Condorcet, Diderot, Rousseau, and Voltaire are among the most influential of the era.

However, the Enlightenment ideas did not necessarily mean the end of monarchies; the idea of the **enlightened despot**—one who was autocratic but was supported by the people—was popular at the time. Democracy was an idea that did not really take off until the 18th century.

The Glorious Revolution

In the late 1600s there was great unrest in England regarding the religious tolerance of **King James II of England**, a Catholic with close ties to France. Those higher up in the political spheres of England were concerned over these troubling facts, and their concern turned to outright alarm when the King issued a male heir, redirecting the line of succession from Mary, the wife of William of Orange and a Protestant. With the support of many from both parties of Parliaments, the Whigs and the Tories, William built political and financial support in order to overthrow the king and assume the throne in 1688.

This revolution, although short and relatively light on bloodshed, had a lasting, and a very detrimental effect, on Catholicism in England. The chance of Catholicism being re-established in any meaningful way in England, at least compared to its past dominance, was completely destroyed. Not only were the future hopes of Catholic growth in the country thwarted, but the immediate effects for practicing English Catholics were severe; they were denied the right to vote or to sit in Parliament (a restriction which lasted for more than a century), they were ineligible to obtain commissions in the army, and the monarchy was restricted from either the practice of Catholicism or marriage to a Catholic.

The American Revolution

The American Revolution took place during 1765–1783, during which time the American Colonies that were owned and operated by the British Monarchy, revolted and claimed independence.

Tensions had been building between the colonies and the monarchy for some time, the worst of which were over the heavy duties, or tariffs, and taxes that were placed on the colonies to help raise funds for England, from which the colonies benefited very little. Due to these frustrations, isolated acts of open violence began to occur between the colonists and the militia of England stationed in America, such as the **Boston Massacre**. By July 1775 Britain acknowledged an open rebellion in the colonies and the American Revolution officially started. With the **Declaration of Independence in 1776**, the American colonies made the "irrevocable" break with England and declared that this would be a war of independence. While there were those who were reticent to break from the mother country, due to both cultural ties and concern over her superior resources in conflict, many were in favor of the separation. A recent immigrant from England, **Thomas Paine**, summed up many of these arguments in his pamphlet *Common Sense*, which assailed the monarchy and appealed to the colonists to form a better government.

General George Washington led the American troops against great odds. He was chosen because he had experience in the French and Indian War and because he could draw his home state of Virginia (the largest state) into the war. The British forces were larger in number, better trained, and supported by the wealth of England, the richest and most powerful nation in the world. However, France was a decisive ally for the Americans. From the beginning, France had secretly supplied weapons and goods to the colonists. Not only did France provide the colonists with a navy crucial for victory, but the country's involvement raised the possibility that Britain might have to fight at home.

Finally, Britain no longer thought it worthwhile to fight the American colonies, especially as other European nations placed military pressure on Britain. American independence was established in the **Treaty of Paris** (1783), two years after the final battle at **Yorktown**.

The Origins of *La Révolution*

In 1789, **King Louis XVI** called the **Estates General**, a council of representatives of three sectors of French society, to discuss the severe economic crisis that France had found itself in as a result of war and taxation issues. The Estates General consisted of the *bourgeoisie*, or urban professional and merchant classes (which led the Third Estate—a group consisting of all commoners) with support from some members of the clergy, the nobility (the Second Estate), and the Church (the First Estate). However, it wasn't just the king who wanted something out of the meeting; the nobility wanted to use the Estates General to create a constitutional government. The Third Estate, however, felt that the nobles were about as bad as the king and the Church. When excluded from the meetings, the Third Estate met on its own and declared itself the **National Assembly** speaking for the people of France. The National Assembly took an oath not to dissolve until a constitution had been written, an event known as the Tennis Court Oath, named after the site where the Assembly convened.

Under pressure, the king ceded power to the National Assembly. The National Assembly then abolished feudalism, noble privilege, and tithes paid to the Church, and issued the *Declaration of the Rights of Man and the Citizen*, which proclaimed the equality of all men in the eyes of the law and the power of the law above any other power. Basic freedoms of religion, speech, thought, and due process under the law were guaranteed to all. The National Assembly eventually produced a constitution in 1791, establishing a constitutional monarchy.

However, things devolved from there. The Assembly was disbanded, and a new National Convention based on universal male suffrage was elected. The Convention soon voted to execute the king, an event that began the "**Second Revolution.**" The aristocracy was actively persecuted as part of a campaign of widespread violence now known as "**The Reign of Terror.**" France was already involved in battles with neighboring countries that both harbored French nobles, and had their own interest in taking advantage of internal conflict to attack France.

The Coming of Napoleon

Napoleon Bonaparte was a general brought in by the Convention to protect it, but Napoleon had other plans. Staging a *coup d'état*, he proclaimed himself First Consul of the Convention and essentially became the head of the government in 1799. The **Napoleonic Wars** pitted France against a coalition led by Austria, Britain (which dominated shipping at the time), and Russia, which supported Britain. Having beaten almost all of his continental opponents, Napoleon lost to Britain at sea at the **Battle of Trafalgar** in 1805, preventing an invasion of England. Also, his invasion of Russia in 1812 was a disaster, costing hundreds of thousands of French soldiers' lives. In France's colonies, Saint-Domingue/**Haiti**, under the leadership of **Pierre Toussaint L'Ouverture**, revolted against its colonial oppressors and, after a decade of bloodshed, gained its independence in 1804, the first successful slave revolt in history. Napoleon eventually was deposed and exiled, and Louis XVIII was installed as king.

"My principle is: France first...."
—Napoleon Bonaparte

Technological Revolution: Industrialization and the Rise of Nations

By the beginning of the 19th century, the **Industrial Revolution** pushed Western European nations—particularly Great Britain—beyond China as the production centers of the globe. The Industrial Revolution affected nearly every aspect of life. Machines were developed that increased production across the board. Agriculture boomed thanks to mechanized methods of sowing seeds and gathering crops. Industrial machines enabled the **mass production** of textiles and durable goods. India, which before the Industrial Revolution manufactured cotton textiles for Britain, was supplanted by Britain once the British had the technology to produce fabrics on their own. India became like other colonies: a source of raw materials, but not manufactured goods. The **cotton gin**, which separated cotton fiber from the pods, revolutionized cotton production in the United States, boosting production and enriching plantation owners.

Slavery and Colonies

Haiti's declaration of independence in 1804 threatened the slave trade across the Caribbean and in the Americas. Britain ended slavery in 1833 in its empire, and the United States stopped importing slaves in 1808 (although slavery continued to be practiced until the end of the Civil War in 1865). The slave trade finally ended once it was abolished in the remaining countries that supported it: Puerto Rico (1876), Cuba (1886), and Brazil (1888).

Other inventions that changed the way goods were moved and people lived include the coal-powered locomotive, which spread like wildfire across Britain and the United States. The **railroads** opened up the western United States to settlers at a pace that had until then been impossible because of the great distances and harsh environments involved. Steam-powered ships could now cross the Atlantic much faster than had previously been possible. In the second half of the 19th century, more inventions arose: steel, chemicals, artificial fertilizers, plastics, and electricity, which, in turn, gave birth to even more innovations. Warfare was changed forever with the development of steel-hulled warships, rapid-fire guns, and heavy artillery.

Women and Industrialization

Working-class women moved into jobs early in the Industrial Revolution, but they were often displaced by men with families, who got paid a higher wage. These women were forced to work any jobs they could to bring in money, including jobs as domestic servants, textile workers, or in the worst cases, as prostitutes. Middle-class women focused their efforts more within the home, but eventually moved into "respectable" "pink-collar" jobs as nurses, shop assistants, and teachers. In the industrial era, women's opportunities to own and operate businesses were much fewer than in previous eras, because of the increasing concentration of economic power in men and the greater need for credit to run a viable industrial business.

Demographic Changes

With the arrival of industrial technologies that mechanized many fields of production that had previously been purely manual, small-scale farming and production along traditional lines became less and less feasible. As a result, many rural folk moved into urban areas to seek jobs in manufacturing, changing the demographic profile of many nations and creating a new class: the urban proletariat.

Industrial giants arose, creating a small but powerful class of industrialists whose economic and political power rivaled—and often surpassed—that of old-world aristocracy. Populations boomed, especially in cities. Women and children joined the industrial workforce in numbers unprecedented in history. Immigration to the United States, Australia, and other former colonies allowed those societies to grow quickly. People lived longer thanks to better hygiene and advancements in medicine, and families could have fewer children, more of whom would survive until adulthood.

But while those who owned the means of production—capitalists—saw their wealth and prestige grow exponentially, the working classes that manned the factories were less rewarded. Wages were low, working conditions dangerous, and urban slums both unsafe and unsanitary. Despite the claim that "a rising tide lifts all boats," the working classes definitely were among the losers in the Industrial Revolution.

The Rise of Labor Unions and Socialism

In reaction to the horrid conditions and abuses suffered by the urban working classes, reforms were instituted in many industrial nations. Labor laws were instituted in Britain and the United States to create safer working conditions, bring an end to child labor, and provide more protections for workers in general.

Labor unions arose in the absence of—or sometimes accompanying—reform, providing workers with collective bargaining power against the industrial ownership.

The capitalist system had created a class hierarchy that shared unhealthy parallels with the old aristocratic system, in which power was held by a select few and the vast majority of people were relatively powerless in comparison. Even in democratic countries such as the United States, the freedoms that were supposedly possessed by everyone were all but illusory to those at the bottom of the class hierarchy. In response to growing inequality in Germany, a new philosophy of protest arose: **socialism**. The fathers of socialism, **Karl Marx** and Friedrich Engels, condemned the abuses of the capitalists and called for a revolution of the working class against their capitalist oppressors. In Marx's view, the **proletariat**—the urban workers—were the ones who made capitalism possible because they provided the labor, without which industry could not survive. Their call for revolution among the proletariat did not happen quite as Marx and Engels predicted. Socialist revolution would not break out until the 20th century, and oddly enough, not (as had been predicted) in those countries where industrialism had made the most gains. Instead, revolution would come in 1917 in Russia, a nation still under a monarchy and not nearly as industrialized as most of the rest of Europe. Subsequent socialist revolutions (in China, for example) have also tended to take place in developing, rather than firmly industrialized, nations.

Nationalism Rears Its (Not So Ugly?) Head

At the same time that industrialization was revolutionizing much of European and American society, Europe's nation-states entered an age of nationalist fervor. Nationalism, formally speaking, is a belief that the nation exists and that it centers on the state and sometimes also a distinct territory, shared language, or shared culture. However, it usually entails the belief that one's own nation is superior to others and ought to be more powerful than other nations. The waning imperial powers—the Ottomans in particular—lost control of their holdings to nationalist separatist movements. Regions that had never before been unified countries—Italy and Germany—formed unified states, and France ended its monarchy once and for all.

At the **Treaty of Vienna**, which ended the Napoleonic Wars in 1815, the participants, led by Austrian minister and prince **Klemens von Metternich**, tried to set limits on nationalism in Europe, but in the end, the gesture was in vain. Prussia, Poland, Italy, Hungary, and Ireland all struggled for and won independence from imperial powers. The age of the nation had arrived.

"Let the ruling classes tremble at a Communist Revolution. The proletarians have nothing to lose but their chains. They have a world to win. Workingmen of all countries, unite!"
—Karl Marx, *The Communist Manifesto*, 1848

Unity at Last!
Unlike England, Spain, and France, which had been unified countries for a long time, Germany and Italy achieved political unification only in the 19th century.

THE MIDDLE EAST: THE EUROPEANS ARE COMING!

The last we checked in on the Ottomans, they were attacking Vienna in 1529 and threatening the coasts of Italy and Spain. By 1566, the **Ottoman Empire** was at its height, controlling North Africa, Egypt, Greece, the Balkans (southeastern Europe), Anatolia, Mesopotamia, the Holy Land, and the edges of the Arabian Peninsula including the holy cities of Islam, Mecca and Medina. The Ottomans controlled the Mediterranean Sea from their capital Istanbul (formerly Constantinople), which they captured from the Byzantine empire in 1453. The city became the showpiece of the Ottomans; the Hagia Sophia, the grand Christian church, was converted to one of largest mosques in all of Islam. The glory of Constantinople was a reflection of the glory of the Ottomans. Until the 17th century, the Ottomans were among the most powerful empires in Europe and the Mediterranean.

Although the Ottoman Empire lasted more than 600 years, it also had its weaknesses. Succession was a particular problem because of the Muslim rules followed—the death of any sultan could spark a struggle over succession. The empire's decline came as a result of the overextension of the empire, the costs of supporting and administering distant borders, and rampant corruption among officials. Other traditions also acted to weaken the empire: for protection, possible successors were kept isolated in the palace until one was called to service. Unfortunately, this isolation meant that new rulers were inexperienced in the real world and not as effective as they could be. The Ottomans also fell behind Europe militarily; the **Janissaries**, who began as elite bodyguards for the sultan, had gained much power on their own and, therefore, stood in the way of any military changes that would improve the army but weaken their own position of power.

The Ottomans' first significant loss was the naval Battle of Lepanto against the Spanish and Italians in 1571, where the empire lost control over the eastern Mediterranean. The Portuguese challenged the Ottomans in the Indian Ocean, weakening the Turks' advantageous (and lucrative) trade with India. Their last siege of Vienna in 1683 was unsuccessful, and losses to neighboring Persia in the 18th century didn't help either. By the end of the 19th century, the empire was also weakened by nationalist movements in the Balkans and came to be known as the "sick man of Europe." In the end, conservatism, inflation, and lack of innovation at home, partnered with the rise of European technology, pushed the Ottomans toward decline.

Asia and the Pacific: Colonial Holdings by 1900

British—Most of India, Bangladesh, Pakistan, Myanmar (Burma), Australia, New Zealand
French—Indochina (Vietnam, Cambodia, Laos)
Dutch—Indonesia
American—The Philippines

THE FAR EAST: ASIA SLOWLY OPENS ITS DOORS

When we last left our discussions of China, the Ming dynasty had rid China of Mongol dominance and had ushered in an era of relative prosperity. However, as with most dynasties, the Ming could not last forever. Invaders from the north (Manchuria) set upon the Ming in the mid-17th century and established the **Qing dynasty**, which would last from 1644 until 1911.

The invaders—the **Manchu**—did not seek to build a new China or a new way of governing; instead, they adopted Chinese language and culture and preserved the existing system. However, over time, some of the changes they did make to the economy and tax system caused the gap between rich and poor to grow even wider. Other weaknesses appeared: The civil service exam system, which used to find and train the best and brightest to serve the state, became riddled with cheating. Those with money could buy their way to privileges and powerful posts. The Confucian system—which was based on the idea that the rich and privileged should use that power to help the common good—was undermined (to the extent that it had ever really been followed), and the government impoverished itself as the powerful steered public funds for their own use. None of these changes were unique to the Qing, but they were all taking their toll by the time the Europeans arrived on the scene in force.

On top of all this, the Manchu-led Qing dynasty let much of the country's infrastructure go to seed, causing massive losses of life because of flooding in heavily populated areas. Something clearly had to change.

Who Can It Be Now? European Contacts with China

When the Chinese came in contact with Europe, they expected Europeans to pay tribute to the emperor like everyone else, a requirement that didn't go over well with the British in particular. After the Napoleonic Wars, trade between China and Europe increased. In 1793, Qing rulers allowed Europeans to pay for goods in silver only, depleting stockpiles of silver in Europe. In reaction to its massive silver depletion, England tried to trade with opium instead. However, the Qing rulers quickly realized that the easy availability of opium only damaged Chinese society, as millions, from the poorest to the richest Chinese, became addicted to the drug.

In reaction, the Qing tried to ban the opium trade in 1838; in response, the English declared war. The **First Opium War** (1839) brought together in battle the huge but antiquated Chinese military and the smaller but far more technologically advanced British navy. Despite their superior numbers, the Chinese were defeated and forced to sign the **Treaty of Nanking**, which opened China to European trade, demanded reparation payments, and ceded **Hong Kong** to England.

The treaty sparked rebellions across China against the Qing. England tried to demand more privileges, sparking a **Second Opium War** (1856–1860), which also ended in a defeat of the Chinese. China's rulers' inability to fend off the encroachment of foreigners into China caused massive revolts across the country. The **Taiping Rebellion** (1851–1864) was among the bloodiest civil wars in history, led by a fanatical Christian convert who amassed thousands in the cause to bring down the Manchus as well as many core symbols of Chinese traditional civilization. The rebellion was eventually suppressed after much loss of life and resources, but the Manchu rulers still refused to institute many of the needed reforms that would bring China into the modern age and help it reach its full potential as a world power. The imperial rulers and the gentry stubbornly adhered to tradition, despite China's defeats at the hands of other countries that had chosen the road to modernity.

Kowtow to the Man
The term "kowtow" comes to us from this time period. All people were expected to *kowtow* (bow down to the ground in a sign of submission) in the presence of the Chinese Emperor. British traders had trouble with this, since it would mean acknowledging their King as a subject of the Emperor.

The Boxer Rebellion: Nothing to Do with Boxing

Anti-foreigner sentiment was at its height by the end of the 19th century, creating the catalyst for the **Boxer Rebellion** of 1899 to 1901, a rebellion against foreign intervention in China. The targets: Christians and foreigners. Although the rebellion was started by an independent group, the Qing government supported the rebels. The Boxer Rebellion is treated differently in different versions of Chinese history. For some, it is a rebellion, a negative act of violence (and one which ultimately hurt China militarily). For others, such as the communists, it is an uprising, a positive act of patriotic defense. But at the time, the presence of dominating foreigners in China was an offense to many, but an offense their military weaknesses forced them to endure. It wasn't just Europeans who threatened China, either—the **Sino-Japanese War** of 1894 to 1895 saw the rise of Japan as a military force in Asia thanks to the Meiji Reforms of 1866 to 1868, which led to the adoption of Western economic and technological innovations there. With the example of Japan just across the water, China's humbling defeats before foreign powers were all the more humiliating and galling. The time was ripe for Western-educated Chinese yearning for true reform to band together to bring down the Qing for good. **Sun Yat-Sen**, one of the period's main revolutionaries, was typical in this regard. The Qing dynasty ended with Sun's **Xinhai Revolution of 1911**, and was replaced by a republic.

Overall, China had experiences similar to Japan and the Islamic civilizations that were impacted by the West during crucial moments of internal instability, events that made them vulnerable to pressures to modernize or be enveloped by Europe's advanced technologies, economies, and militaries. In all these cases, the societies were in continuous contact with Westerners; it was only in moments of internal crisis that the Western influence could no longer be resisted. However, the technology that all of these civilizations gained from the West helped them enter the modern age. Different countries had different degrees of control over how much Western advancement they would accept. China was in a weaker position than Japan in this regard.

India

The **Mughal Empire** was founded in the 1520s by Babur, a man descended from both the Mongols and the Turks. After losing control of his own lands in Central Asia, he moved east into India to plunder the land for its riches, which he hoped would fund his return to his homeland and his fight to gain it back. Eventually he gave up the quest to regain his home turf and turned his efforts completely to capturing northern India on the early 1500s. His grandson **Akbar** (d. 1605), though, was the one who really expanded the power and prestige of the empire, building a military and administrative infrastructure that would serve India for centuries to come, and improving relations between Muslim and Hindu populations. His regime also saw a number of reforms in the treatment of women, including a ban on child marriages and *sati*, the ritual burning of widows on the funeral pyres of their husbands.

The 17th century saw the solid growth of India in world trade, particularly on the basis of its cotton goods, which Indians produced in abundance and dyed in innovative ways. Akbar's successors ushered in an era of artistic achievements in art and architecture of considerable note. Among those successors is Shah Jahan, best known as the man who built the **Taj Mahal** in the mid-17th century as a tomb for his beloved consort. Shah Jahan's son Aurangzeb extended the reach of the Mughal Empire to cover nearly all of the subcontinent, but in doing so, he neglected upkeep on the administrative structures that had become dangerously overextended. He also added to the instability of the empire by actively persecuting Hindus. The Mughal Empire came to an end in 1707, disintegrating as a result of sectarian fighting among rival powers, including the **Marathas**, a Hindu ethnic group.

The Role of Europeans in India

During the 16th century, to counteract Portuguese traders who were monopolizing sea lanes in the Indian Ocean, the English and the Dutch set up trading companies based in India. They built factories there to produce goods that were then shipped to the West. The British East India Company, the Dutch East India Company, and the French East India Company all had factories and Indian communities supporting them. They were often welcomed by Indians, who hoped their presence would help control the Portuguese. The French and British, however, became more and more involved in local politics and wanted to apply their own laws within their jurisdictions in India. The British East India Company even had its own troops, known as **sepoys**, to defend British interests and holdings in India.

The British influence grew over time beyond just the holdings of British traders; the trading companies wanted more land. Eventually, the British-held trading companies moved to expand their control over India in a series of battles with regional princes, which the British, though outnumbered, usually won. Between the 1750s and the 1850s, the British government took control over most of the trading companies' holdings to stem corruption, and thus, Britain came to control much of India, which became part of the British empire. (During this period, one refers to the **raj**, or British political establishment, in India.) Unlike many other colonies, where Europeans outnumbered native peoples, India remained Indian for the most part, although the British resided there, running business and governing the colonies.

The Indians, like other populations who fell sway to a colonial power, did gain some benefits (although many didn't see it that way). The British introduced a formal education system based on the English model, imported various technologies such as the telegraph and railroads, and ended for good the ritual of *sati*. But in the end, being subjugated to a foreign power in one's homeland—a fate shared by many in Asia, Africa, and the Americas—was a state of existence that could last only so long. In the next chapter, we will discuss the independence movements of the 20th century that freed many colonials from their European masters.

Vocab Time!
Sati (or "suttee") was the custom of Hindu widows burning themselves to death (presumably willingly) on the funeral pyre of their husbands as an indication of marital devotion.

Japan

The 16th century in Japan opens with Japan suffering from civil war. Power was diffused throughout the country in the hands of the **daimyo**, Japanese feudal families. It was during this period of instability that Portuguese traders made first contact with the Japanese, introducing **firearms** into Japan in the 1540s. The introduction of Western military technology played an important role in the rise of the first of a series of military leaders in Japan who helped lead the country to unity. Oda Nobunaga was the first such leader, who adopted Western technology and used the arquebus, a precursor of the modern rifle, to great advantage in defeating a much more numerous enemy.

Nobunaga ended the existing shogunate and managed to unify much of central Japan under his rule. After Nobunaga died in battle against a neighboring daimyo, his best general, Toyotomi Hideyoshi, stepped up, taking control of all of Japan by 1590. Having done so, Hideyoshi then tried to move beyond Japan, launching attacks into Korea when he died in 1598. One of Hideyoshi's vassals, a warrior of humble birth named Tokugawa Ieyasu, succeeded Hideyoshi to take control of Japan and, after pulling troops out of Korea, was named shogun by the emperor, an event that ushered in the **Tokugawa shogunate**.

> ### Emperors, Shoguns…Who Runs Japan?
>
> The Japanese **emperor** historically held only a spiritual role; the emperor was literally considered a descendant of the Sun God on earth. Before the Meiji Restoration (more on that soon), the emperor legitimized those who actually ruled; the emperor did not himself rule Japan.
>
> The term **shogun** is a military title that more or less means "general." A shogun may rule a military government or just an administrative area known as a *bafuku*. Much of Japanese history after the 8th century is split into periods named after the reigning shogun.

Tokugawa Shogunate: Why We Care

The Tokugawa shogunate left an important legacy for Japan. First, the capital was moved to the town of Edo, now Tokyo. Second, it was during this period that Japan all but closed its doors to the West. Soon after the Portuguese landed in Japan, Christian missionaries spread across Japan, scoring thousands of converts. They were welcomed by Nobunaga, who used the missionaries to defuse the power of the Buddhist monks who opposed him. However, by the time of Hideyoshi, although there were great benefits to be gained from Western technology and trade, the Japanese were worried that the Europeans' next step would be invasion. By the 1580s, Hideyoshi began to actively persecute the Christian missionaries. Tokugawa banned them outright by 1614, and Japanese converts were forced to renounce their faith.

This banning of Christianity in Japan was the first step toward what would by the mid-17th century develop into Japan's almost total isolation from the West. Japan under Tokugawa would trade only with the Chinese, the Koreans, and the Dutch. No Western goods could come into Japan; Western traders had to pay for Japanese goods in precious metals. The Japanese did not completely cut themselves off; they kept in contact with West on their own terms and borrowed what ideas and technology they needed. What was important was that the Japanese were in control of what aspects of the West came into their country.

Japan Is Opened Up to the West

During the first half of the 19th century Japan found itself weakened internally by economic problems that, in turn, caused social unrest—just in time for American Commodore **Matthew Perry** to land near Tokyo and threaten to attack the city unless the Japanese let the Americans have access to Japanese ports. Many Westerners had been trying to open Japan to Western trade and had always been rebuffed; but this time the Japanese were outgunned, and were forced to concede to American forces. Once that happened, other countries gained access as well. The final opening of Japan to the West caused much upheaval in Japanese society, with shoguns, samurai, and various daimyos all looking for a way to strengthen their own claims to power. Opening to the West also laid bare the simple truth that Japan was in many ways technologically inferior to the West. The year 1866 saw true civil war break out; the war ended two years later with the naming of a new emperor, an event which ushered in the **Meiji Restoration.**

The Meiji Modernizes Japan

The Meiji government did away with the feudal system and centralized political and administrative power. The samurai were first converted to ambassadors who traveled to the West to gather knowledge to bring back to Japan, but they eventually became opponents of the government when a change to the tax system impoverished most of them. The Meiji government replaced the samurai with a normal army and eventually adopted a parliamentary system modeled after England's.

Industrially, Japan grew by leaps and bounds in the second half of the 19th century. The government actively supported the development of industry, modern agriculture, technological education, and transportation infrastructure. The population boomed and public education was instituted, but Japan was missing one thing that put it at a disadvantage as an industrial nation: natural resources. Japan eventually went to war with the Chinese (the **Sino-Japanese War** of 1894–1895) and the Russians (the **Russo-Japanese War** of 1904) over control of Korea, which Japan annexed as a result of its victories. And in an effort to balance traditional culture and Western influence, the government actively promoted a policy of Japanese nationalism centered on the figure of the emperor. As a result, Japan did not suffer the kinds of revolutionary pressures that other nations did in the early 20th century.

THE AMERICAS: INDEPENDENCE IN THE 19TH CENTURY

The Americas continued to be a source of wealth for the Spanish, who controlled most of Latin America until the early 19th century, when all countries in Latin America—inspired by the revolutions in France, North America, and Haiti—declared independence from their colonial masters, pretty much at once. Revolutions in Latin America were led for the most part by the Creole descendants of Spanish colonists, even though earlier attempts at revolt were led by native leaders. Leaders of successful movements include **Simón Bolívar** (Venezuela), Fathers Miguel Hidalgo and José María Morelos (Mexico), José de San Martín (Argentina), Bernardo O'Higgins (Chile), and Antonio José de Sucre (Ecuador).

In the end, the poor in many countries that gained independence from colonial powers traded one dominating power for another. The Creole elite comprised only a very small portion of the population, but they held nearly all the wealth and power. The economies of the region remained largely agrarian, leaving little room for changes to the system. Warfare was rampant in the newly independent states, giving rise to military strongmen who were powerful enough to keep the native and slave populations in check. The Americas' colonial heritage continued to be a challenge internally and internationally, as they still had to contend with the influence of Portugal, Spain, and an ever more powerful United States. **Mexico**, in particular, lost an enormous amount of territory to an expansionist Texas in the early 19th century. Brazil was fairly unique in avoiding the internal breakdown, having been left as a monarchy in the hands of a member of the Portuguese royal family.

AFRICA: THE SHORT END OF THE COLONIAL STICK

The Americas are not the only ones, of course, to have a history so heavily affected by external forces. The history of Africa from 1500 to 1900 is dominated by two institutions perhaps above all others: slavery and colonialism. Before the arrival of the Europeans, northern Africa had benefited from trade with Muslims, and many Africans had converted to Islam. The Muslims did not colonize Africa, although the Ottomans did make North Africa a part of their empire. The Europeans had a different idea in mind; at first they traded with established tribes and kingdoms in Africa, but soon relations turned more aggressive. Christian missionaries tried to convert Africans, and attempts were made by Europeans to replace Africans as controllers of trade. Over time, Europeans colonized Africa to benefit from the wealth of the land and, in the 19th century, to gain strategic advantage over other nations.

But slavery was always a central element to European contacts with Africa. As Europeans began establishing plantations in their Atlantic and American holdings, the slave trade grew exponentially. Slaves were transported to the Americas (a trip known as the **Middle Passage**) and to the Caribbean, but also to the Middle East, the Indian Ocean, and other parts of Africa. In the early days of the slave trade, most were sent to Spanish holdings to work in mines or on sugar plantations. Many died on the voyage, and many more died under the harsh control of colonial slave owners. Later, the trade grew more rapidly in Brazil and the Caribbean, where slaves constituted the vast majority of the population. Despite the importance of slavery to American history, slavery there never reached the heights that it did in Brazil and the Caribbean. By the 17th century, most slaves came from West Africa.

Each European nation that was part of the slave trade established forts in trade centers on the coasts of Africa. Once they gathered the slaves—often with the help of other Africans—the Europeans boarded them onto ships for transport to colonial holdings.

Africans Enslaving Africans

Many African societies had a tradition of enslaving others before the Europeans ever arrived, and they were hardly alone. Most ancient societies functioned this way, as did many later Middle Eastern societies. Therefore, the appearance of Europeans in search of slaves only fueled a practice that had already pitted tribe against tribe, kingdom against kingdom. Those like the Asante and Dahomey in West Africa who could acquire firearms from the Europeans used those weapons to gain advantage over other tribes as they pushed farther into the interior of the continent in search of more slaves. On Africa's eastern coast, Swahili traders facilitated the slave trade to the Middle East and Asia.

South Africa

The southern tip of Africa was colonized in 1652 by the Dutch East India Company but taken over by the British at the turn of the 19th century (the **Boer Wars**). The Dutch farmers—the **Boers**—moved north to get away from the British, but came into contact with the **Zulu** peoples who were consolidating power and aggressively moving south. Britain suffered great losses during the **Zulu Wars**, but eventually won. The colony of South Africa remained in control of the white settlers and their descendants until the 20th century. White settlers also moved north into other areas of Africa, displacing African natives as they spread. Colonialism in Africa left generations of European descendants who knew no other place as home, a situation which would cause unique problems in the 20th century once independence movements came to Africa.

CHAPTER 8 KEY TERMS, PEOPLE, AND EVENTS

Mercantilism

An economic system in which trade and commerce was controlled by governments so that they could ensure sufficient funding for the crown, wars, and the exploration of the non-European world

Capitalism

An economic system in which the generation of private wealth is paramount. Governments are encouraged to take a laissez-faire approach to trade in order to increase wealth broadly throughout society.

Age of Exploration

Time period from the 15th to 17th centuries during which European nations set out to explore and colonize other parts of the world. This was made possible by advancements in maritime technology and navigational instruments, and it was sustained by the large amounts of wealth European nations acquired at the expense of their colonies.

Joint-stock company

The early predecessor of the modern-day stock market. Investors purchased shares in companies, and received a portion of their profits. Examples are the Muscovy Company and the Dutch East India Company.

Scientific Revolution

A massive shift in the way people thought about the world, from a predominantly theological worldview to one more similar to that of modern science. Thinkers such as Nicolaus Copernicus, Galileo Galilei, Tycho Brahe, Francis Bacon, Johannes Kepler, and Sir Isaac Newton made important contributions to the emerging fields of mathematics, physics, astronomy, biology, and chemistry.

Protestant Reformation

A movement started in the 16th century to curb the power of the Catholic Church and to offer alternative religious and political options to those who wanted them. Major figures include Martin Luther, John Calvin, and Ulrich Zwingli.

"Ninety-Five Theses"

The document that started the Protestant Reformation. Martin Luther nailed it to the door of the Castle Church in Wittenberg, and when the Church responded with punishment, he launched his new movement.

King Henry VIII

King of England (1509–1547) who split from the Roman Catholic Church and founded the Church of England. He is well-known for his six marriages.

Council of Trent

The Catholic Church's response to the Protestant Reformation. The Council of Trent was intended to bring Protestants back into the Church but ended up reconfirming the authority of the papacy and condemning many aspects of the new Protestant faith.

Edict of Nantes

After an era of religious warfare, Henry IV of France issued the Edict of Nantes in 1589 as a protective order for Protestants (called Huguenots) in the country.

Peace of Westphalia

Brought an end the Thirty Years War (1618–1648), weakening Spain, Germany, and the Holy Roman Empire. This opened the door for France to dominate the coming century.

Peter the Great

Responsible for turning Russia toward Western Europe. He modernized almost every aspect of Russian government, military, and society.

American Revolution

War to free the 13 American colonies from English rule. Started with the Declaration of Independence, this war represented one of the first major efforts at establishing a modern nation on the principles of the Enlightenment.

Enlightenment

A major shift in European thought, which emphasized secular authority over ecclesiastical authority and the rights of individuals over those of the aristocracy. The major thinkers of the Enlightenment are Thomas Hobbes, John Locke, and Jean-Jacques Rousseau.

French Revolution

Shortly after the American Revolution, King Louis XVI was dethroned and the National Assembly declared itself the author of a new constitution. This plunged France into an era of chaos, broadly known as "The Reign of Terror."

Napoleonic Wars

The period during which Napoleon Bonaparte declared himself First Consul of the Convention and led France in battle against Austria, Britain, and Russia

Industrial Revolution

By the early 19th century, the Industrial Revolution changed the shape of Western Europe. The invention of machines to do many tasks, and the rise in mass production, had profound impacts on European societies.

Karl Marx

In response to industrialization, Marx introduced the concept of socialism, calling for a revolt of the working class against their capitalist oppressors.

Ottoman Empire

Peaking in the 16th century, the Ottoman Empire struggled to keep up with the Western European nations as they progressed through the Scientific Revolution, Enlightenment, and Industrialization. Although still a significant force, by the 19th century it was referred to as the "sick man of Europe."

Opium Wars

A series of battles and treaties that altered the relationship between England and China. Ultimately, the English gained trade rights in China and the territory of Hong Kong.

Sino-Japanese War

Taking place in 1894–1895, this marked the first sign of Japan as a military force in Asia. It also foreshadowed later Japanese imperialism in the 20th century.

Mughal Empire

Founded in the 1520s by Babur, the Mughal Empire in India lasted for almost 200 years and saw incredible growth in Indian trade and wealth.

Tokugawa Shogunate

During this period, Japan almost completely cut itself off from Western Europe. It still had limited contact through trade, but Tokugawa ensured Japan had control over which aspects of Western culture came into its borders.

Meiji Restoration

This era (post-1866) in Japan saw it modernize quickly. The feudal system was abolished, government was centralized, and samurai were replaced with a normal army.

Simón Bolívar

One of many prominent leaders of Latin American revolts of the 19th century. These movements generally advocated for the rights of the poor, but the resulting governments did not always represent those people.

Middle Passage

This time period in Africa is marked mostly by the slave trade. The Middle Passage refers to the trip across the Atlantic Ocean made by slave ships going from Africa to the Americas.

Summary

○ European colonization of the Americas and continental leaders' desire for greater wealth drove the development of mercantilism, capitalism, and eventually, industrialization. Colonization also drove the African slave trade as well as eventual anticolonial independence movements in North and South America and beyond.

○ The Protestant Reformation permanently eroded the power of the Catholic Church in Europe. Both religious and secular leaders questioned the theological and political authority of the Pope. Furthermore, Protestantism put the power of salvation, as well as vernacular Bibles, into the hands of the common people, leading to an increase in literacy rates.

○ The Enlightenment, a philosophical movement that emphasized reason, empiricism, and philosophy above traditional Christian belief, emerged from the religious turmoil of the Reformation. Once Martin Luther questioned the Church, religious and secular leaders questioned the ecclesiastical and philosophical status quo of Europe. Political philosophers began to talk about such radical ideas as man's natural right to life, liberty, and property. Scientific inquiry began to expand rapidly, especially in mathematics and astronomy. Nicolaus Copernicus developed mathematical theories regarding the revolution of planets and the sun that opposed Christian religious doctrine. The scientific method was developed as philosophers and scholars turned to experiment, documentation, and replication rather than reason alone to establish scientific theories.

○ Newfound religious freedom and development of Enlightenment ideals set the stage for an age of revolution, including the Glorious Revolution of England, the American Revolution, and the French Revolution. As scientific inquiry increased, it gave rise to the Technological Revolution, from which came industrialization and mass production, significantly altering historical trading norms across Europe and the East.

o The Ottoman Empire went from controlling the Mediterranean to barely controlling the holy cities of Mecca and Medina. Over-extension, internal struggles, and external pressures, much like the problems of the late Roman Empire, led to the decline of the last great Muslim empire.

o China adhered to tradition, remaining isolated from the West even after conflicts with Britain in the Opium Wars. Meanwhile, China's neighbor, Japan, took advantage of European influence to modernize rapidly and dominate its neighbors.

o Indian society became dominated by European "East India" companies, as French, Dutch, and British interests vied for control of India's lucrative economic potential. By 1850, Great Britain gained control of the subcontinent, introducing India to British-style government, education, and language.

o After losing colonial possessions in the Americas, the European powers competed for imperial holdings in Africa. France, Germany, Belgium, and England carved up North and sub-Saharan Africa in search of natural resources, including gold and diamonds. African colonization proved far less successful for the Europeans than colonization of the Americas, but Africa would feel the effects of European colonization well into the 20th century.

Chapter 8 Drill

Answers and explanations can be found in Part IV.

1. Which of the following events occurred that helped to precipitate the French Revolution?

   (A) The Dreyfus Affair
   (B) The Third Estate establishing the National Assembly
   (C) The Reign of Terror committed by the aristocracy prompting violent reaction from the French people
   (D) The Treaty of Versailles
   (E) The end of the Hundred Years' War with England

2. One of the most direct results of the Protestant Reformation was

   (A) An increase of scientific inquiry
   (B) The Spanish Inquisition
   (C) The translation of Aristotle's works by Ibn-Rushd
   (D) Thomas Aquinas publishing *Summa Theologica*
   (E) Martin Luther nailing his Ninety-Five Theses to the door of Castle Church

3. Which serves as the best analogy between the feudal systems of Europe and Japan?

   (A) Shogun → Emperor, Daimyo → Lords, Samurai → Knights
   (B) Emperor → Monarch, Daimyo → Lords, Samurai → Knights
   (C) Shogun → Monarch, Daimyo → Lords, Samurai → Knights
   (D) Emperor → Monarch, Samurai → Lords, Daimyo → Vassals
   (E) Shogun → Monarch, Samurai → Lords, Daimyo → Vassals

4. All of the following were reasons Britain engaged in the Opium Wars EXCEPT

   (A) the depletion of silver
   (B) anger over China's attempt to repress opium trade within China
   (C) access to opium through trade with India
   (D) China's refusal to accept tea as form of payment from Britain
   (E) strained trade agreements and diplomatic policies

5. What was the outcome of the Treaty of Vienna?

   (A) An increase in nationalism in central Europe, specifically with the formation of nations such as Poland, Italy, and Hungary
   (B) The end of the attempts of Mongol expansion in central Europe
   (C) The dissolution of the Soviet Union, specifically with the establishment of free nations such as Poland, Ukraine, and Estonia
   (D) The end of World War I
   (E) The end of World War II

"I can well appreciate, Holy Father, that as soon as certain people realize that in these books which I have written about the Revolutions of the spheres of the universe I attribute certain motions to the globe of the Earth, they will at once clamor for me to be hooted off the stage with such an opinion."

6. Who wrote the above quote?

   (A) Thomas Aquinas
   (B) René Descartes
   (C) Galileo Galilei
   (D) Nicolaus Copernicus
   (E) Sir Isaac Newton

"As vividly as it teaches me anything, my own nature teaches me that I have a body, that when I feel pain there is something wrong with this body, that when I am hungry or thirsty it needs food and drink, and so on. So I shouldn't doubt that there is some truth in this."

7. The quote above by René Descartes expresses which philosophy most accurately?

(A) Deism
(B) Empiricism
(C) Rationalism
(D) Marxism
(E) Sufism

8. What was a direct effect of the end of the African Slave trade?

(A) An increase in democracy amongst African nations
(B) The payment of reparations to families affected by slave trade
(C) An increase in European Colonization within the African continent
(D) The immediate cessation of slavery in Europe and the New World
(E) The beginning of the Enlightenment in Europe

9. The *encomienda* system eventually failed for what reason?

(A) The Christian missionaries were successful in their pleas for leniency and humane treatment of the laboring slave class within the system.
(B) The imported African slaves could not adapt quickly enough to the New World.
(C) The Creoles were able to revolt against the Peninsulars and Spanish government and demand full rights and higher wages.
(D) The Dutch and French colonial expansion in South and Central America overtook the Spanish colonies.
(E) The Spanish failed to create a sustainable economic infrastructure within their colonies, overpowering their ability to properly govern them.

10. Which of the following granted French Protestants the right to both practice their religions and to arm themselves?

(A) Edict of Nantes
(B) Treaty of Versailles
(C) Estates General
(D) Tennis Court Oath
(E) Treaty of Paris

11. Which of the following did NOT contribute to the xenophobic instigation of the Boxer Rebellion?

(A) Sino-Japanese War
(B) Treaty of Nanjing
(C) Taiping Rebellion
(D) Manchurian rule
(E) Cultural Revolution

Chapter 9
War and Peace:
1900 to Present

At the turn of the 20th century, the "old world" of absolute monarchs and privileged nobles continually clashed with "new world" ideas of nationalism, industrialism, and new political ideologies. In this era, wars and revolutions caused an irrevocable break between these two worlds.

THE 20TH CENTURY: THE PROGRESS PARADOX

The 20th century began with great promise. The French called the period between 1871 and 1914 the Belle Époque (Beautiful Era), nostalgically recalling it as a time of optimism and peace, when the arts flourished and new discoveries in science unraveled many mysteries of the world. While it was true that European civilization made great progress in productivity, technology, and expansion, it was in many respects analogous to what the American author Mark Twain dubbed the Gilded Age in late-19th-century U.S. society: an era of serious social problems that lay beneath a thin veneer of gold.

With the advancement of science and philosophy came new ways of thinking. Anarchism, socialism, racism, nihilism, and nationalism made for an explosive political environment in which emotion and anxiety dictated policy rather than rationality. Moreover, whereas technology allowed for tremendous growth in European societies, it also harbored the means for previously unthinkable destruction. Barely 40 years after the Wright Brothers made their famous 12-second flight at Kitty Hawk, North Carolina in 1903, an American "Superfortress" bomber flew over 1,500 miles and destroyed an entire city with a single atomic bomb. What began as a century of great promise was unfortunately often met with tragedy as the combination of these new social-political philosophies, or ideologies, combined with the awesome power of the Industrial Revolution marred the century with mind-numbing numbers of victims.

Although primarily a European War, **World War I** had far-reaching consequences beyond the continent. The Ottoman Empire was destroyed and replaced by the new country of Turkey. The non-Turkish remnants of the Ottoman Empire were carved up by the victorious Allies who administered these new colonies without much thought given to local realities. The nation of Iraq, for instance, was drawn up to satisfy European convenience and thus ignored the ethnic and religious divisions within those borders (a problem we are unfortunately still living with). The Russian Empire was consumed by revolution and its successor, the Communist Soviet Union, represented a fundamental challenge to the liberal-capitalist system that many believed was bankrupt. Finally, even though the victorious European powers of Great Britain and France saw their empires expand after World War I, they had both suffered terribly, and their empires were increasingly unsustainable. Colonial subjects witnessed the hollowness of the alleged superiority of European civilization as it willingly sent the flower of its youth to die in a ruinous war waged for no clear, let alone good, reason. Ho Chi Minh and Mahatma Gandhi would soon represent two different types of colonial independence movements that European powers were incapable of resisting.

But perhaps the greatest (and most obvious) consequence of World War I was its contribution to sparking **World War II**. The punitive peace that followed the end of World War I humiliated Germany and burdened its newly formed (and weak) democracy with vast reparations that famous English economist John Maynard Keynes argued were both counterproductive and immoral. When **Adolf Hitler** promised the German people that he would throw off the Versailles "slave treaty" and restore Germany's pride, they voted him into office. He subsequently consolidated power and began a military build-up that would start a second world war, bringing previously unimaginable devastation to much of Europe.

Hitler was eventually defeated, as was his Axis ally, Japan. Victory came at a great cost, however, as the scale of destruction of World War II far exceeded that of World War I. Some 60 million people were killed worldwide and two of the means of annihilation left an indelible mark in the historical memory: the extermination camp and the nuclear bomb. Hitler's Third Reich purposely designed mass extermination centers such as Auschwitz with the specific intention of murdering thousands of Jews every day, an event so unprecedented that commentators had to devise a new word for it: genocide. The use of atomic warfare quickly ended the war, but had ushered in a new age in which a Third World War threatened to render the human race extinct. The two Allied **superpowers** that emerged from the ashes of the Second World War, the United States and the Soviet Union, quickly drifted apart due to ideological differences and entered a dangerous chess match called the **Cold War**, in which both jockeyed for global prestige while possessing enough nuclear weapons to destroy each other many times over.

The Cold War was unique because despite their mutual antipathy, the Soviet Union and the United States never engaged in a traditional military conflict. The threat of mutually assured destruction precluded it. But the 45-year diplomatic and ideological conflict between the two nations, characterized by an expensive arms race, huge sums of economic aid to nefarious dictators, and actual "hot" proxy wars such as Vietnam, were perhaps best epitomized by the Berlin Wall, a literal slab of concrete that blocked human traffic from the democratic west side of the city to the Communist east side. The Cold War dominated global affairs until 1989, when, suddenly and surprisingly, the Berlin Wall fell and was quickly dismantled. The Soviet Union gave up communism voluntarily as the future it promised never materialized. Once again, the world hoped for a future without the destruction and fears that marked the 20th century. But events since 1989 such as the violence that accompanied the break-up of Yugoslavia, the terrorist attack on 9/11, and ongoing political disorder in the Middle East are a reminder that we still live in a world shaped and scarred by the events set in motion 100 years ago with the outbreak of the First World War.

EUROPE: WAR, RECOVERY, AND RECONCILIATION

Russia: An Unlikely Revolution

Industrialization not only provided the means for massive economic gains and population growth, but was also a disruptive force that forever changed the fabric of societies. The isolated rural peasant communities that characterized the medieval era were replaced by new urban centers connected by railroads and telegraphs. A new social class emerged, comprised of the millions of people who toiled away in factories for little pay: the **proletariat**, or working class. What rights and roles this new class should have represented the defining political questions with which industrialized societies grappled. Most European governments responded to these social crises by slowly reforming themselves and extending basic rights and civil liberties, such as male suffrage, to their citizens. Nevertheless, acute social tension remained as progressive reformers argued that these measures did not go far enough, whereas conservatives contended that rapid reform would unleash ruinous chaos.

Russia was not the place where socialists envisioned the socialist revolution taking hold since it began to industrialize seriously only in the late 1800s, long after Western Europe and the United States. But revolt Russia did, fueled by the deprivations of World War I and an anachronistic government unresponsive to social change. Liberal ideas had slowly crept into Russia and this was perhaps best epitomized by the decision of Tsar **Alexander II** (reigned 1855–1881) to abolish serfdom in 1861. But Alexander and his successors stopped short of granting meaningful rights and protections to the vast majority of their peasant subjects. By the early 20th century, many sectors in Russian society, from peasant masses to liberal-minded reformers to a growing movement of dedicated socialist revolutionaries, clamored for fundamental change to the Tsarist regime.

In January 1905, several hundred thousand Russian workers gathered in St. Petersburg to petition the Tsar for better working conditions and pay. Government soldiers opened fire, killing hundreds in what became known as Bloody Sunday. This event triggered a revolutionary atmosphere in the months that followed as workers went on strike, peasants seized land, and soldiers mutinied. Tsar **Nicholas II** felt compelled to establish a limited constitution monarchy with the formation of the **Duma**, a state assembly. However, the power of the Duma was restricted as it did not have the authority to govern against the wishes of the Tsar. The reluctance of the Tsar to grant meaningful reforms and the shattered faith that ordinary Russians had in their Tsar as a champion of the people due to the events of Bloody Sunday laid the groundwork for the events of the 1917 revolution.

World War I exacerbated the problems faced by Russia. Economic production slumped, political instability rose, and three million people died due largely to incompetent war leadership. Tsar Nicholas II, recognizing that his legitimacy was at an end and that the country was on the verge of collapse, abdicated power in February 1917 and a new provisional republican government was installed to rule the country. Although the provisional government enacted legitimate civil liberties on behalf of the Russian people, it was a weak body marked by intense internal disagreement and made the fatal mistake to continue fighting a ruinous war no Russian wanted any part of. By November 1917, the provisional government was ousted by **Vladimir Lenin** and his Bolshevik Party, who garnered much appeal by promising Russians "peace, land, bread." Lenin hastened Russia's exit from the war by signing of the **Brest-Litovsk Treaty** with Germany so as to concentrate on consolidating Bolshevik power in Russia against its many enemies. The determination—and ruthlessness—of the Bolsheviks to make a clean break with the past was epitomized by their decision to unceremoniously execute the former Tsar and his family in March 1918.

As with most revolutions, the ascension to power by the Bolsheviks was an easier proposition than maintaining that power against multiple factions vying for control. The ensuing Russian Civil War (1917–1922) pitted the Bolsheviks and their newly formed Red Army against the Whites, a loose coalition of anti-Communist forces. The Bolsheviks emerged victorious primarily because they were unified whereas their opponents were divided and because their uncompromising and brutal policies were effective at asserting control over the territories they governed. Perceived regime opponents, even the workers the Bolshevik cause championed, were summarily executed or exiled into the dreaded **Gulags**, prison-labor camps in the desolate regions of Russia, where many were worked to death. With the forced compliance of Russia's peasantry and the inability of the Whites to dispel the popular image that they represented anti-democratic repression, at war's end the Bolsheviks were firmly—and solely—in control.

Prelude to War

The origins of the First World War, unlike the Second, are not easy to boil down to an obvious event or historical figure. Within the tangle of interconnected factors, the one thread that binds many of them together is the defensive alliance system that divided the European great powers into two camps. These alliances were formed in the late 19th century mostly as a reaction to the unification of Germany, which had upset the balance of power that existed since the end of the Napoleonic wars. Great Britain, France, and Russia all feared German expansion and by the beginning of the 20th century had bound themselves into a military alliance, known as the **Triple Entente**, despite their respective ideological hostility and colonial rivalries. Germany, feeling itself encircled and anxious to enjoy what it believed was its rightful place in world affairs, aligned itself with

-isms, Et Cetera: A Handy Guide

Socialism   A political and economic doctrine that envisions the state playing an active part in distributing wealth and caring for its citizens. Began as a working class movement

Communism   A political and economic ideology according to which society is classless and the nation's economic and productive capital is owned and controlled collectively by the state on behalf of the people

Fascism   A system of government characterized by authoritarian rule and oppression of dissent for the good of the nation. The polar opposite of liberal democracy

Classical liberalism   In economics, classical liberalism champions laissez-faire economics and the free market. In politics, classical liberalism generally champions the rights of the individual over those of the state (yes, we know it's confusing!)

Representative democracy   Political rule of the people through its elected representatives

Austria-Hungary and Italy in the so-called **Triple Alliance**. These alliances meant that should any international crisis trigger even a relatively minor war involving one of the great powers, the war would quickly expand as the others would become sucked into a vortex. The unstable situation in Europe in the early 20th century, with tensions among the allies strained by imperial rivalries, a naval arms race, rampant nationalism, an overly romanticized view of war, and a festering powder keg in the **Balkans**—a region where Austrian and Russian interests constantly clashed—only took one relatively minor spark to explode into a major war.

The Shot Heard 'Round the World

On June 18, 1914, Gavrilo Princip, a Serbian nationalist, assassinated **Archduke Franz Ferdinand** of Austria. The First World War began because of this terrorist attack and subsequent chain of consequences. Austria, reassured by its ally Germany, demanded that Serbia be punished and declared war. Russia, believing its national interests at stake and backed by its ally France, supported Serbia and mobilized its armies in a show of force, an action tantamount to war. This prompted Germany to declare war on Russia and France because its military strategy, the Schlieffen Plan, was predicated on quickly defeating the French before the Russians could fully organize their armies. Great Britain then declared war on Germany in response to that country's violation of Belgium's neutrality (the Schlieffen Plan directed German troops to go around the main French defenses and thus through Belgium). By the beginning of August, all the great powers of Europe had become embroiled in a war that would unleash the full fury of modern industrialized weapons and methods that would last over four years, leave millions dead, and forever shape the landscape of Europe.

But few realized this at the time. Most Europeans from London to Paris to Berlin to St. Petersburg greeted the war with enthusiasm, believing that a rapid victory would usher in a Renaissance. These hopes were quickly dashed when every offensive failed, resulting in hundreds of thousands of casualties. By the end of 1914, the Central Powers (Germany, Austria-Hungary, and the Ottoman Empire) and the Allied Powers (Great Britain, France, Russia, later joined by Italy) were locked in a military stalemate, characterized by trench warfare in which battles were exceedingly long, brutal, and costly in terms of lives and material.

This equilibrium resulted primarily from two factors. First, the economies of the two sides were evenly matched (for instance the amount of steel produced in 1914 by the two warring factions was virtually the same). A modern and industrialized economy was particularly important to fight this new type of Total War, in which nations geared their entire populations and industries to the war effort. Second, the military technology at the time, specifically the machine gun, favored the defensive. Although new weapons such as tanks and aircraft made their appearance on European battlefields, these machines were too primitive to overcome entrenched positions that were protected by barbed-wire, overlapping fields of fire, poison gas, and murderous quick firing artillery. The battles of the Somme and Verdun, both fought on the Western Front in France in 1916, saw hundreds of thousands of men on both sides fall just to see the battle lines shift a few miles.

Battles under such conditions revealed the horrors of industrial warfare as bravery counted for little in a virtual slaughterhouse.

The year 1917 saw two developments that broke the stalemate: the entry of the United States into the war on the Allied side in April and the Russian Revolution that eventually caused that nation to exit the war. President **Woodrow Wilson** was angered by Germany's submarine warfare and resolved that the United States should enter the war to "make the world safe for democracy." However, the Germany of the First World War was not the dictatorial murderous regime of the Second (although it was portrayed that way in propaganda). In any event, although the United States had by far the largest economy in the world, it had virtually no standing army and would have to build one from scratch. When Lenin's Bolshevik Russia dropped out of the war, Germany was freed from the burden of fighting on two fronts and was able to shift over one million soldiers to the Western Front.

Germany thus had a temporary advantage, but its window of opportunity was decidedly narrow; it had to mount a war-winning offensive against the British and French before the summer of 1918 when the Americans would ship 10,000 fresh soldiers to France every day. A tremendous German offensive in the spring of 1918 cost the Germans over half a million causalities (and the Allies more) and came tantalizing close to Paris, but in the end the offensive was halted. Afterward Allied forces advanced continuously against increasingly demoralized German troops. By November 1918, the German supreme commander counseled his government to ask for an armistice on the basis of Wilson's Fourteen Points. The German Kaiser, fearing revolution, abdicated his throne and fled, while a moderate and democratic socialist government assumed control. Crucially, it was this new government, the **Weimar Republic**, that agreed to the armistice and signed the peace accords that ended the First World War in defeat for Germany: the **Treaty of Versailles**.

Treaty of Versailles: How NOT to Make a Treaty

World War I had brought unprecedented suffering to the countries of Europe. Although the fault for the war lay mostly in the system of interconnected alliances, great power rivalries, and misguided nationalism, the victorious Allied Powers wanted someone to blame and someone to make pay—that "someone" was Germany. Diplomats of the victorious powers converged on Versailles to arrange a settlement—Germany was intentionally shut out (as were Russia and the other Central Powers). The talks were dominated by President Woodrow Wilson of the United States, Prime Minister **David Lloyd George** of Great Britain, and Premier **Georges Clemenceau** of France.

Wilson had hoped that the Versailles peace would augur in a new **liberal** age in which international cooperation would render the old great power diplomacy obsolete. His **Fourteen Points** reflected these desires and he called for the creation of a joint council of nations called the **League of Nations** that was to arbitrate international disputes and prevent another terrible war from breaking out. Clemenceau was dubious of Wilson's idealism and determined to enact a harsh peace because France had suffered greatly during the war and feared a future German invasion.

The resulting peace was a compromise of these extremes and was based on the principle of national self-determination, the notion that an ethnic group ought to be sovereign and free from foreign domination. Consequently, the great empires of Europe: Russian, Austrian, German, and Ottoman were all dismantled and new nations such as Poland and Czechoslovakia emerged. This was admirable in theory, but the arbitrary manner in which these borders were drawn laid the groundwork for future problems. For example, millions of Germans now lived under Polish and Czech rule (ideal fodder Hitler would exploit later) and although nobody had ever claimed to be a Yugoslavian, the nation of Yugoslavia was created as a home for an assortment of Balkan people who had very different linguistic, ethnic, and religious traits.

As for Germany, that nation was stripped of all its colonies, lost territory to France and Poland, had its armed forces dismantled, and was told to sign a virtual blank check. Included in the treaty was a specific clause that blamed Germany for the entire war and all its destruction. Although the new Weimar government protested the severity of these conditions, it had no choice but to sign because the Allied Powers continued their blockade and threatened to invade the country.

The Versailles Treaty was an abject failure. The United States refused to join the League of Nations because of Wilson's refusal to consult Congress. Without America's economic might, the League lacked the means to meaningfully punish aggressor nations. Furthermore, the burdensome indemnities placed on Germany generated all sorts of problems. When the Germans claimed that they could not pay, the French sent in troops to forcibly collect, the British condemned their former French allies, and the Americans artificially propped up the whole system with loans to Germany (with disastrous consequences when the stock market crashed in 1929). Most significantly, the "slave treaty," as the many resentful Germans dubbed it, irreparably delegitimized the nascent Weimar Republic. Because it had signed the treaty, the Weimar government was unfairly blamed for Germany's defeat even though it did not start the war or have any realistic alternatives. Germany had been disarmed and humiliated, but with so many of its people feeling resentment and hardship over the treaty, its large industrial capacity, and its technical knowhow, a skillful leader could exploit these circumstances and build Germany into the most powerful country in Europe.

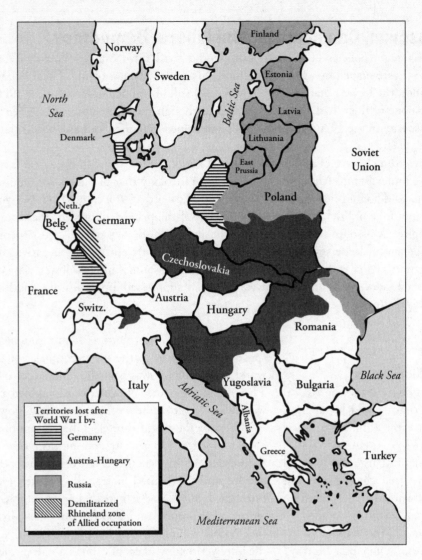

Europe After World War I

Territories lost after World War I by:
- Germany
- Austria-Hungary
- Russia
- Demilitarized Rhineland zone of Allied occupation

ANOTHER WAR TO END ALL WARS

World War I had been called the "War to End all Wars," and it was inconceivable in 1920 that another world war could break out so soon after the first. Yet the Treaty of Versailles and growing nationalism contributed heavily to the post–World War I atmosphere of discontent among the European powers. Three starkly opposing political ideologies would emerge: liberal democracy, fascism, and communism. The United States, whose response to these developments was isolationism, would end up playing an important role in the era. And the economic pressures of costly postwar reconstruction and burdensome reparations on Germany would contribute to a worldwide depression in the 1930s.

Fascism, Communism, and Liberal Democracy

The foreign policies of Western Europe and the United States following World War I were shaped by a fear of communism and a weariness of war. Great Britain, France, the United States, and Germany were all liberal democracies in the 1920s, but none of them had strong leadership. Although the United States experienced prosperity in the 1920s, most of Europe remained desperate for basic necessities.

Italy, riding a wave of anticommunist and nationalist sentiments, became a fascist state under **Benito Mussolini**. **Fascism** is an ideology that promotes nationalism, glory, and honor under an iron dictatorship; the word *fascism* comes from the word for a bundle of birch rods used as a symbol of the penal authority of the Roman Empire. Mussolini's charisma and rousing patriotism seduced many people desperate for leadership and strength in the war-torn country. The negative connotation of the word *fascist* is well-deserved; Mussolini came to power via gang warfare tactics and, once in power, ruthlessly suppressed any political opposition to his regime.

Social Changes of the Early 20th Century

The 20th century was not just about wars; the rise of industrialism in the 19th century and of labor unions in the late 19th and early 20th centuries also spurred other "rights" movements elsewhere in the West. **Women's movements** in particular were popping up in many industrialized countries, demanding labor laws to protect women and children in the workplace. **Suffragist** movements demanded the vote for women: Figures such as the Pankhursts in England and Susan B. Anthony, Lucretia Mott, and Elizabeth Cady Stanton in the United States fought for and won the right of women to vote.

After the Russian Revolution, Lenin sought to spread **communism** to the other countries of the world. Communism was never intended to be only a Russian movement, but rather was imagined as a worldwide revolt of the workers, hence the slogan "Workers of the world, unite!" The communists' concerted efforts to spread communism beyond the borders of Russia threatened other European nations and the United States, all of which (yes, even the United States) had their own problems with worker protests and labor unions—socialism, they feared, would seem an attractive alternative to the impoverished workers of capitalist nations, just as Marx and Engels had imagined. As a result, the Union of Soviet Socialist Republics (USSR) was isolated economically and politically from the rest of the world, a fact that actually helped the USSR avoid the Great Depression.

Meanwhile, Back at the Gulag...

While Europe and the United States were busy dealing with the Depression and other issues, the Soviets concentrated on their own domestic problems. Lenin first instituted the **New Economic Policy**, which had such capitalistic aspects as allowing farmers to sell portions of their grain. This plan was successful for agriculture, but Lenin did not live long enough to encourage its expansion into other parts of the Soviet economy. Lenin died in 1924, and two successors, **Leon Trotsky** and **Joseph Stalin**, battled for supremacy over the Communist Party—it was Stalin who triumphed.

As General Secretary of the Communist Party, Stalin imposed an economic policy of aggressive agricultural collectivization and the construction of large, nationalized factories. The program was carried out in a series of **Five-Year Plans**. **Collectivization** of agriculture ended private ownership of land in the hopes that by combining all the farms, agricultural production would be more efficient and productive, and that once the peasants weren't needed in the fields, they would willingly go to work in the new factories. Many peasants resisted—and often paid with their freedom or lives.

Notwithstanding his ruthlessness, Stalin's plan did finally industrialize the USSR; by the outbreak of World War II, Russia had become an industrial force to be reckoned with. Still, to retain firm control of the Communist Party (and of life in general in the Soviet Union), Stalin used terror tactics that he borrowed from the tsar, such as a secret police force, bogus trials, and assassinations. Taking a cue from Lenin as well, Stalin made copious use of the Gulag system to suppress any and all opposition to his policies, shipping millions to work and die in the wilds of Siberia. Stalin's rule is now called the **Great Terror**; up to 20 million people may have been killed by his government.

The Rise of Hitler

The **Weimar Republic** of Germany was greatly disliked by the German people because of its association with defeat, both in the war and at the various treaty signings. Also, inflation was rampant in Germany, caused by both the large war debt and the worldwide depression. In this atmosphere Adolf Hitler rose to power. Like Mussolini's Fascism, Hitler's Nazism fed on extreme nationalism and dreams of the renewed greatness of a long-lost empire.

But Hitler's philosophies were more insidious than Mussolini's. Hitler believed in the superiority of one race over others. He felt that the "Aryan" race (characterized by tall, white, blond, blue-eyed people, even though Hitler himself was rather small and dark-haired) was superior, and that the Aryan race was being corrupted by "inferior" races, especially the Jews. He thought that the Jews should be eliminated and the German people should take over Europe. The Germans, Hitler argued, needed the extra living space (*lebensraum*) and resources to develop fully as a race.

The Nazi Party (short for the National Socialist German Workers Party) began to gain political power in the 1920s with Hitler as its leader, or *führer*. At first, the Nazi Party gained votes democratically and participated in the **Reichstag**, Germany's parliament. But when the country found itself caught in the middle of the economic depression in the early 1930s, Hitler gained political clout. Many who disagreed with Hitler's philosophy still backed him because they felt he was the country's only hope. In 1933, Hitler was named chancellor, and, when the president of the Weimar Republic died, Hitler was solely in control. Under his domination, German society was as rigidly controlled as the Soviet Union's. The Nazi regime did revive the economy, thanks to Hitler's massive arms build-up. The making of weapons and the training of soldiers and police soon rectified the unemployment problem. Meanwhile, Hitler began to round up primarily Jews, but also Gypsies, homosexuals, Catholics, and other "outsiders," sending them to concentration camps.

Germany proceeded with what it called the "Final Solution" to the Jewish problem. The "solution" was the systematic mass murder of millions of people through the use of gas chambers and other methods of slaughter. Six million Jews and as many as 15 million people total were killed in what is now remembered as the **Holocaust**.

World War II

Although the nations of the world could easily see the growing aggression of the Nazi and fascist regimes, the other European nations, remembering the massive loss of life that resulted from the previous war, sought **appeasement**, while the United States favored isolation from the events. The primary advocate for diplomacy over war was Prime Minister **Neville Chamberlain** of Great Britain.

In 1936, Hitler began his military advance by occupying the **Rhineland**, a strip of German territory that bordered France. He joined in an alliance with Italy to create the **Axis Powers**; later Japan would enter into this alliance. Mussolini had also begun military expansion by invading Ethiopia. In 1938, Germany annexed Austria and threatened to invade Czechoslovakia. The **Munich Conference of 1938**, which included Hitler, Mussolini, and Chamberlain, was called to avert the invasion (called the **Sudetenland crisis**), but Hitler's march was only stayed for about a year. In 1939, Hitler invaded **Czechoslovakia** and signed the secret **Nazi-Soviet Pact**: Stalin and Hitler, though ideological enemies, agreed that Germany would not invade the USSR if the Soviets stayed out of Germany's military affairs. So Stalin got a measure of security and Hitler got a clear path by which to take Poland. Hitler invaded **Poland** shortly thereafter in 1939; Great Britain, realizing that all diplomacy had failed, declared war on Germany, with France reluctantly following suit.

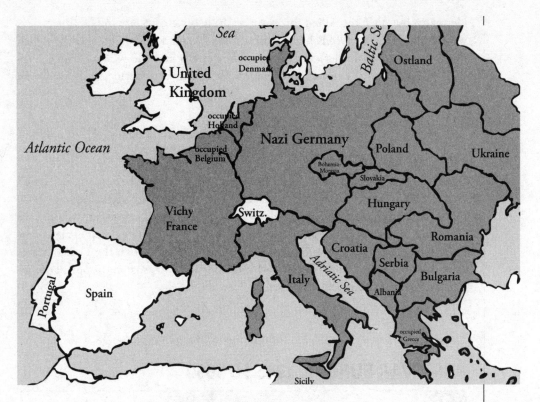

Nazi Germany's Occupation, 1943

Hitler's forces were devastating. Using new forms of mechanized warfare, they employed motorized tanks, planes, and trucks, rather than just moving men and equipment on foot. This tactic was known as *blitzkreig*, or "lightning war," because it destroyed everything in its path with unprecedented speed. Within a year, the Axis Powers controlled most of continental Europe. Great Britain, under the determined leadership of new Prime Minister **Winston Churchill**, faced Germany alone. Hitler tried to air bomb Great Britain into submission, but Britain survived the **Battle of Britain**, aided by U.S. supplies and the new technology of radar, which helped the British air force locate German planes. Also, Hitler decided to nullify the Nazi-Soviet Pact and invade the USSR. The movement of men and supplies into Russia alleviated some of the pressure on Great Britain.

In the Pacific theater, **Japan** was invading other Asian countries. Like the Nazis, Japan's leaders believed themselves racially superior to those they dominated. By 1941, Japan had invaded Korea, Manchuria, and other significant parts of China, and was threatening action in Indochina. For trade reasons, the United States viewed this action as hostile. But the ultimate hostility came on December 7, 1941, when the Japanese bombed **Pearl Harbor** in Hawaii. This action would greatly affect the outcome of the war, as it prompted the United States to enter into the war against Japan. In response to the U.S. declaration of war, Germany declared war on the United States.

By 1941, the **Allied Powers** included Great Britain, France, the Soviet Union, and the United States. The Axis Powers were Germany, Italy, and Japan. It took several years before the United States and Great Britain could launch a land attack against

Those Who Do Not Learn From History...
Both Napoleon Bonaparte and Adolf Hitler thought they could take over all of Europe. Both men made the same mistake: invading Russia.

Allied Powers.
Great Britain, France, the Soviet Union, and the United States

Central Powers
Germany, Italy, and Japan

Germany, but once the Allied forces successfully invaded Normandy, Hitler's days were numbered. The USSR had withstood the German onslaught, and the Allied forces closed in on Hitler's troops from the eastern and the western fronts until they reached Berlin. It is believed that Hitler committed suicide, and the war in Europe came to an end.

How to End a War?

But the war in the Pacific dragged on. The Japanese were particularly dedicated to their cause and often fought hopeless battles to the death. Casualties on both sides were very high. A land war victory over Japan, it was thought, would have claimed an enormous number of casualties, so the United States used nuclear warfare to force the Japanese into submission. On August 6, 1945, the United States exploded an atomic bomb over **Hiroshima** and, a few days later, dropped another bomb on **Nagasaki**. Japan surrendered.

POSTWAR EUROPE, 1945 TO 1990

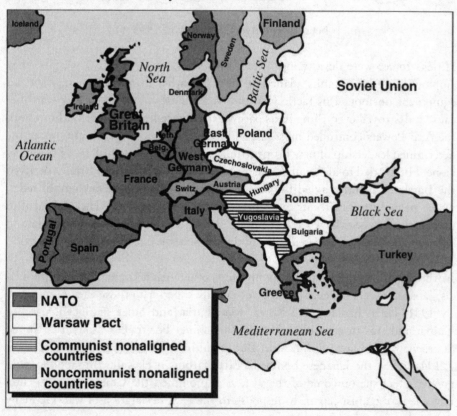

Cold War Europe

Prior to 1991, when the Soviet Union disbanded, it was hard to imagine that the USSR and the United States had ever been allies. That's because Cold War tensions between these two superpowers shaped international diplomacy for nearly 50 years. During the Cold War, the United States and Soviet Union never actually engaged in a shooting war, but they wrestled for ideological dominance of the globe through intervention into the affairs of other nations, using diplomatic, economic, subversive, and military means.

Much of the mutual distrust between superpowers emerged because of questions concerning what to do with Hitler's defeated Third Reich. Russia had a long history of being invaded by Western European powers and the Soviet leadership was determined to ensure that Germany was punished and that friendly socialist nations would border the Soviet Union after it had been on the winning side of a war in which over twenty million of its citizens died. The United States interpreted Soviet intentions as aggressive and expansionist, simply replacing one totalitarian regime in Eastern Europe with another. In effect, both nations wished to remake Germany (and the rest of Europe) in accordance with their respective ideologies, communism and liberal democracy. By 1947, just two years after the war, it became apparent that no European settlement would ever be agreed to and both superpowers entrenched their political and economic influence upon the regions in which their armies had defeated Hitler's Third Reich. Eastern European countries (including the new nation of East Germany) became Soviet satellites compliant to Moscow's wishes, while Western European countries (including the new nation West Germany) remained democratic and consented to Washington's anti-communist stance. Winston Churchill famously referred to Cold War Europe as being divided by an "**iron curtain**," which separated the communist east from the democratic west.

> ### The United Nations
>
> Woodrow Wilson's dream of an international body to legislate diplomatic differences emerged after World War II as the **United Nations**. Founded in 1945, the United Nations originally began with 51 member countries whose guiding principles were international law and security, economic development, and social equity. It was created in the hopes that an international adjudicating body would prevent the world from ever seeing another world war. The five permanent members of the **Security Council** are those countries (or their successor states) that came out of World War II as its most powerful victors: the United States, the People's Republic of China, Russia, France, and the United Kingdom. As of 2011, there were 193 member countries.

U.S. President Harry S. Truman instituted a policy of **containment** by means of the **Truman Doctrine**. He felt that U.S. support of anti-communist nations would help "contain" the spread of communism. The **Marshall Plan** (1947) built on this idea by offering significant economic assistance to the war-torn nations of Europe, including Germany. The Soviet-led Eastern bloc refused the aid and, in retaliation, blockaded West Berlin from American supplies. (Although Berlin was located in East Germany, half the city was administered by western nations and was considered legally part of West Germany.) The United States and Great Britain overcame the blockade by bringing supplies in by air, an action known as the Berlin Airlift. Next, much of Western Europe allied with the United States and Canada in a common defensive alliance against a potential communist attack, the North Atlantic Treaty Organization (NATO). The Soviet Union, viewing the formation of NATO (established in 1949) as

The Warsaw Pact: Members Only
Soviet Union
East Germany
Poland
Czechoslovakia
Hungary
Romania
Bulgaria
Albania

a provocation, signed a similar treaty with its satellites in Eastern Europe, the **Warsaw Pact** (established in 1955).

The Cold War was not a traditional territory dispute. It centered on ideological clashes and was thus mostly "fought" by means of propaganda, diplomacy, economics, and covert operations. Occasionally, the Cold War got "hot" in what are considered proxy wars, meaning wars in which the actual combatants were overshadowed by the massive sponsorship they received from the Soviet Union or the United States. As the United States and the U.S.S.R. were reluctant to risk escalating local conflicts into a potentially nuclear Armageddon, support typically meant economic assistance, delivering arms and advisors, and diplomatic arrangements. The two superpowers became so concerned about the prospect of "losing" any country in the world to their ideological adversaries that both sides were willing to support nefarious dictators and corrupt regimes that contradicted the very principles the Cold War combatants claimed to be fighting for. As a consequence, many of the major conflicts after 1945 were in some way connected with the underlying tensions of the Cold War, even though most of these wars were primarily fought because of local conditions and had little to do with the American-Soviet ideological conflict.

Things That Go Boom: Nuclear Proliferation

The primary feature—and fear—of the Cold War was the build-up of massive stockpiles of increasingly more destructive nuclear arms in the United States and the Soviet Union. The destructive power of nuclear weapons had already been demonstrated by the destruction of Hiroshima, an event neither side wished to repeat. Massive retaliation that would lead to mutually assured destruction (MAD) seemed to be the only means to deter one side from starting World War III. This arms "race" quickly led both superpowers into a rush to create space technology, particularly satellites for surveillance and communication and to monitor and guard against a potential surprise missile attack. By the 1960s, both sides possessed arsenals large enough to destroy the world several times over and made tremendous strides in space technology; the Soviet Union launched the first orbital satellite Sputnik in 1957 and the United States landed the first man on the moon in 1969 as part of the Apollo Program.

The **Cuban Missile Crisis** in 1962 was a sobering example of how easily tensions could flare up into nuclear Armageddon. After the failure of the American-financed **Bay of Pigs** invasion of Cuba (intended to oust the communists who had taken power), the Soviet Union placed missile bases in Cuba in order to deter another invasion. U.S. President John F. Kennedy demanded that the Soviet Union remove these missiles (as they constituted an unacceptable nuclear threat just 90 miles from the U.S. mainland) and blockaded Cuba with warships. Soviet Premier Nikita Khrushchev, after some two weeks of tense negotiations when war seemed imminent, agreed to remove the missiles provided that the U.S. publicly agree never to invade Cuba. The crisis was resolved peacefully, but both the United States and the Soviet Union recognized the danger inherent to the Cold War. Both quickly agreed to takes steps toward moderation and discussion rather than silent aggression in what was called détente. An instant communication hotline between Moscow and Washington was quickly established and a series of international treaties designed to limit the nuclear arms race were negotiated, culminating in the **Strategic Arms Limitation Talks** (SALT I and SALT II) during the 1970s.

The early 1980s brought a series of crises that renewed tensions between the United States and the USSR under Ronald Reagan and Leonid Brezhnev. When **Mikhail Gorbachev** came to power in the USSR in 1985, he began a series of policies known as *glasnost* ("openness") and *perestroika* ("restructuring") intended to reform the Party along more liberal lines. This led to improved relations with the United States but had the unintended consequence of weakening the communists' hold on power and ultimately led to the dissolution of the Soviet Union in 1991. Communism's grasp across Europe had noticeably weakened by the late 1980s, best exemplified by the collapse of the Berlin Wall in 1989 and the peaceful revolutions that swept away the communist governments in the old Soviet bloc. Indeed, by 1991, with the United States as the sole remaining superpower, the Cold War, which had threatened nuclear annihilation for some forty years, was suddenly over. However, the ending of the Cold War revealed tensions, ethnic and religious antagonisms, and age-old rivalries that had never gone away, that is, that were merely masked during the Cold War. The wars and ethnic cleansing that marked the breakup up the former Yugoslavia in the mid 1990s were a sobering reminder that although the threat of nuclear annihilation had become but a memory, history had not "ended" as some had hoped. Indeed, a new historical post-Cold War era had begun.

MIDDLE EAST: AN EMPIRE FALLS, NATIONS EMERGE

Down with the Ottomans, Up with the Modern Middle East

When we last left off with the Ottoman Empire, it had earned the title "the sick man of Europe" thanks to internal political and economic weaknesses that were slowly but surely eroding the empire both at home and abroad. At home, the sultan's power was under attack by the **Young Turks**, a group of liberal-minded intellectuals and military personnel, who arose in 1908. Abroad, the Ottoman Empire lost control over its holdings in North Africa to Italy and in the Balkans to the Austro-Hungarian Empire (Bosnia), or to the nations themselves as they declared independence (Bulgaria, Serbia, Greece, and Albania) by 1912.

The Ottomans joined the Central Powers (Germany and Austria-Hungary) in World War I, mainly meeting the British in battle. Britain supported the Arabs in their desire to break from Ottoman rule, defeating the Ottomans in a series of battles that recaptured Damascus, Jerusalem, and Baghdad from Turkish control. By 1918, the Ottomans conceded to the British. As a result of the Allied victories in World War I and Woodrow Wilson's **Fourteen Points,** the Ottoman Empire came to an end as its former territories became protectorates or other dependent states of various Allied forces (Syria, Egypt, Palestine, Lebanon, Iraq) or independent entities (Turkey, Saudi Arabia). But the seeds of further discontent in the region were sown by the **Balfour Declaration** of 1917. Named after the British Foreign Secretary Lord Arthur Balfour, this declaration seemed to simultaneously support both an independent Jewish state and the rights of Palestinians, an incompatibility which would worsen over time. The **Peace of Paris** (1919) essentially redrew the borders of the Middle East, more or less creating the nations we know today.

After World War II: More Independence in the Middle East

After the end of World War II, which really was the beginning of the end of colonialism in Africa and Asia, the Middle East gradually came into its own and freed itself of the remaining European influences that had defined it diplomatically for so long.

In many ways the most problematic new nation was **Israel**, which was recognized as an independent state in 1948 after claiming about half of Palestine. Although attacked from all sides by Arab forces, the new state survived, driving many Palestinian Arabs to neighboring countries. Israel even expanded its territory by seizing the **Gaza Strip** and **West Bank** in 1967 in the Six-Day War (when it also took over the entire Sinai Peninsula, which it returned to Egypt in 1979). The idea of establishing a new **Zion**—a homeland for Jews—dated from at least the turn of the century but really took off after the Holocaust created a desire among Jews worldwide for a safe haven for their people; this movement became known as **Zionism**. Unfortunately for those Palestinians who fled the new state, a homeland for the Jews meant losing their own homes. Surrounding Arab states did not absorb the refugees, who found themselves living permanently in refugee camps. The **Palestinian Liberation Organization**, or PLO, was created to represent those displaced by the establishment of Israel. Israeli-Arab relations have had their ups and downs, from peace treaties with Egypt in 1979 and the Oslo Accords in 1993 to the *intifada* (Palestinian uprising) of 1987 and violence arising from the assassination of Israeli prime minister Yitzhak Rabin in 1995, and tensions have continued into the 21st century.

Egypt's military took control of its government in 1952, claiming to be independent of British control. Central to the fight to rid **Egypt** of foreign influence was the **Suez Canal**, which connected the Mediterranean and Red Seas and allowed European trade through a passageway to Asia. In answer to Israel's pleas for help, Britain and France tried to retake the canal from the Egyptians, but were sharply rebuked by U.S. President Dwight D. Eisenhower for their inappropriate meddling in the internal affairs of a sovereign power. One of the officers who led the insurgence against the British was Gamal Abdel Nasser, who went on to rule Egypt until 1970.

In the 1970s, the nations of the Middle East gained significant political power because the region is rich in **oil**, a necessity in modern industrial societies. The countries of this region formed a cartel, the Organization of Petroleum Exporting Countries (**OPEC**), to better control the availability and thus the price of world oil reserves. Because of the wealth of the area's resources, the United States and the Soviet Union exerted Cold War influence in this region, a pattern seen in many areas freeing themselves from colonialism. The region has also been historically volatile because of religious conflicts: Jews, Muslims, and Christians all have religious ties to the region. Arab and Israeli forces engaged in military conflicts intermittently throughout the 1970s, 1980s, and 1990s. Other important conflicts in the region include the invasion of **Afghanistan** by the Soviet Union in 1979; the **Iran hostage crisis** (1979–1980) in which Islamic revolutionaries, under the **Ayatollah Khomeini**, held American hostages for more than a year; and the devastating Iran-Iraq War of the 1980s. In 1990, Iraq, under the leadership of **Saddam Hussein**, invaded the wealthy and oil-rich Arab nation of Kuwait. An international coalition led by the United States launched the **Persian Gulf War** to push Iraq out of Kuwait.

CHINA: THE PATH FROM COMMUNISM TO CAPITALISM

From Empire to Republic

When we last left the Chinese, the 2,000-year-old empire was brought to an end in 1911; the last emperor was deposed, and a new nation was born into an atmosphere of considerable instability. The two major groups fought for power—the Guomindang (GMD), or National People's Party, led by **Chiang Kai-Shek**, and the **Communist** Party, led by **Mao Tse-tung**. In the end, the communists were victorious, despite foreign support for the GMD; the nationalists could not control rampant corruption or fend off the invading Japanese, and thus lost the support of the masses. Mao and the Communist Party, on the other hand, were able to organize first urban workers and then the peasantry, who were extremely sympathetic to the communist call for the redistribution of land and the spread of universal education. The communists eventually drove the GMD forces to the island of Taiwan. Once its main opponent in the civil wars was gone, the communists took control once and for all, establishing the communist **People's Republic of China** in 1949.

GMD?
In the dominant modern alphabetic spelling system for Chinese, *pinyin*, the name of this party is the Guomindang, GMD. However, older sources may refer to the Kuomintang, or KMT. It's the same people either way!

A Republic Matures, Then Revolts From Within

The polices of the new republic were born of Mao's civil war experiences, especially the Long March (1934–1935), during which Mao and his forces evaded the GMD to establish a soviet in Yan'an, where the communists set up headquarters and formulated their guiding principles. The communists did implement some of the policies that had endeared them to the people, such as land distribution and massive investment in better technology and agricultural practices, but they drove out foreigners, leaving themselves with only the Soviet Union as a major supporter. The communists then embarked on a number of large-scale policies to jump-start industrialization in the form of those Five-Year Plans that had been so popular in the Soviet Union. The first plan from 1952 to 1957 focused on increasing industrial output. At the same time, Mao encouraged political openness with the call to "Let a hundred flowers bloom, let a hundred schools of thought contend." In the end, though, the communists repressed protest for fear of growing instability.

The next plan, instituted from 1957 to 1960, was known as the **Great Leap Forward**, and was intended to bring both agriculture and industry into a state of high development immediately, by using the manpower of China's massive population instead of expensive industrial equipment. The policy was an unmitigated failure: The spirit of over-optimism, coupled with lack of know-how and poorly chosen priorities, led to crop failures and poor harvests despite incredibly optimistic overestimates of agricultural output. Widespread starvation followed when the food ran out. On the industrial side, Mao had set a goal of doubling the country's steel production in one year, mainly through the use of backyard furnaces; despite significant economic hardship (as pots and pans were requisitioned to meet the steel production quota) and environmental devastation (as everything burnable was used to operate the furnaces), the plan was useless, because the backyard furnaces could not burn hot enough to create high-quality steel.

Maoist China's Foreign Relations

Under Mao, China was both the target and the perpetrator of territorial aggression. Here are just a few examples:

- China invades Tibet in 1950, driving the Dalai Lama into exile in India.
- China fights the United States in the Korean War (1950–1953).
- China experiences border skirmishes with the Soviet Union and India in the 1960s and 1970s.
- China backs Pol Pot and the Khmer Rouge in Cambodia in the 1970s.

Soon after, Mao launched the **Cultural Revolution** of 1966–1969, which aimed to curb protest and corruption further and to reinvigorate the revolutionary spirit. The Cultural Revolution saw the rise of the Red Guard—students and soldiers devoted to the revolutionary ideal as embodied in Mao's *Little Red Book*—to the detriment of intellectuals, the economy, and the famine-stricken masses. Eventually the Red Guard was suppressed and China's leaders faced the prospect of undoing the damage the Cultural Revolution had caused.

By the 1970s, China's industrial and agricultural outputs were growing, and it began to open itself up to the outside world in reaction to souring relations with an ever more territorially aggressive Soviet Union, with which China cut off diplomatic relations in 1961. Worried by Soviet takeovers of its satellite states in Eastern Europe in the 1960s, China ended its political isolation with the 1972 visit of U.S. President Richard Nixon and soon reaped the economic benefits of opening its markets to the West.

After the Revolution

Mao's death in 1976 ended an age of revolutionary fervor; the Gang of Four, four revolutionary leaders seen as the driving force behind the most destructive policies of the Cultural Revolution, were removed from power. A former revolutionary condemned for his moderation during the Cultural Revolution, **Deng Xiaoping** gained control of the Communist Party after Mao and proceeded to create a China that was both communist *and* capitalist. Under Deng's leadership, China became an industrial powerhouse; life expectancy grew and the population boomed, necessitating the institution of a "one family, one child" policy in the mid-1970s to curb further growth. China has since joined the World Trade Organization (2001) and has risen to the status of economic superpower. But China's rulers have been continually challenged as they try to balance market-based economic reforms with communist ideology, suppressing nascent democratic movements fueled by economic and cultural globalization. Student pro-democracy demonstrations—and the government's violent reaction—in **Tiananmen Square** in 1989 were the most visible examples of this clash of ideologies, played out globally on television screens.

JAPAN: FROM EMPIRE TO CAPITALISM

Japan welcomed the 21st century poised for growth, having defeated two larger enemies (Russia and China), occupied Taiwan and Korea, and borrowed copiously from the West to build its technological and military strength. When Europe was entangled in World War I, Japan took advantage of the downturn in industrial production caused by the war and moved to a prominent place as a world economic power. Thanks to its contributions against the Germans in the Pacific theater, Japan was represented at the signing of the Treaty of Versailles in 1919 (which ended World War I), and was a member of the League of Nations.

Japan was far from Westernized at this time; despite ever greater contacts with the West, Japan's unique domestic policies—both social and political—kept it from fully embracing democratic governance. *Zaibatsu*, large corporate conglomerates funded by the government but privately held, and the military had a disproportionate amount of control over Japanese economics and politics, and pushed Japan toward a more militaristic attitude after the United States's Great Depression sent the Japanese economy into a severe downturn. This militarism, along with Japan's desperate need for industrial resources, is clear in Japan's actions leading up to World War II: the invasion into Manchuria in 1931 and into China proper in 1937 demonstrated the victory of an aggressive stance toward Japan's neighbors. Japan became a part of the Axis Powers in 1941 upon signing the Tripartite Pact with Germany and Italy. Instead of invading Russia, Japan turned its sights on France's holdings in French Indochina (now Cambodia, Laos, and Vietnam) and eventually U.S. territory in Hawaii in response to American embargoes of Japanese goods. Japan captured a number of territories in the South Pacific but was unable to hold them; local resistance and American incursions into the Pacific drove the Japanese out of newly acquired lands. By 1944, Japan itself was under attack by American forces and unconditionally surrendered in August 1945 after American forces dropped atomic bombs on Hiroshima and Nagasaki. The war devastated Japan's population and industrial infrastructure.

Japan After World War II

The U.S. military occupied Japan until 1952, helping to try war criminals, rebuild the economy, and establish democratic institutions. The Americans allowed the Japanese monarchy to continue, though with greatly diminished powers. Although the occupation officially ended in 1952, the American presence in Japan remained strong; U.S. military bases remained in Japan for decades, giving the American military a Pacific foothold in the Cold War, against communism in general, and in its battles in the Korean War (1950–1953) and later Vietnam. American investment in Japan played a central role in Japan's return to industrial strength in the decades following the war; Japan eventually outpaced the United States in industrial efficiency and management, particularly in the technology sector. Even after a severe recession in the 1990s, Japan remains one of the world's most powerful economic players.

KOREA AND VIETNAM: COLD WAR BATTLEGROUNDS

Korea and Vietnam are both countries in Eastern Asia whose histories are closely intertwined with those of their larger, more powerful neighbors. Both countries were occupied by foreign powers and had attained their independence soon after World War II. Korea was liberated from Japan with that nation's unconditional surrender and Vietnamese nationalists successfully overthrew French rule by winning a war of independence ending in 1954. Due to a number of complex reasons, both would also become Cold War battlegrounds that saw the deployment of hundreds of thousands of American troops in what were the most extreme examples of Washington's policy of containment.

Korea

The Allied victory over Japan in the Second World War brought an end to Japanese colonial rule over Korea, which had been formally established in 1910. The Untied States and the Soviet Union agreed to jointly administer the country and divided responsibilities along the 38th parallel, the U.S. overseeing the south while the USSR the north. Plans for free national elections unifying the country under a single government never took place as the Soviet Union first opposed, then boycotted, a 1948 United Nations–supervised general election. By 1950 Korea was essentially two countries, a communist North headed by the Stalinist autocrat Kim Il-sung and a right-wing anti-communist South led by strongman Syngman Rhee. Border skirmishes escalated dramatically when North Korea invaded the South in June 1950 and this marked the beginning of the **Korean War**, believing its superior armed forces could achieve unification by force.

North Korean forces swept aside Southern resistance and were soon poised to over-run the entire country. The United States, interpreting the naked communist ag-gression as a test of its resolve, intervened under a United Nations resolution ap-proving the use of military force to aid South Korea. American-led forces, after some initial embarrassing defeats, soon drove the North Koreans back beyond the 38th parallel, but then—in a decision underestimating the perspective of border-ing communist China—continued into North Korea in pursuit of a complete vic-tory. China, under the leadership of Mao Zedong, interpreted the move as Ameri-can aggression and sent hundreds of thousands of its troops to aid its communist neighbor. The Chinese intervention established a military equilibrium in which both sides were locked in a stalemate that saw many battles, but little exchange of territory. In 1953, an armistice was signed that ended the conflict and left the Korean peninsula divided into two nations—a division that is still in effect. North Korea remains an authoritarian communist state, while South Korea has since overthrown its anti-communist virtual dictatorship and become a parliamentary democracy.

Vietnam

Unlike Korea, where it could be argued that American intervention was successful in containing Communism, the **Vietnam War** represented eight years of military frustration as American forces won many battles but were incapable of preventing a communist takeover of that country.

Vietnam had been a French colony since the 19th century, but numerous factors had undermined French rule, the most obvious being that nation's humiliating defeat by Nazi Germany. After the Second World War, the French tried to reclaim their Vietnamese colony, but to no avail; communist nationals led by **Ho Chi Minh** successfully resisted, defeating the French decisively in 1954 at the battle of Dien Bien Phu. The treaty that ended this **First Indochina War** split Vietnam along the 17th parallel into a communist north (ruled by Ho Chi Minh and Viet Minh forces) and the anticommunist south (led by strongman Ngo Dinh Diem), a situation that was intended to be temporary until free and fair national elections unified the country. But neither the North nor the South honored this agreement as both staged rigged elections in which their respective rules won over 95 per-cent of the vote. In 1955, Diem formally declared South Vietnam an independent country and decided the issue.

The communist North, however, wanted a unified communist Vietnam. To this end they encouraged the Viet Cong, South Vietnamese revolutionary insurgents dedicated to unifying the country with the North, to stir up civil war. By the early

1960s, the Viet Cong, in large measure due to the corruption of the Diem regime, had considerable success in recruiting new members, staging guerilla attacks, and creating general havoc in the south.

Many in the United States viewed these developments with alarm. According to the widely held domino theory, if one nation became communist, then other neighboring regions would soon follow. As the South Vietnamese situation deteriorated, the United States steadily escalated its military forces in the region until reaching a peak strength of over half a million by 1968. This was not a traditional war. In fact, the United States never formally declared war; the **Gulf of Tonkin Resolution** gave U.S. President Lyndon B. Johnson the authority to commit troops. Rather than capturing territory or seeking to defeat and occupy an enemy country, U.S. policy was predicated on eliminating Viet Cong guerillas through "search and destroy" missions with the expressed purpose of maintaining an anti-communist South Vietnam. This strategy produced mixed military results as U.S. military forces were not trained to fight such a war and winning battles did nothing to solve the root cause of the Viet Cong insurgency: a dictatorial and corrupt South Vietnamese regime that alienated its people. The **Tet Offensive** of 1968, a massive Viet Cong surprise attack, represented the pattern of much of the fighting. Although this campaign failed from a traditional military perspective as U.S. and South Vietnamese forces thwarted these attacks and inflicted heavy casualties, the audacity and sheer scale of the Viet Cong insurgency had a considerable psychological effect. It shocked an American public that had repeatedly been told that the communists were incapable of such an effort and very much contributed to an already growing anti-war movement. President Johnson opted not to seek re-election and his successor, Richard M. Nixon, promised Americans that he would negotiate with North Vietnam and oversee the withdrawal of U.S. forces. Thus from a political perspective, the Tet Offensive was a significant success for the communists.

Nixon eventually did withdraw U.S. forces from Vietnam in 1973. With the American public firmly against the war and highly skeptical of its government, there was little alternative. Under the policy of Vietnamization, U.S. troops were withdrawn and replaced with South Vietnamese troops who ideally would continue the defense against communist forces. Some 58,000 U.S. soldiers had died by that point and although Nixon did sign an armistice that ended the fighting, nothing in that agreement prevented the North Vietnamese from eventually taking total control over Vietnam (which they would do just two years later). In the end, U.S. military involvement failed to prevent a communist takeover of Vietnam. The root cause of this failure was political, not military. However many battles U.S. forces won, none of these victories delivered the food, land reform, and hope that most South Vietnamese wanted. Because the authoritative South Vietnamese regime failed to provide for the basic wants of its people, many of them believed a unified and independent communist Vietnam free from foreign influence could.

INDIA: INDEPENDENCE, PARTITION, INDUSTRIALIZATION

India had traditionally been politically fragmented and its society rigidly classified according to the religious caste system suggested by Hinduism. Thus, India was unprepared to defend itself against the mercantile interests of the British trading companies in the 18th century. Through colonial domination, the British East India Trading Company came to own or control most of India. After the **Indian (Sepoy) Mutiny of 1857**, the British government assumed control of the colony, but nationalistic fervor was rising.

To stem the rising tide of Indian nationalism, the British government encouraged the establishment of the **Indian National Congress** in 1885, which it hoped would allow Indian leaders a forum to air their views. Over the course of the next few decades Indian leaders educated in British schools or in Britain itself were courted by the British, who claimed they planned to train Indians gradually to rule themselves. By 1917, dual governments were created by the Government of India Act, which gave real administrative power to Indian officials. However, the partnership was an uneasy one, and changes did not come fast enough to suit many Indians—as early as 1907, leaders in the Indian National Congress called for the ouster of the British from India altogether. As Indians demanded more and more control, the British often responded by taking away rights and powers it had already granted.

The Rowlatt Act of 1919, which extended Britain's wartime powers to the right to imprison without trial anyone suspected of terrorism or other political crimes, set more dangerous events in motion. In response to the act, many Indians declared a *hartal*, or labor strike, and protested publicly. One such protest in **Amritsar** led to British troops firing on the crowds, killing almost 400 unarmed men, women, and children and injuring 1,000 or more.

The Rise of Gandhi

It was in this time of widespread unrest that an English-educated lawyer named **Mohandas Gandhi** rose to prominence among India's leadership. Gandhi had spent 21 years in South Africa, where he worked for the rights of Indians there, developing a method of resistance by way of **nonviolent protest** and **civil disobedience**. Once he returned to India, he lent his considerable experience and organizational skills to the cause of Indian independence, harnessing the power of grassroots movements and the overwhelming numerical superiority Indians had over their colonial overlords.

Gandhi's methods were deceptively simple and steeped in Hindu spirituality: known collectively as *satyagraha*, or "truth force," these methods included mass demonstrations; *ahimsa*, or nonviolence; and *swadeshi*, a boycott of foreign-made goods, which encouraged Indian economic self-reliance. His ideas had received Western influence as well: The ideas of civil disobedience were first advocated by American Henry David Thoreau. Gandhi's influence extended beyond India;

future leaders such as Martin Luther King Jr. and **Nelson Mandela** used similar methods inspired by Gandhi's teachings in their fights against oppressive governmental policies in the United States and South Africa, respectively.

Gandhi was not universally admired in India, though; his philosophies were based in Hindu belief, which alienated many Muslims, and his nondiscriminatory stance toward Muslims angered radical Hindus. Despite his concerted efforts to reach out to Muslims, Hindu and Muslim tensions remained high. In 1948, Gandhi was assassinated by a Hindu fanatic who believed Gandhi had gone too far in appeasing the Muslim minority.

India Before and After Independence

Independence for India came as a result of years of concerted efforts on the part of India's resistance movements. A series of *satyagraha* movements sealed the deal for India: First, Indians boycotted British institutions, including schools; then came the Salt March in the early 1930s, which simultaneously called attention to and mocked the British monopoly on salt production; and the Quit India campaign of 1942, which withheld India's official support of British efforts in World War II until India was granted its independence. Independence came in 1947, two years after the end of World War II. India became a secular, Hindu-majority state.

India elected its first prime minister, Jawaharlal Nehru (1889–1964), in 1947. India's democratic secular government for the next 30 years was led by a succession of Nehru's family members: Nehru's daughter Indira Gandhi (no relation to Mohandas) served as prime minister between 1966 and 1977 and again from 1980 to 1984 until she was assassinated. Her son Rajiv Gandhi took her place until 1989 when he, too, was assassinated.

Hindu-Muslim Relations: How Are They Resolved?

Muslim **Pakistan**, at the time the northeast and northwest corners of India, broke off as an independent country in 1947, kicking off a large-scale, often deadly two-way migration of Muslims into Pakistan and Hindus into India. Clashes between Hindus and Muslims continued: The disputed territory of **Kashmir**, sandwiched between Pakistan and northern India, to this day is split under Indian and Pakistani control and is a site of sporadic armed conflict. An area located in the northeast of India but officially a part of Pakistan, Bangladesh declared independence from Pakistan in 1971 with the support of India. In the wake of European colonialism, religious tension on the Indian subcontinent became a major motivator for state formation.

Industrialization and the Green Revolution

As India's population increased, the need for comparable growth in the economy and in agriculture posed a significant challenge to the nation. However, the 1960s brought the Green Revolution to India with the help of other nations, including the United States. With better technology and agricultural practices, India was able to feed itself and its ever-burgeoning population. The advent of technology and agricultural growth helped the rich get richer, but left many others in severe poverty; more technology did not necessarily create new jobs, which meant that the promise of advancement did not lead to a wider spread of wealth or opportunity.

Today, India, a nation of more than one billion inhabitants, continues to exist as one of world's largest democracies. It still faces challenges posed by its dense, multiethnic, multilingual population and massive disparities between its poorest and richest citizens.

THE AMERICAS

The 20th century ushered in profound changes in the Americas, perhaps more profound than anywhere else, thanks to the United States' rise from an insurrectionist colony to one of the world's most dominant economic, political, and military nations.

Latin and South America: The Search for Stability and Opportunity

Latin American Nations

Latin America has a Western heritage, because its countries were among the first colonized by Europe. But its economic and political development has diverged sharply from the European continent, and the legacy of colonialism at the hands of Europeans has become a part of the social structure in many countries in this area. After Latin American countries gained their independence, most established authoritarian rule. The primary economic bases were mining and the **plantation** system of agriculture, a farming method requiring a large, low-paid workforce. Its products were cash crops such as tobacco and cotton sold to other countries, rather than food to feed the local population. With this system in place, the wealthy landowners had no incentive to industrialize. In most countries a two-class dynamic emerged—the very poor working for the very wealthy. However, others gradually rose to challenge the wealthy landowners for political power: middle-class businessmen, the military, and European immigrants who brought traditions of labor unions and industrial development. More revolutionary forces often came from among the poor.

The **Mexican Revolution** was fought between 1910 and 1920 by radicals seeking greater representation in governance and fairer distribution of land. Mexico had an autocratic ruler before the revolution, and much of the land was dominated by only a few hundred elite families. Francisco "Pancho" Villa and Emiliano Zapata, two revolutionaries, led the fight against elites, but it was Álvaro Obregón and Venustiano Carranza who eventually rose to power, resisting autocratic pretenders. Obregón became president in 1920, overseeing the establishment of a constitution and the redistribution of millions of acres of land.

American colonial intervention in many cases stunted Latin American development. U.S. President Theodore Roosevelt was especially paternalistic toward Latin America, because he felt it was within the U.S. sphere of influence. He oversaw the construction of the **Panama Canal**, which resulted in massive cost savings for merchant ships. The canal was owned by the United States, because that country constructed it and had obtained permanent rights to the land on either side of it, though, obviously, it was built in Panama. The canal was returned to Panama on January 1, 2000.

In the age of the Cold War, America fought any signs of the spread of communism wherever they appeared: North Korea, North Vietnam, and—closer to home— **Cuba**. The revolutionary **Fidel Castro** led the fight to overthrow the dictatorship of Fulgencio Batista in 1959, installing a communist government with close ties to the Soviet Union. It was one thing to have communism spreading in Eastern Europe, but quite another to have it sprouting up practically within sight of American shores. Socialist revolutionaries in Nicaragua, Guatemala, and Chile received no support from the United States, which backed right-wing dictatorships in these countries instead, in the name of controlling the spread of communist sympathizers in the Americas.

AFRICA'S LONG COLONIAL AILMENT: CORRUPTION, CHAOS, AND CONFLICT

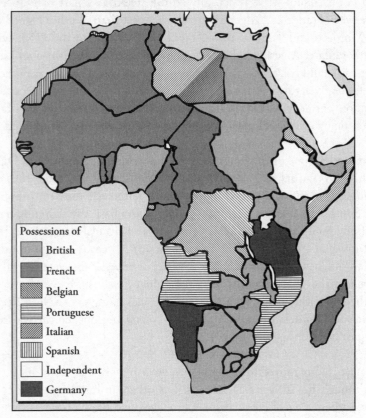

European Colonies in Africa, 1914

Since the Age of Discovery, Africa's resources have been thoroughly abused by European countries. Its people have been kidnapped and sold into slavery to supply much of the manpower used in the colonization of the Americas. The landscape of the continent (deserts, jungles, savannas) has also made it difficult for the African countries to become self-sufficient in large-scale, industrialized agriculture, which would permit a non-agrarian economy.

In the 19th century, Africa was colonized by European powers, primarily by Great Britain and France. The continent of Africa is a mix of different cultures, religions, and ethnicities, but the colonial powers usually did not respect the divergent cultural roots of the tribes when they established colonial states. In addition to controlling the political and economic institutions, the colonists sought to indoctrinate the African natives in more Western ways of thinking, bringing in missionaries to convert Africans to Christianity, without respect for the cultures and religions that the tribes historically held.

The end of World War II and the rise of the Cold War worked in tandem to break the bonds of colonialism on the African continent. One by one, African nations declared their independence from their colonial overlords.

Algeria claimed its independence from France in 1962 after many years of resistance. Algeria's claims to independence were complicated by the fact that so many French citizens were born, lived, and were property owners in the country. Algeria was also not a colony—it was actually administered as a part of France, so the bonds between France and Algeria were much closer than in other French colonies such as Morocco and Tunisia, which broke from France in the 1950s with relatively little fanfare. Algeria's fight for freedom was led by the National Liberation Front, or FLN, and backed by other Islamic nations in the region. A France weakened at home by its own internal struggles granted Algeria its independence in 1962, but only after thousands of deaths on both sides. Nearly a million European Africans—many of whom knew no other home than Algeria—emigrated.

South Africa had one of the longest colonial histories, beginning as a Dutch colony in the 17th century and then becoming a British holding in the 18th century. The Europeans eventually joined together to rule the native African population, limiting South Africans' ownership of property and basically stripping native Africans of any political rights. The system of **apartheid** institutionalized the separate and unequal treatment of the races in South Africa. Although South Africa became an independent nation in the 1960s, native Africans were not allowed to participate in the government until 1994, when President F. W. de Klerk ended apartheid and the ban on the African National Congress (ANC), freed ANC leader **Nelson Mandela** from prison after 27 years, and opened the way to native African participation in government.

Colony after colony moved toward independence between the early 1950s and late 1970s, although not all were as successful as others in building stable countries. From the earliest days of colonialism, Europeans had drawn borders that did not coincide with preexisting linguistic or ethnic boundaries. Therefore, when colonial governments were gone, many new African nations were left with the legacy of tribal conflicts that had been suppressed by the presence of the colonial powers but not eradicated. Once the Europeans were gone, many longstanding conflicts arose to cause instability, civil war, and death in many nations.

Congo, Somalia, Ethiopia, Mozambique, and Sierra Leone are just a few countries that have recently struggled or continue to struggle with civil war, violence, and poverty.

In some cases—like that of **Rwanda**—the way colonial powers ran the country created conflicts that didn't necessarily exist before. Rwanda was a colony of Belgium, which forced the native populations to identify and differentiate themselves by their ethnicity for the first time. Tutsis were the favored ethnicity in the colonial system, which created resentment among the Hutu, who constituted the majority of the population. Upon independence in 1962, the Hutu majority took control of the country, starting a cycle of Hutu-Tutsi violence that reached a fever pitch in the early 1990s. The death of Hutu leader Juvénal Habyarimana in a plane crash sparked a widespread campaign of violence against the Tutsi minority in 1994, leading to the deaths of 800,000 Tutsis in the span of only four months—the Rwandan genocide.

THE 20TH CENTURY: CONTINUITY AND CHANGE

As the opening decades of the 21st century continue with conflict in the Middle East, we are reminded of the conflicts that beset the region throughout the 20th century; as time progresses, conflict in that area seems endless. Other constants have remained with us through the turn of the century: North Korea remains in the hands of a communist, totalitarian state, just as it did 60 years ago (except now with nuclear capabilities), and Afghanistan remains war-torn and politically unstable, not unlike 30 years ago. In addition, ethnic tensions still simmer below the surface in the Balkan peninsula just as they did at the outset of World War I, and postcolonial divisions and corruption continue to plague many of the governments of Africa.

However, on many levels much changed over the course of the 1900s. Soviet communism emerged at the beginning of the century only to fade away by the end of it. China, too, once a bastion of communist teachings, has embraced the economics of the free market and is poised to become the industrial power of the coming decades—will political reform follow? And of course technology has progressed tremendously since the invention of the automobile and the lightbulb. The invention of the microprocessor and the resulting Internet age have changed human civilization forever. Libraries of information can be stored on devices the size of your thumb, and Google search gives anyone with access to the Internet a satellite view of his or her home.

But the 21st century began with the legacy of the last—that of violence. The nations of the world continue to struggle with conflict and violence from abroad and from within, increasingly from various rebel and extremist groups. The darker side of the economic globalization that took off in the last century has shown itself in the intertwined economic crises of 2008. Even the superpower of the 20th century, the United States, struggles for influence in a world that is still healing from pre– and post–Cold War wounds. This century poses many of the same challenges as the last. Will ethnic and religious politics continue to dominate relations in the Middle East? Will Africa overcome its own economic and political challenges over the next century? Central and South America, too, continue to struggle with economic and political reform more than a century after their independence from European control.

To be sure, some of these issues will come to peaceful and progressive solutions; others, however, will not. The history of some parts of the world will look drastically different 100 years from now. Others will be starkly similar. Yet the 20th and 21st centuries are, ultimately, no different from any of the time periods that came before; some things change, others remain the same. Today, we are just as human as the ancient civilizations with which we began this text, with all of their flaws and with all of their potential. We carry on their collective cultural memory, and in the end, two themes of world history will remain the same—continuity and change.

CHAPTER 9 KEY TERMS, PEOPLE, AND EVENTS

Archduke Franz Ferdinand
The man whose assassination in June 1914 started the First World War. This murder set off a chain of events leading to one of the bloodiest and most brutal wars in history.

Treaty of Versailles
Brought World War I to an end in 1919, but its terrible terms set the stage for the Second World War

Peace of Paris (1919)
After World War I ended and the Ottoman Empire finally fell apart, this treaty essentially redrew the boundaries of the Middle East, creating the basic outlines of the nations we know there today.

Weimar Republic
The German government that agreed to the Treaty of Versailles and ruled between the two World Wars

League of Nations
An early attempt by Woodrow Wilson to bring together the nations of the world in a council meant to prevent another World War

Fascism
A system of government characterized by authoritarian rule and oppression of dissent for the good of the nation; the polar opposite of liberal democracy

Vladimir Lenin, Leon Trotsky, and Joseph Stalin
The primary figures of the Russian Revolution of 1917 and the government that followed. While Lenin led the revolution itself, Stalin ultimately defeated Trotsky in a power struggle for control of the new Soviet Union.

Reichstag
German parliament

Appeasement
The political response to Nazi and other fascist aggression in the 1930s; favored most by Great Britain's Prime Minister Neville Chamberlain

Battle of Britain
A major turning point in the Second World War, during which Britain survived a massive wave of bombing by Germany. Soon after, the USSR's attack of Germany's eastern front alleviated some of the pressure on Great Britain.

Pearl Harbor
The Japanese attack on Pearl Harbor on December 7, 1941 spurred the United States to enter the Second World War against Japan. This had a great impact on the outcome of the war.

Hiroshima and Nagasaki
These two cities were bombed by the United States using nuclear weapons, the first and only time in history this has happened. The destruction of these cities brought World War II to an abrupt end.

"Iron Curtain"
A term coined by Winston Churchill to refer to the separation between Western Europe and soviet-controlled Eastern Europe in the time after the Second World War

Containment
A U.S. policy instituted by President Harry S. Truman of supporting anti-communist nations in order to contain the spread of the Soviet Union's power

Cuban Missile Crisis
A close call in the early 1960s during which Soviet and American forces almost came to war due to the tensions inherent to the Cold War

Mikhail Gorbachev
Came to power in the USSR in 1985 and immediately eased tensions with the United States by instituting policies such as glasnost ("openness) and perestroika ("restructuring"). His leadership and these policies ultimately led to the dissolution of the Soviet Union in 1991.

Zionism

A Jewish belief that they would re-inherit their homeland of Israel. This morphed into a real political movement after the two World Wars, and modern-day Israel was founded in 1948.

Palestinian Liberation Organization (PLO)

The Arab response to the founding of Israel, the PLO was founded to represent the people displaced by the new country. To this day, the Palestinians continue not to have an internationally recognized nation-state.

Mao Tse-tung

Leader of the Chinese Communist Party, Mao defeated Chiang Kai-Shek for control of the nation and established the People's Republic of China in 1949. Mao would institute several oppressive policies throughout his rule, including the Great Leap Forward and the Cultural Revolution.

Tiananmen Square

A visible clash of ideologies in modern China. Student pro-democracy demonstrations were put down in 1989 with excessive force, most notably represented by the famous photo of the protestor facing down a tank in the square.

Korean War

This was the first post-World War II war to result as part of the ongoing conflict between the United States and communist countries. North Korea invaded the South and the United States stepped in to defend it. These nations continue to have a tense relationship to this day.

Vietnam War

Another example of America's containment policy, this war was not as successful as the Korean War. The United States spent eight years fighting along South Vietnam's forces against their northern adversaries, only to pull out of the country entirely in 1973.

Indian National Congress

This body was established by the British in India to help stem the growing tide of nationalism and anti-colonialism there.

Mohandas Gandhi

The early 20th century leader of the Indian independence movement against Great Britain. His unique method of nonviolent protest garnered international support and eventually led to the establishment of an independent Indian nation in 1947.

Mexican Revolution

An early 20th century revolt against autocratic rule that resulted in the establishment of a constitutional government in 1920

Fidel Castro

The revolutionary leader of Cuba who became a communist dictator. The presence of a communist nation so close to America made the United States uneasy.

Apartheid

The South African system of separation and inequality based on race, established during colonial rule but continued after South Africa became an independent nation in the 1960s. Apartheid lasted until 1994.

Nelson Mandela

A leader of the African National Congress and outspoken opponent of apartheid in South Africa. He spent 27 years in jail as a political prisoner, only to be freed in 1994 when apartheid came to an end, and later was elected president.

Summary

○ Nationalism and industrialism combined to ignite two world wars on a scale of destruction never seen before.

○ The emergence of two superpowers, the United States and the U.S.S.R., and Cold War politics dominated the history of the second half of the 20th century.

○ The age of the empire ended in the Middle East, but European influence and Cold War politics fostered unstable regimes and decades of conflict.

○ China embraced the modern world by adopting communist political rule, yet eventually chose free-market policies to guide its economic reforms.

○ Japan emerged as an imperial power only to suffer defeat in World War II. Later it rebuilt itself as a model of democratic and economic reform in the second half of the 20th century.

○ India gained independence from Britain, but differences between Muslims and Hindus resulted in separate states.

○ South and Central America fought for independence and identity in a hemisphere dominated by the United States.

○ Africa, too, fought for independence from colonial powers but struggled with continued ethnic conflicts as well as political instability and corruption.

Chapter 9 Drill

Answers and explanations can be found in Part IV.

1. Which three countries made up the Axis Powers during World War II?

   (A) Italy, France, and Spain
   (B) Germany, the Soviet Union, and Italy
   (C) Germany, Japan, and the Soviet Union
   (D) Italy, Japan, and Germany
   (E) Switzerland, Germany, and Sweden

2. Which of the following is the name of the peace accord that marked the end of World War I?

   (A) The Treaty of Versailles
   (B) The Treaty of Berlin
   (C) The Treaty of London
   (D) The Treaty of Alexandropol
   (E) The Treaty of Vereeniging

3. Which of the following is NOT a characteristic of "cold war"?

   (A) Widespread espionage
   (B) Direct military action
   (C) Propaganda campaigns
   (D) Proxy wars waged by surrogates
   (E) Economic competition

   "We must recognize that ending the war is only the first step toward building the peace. All parties must now see to it that this is a peace that lasts, and also a peace that heals--and a peace that not only ends the war in Southeast Asia but contributes to the prospects of peace in the whole world."

4. The quote by U.S. President Richard M. Nixon above most likely refers to which of the following?

   (A) The end of the Korean War
   (B) The end of the Pacific Campaign of World War II
   (C) The end of the Vietnam War
   (D) The end of the War in Afghanistan
   (E) The end of the Cold War

5. Which military campaign by the North Vietnamese communists shocked the U.S. government and the American public in 1968?

   (A) The Easter Offensive
   (B) Operation Rolling Thunder
   (C) Operation Barrel Roll
   (D) The Spring Offensive
   (E) The Tet Offensive

6. Which of the following presents the selected events of the Cold War listed in the proper chronological order?

   (A) The Berlin Airlift; the establishment of NATO; the Warsaw Pact; the Bay of Pigs invasion
   (B) The establishment of NATO; the Bay of Pigs invasion; the Berlin Airlift; the Warsaw Pact
   (C) The Warsaw Pact; the Bay of Pigs invasion; the Berlin Airlift; the establishment of NATO
   (D) The Bay of Pigs invasion; the Berlin Airlift; the establishment of NATO; the Warsaw Pact
   (E) The Berlin Airlift; the Bay of Pigs invasion; the Warsaw Pact; the establishment of NATO

7. Which of the following events is often viewed as the catalyst for the beginning of World War I?

   (A) The assassination of Alexander Litvinenko
   (B) The assassination of Archduke Franz Feridinand
   (C) The assassination of Lee Harvey Oswald
   (D) The assassination of James Garfield
   (E) The assassination of Benito Mussolini

8. Which of the following was an American policy designed to contain the spread of communism during the Cold War?

   (A) The Monroe Doctrine
   (B) The Rumsfeld Doctrine
   (C) The Brezhnev Doctrine
   (D) The Calvo Doctrine
   (E) The Truman Doctrine

9. Which of the following was a major consequence of the end of World War I?

   (A) The beginning of American intervention in global affairs
   (B) The replacement of a military draft with an all-volunteer force in the United States
   (C) The establishment of the Third French Republic and the German Empire
   (D) The breakup of the former Ottoman Empire into several new states
   (E) The fall of the Spanish monarchy

10. Who was the communist leader of North Korea from the country's establishment in 1948 until his death in 1994?

    (A) Kim Il-sung
    (B) Kim Jong-un
    (C) Syngman Rhee
    (D) Kim Jong-il
    (E) Ho Chi Minh

Part IV
Chapter Drill
Answers and
Explanations

CHAPTER 4 DRILL ANSWERS AND EXPLANATIONS

1. **E** In the ancient world, civilizations arose in a number of different physical environments. Agriculture was vitally important to these early groups of people because large populations needed reliable food sources in order to thrive. The majority of ancient civilizations thus developed in fertile river valleys; the most advanced societies of Mesoamerica—the Olmec, the Teotihuacán, and the Maya, (E)—are unique in the ancient world because they developed according to a different pattern (there are no major rivers in the region). The Egyptian civilization, (A), developed along the Nile River Valley in North Africa; the Harappan civilization, (B), developed along the Indus River Valley in modern-day Afghanistan, Pakistan, and India; the Sumerian and Babylonian civilizations, (C) and (D), respectively, developed along the Tigris-Euphrates river system in Mesopotamia.

2. **E** The quotation cited in this question comes from *The Analects of Confucius,* (E). It describes the important Confucian ideal of filial piety, or the virtue of respect for parents and ancestors. Obedience was thought to be vital to the development of a strong society, and thus was a central component of Confucian ethical teaching. The *Art of War,* (A), is an influential Chinese treatise about military strategy and tactics; the *Avesta,* (B), is a Persian religious work associated with Zoroastrianism; the *Tao Te Ching,* (C), is a Chinese text of unknown origin that deals with Taoist philosophy and religion; the *Bhagavad Gita,* (D), is a Hindu sacred text that takes the form of a dialogue between Prince Arjuna and Lord Krishna.

3. **A** The *Epic of Gilgamesh,* (A), is an Akkadian epic poem from Mesopotamia whose standard Babylonian version dates as far back as the 13th century B.C.E. (although the literary traditions out of which it was compiled are even older). *Gilgamesh* tells the story of a king (Gilgamesh) and his doomed friend, Enkidu. *Gilgamesh* contains several plot elements that have parallels in the Hebrew Bible, such as a paradisiacal garden and a flood narrative. The *New Testament,* (B), is the second part of the Christian Bible. Its contents were written and edited primarily in the 1st and 2nd centuries C.E., but the list of recognized books (canon) was not agreed upon until the 4th century C.E.; the *Iliad,* (C), is a Greek epic poem, traditionally attributed to Homer, probably from the 8th century B.C.E.; the Egyptian *Book of the Dead,* (D), is a collection of funerary texts with religious content, spells, and accompanying illustrations, compiled over many centuries but whose origins date as far back as 2400 B.C.E. (While the *Book of the Dead* is much older than the *Epic of Gilgamesh,* it is not really literature as we understand it today; rather, its cultic purpose was to protect the dead and provide guidance in the afterlife.) The *Fables* traditionally attributed to Aesop, (E), are moralistic stories that survive in a number of textual versions and date back as far as the 6th century B.C.E.

4. **B** Agriculture in sub-Saharan Africa began to spread as early as 3000 B.C.E., and African populations grew concurrently. Because much of the continent's land did not contain favorable conditions for farming, many early African peoples were nomadic pastoralists. Beginning around 1500 B.C.E., the Bantu people from West Africa's Niger River region migrated to other parts of the continent, and gradually farming communities and settled societies grew in number. While settlements of

thousands of people existed in Africa during these years, historians know very little about the early African societies as compared to those in the Egypt, the Near East, Asia, and the Americas. The primary reason for this dearth of knowledge is the relative scarcity of archaeological finds and the fact that early African cultures did not develop systems of writing—and thus there is no textual record of these societies, (B). Choices (A) and (C) do not describe actual historical events. Choice (D) is partially correct; much of sub-Saharan Africa is tropical, and tropical climates are very destructive to organic materials. The civilizations of Mesoamerica, however, thrived in tropical climates. We know about them in part due to their monumental architecture and writings on stone. Choice (E) is incorrect because there was no system of writing in early sub-Saharan Africa.

5.   C   During the first few millennia B.C.E., when Hinduism was taking shape, society in South Asia became increasingly stratified. Hierarchically ranked groups were commonly referred to as *varnas*. These distinctions were class-based, not racially based, and were designed to organize society along economic lines. People living under this system were born, lived, and died in the same caste, and rarely mixed with those of other castes. The *Brahmins*, or priests, (C), were the highest caste in this hierarchy, and were responsible for education, overseeing religious ritual, and legal affairs. The *Kshatriya*, or warrior caste, (A), ran the government and the military, and was second in the hierarchy. Members of the third caste, the *Vaishya*, were skilled farmers, merchants, (D), and artisans or craftspeople, (E). Beneath these top three castes were the *Sudra*, or peasants, (B), unskilled farmworkers, laborers, and servants. At the bottom of the hierarchy (actually, not formally even part of the hierarchy) were the so-called "Untouchables," who were outcasts and commonly performed the most menial tasks, such as street-sweeping and cleaning latrines.

6.   D   The Olmec civilization of Mesoamerica, (D), is well known for its artwork, much of which depicted humans and animals in a naturalistic manner. Most of the surviving Olmec artwork took the form of sculpture (made of jade, basalt, clay, and other raw materials). The colossal representation of a human head pictured above this question is typical of Olmec monumental stone sculpture, which often depicts male subjects with somewhat flat, round faces and helmets. Historians have not been able to date the colossal heads precisely, but some of those found may date as early as 900 B.C.E. The most prominent art known from the Hittite civilization, (A), consists primarily of gold and bronze ornaments. The Hittites did produce stone sculpture depicting humans, but the men usually had full beards. The Egyptians, (B), produced a lot of monumental stonework, but the subjects were typically gods, pharaohs, and their queens. In Egyptian statuary, most men were portrayed with a long, thin beard or a short tufted beard as well as headgear with two large flaps. The most well-known Chinese, (C), sculpture depicting humans comes from the Qin dynasty, exemplified by the so-called "terra cotta" warriors (3rd century B.C.E.). These sculptures, however, depicted the whole human body and were life-sized. The Aztecs, (E), produced large stone sculptures of gods and goddesses. Male gods were typically depicted with deeply inlaid eyes and partially open mouths (in contrast to the closed mouths of the Olmec statuary).

7.   E   Hammurabi was a Babylonian king who ruled for almost half a century. He conquered a fair amount of land in Mesopotamia, but is most well known for the so-called Code of Hammurabi,

(E), which contains a record of one of the earliest legal systems in history. The Code, which dates to around 1750 B.C.E., consists of 282 laws and was written on a large stone stele (inscribed tablet) as well as various clay objects. The laws contained in the code deal with all sorts of matters, including contracts and transactions, religion, food and agriculture, slavery, family relationships, and sexual behavior. Written in the cuneiform Akkadian script, the Code is extremely important not only because of its place in legal history, but also because it is one of the oldest deciphered texts of its length from the ancient world.

8.   C   The term "Mandate of Heaven," (C), comes from the Chinese term *tian*, which is difficult to translate into English but concerns the cosmos or heaven (as opposed to Earth). The Mandate of Heaven was the idea, similar to the divine right of kings in Western Europe, that emperors had the right to rule and that their legitimacy derived from heaven. In certain instances, conquering emperors used this concept to justify their own usurpation of other emperors, claiming that the Mandate of Heaven permitted just rulers to take the place of unjust rulers. The concept was first used in a major way to justify the Zhou dynasty's takeover of the Shang dynasty in the 11th century B.C.E. (much earlier than the advent of Buddhism in China). The term "Four Noble Truths," (A), refers to the central Buddhist teachings about *dukkha*, commonly translated as "suffering." The Four Noble Truths illuminate what *dukkha* is, where it comes from, how it ends, and what the path to its end looks like. The Eightfold Path, (B), refers to the fourth Noble Truth, dealing with the path to ending *dukkha*. The steps of the Eightfold Path are Right Understanding, Right Thought, Right Speech, Right Action, Right Livelihood, Right Effort, Right Mindfulness and Right Concentration. The Buddhist concept of nirvana, (D), or enlightenment, is a component of the third Noble Truth and refers to a transcendent state characterized by freedom from the earthly cycle of birth, rebirth, and suffering. The Buddhist concept of karma (good and bad deeds and thoughts) is closely related to the notion of rebirth, (E). In Buddhist thought, good karma increases a living being's likelihood of being reborn into one of the favorable planes of existence (gods, demi-gods, and humans).

9.   A   Among their many notable achievements, the Maya are known for their monumental architecture, complex religious ritual, widespread agriculture, and highly organized urban society, (A). Over the course of several thousand years, the Maya built countless temples, palaces, and other structures, the most recognizable of which are probably the giant stepped pyramids discovered at sites such as Chichen Itza (modern-day Mexico) and Tikal (modern-day Guatemala). Maya religious ritual was very complex. Temples were laid out according to geographical patterns and were aligned with the calendar, and religious ceremonies involved the worship of numerous gods as well as blood sacrifice. The relatively large Maya population depended on widespread agriculture in order to sustain the cities' food needs. In densely forested areas, slash-and-burn agriculture was employed, as were irrigation systems. Maya civilizations were centered in highly organized cities, as evidenced by the remnants of residential structures surrounding many of the ancient temple sites. Choices (B), (C), and (E) can be eliminated because the Maya were not pastoralists. Choice (D) can be eliminated because the Mayan civilization did not develop in a river valley.

10. **B** The first real urban society in ancient China was the Shang, (B), prominent between around 1500 to 1100 B.C.E. While many Shang were nomads, the dynasty was ruled by kings who built imperial capitals to house temples, palaces, and administrative buildings from which to oversee their lands. These imperial cities as well as smaller provincial cities were fortified and surrounded by walls for safety. There was probably cultivated land used for agriculture both inside and outside of these walled cities. Historians do not know this for certain, but it appears that Shang society was highly stratified and peasants probably did not live within the cities' boundaries. The Zhou, (A), came after the Shang, ruling approximately 1100–400 B.C.E. The Qin, (C), came after the Zhou, ruling approximately 221–206 B.C.E. The Tang, (D), came much later, ruling approximately 618–907 C.E. The Xia, (E), prominent between around 2200 B.C.E. and 1700 B.C.E., were the first major Chinese dynasty, but the Chinese population during this period was not very centralized and there are few archaeological remains that would indicate any widespread urbanization.

CHAPTER 5 DRILL ANSWERS AND EXPLANATIONS

1. **B** The "Warring States" period of Chinese history lasted from the 5th to the 3rd centuries B.C.E. At the end of this period, the Qin dynasty, (B), emerged victorious and successfully unified various competing groups within the region. The Qin rulers established the first real Chinese empire, organizing a complex political system with a large army, supported by a relatively stable economy. The Han dynasty, (A), was indeed an imperial Chinese dynasty, but followed the Qin chronologically (c. 206 B.C.E.–220 C.E.). The Tang dynasty, (D), ruled China much later, c. 618–907 C.E. The Zhou dynasty, (E), was prominent in China prior to the Warring States period, 1100–256 B.C.E. Finally, the Gupta, (C), were not Chinese at all, but rather were a major force in India c. 240–540 C.E.

2. **E** The Draconian Constitution, (B), otherwise known as Draco's Code, was named after the Greek legal theorist Draco, who organized this written law code in response to the difficulty of accessing and systematically using the numerous oral laws dominating Athens during the beginning of its democratization process. Written around 620 B.C.E., the Draconian Constitution was well known for its harshness (hence the modern English adjective "draconian," referring to any law or punishment that is excessively severe). The Twelve Tables, (C), were the ancient Roman law codes that established the foundation of the Roman Republic. Written around 449 B.C.E., the Twelve Tables were not really comprehensive, but dealt mainly with contracts and other transactions. Like the Draconian Constitution, the Twelve Tables contained quite a few prescriptive punishments. The Code of the Assura, (D), was an Assyrian law code written around 1075 B.C.E. In many ways it is similar to the Code of Hammurabi, (A), but some historians characterize it as being harsher. The Code of Justinian, (E), was the major legal achievement of the Byzantine Empire. Compiled at the order of the emperor Justinian around 529 C.E., this massive undertaking sought to collect and organize all of the laws and imperial decrees that had been issued from the time of Hadrian (emperor from 117–138 C.E.) up to Justinian's own time.

3. **D**   Choice (D) presents the events in the correct chronological order. The Roman Republic was founded in 509 B.C.E.; the Punic Wars, fought between Rome and Carthage, occurred from 264–146 B.C.E.; Julius Caesar was assassinated in 44 B.C.E.; Constantinople became Emperor Constantine the Great's eastern capital in 330 C.E.

4. **C**   All of the answers except (C) are characteristics of major world empires in antiquity. Because ancient empires generally covered quite a bit of geographical ground, people who spoke multiple languages (or who were bilingual) often lived under the same rulers. For example, in the Roman Empire, both Latin and Greek were widely spoken, as were regional languages such as Coptic (in Egypt) and Syriac (in the Near East). Similarly, while Prakrit was the official language of the Mauryan Empire, significant portions of the population also spoke Greek.

5. **A**   The text is excerpted from the *Hymns of Zarathustra*, one of the major religious works of the Zoroastrian religion (probably written sometime in the 18th century B.C.E.). There are two clues in the quote: 1) the emphasis on truth is a major characteristic of Zoroastrian belief; 2) Ahuramazda, to whom the hymn is addressed, was the god of the Zoroastrians. The *Hebrew Bible*, (B), is one of the major texts of Judaism and Christianity (dates debated); the *Upanishads*, (C), are a collection of Vedic texts that contain some of the principal teachings of Hinduism, Buddhism, and Jainism (dates debated); the *Oxyrhynchus Hymn*, (D), named after the location where it was found in southern Egypt, is the earliest known Christian hymn to contain both musical notes and lyrics (3rd century C.E.); the *Ramayana*, (E), is a Hindu epic dating back to the 4th or 5th century B.C.E. that explores the concept of *dharma*, among other topics.

6. **C**   The image in question depicts the Acropolis of Athens, (C). The big giveaway is that ancient Athens, along with many other Greek city-states, had monumental temples with large marble pillars placed on top of high hills in the center of town. The Pyramids of Giza, (A), are surrounded by flat desert; the Church of Hagia Sophia, (B), has a prominent domed roof; the Royal Treasury at Petra, (D), is carved into the side of a cliff (think *Indiana Jones and the Temple of Doom*); the Temple of Borobudur, (E), is pyramid-shaped and is in the middle of the jungle.

7. **A**   In 260 B.C.E. the Mauryan Emperor Asoka, (A), made Buddhism the official state religion, thus weakening the Hindu establishment. Asoka undertook a fairly widespread building program, commissioning the construction of many Buddhist temples. It was also under Asoka's rule that Buddhism spread from India to China and elsewhere around the Asian world.

8. **E**   One of the most well-known aspects of political life in the Roman Republic was the separation of powers among different branches of government, (A), with the Senate composed of the elites and the common assemblies composed of citizens of lower class (plebeians). The Republic also placed term limits on political leaders, (B), to prevent any one person gaining too much power. The Republic had off-and-on (more often on) conflict with the Carthaginians, (C), for many decades—these were the Punic Wars. The legend of Rome's founding includes a mythical story about the brothers Romulus and Remus, (D). Choice (E) is NOT a characteristic: while the Republic's divided political system was unusual in the ancient world, most political power was still held by landowning (male) aristocratic elites.

9.   C   The Romans, (A), controlled Egypt politically from 30 B.C.E. to the time of the Arab conquest, (B), in 642 C.E. Alexander the Great conquered Egypt in 332 B.C.E., so during the year in question it was ruled by the Greeks, (C). Alexander himself was only there for a brief period of time during his wide-ranging military campaigns, but after Alexander's departure his influence was felt for hundreds of years. Even after the Romans came to dominate Egypt, it remained culturally Greek in many ways. The Persians, (D), controlled Egypt starting around 525 B.C.E. during the reign of Darius the Great.

10.   D   The Han emperor Liu Bang ended the domination of Legalism in China and replaced it with Confucianism. Legalism, of course, still influenced many aspects of society, but during the Han period Confucianism had the largest impact on societal developments. One of these was the creation of a civil service that was, at least in theory, open to anyone through hard work and ability (although the system still favored the elites). The creation of a terra cotta army, (A), and the standardization of state currency, (B), both occurred during the Qin dynasty, which preceded the Han dynasty; the completion of the Grand Canal, (C), occurred during the Sui dynasty, which followed the Han dynasty; the invention of the block printing system, (E), occurred during the Tang dynasty, which followed the Sui dynasty.

CHAPTER 6 DRILL ANSWERS AND EXPLANATIONS

1.   B   While it is impossible to pinpoint exact dates for some of the major religious movements in world history, (B) presents the religions listed in the correct chronological order. Judaism began with the patriarch Abraham sometime around 2000 B.C.E. Hinduism had prehistoric roots, but the religion proper can be traced to the Vedic period beginning around 1500 B.C.E. Buddhism arose from Hinduism and can best be marked by the birth of Siddhartha Gautama around 563 B.C.E. Christianity began with the birth of Jesus around 4 B.C.E. Islam began with the birth of Muhammad around 570 C.E.

2.   C   Shintoism, (C), the native religion of Japan, is centered on belief in the importance of the natural world and the ways in which the forces of nature are manifest in physical objects. Part of this belief system includes the notion that there are good and evil spirits that dwell within plants, animals, and the earth itself. Other than the belief that God created the earth and everything on it, Christianity, (A), and Judaism, (B), do not focus extensively on the natural world (at least not in terms of primary theological concerns). Jainism, (D), focuses on the essence of truth and broad metaphysical questions about the soul and the universe. Hinduism, (E), views the natural world as part of divine reality, but Hinduism is not nature-centric to the same degree as Shintoism.

3.   E   The belief that the Messiah came to earth in the 1st century C.E., (E), is a Christian belief about Jesus. While Jesus was a Jew, and the concept of the Messiah is originally a Jewish one, the vast majority of Jewish leaders and individual believers did not think that Jesus was the Messiah about whom the prophets of the Hebrew Bible had spoken. The other answer choices are all prominent characteristics of ancient Judaism.

4. **A** The Edict of Milan (313 C.E.) was a proclamation made by the Emperor Constantine the Great, stating that Christianity would be tolerated throughout the Roman Empire. The passing of this edict marked a major turning point in the history of Christianity, which up until that point had been periodically persecuted and driven underground. The Nicene Creed, (B), is the profession of faith that arose out of the Council of Nicaea in 325 C.E. Widely accepted by most Christian groups since the 4th century, the Nicene Creed contains many of the foundational tenets of Christian theology, including the nature of God, Jesus, and the Holy Spirit. The Apostolic Constitutions, (C), date to around 380 C.E. and contain teachings about ethical and ritual behavior. It is believed that this text was intended primarily as a manual for early Christian leaders. The Institutes of Gaius, (D), have nothing whatsoever to do with Christianity, but rather constituted a textbook of Roman law dating to around 160 C.E. The Chalcedonian Creed, (E), also known as the Chalcedonian Definition, is a proclamation of faith that arose out of the Council of Chalcedon in 451 C.E. This creed builds on the creeds established during some of the earlier church councils and contains a more specific definition of the nature of Jesus; it is the first creed that was not accepted by the majority of bishops in the eastern churches and its passing marked the first major split between eastern and western Christianity.

5. **B** The Maccabean or Hasmonean Revolt, (B), took place in 167–165 B.C.E. The leaders of this revolt were a prominent group of Jewish military leaders who were extremely unhappy after the conquest of Alexander the Great and the growing influence of Hellenism in their society. The Maccabees were successful for a time, but after about 100 years of Hasmonean rule the Romans ushered in a new era of foreign occupation in Israel. The civilizations in the other answer choices all occupied Jewish lands at some point in time, but not during the time of the Maccabees.

6. **D** The quote cited comes from the *Upanishads*, one of the foundational texts of Hinduism. The key is the mention of the *atman*, the Hindu term for the soul and a major focus of Hindu religious writings.

7. **A** The Shi'ites, (A), are the sect of Islam that broke with the Sunnis, (B), over the issue of who should have authority over the Muslim faith in the years following the death of Muhammad in the 7th century C.E. The Shi'ites wanted to follow Muhammad's son-in-law Ali, while the Sunnis wanted to follow Muhammad's friend Abu Bakr. The Gnostics, (C), were a Christian group that emphasized secret teachings and esoteric knowledge. They were active during the first few centuries after Jesus' death but were generally regarded as heretical by the mainstream Christian leaders. The Moors, (D), were the medieval Muslim inhabitants of the Iberian Peninsula. The Sufis, (E), are a mystical sect of Islam dating back to the end of the 7th century C.E. Sufis preach conversion of the heart and seek to perfect the process of worshipping the one true God.

8. **E** The map in question shows the extent of the spread of Islam as of about 750 C.E., (E), when Muslim armies had greatly expanded their geographical holdings from the homeland of Islam (the Arabian Peninsula) to the rest of the Middle East, parts of North Africa, and the Iberian Peninsula. The other answer choices are not correct.

9. D   While the various reasons for which some Roman authorities periodically persecuted early Christians were complex, one of the primary aspects of early Christian belief that irked the Romans was the Christians' refusal to worship the emperor as a god, (D) (the belief in the divinity of the emperor was sometimes known as the "imperial cult"). The Jews also refused to participate in the imperial cult, but were left alone more often than not because Judaism had much older historical roots and the Romans tended to respect long-standing traditions. Christianity, on the other hand, was viewed as an upstart new religion (even though it emerged out of Judaism). The other answer choices are incorrect.

10. C   The pilgrimage site depicted in the image in question is the Muslim holy site of the Ka'aba, (C), in Mecca, Saudi Arabia. The distinctive black box in the middle of the picture is the central point of the most important mosque in the Islamic world, and is the place towards which Muslims pray and are to which they are expected to travel if they are able to do so. If the black box didn't give it away, you can also see the minarets of the mosque in the background of the photo. The Western Wall in Jerusalem, (A), is a holy site for Jews; Lumbini in Nepal, (B), is the place where Siddhartha Gautama is believed to have been born, and thus is a major pilgrimage site for Buddhists; the Church of the Holy Sepulcher in Jerusalem, (D), is built over the site where early Christians believed Jesus was crucified. (The church was built during the reign of Constantine the Great in the 4th century c.e.) Vatican City in Rome, (E), is the central authority of the Roman Catholic Church and is a major pilgrimage site for Catholics from around the world.

CHAPTER 7 DRILL ANSWERS AND EXPLANATIONS

1. D   After the failed campaigns of the Crusades, the Catholic Church reacted by coming down even more strongly against Muslims in the Roman Catholic Empire, leading Pope Gregory IX to instigate the Inquisition, (D). The recapturing of Israel, (A), had been the goal of the initial Crusade, which was accomplished for a time. The Great Schism came before the Crusades, making (B) incorrect. The Protestant Revolution of England occurred much later in time and was not connected to the Crusades, (C). And the development of Islamic sects occurred much earlier in history, which eliminates (E).

2. B   The Black Plague decreased roughly one-third of the world population, leaving every part of medieval society greatly reduced. No one was safe from its reach, including the clergy who tried to abate the disease by tending to the sick. With the large number of vacancies in the local clergy left by the Black Death, many who saw an opportunity to take advantage of a position of relative local power at that time moved in to those roles, (B). Due to the extreme loss of life, famine was no longer the issue it had been prior to the Black Plague as there were so many fewer mouths to feed, (A). Since no one was safe from the reach of the Black Plague, and so there was a decrease in the merchant and artisan class, (C), which led to the ability to demand higher wages, (D), with fewer

people available to offer their services. The merchant class began to grow due to this newfound leverage, and economic stability for a greater number of people began to rise in the form of land ownership, (E), that would have been almost impossible previously.

3. **E** The Magna Carta was a document that acted much in the same way as the Bill of Rights, giving limited power to the public as well as the king, as they were all subject to the same law. Once it was signed by James I, the Barons called together an assembly, (E), which was an early version of what would become Parliament. The War of the Roses, (A), was fought two hundred years later over succession of the English throne, not the rights of the people. The Triple Entente, (B), was formed in a different era in anticipation of World War I. The Protestant Reformation of England, (C), occurred well after both the signing of the Magna Carta and the War of the Roses when Henry the VIII broke from the Catholic Church. And the American Revolution was a result of, amongst other things, the signing of the Declaration of Independence, (D), not the Magna Carta.

4. **B** The Renaissance was propelled by the philosophical approach of humanism, (B), which placed man rather than god as the focal point of study/inquiry. Deism, (A), God as a passive watcher of that which he created, was a result of the Scientific Revolution, which came after the Renaissance. Copernican Theory, (C), the heliocentric view of the universe, was a part of the Scientific Revolution as well. The social contract, (D), was part of the Enlightenment, which the Scientific Revolution was a part of, and came well after the Renaissance. Mercantilism, (E), refers to government control of trade and is not related directly to the Renaissance.

5. **D** Niccolo Machiavelli was the author of *The Prince*, a political work which focused on the attainment of goals even at the cost of morality. The goal-oriented, amoralistic aspect of the work aligns most closely with capitalism, (D). The development of socialism, (A), and communism, (B), is closely tied to the moral inequities of capitalism, making those choices incorrect. Laissez-faire economics, (C), has more to do with the lack of supervision/control over an economy, as opposed to the goal-oriented nature of capitalism. And utopianism, (E), engaged in the opposite belief system as outlined in *The Prince;* it held that men should work together to create and ideal society of equality and sharing.

6. **A** This a very tricky answer, as Florence, Italy, (A), is considered by many historians to be the birthplace of the Renaissance, due to the Medicis of Florence becoming major patrons of some of the most prominent artists during this period. However, all other cities listed built universities during the Renaissance, while Florence did not.

7. **E** The Vikings and the Ottoman Turks were different in almost every way imaginable, except they did share one thing in common: they were both able to overtake the city of Constantinople (the Vikings three times as raids, the Ottomans as a full invasion resulting in dominance of the region to become the Ottoman Empire), making (E) the best choice. Only the Vikings were known as masterful sailors of long-oared boats, (A), and only they eventually converted to Christianity out of the two groups, (B). The Ottoman Turks, on the other hand, did greatly expand the reach of Islam through the establishment of the Ottoman Empire, (C), which lasted until 1922, (D).

8.   D   Despite their ability to conquer an astounding amount of Asia and parts of Europe, the Mongols were never able to establish rule in Japan (despite multiple attempts), making (D) the best answer.

9.   B   The Great Schism between the Roman Catholic Church and the Orthodox Christian Church had been a long time coming before 1054, due to several disagreements over doctrine. These included disagreements over the sacrament of communion, (A); God as Trinity, (C); whether or not those in the priesthood could marry, (D); and the appropriateness of local language being used during church services, (E). One thing they did not disagree on was whether or not Mary (mother of Jesus) was born through immaculate conception (kept free from original sin), making (B) the best answer.

10. A   The Aztecs built an empire on par with even those of the most advanced Europeans during the 15th century, despite their lack of similar, or even comparable, technology. This included the lack of efficient food production, (A), as the Aztecs did not possess basic farming tools such as the plow and did not domesticate their livestock. It did, however, share many other attribute of the Empires of Europe. It had a strong centralized government, (B); a strong standing military, (C); and a social class system, (E). It did not have a written language, unlike the written languages of Europe, making (D) incorrect (and a very tricky answer).

11. C   The Ming dynasty was a great time of agricultural and economic prosperity for China. Zhu Yuanzhang, who became leader immediately following the overthrow of the Mongols in the Yuan dynasty, focused primarily on irrigation and intense farming of land in his agricultural pursuits. At this point in history, the Chinese had been utilizing domesticated livestock and steppes for centuries, so eliminate (A) and (E). The exchange of tea for silver, (B), came after the Zhu Yuanzhang, when China opened up to trade with the west (specifically England). Zhu Yuanzhang concentrated on the method of increasing production in agriculture, not the distribution/ownership of land, making (D) incorrect.

CHAPTER 8 DRILL ANSWERS AND EXPLANATIONS

1.   B   When King Louis XVI called together the Estates General, he omitted the Third Estate, which was made up of commoners. Believing that neither the King nor the other two Estates, made up of noblemen and members of the church, had the common people's best interests at heart, the Third Estate collected and formed the National Assembly, vowing to create a constitution, (B). The Dreyfus Affair did not begin until the late 19th century, making (A) a clear anti-era choice. The Reign of Terror came after the initial French Revolution, and was committed by the common people against the aristocracy, (C). The Treaty of Versailles, (D), and the Hundred Years' War, (E), are both far removed from the French Revolution in history; the former occurred in the early 20th century and the latter occurred in the mid-15th century.

2. **A** The Protestant Reformation accomplished a break from the Catholic Church, and thereby much greater freedom from the religious dogma that had ruled scientific inquiry up until that break, resulting in a vast increase in scientific inquiry and accomplishment, (A). The Protestant Reformation occurred after the Spanish Inquisition began, (B), as opposed to the other way around. Both (C) and (D) also happened well before the Protestant Reformation; Thomas Aquinas worked on his *Summa Theologica* from 1265–1274, although he never published it, and Ibn Rushd began his translation of Aristotle in 1169. Martin Luther's nailing of his Ninety-Five Theses to the door of Castle Church, (E), helped to precipitate the Protestant Reformation rather than be motivated by it.

3. **C** In the feudal systems of Japan, the Emperor was a powerless figurehead, with real power resting in the hands of the shoguns. Below the shoguns were differing classes of samurai, the highest of which was the daimyo. Due to this level of class system, the shogun is most analogous the monarch, the daimyo are most analogous to lords, and the samurai are most analogous to knights, making (C) the correct answer.

4. **D** There were several reasons that Britain engaged in the Opium Wars with China. Trade with China was a very lucrative and necessary aspect to the British economy, but it came with many drawbacks. China would only accept silver as a form of payment for the goods that were in high demand in England, such as tea, which led to a depletion of silver held by Britain, (A). Instead, Britain tried to use opium as a form of payment to China for the goods it sought, since it had a surplus from India, (C). The Chinese government was weary of the effects opium would (and did) have on the populace, so they not only refused opium as s a form of payment but also actively destroyed cargos of opium owned by the British, which greatly angered Britain, (B), and led to strained diplomatic relations between the counties, (E). The only one of the answer choices listed that did not contribute to Britain's involvement in the Opium Wars is, (D), as it was Britain who sought to buy tea from China rather than the other way around.

5. **A** The Treaty of Vienna ended the Napoleonic Wars in 1815. These series of wars, which lasted for roughly a decade, were aimed to expand the French Empire under Napoleon. When the treaty was drawn up, the result was that several new nations were formed, including Prussia, Poland, Italy, Hungary, and Ireland, leading to an increase in nationalism within Europe, (A). By this time the Mongols had lost power in its previous holdings, making (B) incorrect. Choices (C), (D), and (E) all occurred in the 20th century and are therefore incorrect.

6. **D** Nicolaus Copernicus, (D), wrote *On the Revolutions of Heavenly Spheres,* a completely radical work at the time it was published. Copernicus was the creator of Copernican Theory, a heliocentric approach to the universe. Church dogma stated that the Earth was the center of the universe; prior to Copernicus, no one had publicly claimed otherwise. This meant that what Copernicus was stating was heresy. Thomas Aquinas, (A), was a philosopher of scholasticism, who staunchly defended church doctrine, even when faced with contradictory information. René Descartes, (B), was an

empiricist and mathematician who focused on the acquisition of knowledge through sensory experience. Galileo, (C), was a believer of Copernican Theory, who was forced to recant his beliefs as part of the Inquisition of the Church against heresy. And Sir Isaac Newton, (E), was a follower of Copernican Theory who was able to explain not only the motion of the planets but other natural laws such as gravity.

7. **B** René Descartes, (B), was an empiricist and mathematician, who focused on the acquirement of knowledge through sensory experience. Deism, (A), was a belief in God as a passive watcher of that which he created, a theory not based on observation or sensory experience. Rationalism, (C), is a theory which states that knowledge is not sensory but rather intellectual or deductive, which is in direct opposition of empiricism. Marxism, (D), is a theoretical approach based on class conflict, so is not related to this quote. Sufism, (E), was the attempt of the Sufis to convert individuals to Islam, so it is also incorrect.

8. **C** During the African slave trade, Africans were shipped from Africa to newly formed colonies to work as unpaid manual labor. Most of these colonies were located in the New World, and Africa functioned as a provider of free (since they were stolen) natural resources for European colonizers. Once the slave trade ended, European focus was turned to Africa as an opportunity for colonization, (C). The end of the slave trade did little to change anything but the process of trade itself. African nations suffered even more post–colonization than before the end of the trade, refuting (A). No reparations were paid; Africans were exploited to an even greater extent in Africa, (B). Despite the slave trade ending, slavery in the New World would not end for another several decades, (D). The Enlightenment was one of the factors that lead to the abolishment of the slave trade, as opposed to the other way around, (E).

9. **E** Despite being a profitable area of colonization, the Spanish Empire eventually failed to to capitalize on the New World as effectively as it could have. Despite the implementation of the encomienda system, which established a strict class system in the new world for the purposes of labor and taxation, the Spanish failed to create sustainable economic infrastructure within their colonies and were therefore unable to govern them effectively, (E). The Christian missionaries who called for more humane treatment of the slave labor in the colonies, (A), were not successful in their attempts; in fact their requests only resulted in more slaves brought in from Africa, (B). While the creoles were eventually able to organize and demand specific rights from the Spanish government, they were not directly connected to the failure of the encomienda system, (C). The Dutch and French were not directly involved in the failure of the Spanish colonies, (D); they were busy making money with colonies of their own that were better managed.

10. **A** The Huguenots, the French Protestants, were protected by Henry IV of France by the signing of the Edict of Nantes in 1589, (A), which gave them protection to practice their religion as well as arm themselves. The Treaty of Versailles, (B), ended World War I, while the Treaty of Paris, (E), ended the American Revolution, making both of those answers incorrect. The Estates-General, (C), and the Tennis Court Oath, (D), were both connected to the French Revolution.

11.   E   The Boxer Rebellion was an internal Chinese rebellion against the Manchurian controlled government, Christians, and foreigners. China had been humiliated for decades by foreign military defeat, including the invasion of the Manchu, (D); the Sino–Japanese War, (A); the Opium Wars and the Treaty of Nanjing, (B), as well as by failed internal rebellions such as the Taiping Rebellion, (C). The growing frustration of some of the Chinese people eventually found its way out in 1899 in the Boxer Rebellion. The Cultural Revolution, (E), did not take place until the 1960s under the leadership of Mao Tse–Tung, which makes it the correct answer.

CHAPTER 9 DRILL ANSWERS AND EXPLANATIONS

1.   D   The three major countries that made up the Axis Powers during World War II were Italy, Japan, and Germany, (D). The major Allied powers were the United States, the United Kingdom, France, the Soviet Union, and China.

2.   A   The Treaty of Versailles, (A), ended the state of war between Germany and the Allied Powers in 1919. The Treaty of Berlin, (B), was a separate post–World War I agreement between the United States and Germany, signed in 1921. The Treaty of London, (C), was a secret pact between the Triple Entente and Italy, signed in 1915 and intended to entice Italy to turn against its former ally, Germany. The Treaty of Alexandropol, (D), ended the war between Turkish nationalists and the Armenian Republic in 1920. The Treaty of Vereeniging, (E), ended the Second Boer War in South Africa in 1905.

3.   B   The difference between "cold wars" and regular wars is that cold wars do not involve direct military action, (B). Widespread espionage, (A); propaganda campaigns, (C); proxy wars waged by surrogates, (D); and economic competition, (E), are all characteristics of cold wars, as illustrated by the cold war between the United States and the Soviet Union.

4.   C   The quote comes from President Nixon's "Address to the Nation Announcing Conclusion of an Agreement on Ending the War and Restoring Peace in Vietnam" (January 23, 1973). The Korean War, (A), formally ended in 1953 and the Pacific Campaign of World War II, (B), ended in 1945, long before Nixon was president. The War in Afghanistan, (D), is still ongoing today, and the Cold War, (E), ended with the dissolution of the Soviet Union in 1991, long after Nixon's presidency.

5.   E   The Tet Offensive, (E), was a major military campaign by the North Vietnamese communists that took both American and South Vietnamese troops by surprise. Although the offensive ultimately ended up in defeat for the Viet Cong, it had a profound psychological effect on the Americans, who did not think the North Vietnamese were capable of such a broad-based assault. The Easter Offensive, (A), was a 1972 campaign by the North Vietnamese that was designed to gain land and thereby improve their negotiating position at the end of the war. Operation Rolling Thunder, (B), and Operation Barrel Roll, (C), were both American air campaigns. The Spring Offensive, (D), of 1975 was a North Vietnamese operation that led to the surrender of South Vietnamese forces.

6. **A** The correct order of Cold War events is: the Berlin Airlift (1948); the establishment of NATO (1949); the Warsaw Pact (1955); the Bay of Pigs invasion (1961).

7. **B** The assassination of Archduke Franz Ferdinand, (B), in 1914 led to Austria–Hungary's declaration of war against Serbia, which caused a chain reaction across Europe and ultimately resulted in war. Alexander Litvinenko, (A), was a Russian KGB agent who was assassinated in London in 2006. Lee Harvey Oswald, (C), was the sniper who killed president John F. Kennedy and who was himself killed by Jack Ruby in 1963. James Garfield was the American president who was assassinated in 1881. Benito Mussolini was the World War II–era Italian fascist leader who was killed by Italian partisans in 1945.

8. **E** The Truman Doctrine, (E), was a policy enacted by U.S. President Harry Truman after World War II, designed to stop the expansion of communism under the Soviet Union. The Monroe Doctrine, (A), was a policy enacted by U.S. President James Monroe in 1823, stating that any further attempts by European nations to interfere in North or South American affairs would be viewed as acts of aggression. The Rumsfeld Doctrine, (B), named after U.S. President George W. Bush's Secretary of Defense Donald Rumsfeld, was the way in which journalists commonly referred to Rumsfeld's policy of transforming the American military into a smaller and more nimble force (in part through an increased use of air power and advanced technology). The Brezhnev Doctrine, (C), was a foreign policy platform of Soviet leader Leonid Brezhnev designed to halt liberalization efforts in Soviet satellite states. The Calvo Doctrine, (D), is an international legal doctrine that deals with jurisdictional issues and diplomatic affairs.

9. **D** One of the most long-lasting consequences of the end of World War I was the breakup of the former Ottoman Empire into a number of new states, (D), such as Turkey. The beginning of American intervention in global affairs, (A), is generally described as occurring as a result of the Spanish-American war in the late 19th century. The end of the military draft in the United States, (B), occurred after the end of the Vietnam War. The establishment of the Third French Republic and the German Empire, (C), occurred at the end of the Franco-Prussian War in the 1870s. The fall of the Spanish monarchy, (E), occurred in 1931 and precipitated the events leading up to the Spanish Civil War.

10. **A** Kim Il-sung, (A), was the long-serving dictator of North Korea from the time of the country's founding until his death in 1994. Kim Jong-un, (B), is the current Supreme Leader of North Korea; he assumed the role after his father Kim Jong-il's, (D), death in 2011. Syngman Rhee, (C), was the first president of South Korea after Korea's division; he served three terms, from 1948–1960. Ho Chi Minh, (E), was a communist revolutionary leader during the Vietnam War; he was the prime minister and president of North Vietnam and was instrumental in shaping the military strategies employed against the American and South Vietnamese forces.

Part V
Practice Test 2

- Practice Test 2
- Practice Test 2: Answers and Explanations

Practice Test 2

WORLD HISTORY
TEST 2

Your responses to the Subject Test in World History questions must be filled in on the Test 2 answer sheet (at the back of the book). Marks on any other section will not be counted toward your Subject Test in World History score.

When your supervisor gives the signal, turn the page and begin the Subject Test in World History.

WORLD HISTORY TEST 2

Directions: Each of the questions or incomplete statements below is followed by five suggested answers or completions. Select one that is best in each case and then fill in the corresponding oval on the answer sheet.

Note: The SAT World History Subject Test uses the chronological designations B.C.E. (before the Common Era) and C.E. (Common Era). These labels correspond to B.C. (before Christ) and A.D. (*anno Domini*), which are used in some world history textbooks.

1. During the Tang dynasty (618–881 C.E.), China had a powerful influence on all of the following surrounding countries EXCEPT

    (A) Bengal
    (B) Kashmir
    (C) Tibet
    (D) Korea
    (E) Vietnam

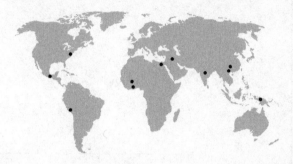

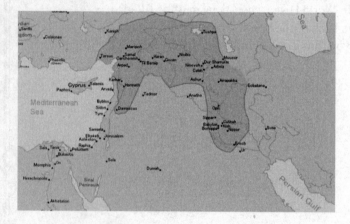

2. The map above shows the borders of

    (A) the Assyrian Empire around 850 B.C.E.
    (B) Alexander the Great's Empire c. 326 B.C.E.
    (C) the Byzantine Empire in 1200 C.E.
    (D) the Egyptian Empire around 1700 B.C.E.
    (E) the Safavid Empire around 700 C.E.

3. The dots in the map above indicate regions in which

    (A) major world religions were founded
    (B) food production arose independently
    (C) the first alphabets were invented
    (D) major ancient iron deposits were located
    (E) the earliest human skeletons have been found

4. The decision of Tsar Nicholas II to allow a national legislature in Russia in 1905 led to

    (A) the emancipation of the serfs
    (B) the establishment of a vigorous democratic tradition
    (C) the appeasement of Orthodox Church leaders
    (D) the creation of long-term plans for economic reform
    (E) the introduction of limited representative government

GO ON TO THE NEXT PAGE

Source: Jeff Soules

5. The building in this picture is

(A) a Confucian *stela*
(B) a Buddhist *stupa*
(C) a Sufi sculpture
(D) a Taoist *gong dian*
(E) an Indian war memorial

6. India's caste system, Japan's samurai class, and France's Three Estates all embody the principles of

(A) social Darwinism
(B) Marxism
(C) social stratification
(D) dynasticism
(E) egalitarianism

7. Saudi Arabia can best be described as a

(A) conservative constitutional monarchy
(B) moderate representative democracy
(C) radical communist dictatorship
(D) theocratic absolutist monarchy
(E) repressive Islamic oligarchy

8. Ghana, the first West African empire, was able to form around 750 C.E. because

(A) desertification of the Sahara led to increasing concentration of population, requiring central organization
(B) the collapse of Roman government in the region created a power vacuum that the new empire could fill
(C) social upheavals after the bubonic plague caused a complete restructuring of the pastoral society
(D) introduction of the camel first allowed the possibility of cross-Sahara gold trade, funding a centralized government
(E) military innovations introduced by the first warrior-king allowed one tribe to conquer the others by force

9. "We plan to eliminate the state of Israel and establish a purely Palestinian state. We will make life unbearable for Jews by psychological warfare and population explosion . . . . "

This speech was given before an Arab audience by

(A) Gamal Nasser
(B) Ayatollah Khomeini
(C) Al-Qadhafi
(D) Salman Rushdie
(E) Yasser Arafat

10. Pol Pot, a Cambodian revolutionary leader, believed that

(A) society must be purged of intellectuals and city-dwellers
(B) national independence depended on rapid industrialization
(C) ethnic minorities, mainly Jewish, threatened national unity
(D) peasants were inherently backward and unfit for modern life
(E) about a quarter of all people were naturally lazy and worthless

GO ON TO THE NEXT PAGE

11. Which of the following best describes the economic system that existed in Brazil and Argentina in the early twentieth century?

   (A) Colonial rule by Western European powers
   (B) A plantation system based on large-scale agriculture
   (C) Guilds of artists and craftsmen preserving traditional products
   (D) A factory system dependent on heavy industrial manufacture
   (E) An office-based workforce predominated by white-collar workers

Questions 12-13 refer to the following map. For each question, select the appropriate location on the map.

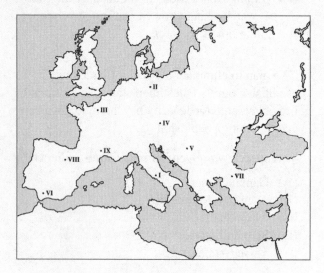

12. The site at which Charlemagne was declared emperor of Rome

   (A) I
   (B) II
   (C) III
   (D) IV
   (E) V

13. The site of the capital of the eastern Roman (Byzantine) empire

   (A) I
   (B) II
   (C) III
   (D) VI
   (E) VII

14. Herbert Spencer contributed to the development of Charles Darwin's theories by

   (A) applying Darwin's ideas to human behavior
   (B) supplying genetic evidence to prove Darwin correct
   (C) using Darwin's theories to prove the continuity of several species
   (D) proving the impracticality of Darwin's original theoretical work
   (E) tracing all existing species to a single ancestor

15. Which of the following is a system of thought based on the ideas of Saint Thomas Aquinas and Aristotle?

   (A) Scholasticism
   (B) Neo-Platonism
   (C) Capitalism
   (D) Socialism
   (E) Determinism

16. Which of the following attributes gave the Hittites a vast advantage over neighboring tribes?

   (A) A more efficient, Indo-European language
   (B) Superior social and political organization
   (C) A large slave population
   (D) Very early adoption of iron weapons and tools
   (E) Use of writing to administer a large empire

17. Foot binding in dynastic China was most similar in function and effect to

   (A) hoopskirts in revolutionary America
   (B) copper neck rings in Padaung culture
   (C) heavy tattooing among Maori groups
   (D) decorative scarification among Bantu tribes
   (E) tight-laced corsets in Victorian Europe

18. Which of the following overthrew the Ming dynasty?

   (A) The Mongols
   (B) The Manchu
   (C) Yuan dynasty
   (D) Song dynasty
   (E) Tokugawa shogunate

GO ON TO THE NEXT PAGE

19. The cartoon above depicts

   (A) the tragic role of Archduke Franz Ferdinand in World War I
   (B) Napoleon's indifference to popular criticism of his rule
   (C) Tsar Nicholas II's obstinance in the face of the Bolshevik Revolution
   (D) the Holy Roman Empire's collapse because of poor leadership
   (E) the spread of democracy in the late nineteenth and early twentieth centuries

Questions 20-21 refer to the following passage.

"The West has been through the trials brought about through excessive nationalism and yet sits idly by while millions of people are ruthlessly oppressed in search of the elusive quality of independence. When will the West learn that it must share its wisdom with these communities that are willing to sacrifice lives for the ability to govern themselves? The West should, and even must, take the lead in enforcing the peace."

20. The passage above is advocating a course of action best described as

   (A) isolationist
   (B) interventionist
   (C) colonialist
   (D) nationalistic
   (E) Realpolitik

21. Which of the following best exemplifies a failure to act according to the principles described above?

   (A) The United States during the disturbances in Central America in the 1960s
   (B) The Soviet Union during the Vietnam War from the 1950s through 1970s
   (C) The United States during the Yom Kippur War in 1973
   (D) France during the War of the Spanish Succession
   (E) France and England during World War I

22. Which of the following best describes the commercial organization of the earliest human societies?

   (A) All goods were held in common.
   (B) Trade was conducted based on a gold economy.
   (C) Written accounts were kept to track debts.
   (D) Goods were exchanged through a barter system.
   (E) Chiefs or kings managed the exchange of goods.

23. The public ceremonies of the earliest human religions were meant to

   (A) maintain the spiritual salvation of the people
   (B) ask the gods to look after the dead
   (C) atone for each believer's individual sins
   (D) teach the people to be morally upright
   (E) ensure good weather and a safe future

24. Which of the following is true of Buddhism?

   (A) Peace and enlightenment are sought through meditation.
   (B) Confucianism is the basis of its belief system.
   (C) True believers pay tribute to Buddhist priests in exchange for the absolution of sins.
   (D) It has its origins in Chinese philosophy.
   (E) Buddhists believe that faith alone justifies their beliefs.

GO ON TO THE NEXT PAGE

25. Which American ally from World War II became a major foe in the years that followed?

    (A) The Soviet Union
    (B) The United Kingdom
    (C) France
    (D) Japan
    (E) Italy

26. Which nation's merchants were allowed to trade with Japan during the isolationist policy of the Tokugawa shogunate?

    (A) Germany
    (B) Vietnam
    (C) France
    (D) The Netherlands
    (E) Great Britain

27. The figures in the image above are usually associated with the culture of which region?

    (A) Europe
    (B) Asia
    (C) Africa
    (D) North America
    (E) South America

28. Which architectural feature is shared by both Gothic cathedrals and most mosques?

    (A) Flying buttresses
    (B) Arched doorways
    (C) Painted geometric designs
    (D) Sculptures of religious figures
    (E) Large domes

29. All of the following are characteristics of West Germany after World War II EXCEPT

    (A) a free market economy
    (B) membership in the North Atlantic Treaty Organization
    (C) a stable, democratic government
    (D) a deemphasis on public welfare spending
    (E) the growth of industry

30. The Christian figure of the Virgin Mary is most similar to which of the following Buddhist figures?

    (A) Maitreya Buddha
    (B) Xuanzang
    (C) Bodhidharma
    (D) Kuan Yin
    (E) Dogen

31. The Chinese Imperial Court in the 1700s viewed trade relations with other countries primarily as

    (A) profitable exchanges to fund the Imperial government
    (B) a private matter between different countries' merchants
    (C) a means of maintaining cultural exchange with the world
    (D) tributary gifts offered to show respect from lesser nations
    (E) a nuisance that threatened the purity of Chinese culture

32. Which two philosophical schools were prominent in Han China?

    (A) Legalism and Confucianism
    (B) Shintoism and Legalism
    (C) Buddhism and Islam
    (D) Confucianism and Rationalism
    (E) Legalism and Buddhism

GO ON TO THE NEXT PAGE

33. "Brothers, you came from our own people. You are killing your own brothers. Any human order to kill must be subordinate to the law of God, which says, 'Thou shalt not kill.' No soldier is obliged to obey an order contrary to the law of God. No one has to obey an immoral law. It is high time you obeyed your consciences rather than sinful orders. The church cannot remain silent before such an abomination . . . . In the name of God, in the name of this suffering people whose cry rises to heaven more loudly each day, I implore you, I beg you, I order you: stop the repression."

The view of God held in this request most strongly resembles that of the Latin American school of thought known as

(A) Christian socialism
(B) Counter-Reform
(C) liberation theology
(D) *Pax Catholica*
(E) the Priesthood of All Believers

Source: Erik Kolb

34. The statue pictured in the photograph above displays the artistic influence of which of the following civilizations?

(A) Persian
(B) Greek
(C) Egyptian
(D) Olmec
(E) Berber

GO ON TO THE NEXT PAGE

"Since we long ago resolved never to be servants to the Romans, nor to any other than God himself, the time has now come that obliges us to make that resolution true in practice. It is very clear that we shall be taken within a day's time; but it is still an eligible thing to die after a glorious manner, together with our dearest friends . . . for it will be a testimonial when we are dead that we were not conquered for want of provisions; but that, according to our original resolution, we have preferred death before slavery."

35. The quote cited above most likely refers to which of the following events?

(A) Leonidas' last stand at Thermopylae, c. 480 B.C.E.
(B) The Battle of Marathon, c. 490 B.C.E.
(C) The Battle of Actium, 31 B.C.E.
(D) The Jews' last stand at Masada, 73 C.E.
(E) Battle of Edessa, 259 C.E.

36. Both Bismarck and Cavour began their respective unification movements

(A) with the support of the Vatican
(B) by petitioning the United States for assistance
(C) while fighting against Napoleon Bonaparte
(D) by extending the borders of their home countries
(E) by invading France

37. Which answer choice best describes the decolonization process of the following countries in the correct chronological order?

(A) India, Bolivia, Vietnam, Hong Kong
(B) Bolivia, India, Vietnam, Hong Kong
(C) Hong Kong, Vietnam, Bolivia, India
(D) Hong Kong, India, Bolivia, Vietnam
(E) Bolivia, Hong Kong, India, Vietnam

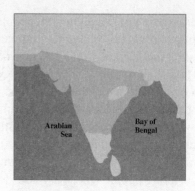

38. The shaded portion of the map above indicates areas that, around 230 B.C.E., would have been controlled by

(A) the Mughal Empire
(B) the Chagatai Khanate
(C) the Mauryan Empire
(D) the Gupta Empire
(E) the Delhi Sultanate

39. The jade carving above is representative of art styles associated with ancient

(A) South American civilizations
(B) Mesoamerican civilizations
(C) North American civilizations
(D) Chinese civilization
(E) central Asian civilizations

GO ON TO THE NEXT PAGE

40. The first independent governments of many nineteenth-century nations of the Americas, such as Mexico and Brazil, were

    (A) absolute dictatorships
    (B) representative democracies
    (C) rational anarchies
    (D) constitutional monarchies
    (E) communist republics

41. Which of the following civilizations is best known for its building accomplishments at Machu Picchu?

    (A) Zapotec
    (B) Olmec
    (C) Aztec
    (D) Maya
    (E) Inca

42. Which of the following statements about the countries of sub-Saharan Africa is LEAST accurate?

    (A) Their people have a lower per capita income than do Europeans.
    (B) Many were colonized by Europeans during the nineteenth and twentieth centuries.
    (C) Most have gained their independence from colonial powers since World War II.
    (D) They share a common culture, language, and religion.
    (E) Their economies depend more upon natural resources than upon manufacturing.

43. Which segment of society was most highly revered in most ancient societies?

    (A) Farmers
    (B) Warriors
    (C) Merchants
    (D) Hunters
    (E) Craftspeople

44. Under the *encomienda* system, Spanish conquistadors

    (A) compelled Native Americans to work on plantations essentially as serfs
    (B) established representative governments that respected native rights
    (C) were made governors and judges of specific New World territories
    (D) formed private holdings out of previously native-owned lands
    (E) provided a more humane alternative to the slavery practiced in North America

45. Which of the following religions does NOT involve the worship of many gods?

    (A) Hinduism
    (B) Jainism
    (C) Ásatrú
    (D) Taoism
    (E) Aztec faith

46. All of the following were languages commonly spoken in the Safavid Empire EXCEPT

    (A) Hindi
    (B) Azerbaijani
    (C) Turkish
    (D) Arabic
    (E) Persian

GO ON TO THE NEXT PAGE

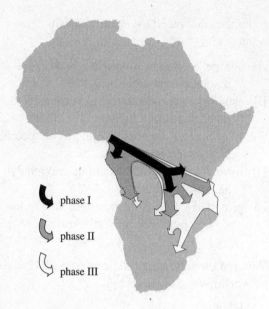

phase I

phase II

phase III

47. What does the map above show?

(A) The spread of Sahel farming technology around 1200 C.E.

(B) Exploration routes used by European explorers in Africa circa 1800

(C) The spread of the Bantu language family in the first 1,000 years C.E.

(D) The settlement path of the Dutch in Africa in the nineteenth century

(E) The growth of the Zulu Empire in the late 1800s

48. The earliest human civilizations were able to develop because

(A) abundant local resources made farming unnecessary to ensure population growth

(B) large irrigation projects permitted farming for the first time, creating a specialized nonfarming population

(C) advances in military technology enabled them to subjugate their neighbors and capture slaves

(D) local crops were fit for farming, enabling food surpluses and a large, sedentary population

(E) following their herd animals exposed them to many different environments and ideas, stimulating progress

"The mode of production of material life conditions the social, political, and intellectual life process in general. It is not the consciousness of men that determines their being, but on the contrary, their social being that determines their consciousness."

49. The philosophy that this quote promotes was instigated most strongly by which of the follow revolutions?

(A) Protestant Revolution

(B) Scientific Revolution

(C) Glorious Revolution

(D) Copernican Revolution

(E) Industrial Revolution

50. In the years immediately following World War I, the economies of France and England

(A) flourished as a result of the "peace dividend"

(B) faltered because of high unemployment

(C) grew slowly because of increased exports to the United States

(D) suffered as a result of the worldwide Great Depression

(E) prospered as a result of receiving massive German war reparations

GO ON TO THE NEXT PAGE

51. The image above most likely depicts a harvest that took place along the banks of which of the following rivers?

    (A) The Yellow River, China
    (B) The Indus River, Indian subcontinent
    (C) The Mississippi River, North America
    (D) The Tigris and Euphrates Rivers, Mesopotamia
    (E) The Nile, Egypt

52. Which of the following is a common characteristic of ancient religions?

    (A) Belief in a single god with the power to save mankind
    (B) Belief that humans must be sacrificed to appease angry gods
    (C) Belief that in the afterlife good deeds will be rewarded and evil deeds punished
    (D) Belief in communication with the spirit world through transcendent experience
    (E) Belief that spirits must be worshipped in a structure used for veneration alone

Questions 53-54 refer to the following passage.

"Attention, all people in markets and villages of all provinces in China: Now, owing to the fact that Catholics and Protestants have vilified our gods and sages, have deceived our emperors and ministers above, and oppressed the Chinese people below, both our gods and our people are angry at them, yet we have to keep silent. This forces us to practice the I-ho magic boxing so as to protect our country in order to save our people from miserable suffering."

53. The passage above was most likely written in

    (A) 1815
    (B) 1853
    (C) 1900
    (D) 1938
    (E) 1949

54. The revolt encouraged by the author of the passage above

    (A) was suppressed by a coalition of Western nations
    (B) led to the Japanese invasion of Manchuria
    (C) was a direct response to the United States' "opening" of Japan
    (D) brought an end to the Opium Wars
    (E) led to the installation of a Chinese communist government

55. Which conflict marked the beginning of Japan's rise to dominance in East Asia?

    (A) The Russo-Japanese War
    (B) The First Sino-Japanese War
    (C) The Second Sino-Japanese War
    (D) World War I
    (E) World War II

GO ON TO THE NEXT PAGE

Source: Erik Kolb. Circle of ceremonial
standing stones, northwest Portugal.

56. The giant stones pictured in the photograph above
most likely come from which period of human
history?

(A) Paleolithic
(B) Neolithic
(C) Mesozoic
(D) Iron Age
(E) Classical Antiquity

57. The statue shown above reflects which of the
following artistic influences?

(A) Ancient Roman and French Gothic
(B) Celtic and Viking
(C) Sung-dynasty Chinese
(D) Spanish Baroque
(E) Ottoman and Byzantine

58. The investiture controversy of the Middle Ages was

(A) a disagreement between the Pope and secular
rulers over the appointment of bishops
(B) a widespread heresy that Pope Innocent III
sought to eliminate by launching a crusade
(C) a quarrel between Florentine political factions
(D) a scandal involving King John that led to the
church interdict over England
(E) a dispute over the orthodoxy of granting land
to monasteries

59. "Stability and authority are more important to
the success of communist revolutions than the
presence or absence of a certain economic system.
Authoritarian command is necessary to determine
the country's economic and political future and
ultimately its success in achieving the ideal
communist state."

The quote above can be attributed to

(A) Karl Marx
(B) Peter the Great
(C) Nicholas II
(D) Joseph Stalin
(E) Dean Acheson

60. People first arrived in Polynesia and Micronesia
traveling via

(A) outrigger canoes
(B) swimming
(C) caravels
(D) small rafts
(E) steamships

GO ON TO THE NEXT PAGE

61. In 1529, the Christian world was disturbed when Vienna was besieged by

    (A) the Polish-Lithuanian Commonwealth
    (B) the Hapsburg Empire
    (C) the Byzantine Empire
    (D) the Ottoman Empire
    (E) the Kingdom of Granada

62. Which of the following was common to the diet of both the ancient Mesoamerican and, later on, the Northeast American peoples?

    (A) Barley
    (B) Maize
    (C) Wheat
    (D) Llama
    (E) Goosefoot

63. The Pueblo of the American Southwest traditionally lived in

    (A) villages of conjoined adobe buildings
    (B) movable shelters made of tanned hides
    (C) longhouses built of wood and earth
    (D) dugout residences built below the ground
    (E) individual, mostly isolated, family farm settlements

64. Each of the following was an immediate effect of the events surrounding World War II EXCEPT

    (A) the development of sophisticated weapons systems
    (B) the emergence of the United States and the Soviet Union as major superpowers
    (C) the end of the Great Depression
    (D) the end of European colonialism in Africa
    (E) the creation of the International Monetary Fund

65. In most world cultures, eunuchs performed the tasks of

    (A) military leadership within the armed forces
    (B) direct rule over the country or nation
    (C) finding and evaluating women for the royal harem
    (D) administration and maintaining the royal household
    (E) planning and executing large public projects

66. Which of the following was a similarity between the Khoi people of South Africa and the Berbers of Algeria around 1000 C.E.?

    (A) Both groups had been converted to Islam.
    (B) Both groups were nomadic herders.
    (C) Both groups had been colonized by Europeans.
    (D) Both groups engaged in extensive agriculture.
    (E) Both groups were part of large trade networks.

67. All of the following weapons were in use in both Japan and England in the seventeenth century EXCEPT the

    (A) halberd
    (B) arquebus
    (C) sword
    (D) bow
    (E) staff

68. Julius Caesar of the Roman Empire and Zhu Di of the Ming dynasty were similar in which way?

    (A) Both were sons of the emperor.
    (B) Both were generals who took over the government.
    (C) Both were famous for expanding their countries' borders.
    (D) Both wrote books about their conquests.
    (E) Both were eventually assassinated.

GO ON TO THE NEXT PAGE

Source: Erik Kolb

69. The image of the Buddha shown above was one of two destroyed in 2001 by

   (A) Sri Lankan rebels
   (B) the Taliban government
   (C) improper restoration attempts
   (D) an earthquake in Kazakhstan
   (E) local vandalism

70. "The Master said, 'Those who are not benevolent cannot for long reside in straightened conditions, cannot for long reside in happiness; the benevolent one is secure in benevolence, the knowing man seeks profit from benevolence."

   The quotation above is most likely from the

   (A) Ibn Rushd
   (B) Great Code of Charlemagne
   (C) *Analects* of Confucius
   (D) Egyptian Book of the Dead
   (E) Rig Veda

71. The enormous church-turned-mosque called Hagia Sophia, depicted in the photograph above, was built under which of the following Emperors?

   (A) Constantine
   (B) Diocletian
   (C) Decius
   (D) Augustus
   (E) Justinian

72. The discovery of the Rosetta Stone led to which of the following?

   (A) The ability of archaeologists to read and understand Egyptian hieroglyphics
   (B) The discovery that Egyptian culture predated that of Babylon
   (C) The development of a theory of a universal language
   (D) An understanding of the Babylonian political system
   (E) Innovations in Italian Renaissance architecture

GO ON TO THE NEXT PAGE

73. Of the following empires, which one established a state religion that originated in India?

    (A) Meiji Japan
    (B) The Safavid Empire
    (C) The Mughal Empire
    (D) The Tang dynasty
    (E) The Mali Empire

74. Napoleon's empire and the empire of the Mongols were similar in all of the following ways EXCEPT:

    (A) Both successfully invaded and conquered Russia.
    (B) Neither was able to unify Europe completely.
    (C) Both led to large exchanges of ideas between regions.
    (D) Both disrupted traditional monarchies in the conquered areas.
    (E) Both inspired fear and hatred throughout Europe.

75. Which of the following is most responsible for the rise of the Muscovite princes in fourteenth- and fifteenth-century Russia?

    (A) The collection of tribute on behalf of the Golden Horde, which enriched the local princes
    (B) The retreat of the Golden Horde, which was concentrating military efforts in India
    (C) The defeat of Polish forces by the Swedes, which eliminated a major threat in the west
    (D) The autocratic policies of Peter the Great, which consolidated the principality
    (E) Military partnership with Sweden, which strengthened Muscovy's standing in the region

76. Which of the following religions mandates that its adherents make a pilgrimage to Mecca at least once in their lifetime if they are able to do so?

    (A) Islam
    (B) Judaism
    (C) Zoroastrianism
    (D) Hinduism
    (E) Buddhism

77. Which country currently has the world's largest population of Muslims?

    (A) Saudi Arabia
    (B) Indonesia
    (C) Iraq
    (D) Iran
    (E) Singapore

Source: Erik Kolb

78. The aqueduct pictured in the photograph above was characteristic of the engineering achievements of which of the following civilizations?

    (A) Roman
    (B) Babylonian
    (C) Israelite
    (D) Inca
    (E) Gupta

GO ON TO THE NEXT PAGE

79. Which best describes how the Navajo way of life changed between 1500 and 1800?

    (A) The Navajo were originally hunter-gatherers and then took to raiding other tribes.
    (B) The Navajo were originally settled farmers who became nomadic herders.
    (C) The Navajo were originally peaceful nomads who became exclusively traders.
    (D) The Navajo were originally nomadic hunters who became settled farmers.
    (E) The Navajo were originally sedentary farmers who developed intertribal trade.

80. The sine law, algebra, and irrational numbers are just a few of the major mathematical concepts known to the West primarily through

    (A) Arabic scholars around 1000 C.E.
    (B) Greek philosophers around 300 B.C.E.
    (C) Renaissance mathematicians around 1600 C.E.
    (D) Indian philosophers around 600 C.E.
    (E) Babylonian scribes around 1200 B.C.E.

81. All of the following were important reasons for the flourishing of art and literature in fourteenth-century Europe EXCEPT

    (A) improvements in clerical education
    (B) the desire of popes and kings to assert their power over one another
    (C) contact with the sophisticated societies of the Islamic world
    (D) a steady revival of the European economy
    (E) the widespread availability of ancient Greek literature

82. Louis XIV encouraged nobles to live at Versailles in order to isolate them from powerful allies in their home regions. This is most similar to which of the following practices?

    (A) Medieval European priests were often made bishops far from their homelands.
    (B) European nobles, like the Duke of Burgundy, often held multiple separate fiefdoms.
    (C) The office of the Papacy was never considered to be hereditary.
    (D) Bureaucrats in Ming China were sent to serve in districts far from their hometowns.
    (E) Islamic mamluks were kidnapped as children and raised far from their homes.

83. India's largest export product during the period of British colonization was

    (A) cotton
    (B) opium
    (C) spices
    (D) palm oil
    (E) teak

84. Which country was temporarily ruled by the Mamluks in the 1200s ?

    (A) France
    (B) The Ottoman Empire
    (C) The Abbasid caliphate
    (D) Egypt
    (E) Turkey

GO ON TO THE NEXT PAGE

85. Which of the following statements about the Glorious, American, and French Revolutions is correct?

   (A) The Glorious Revolution was instigated over concerns regarding the monarchy's religious affiliations, while the American and French Revolutions were fought to gain independence from Britain.
   (B) Each Revolution resulted in the reclamation of power by the general population of each nation and formation of a democratic governing body.
   (C) Religious tolerance was the impetus for each Revolution.
   (D) The Glorious Revolution was both the shortest and least violent of the three.
   (E) Each revolution proved beneficial to all members of society.

86. "When thy LORD said unto the angels, I am going to place a substitute on earth; they said, Wilt thou place there one who will do evil therein, and shed blood? but we celebrate thy praise, and sanctify thee. GOD answered, Verily I know that which ye know not; and he taught Adam the names of all things, and then proposed them to the angels, and said, Declare unto me the names of these things if ye say truth. They answered, Praise be unto thee; we have no knowledge but what thou teachest us, for thou art knowing and wise. GOD said, O Adam, tell them their names. And when he had told them their names, GOD said, Did I not tell you that I know the secrets of heaven and earth, and know that which ye discover, and that which ye conceal?"

   The text above is a selection from the holy book of the

   (A) Greeks
   (B) Hindus
   (C) Babylonians
   (D) Buddhists
   (E) Muslims

87. An archaeologist examining the mask pictured above would NOT be able to prove that the object

   (A) had a religious significance to its creator
   (B) is 30 centimeters high
   (C) was made with metal tools
   (D) resembles other objects found in South America
   (E) is constructed of tropical hardwood

88. Which of the following civilizations had the most rigid caste system?

   (A) Tang China
   (B) Medieval Europe
   (C) Ancient India
   (D) The Aztec Empire
   (E) The Ottoman Empire

89. How were fifteenth-century funeral customs in East Asia different from those in Europe?

   (A) In Europe the dead were buried with precious objects.
   (B) In Europe the spirits of the dead were worshipped.
   (C) East Asian mourners always cremated their dead.
   (D) Mourners wore white clothing in East Asia.
   (E) Mourners left gifts of flowers at East Asian gravesites.

GO ON TO THE NEXT PAGE

90. All of the following were once part of the French colonial empire EXCEPT

    (A) Vietnam
    (B) the Philippines
    (C) southern India
    (D) Madagascar
    (E) Algeria

91. The Islamic Golden Age (750–1200 C.E.) most contributed to worldwide scientific and cultural development by

    (A) preserving and extending the classical traditions of the Mediterranean and southwestern Asia
    (B) ensuring a peaceful environment in which new scientific progress could begin
    (C) supplying ample funds for public-sponsored scientific research
    (D) creating interstate competition that spurred new ideas
    (E) providing a religious justification for expanding the frontiers of human knowledge

92. Enkidu, Hanuman, and Sun Wukong are similar because they are each

    (A) important figures in Indian mythology
    (B) supernatural beings who each took the form of a monkey
    (C) major figures in Buddhist religious practice
    (D) the embodiment of an ideal moral model for their believers
    (E) a companion to a mythic hero on a major journey

93. "The Tiger doesn't need to land one mighty killing blow. If the Tiger does not stop fighting the Elephant, the Elephant will die of exhaustion."

    The quote above describes the events that occurred during

    (A) the Korean War
    (B) World War I
    (C) World War II
    (D) the Iran-Iraq War
    (E) the Vietnam War

"As he was traveling, it happened that he was approaching Damascus, and suddenly a light from heaven flashed around him; and he fell to the ground and heard a voice saying to him, 'Saul, Saul, why are you persecuting Me?' And he said, 'Who are You, Lord?' And He said, 'I am Jesus, whom you are persecuting.'"

94. The quotation cited above most likely describes the conversion experience of which of the following religious figures?

    (A) The Apostle Peter
    (B) John the Baptist
    (C) Pontius Pilate
    (D) The Apostle Paul
    (E) The Disciple John

95. Plato, Zhuangzi, and Averroes were all ancient

    (A) philosophers
    (B) religious leaders
    (C) healers
    (D) military leaders
    (E) debaters

STOP
If you finish before time is called, you may check your work on this test only.
Do not turn to any other test in this book.

Practice Test 2: Answers and Explanations

- Practice Test 2 Answer Key
- Practice Test 2 Explanations
- How to Score Practice Test 2

PRACTICE TEST 2 ANSWER KEY

Question Number	Correct Answer	Right	Wrong	Question Number	Correct Answer	Right	Wrong	Question Number	Correct Answer	Right	Wrong
1.	A	___	___	33.	C	___	___	65.	D	___	___
2.	A	___	___	34.	B	___	___	66.	B	___	___
3.	B	___	___	35.	D	___	___	67.	B	___	___
4.	E	___	___	36.	D	___	___	68.	B	___	___
5.	B	___	___	37.	B	___	___	69.	B	___	___
6.	C	___	___	38.	C	___	___	70.	C	___	___
7.	D	___	___	39.	B	___	___	71.	E	___	___
8.	D	___	___	40.	D	___	___	72.	A	___	___
9.	E	___	___	41.	E	___	___	73.	D	___	___
10.	A	___	___	42.	D	___	___	74.	A	___	___
11.	B	___	___	43.	B	___	___	75.	A	___	___
12.	A	___	___	44.	A	___	___	76.	A	___	___
13.	E	___	___	45.	B	___	___	77.	B	___	___
14.	A	___	___	46.	A	___	___	78.	A	___	___
15.	A	___	___	47.	C	___	___	79.	D	___	___
16.	D	___	___	48.	D	___	___	80.	A	___	___
17.	E	___	___	49.	E	___	___	81.	E	___	___
18.	B	___	___	50.	B	___	___	82.	D	___	___
19.	C	___	___	51.	E	___	___	83.	A	___	___
20.	B	___	___	52.	D	___	___	84.	D	___	___
21.	A	___	___	53.	C	___	___	85.	D	___	___
22.	D	___	___	54.	A	___	___	86.	E	___	___
23.	E	___	___	55.	B	___	___	87.	A	___	___
24.	A	___	___	56.	B	___	___	88.	C	___	___
25.	A	___	___	57.	A	___	___	89.	D	___	___
26.	D	___	___	58.	A	___	___	90.	B	___	___
27.	B	___	___	59.	D	___	___	91.	A	___	___
28.	B	___	___	60.	A	___	___	92.	E	___	___
29.	D	___	___	61.	D	___	___	93.	E	___	___
30.	D	___	___	62.	B	___	___	94.	D	___	___
31.	D	___	___	63.	A	___	___	95.	A	___	___
32.	A	___	___	64.	D	___	___				

PRACTICE TEST 2 EXPLANATIONS

1. **A** The Tang dynasty was a high point in Chinese cultural and political influence, such that the Chinese controlled, culturally influenced, or at least received regular tribute from most of the other national groups in the region. Bengal, (A), did not pay tribute to China or receive major direct cultural influence at this time; the Himalayas and the mountainous regions of modern-day Bhutan and Myanmar provided a barrier against political influence or cultural diffusion. The rest of the countries listed were integrated into a trade network that centered on China, and had substantial subservient dealings with the Tang empire. This group includes even the cultures of Kashmir, (B), which were tied into the Chinese sphere of influence by the Silk Road trade.

2. **A** This map shows an area stretching from the north and east of the Levant, in an arc that does not quite reach the Persian Gulf, through what is now the southern part of modern-day Turkey. These are the borders of the area controlled by the early Assyrian Empire, (A). The region shown does not include Greece, so it could not be Alexander's empire, (B), or the Byzantine Empire, (C). Because it does not include the Nile, it could not be Egypt, (D). And the Safavid Empire, (E), would include access to the Persian Gulf, so that choice is also incorrect.

3. **B** These dots list all of the places where paleobotanical and anthropological evidence suggests that food production, (B), arose independently as the first local crops were domesticated. No major world religion, (A), was founded in the Andes, nor were alphabets, (C), in use in the Americas prior to the arrival of Europeans. Similarly, American societies did not use iron before the Europeans, which rules out, (D). Last, the earliest human skeletons have been found in Africa and date to well before the arrival of humans in the Americas or in New Guinea, so (E) is also incorrect.

4. **E** Tsar Nicholas II created the Russian legislature, called the Duma, in 1905 in order to appease critics of the government. The Duma soon demanded greater power, and Nicholas angrily moved to limit its powers. Eventually, though, the Duma regained power and persuaded the military to abandon the tsar, leading to Nicholas's abdication. Russian serfdom, (A), had been abolished in 1861 by Tsar Alexander II. Vigorous democracy, (B), was not a part of the Russian experience of the early 20th century. The Orthodox Church, (C), lost influence with the rise of revolutionary forces, so a national assembly did not help it. Finally, the calling of the national assembly had more to do with politics than economics, so (E) is the correct answer.

5. **B** The solid stone construction, stacked sloping eaves, tall tower on the top, and images of the meditating Buddha identify this as an East Asian–style Buddhist *stupa*. Originally built as reliquaries holding pieces of or objects associated with highly revered figures, *stupas* eventually became buildings built as temple statuary or as places of reverence. A Confucian *stela*, (A), would have something written on it—*stelae* are upright stones with inscriptions of some kind. The Sufis, (C), were Islamic mystics; because Islam prohibits the depiction of the human form, especially in religious contexts, this could not be an Islamic artifact. *Gong dian*, (D), means "palace" in Chinese, but there is no particular building in Taoism referred to as a *gong dian*. This is not a war memorial, (E): no martial images or text referring to military conflict appears on the carving.

6. **C** Each of the systems identified in the question defines individuals by social class. Each creates rigid laws pertaining to the ways in which members of each group may behave toward one another. Social Darwinism, (A), is the belief that Darwin's theories of physical evolution apply also to human interaction. Marxism, (B), is an economic and political philosophy that holds that communism is the natural conclusion of economic history. Dynasticism, (D), is a term used to describe the system by which one family continues to rule, for example, by creating a dynasty. Egalitarianism, (E), is the opposite of social stratification: it demands that all members of a society be treated as equals.

7. **D** Saudi Arabia is ruled by the Saud family, which has been in power since the 1930s, after gradually consolidating large portions of the Arabian Peninsula. The Saudis are a royal dynasty, which eliminates (B), (C), and (E). Saudi Arabia is more closely associated with theocracy, or rule by religious authorities, than with constitutional limitations, so choose (D). Indeed, the Saudi Basic Law passed in 1992 states that the only constitution in Saudi Arabia is the Qu'ran, which clearly means that religion plays a role in governance.

8. **D** The Ghanaian Empire (8th to 11th centuries C.E.) grew thanks to trade to the north and east, made possible primarily by the camel. Without camels, goods could not be transported across the harsh landscape of the Saharan desert, making (D) the correct answer. Centralization, (A), was not in and of itself the reason Ghana became powerful; the growth of local wealth, however, was. Rome was not influential in the part of western Africa in which the Ghanaian Empire arose, so eliminate (B). Widespread plague, (C), did not affect Africa until much later. Ghana's growth in this period is not the result of a single warrior-king, so eliminate (E).

9. **E** Yasser Arafat was the principal leader of the Palestinian statehood movement from the founding of Fatah in 1957 until his death in 2004. He was a highly controversial figure for most of that time, with staunch supporters and detractors on all sides, including allegations of making one statement to the international world and another to the Arab world, as he did in this quote, (E). Gamal Nasser, (A), was a pan-Arab nationalist leader of Egypt from 1954 to 1970, but he was more concerned with direct action to establish a Palestinian state at Israel's expense than with a slow psychological war. The Ayatollah Khomeini, (B), was the political leader of the 1979 Iranian revolution; he was no fan of Israel, but he was not interested in establishing a Palestinian state either. Libyan leader Al-Qadhafi, (C), was, like Nasser, interested in pan-Arabism and a Palestinian state, but he would not have advocated population explosion as a means to this end. Salman Rushdie, (D), is an expatriate Indian novelist living in England; he is not known to have any relation to the Palestinian statehood movement.

10. **A** Pol Pot was a Cambodian dictator who led a quasi-communist revolution in the 1960s and 1970s. The Khmer Rouge, Pol Pot's revolutionary group in Cambodia, believed that the true leading class of socialist revolution was the agrarian peasants and that the ideal communist paradise in Cambodia would require only a few million farming inhabitants;. He was, therefore, determined to kill urbanites and intellectuals, (A), and any non-rural workers in general. Although Pol Pot did believe in national independence, he did not believe in rapid industrialization, (B). The Khmer Rouge

discriminated against ethnic minorities, dispersing them and forbidding them to speak their languages, but they were not primarily Jewish groups, (C)—the Cambodian Jewish population is not very large. The Khmer Rouge believed that peasants were the most important and most forward-thinking class of society, not the least, (D), and the party never indicated that a quarter of all people were worthless because of laziness, (E)—only because of class background.

11. **B** Connect to the era and the country: in the early 20th century, South American countries were no longer influenced by colonial rule, but they were not in the late-20th-century stage of having an office-based workforce, eliminating (A) and (E). Choice (B), a plantation system of large-scale agriculture, best describes the economic systems of these two countries. Following colonial rule, many Latin American countries became authoritarian regimes and continued to harvest cash crops for export. This created two economic tiers, the wealthy plantation owners and the lower classes that made up most of the farm labor. Industrial development did not occur in Latin America until later in the century, eliminating (D).

12. **A** The place where Charlemagne was declared emperor of Rome…hmm, Rome would be a good guess, don't you think? Roman numeral I on the map shows the location of Rome, the correct answer to this question.

13. **E** Constantinople (now Istanbul), Turkey, was the capital of the Byzantine Empire.

14. **A** Herbert Spencer applied Darwin's theory of biological evolution to human societies, thus laying the groundwork for the study of cultural anthropology. Spencer compared societies to living organisms, theorizing that many of the same laws that govern evolution—for example, adaptation and survival of the fittest—also applied to the history of civilization.

15. **A** Scholasticism is characterized by its reliance on human reason and science. It was developed by the ancient Greek philosopher Aristotle. Scholasticism stood in direct contrast to the more theoretical, idealistic philosophy of Plato, Aristotle's contemporary. In the Middle Ages, Saint Thomas Aquinas revived Aristotle's philosophy, attempting in his *Summa Theologica* to use reason and science to prove the existence of God.

16. **D** The Hittites (or, as they probably called themselves, the Neshites) were one of the early peoples establishing an empire in the Mesopotamian and Anatolian region, which existed from the 18th to the early 12th centuries B.C.E. Their political organization does not appear to have been unusually good, but their weapons certainly were: the Hittites were the first, or one of the first, peoples in the world to begin using mainly iron for weapons and tools, making (D) the best answer. The Hittites were the first Indo-European-speaking people to become dominant in the area, but linguistic differences, (A), did not have any significant role in establishing their empire. The Hittites were also not known for owning slaves, so eliminate (C). Their use of writing, (E), was most likely not remarkable, because the Sumerians had introduced written record keeping a thousand years earlier.

17. **E** Foot binding was a well-known body modification practice carried out in China during the later imperial period, reaching its peak under the late Qing dynasty. By tightly wrapping young girls' feet with cloth, parents could cause their daughters to grow up with tiny feet as the bones broke and the muscles merged together. This was considered attractive, and perhaps also a status symbol, as bound feet made it very difficult for a woman to walk and impossible for her to do any kind of manual labor except for sewing or handicrafts. This practice resembles wearing tightly laced corsets, (E), which also cause semipermanent body modification due to external constriction, though the negative effects of tight lacing are nowhere near as severe as with foot binding: Women who wore tightly laced corests could certainly walk and function socially, although they would be unlikely to be able to perform heavy labor while wearing such a restrictive garment. Hoopskirts, (A), were inconvenient but caused no body modification; tattooing, (C), and scarification, (D), both result in permanent changes in appearance, but do not limit the body's functionality in any way. In Padaung Thai culture and in Ndebele South African culture, women wear large copper or brass rings, (B), that cause the appearance of a lengthened neck by compressing the rib cage. Again, though, this body modification, while permanent, is not debilitating or damaging to the woman's ability to work nor is it as notoriously painful as foot binding.

18. **B** The Ming dynasty (1368–1644) was a period of agricultural and economic prosperity for China. It was overthrown by the Manchu—invaders from the north (Manchuria)—in the mid-17th century, and the Qing dynasty was established under their rule. The Mongols, (A), immediately preceded the Ming dynasty with the Yuan dynasty, (C), which means both of those answer choices can be eliminated. The Song dynasty, (D), preceded the Mongol invasion (Yuan dynasty) of China, and the Tokugawa shogunate, (E), took place in Japan.

19. **C** This cartoon depicts Tsar Nicholas II at the end of his reign. How do we know? The cartoon depicts a noble figure riding "despotism" off a cliff. This eliminates Franz Ferdinand, (A), who was not a despot. The figure is obviously a monarch, as can be determined from his crown, the scepter, and the orb beside him. This figure's attitude is one of disinterest or disregard for the fact that he is about to fall into an abyss, and he wears a mustache, eliminating (B) because it is clearly not a picture of Napoleon. You can also safely eliminate (D): this monarch is disinterested, but the Holy Roman Empire officially came to an end when Francis II abdicated after a military loss to Napoleon. In other words, the last Holy Roman Emperor went down fighting. Last, there is no indication of democracy anywhere here, leaving (C) as the correct answer.

20. **B** Interventionists, as their name implies, favor intervening in the affairs of other countries. It doesn't matter that the speaker here has noble aims, namely, to help ease the transition of other societies to democracy. Isolationists, (A), seek to avoid involvement with foreign nations, preferring, as their name implies, to isolate themselves from the rest of the world. Colonialists, (C), seek to colonize foreign lands for economic gain. Nationalists, (D), believe that their country is superior to others. They are fiercely loyal to their nation and regard all others with suspicion and contempt. Advocates of Realpolitik, (E), take a practical approach to politics, shunning ethical and moral considerations when they necessitate impractical actions.

21. **A** Guatemala, Cuba, El Salvador, Honduras, and Panama are among the Central American nations that experienced war and political upheaval in the 1960s. Often the turmoil was the result of citizens seeking increased democratization and human rights. The United States, embroiled in political unrest at home and already committed to an unpopular war in Vietnam, did not act to shore up democratic movements in the region. To eliminate incorrect answers, you need to realize that the quote focuses on the necessity for democratic nations to help democratic revolutionaries within oppressive regimes. The Soviet Union does not qualify as a democratic nation, allowing you to eliminate (B). Similarly, the War of Spanish Succession, (D), involved succession to the Spanish throne, not a popular democratic uprising. France and England did not "sit idly by" during World War I, so you can eliminate (E). The Yom Kippur War, (C), was fought over territorial rights; it was not a revolution and, therefore, does not fit the parameters laid out by the quotation.

22. **D** The earliest human societies exchanged goods without currency or writing, which suggests a barter system, (D), as the correct answer and eliminates (B) and (C). Not all early societies held goods in common, so (A) is also incorrect. Although many early governments took great care to regulate trade, they usually did not personally take goods from one party to give them to another, so (E) is overly ambitious and should be eliminated.

23. **E** The earliest forms of human religion have been mostly forgotten because of the passage of time and the advent of later religious traditions. However, evidence suggests that early religious ceremonies were dedicated to ensuring the favor of the gods, as represented in good weather, good harvests, and a safe future, which means that (E) is correct. The ideas of spiritual salvation, (A), and atonement for personal sins, (C), did not become part of religious traditions until around the advent of the great religions, nor was the role of religion in moral instruction, (D), prominent until the historic period. Although it is possible that early religious ceremonies existed to ask the gods to protect the dead, (B), that focus on the well-being of the individual is more characteristic of later religious practice and of personal belief rather than public ceremony.

24. **A** Meditation is a central practice of most sects of Buddhism. (Pure Land Buddhists are among the few who do not stress the importance of meditation; instead, they advocate the importance of faith in achieving enlightenment.) It should be noted that no blanket statement could correctly describe the multifaceted Buddhist faith, particularly because its progenitor, Siddhartha Gautama, rejected all dogma as unnecessarily restrictive. It is easy to say, however, what Buddhism is not: it is not based on Confucianism, (B), or any Chinese philosophy, (D). Rather, it developed in India as a reaction to Hinduism and other indigenous religions. The notion of sin, (C), is foreign to Buddhism, and so too is the practice of paying for the absolution of one's sins. For the majority of Buddhists, Buddhism is not a faith-based religion, (E), but rather a spiritual and philosophical approach to living.

25. **A** The Soviet Union, (A), along with the United Kingdom, France, and others, was an American ally during World War II. In the years (the Cold War years) that followed, however, the United States and the Soviet Union were at odds.

26. **D** Under the Tokugawa shogunate's *Sakoku* policy, Japanese people were not allowed to leave Japan, and foreigners were not allowed to visit. There were some exceptions that permitted a certain amount of trade to take place: most of these were with other East Asian nations, but the Dutch, (D), were also allowed to maintain their trading contact in Nagasaki. Not all nations in Pacific Asia were permitted trade, either; the Vietnamese, (B), were not allowed trading contacts with Japan. The other European countries listed in the answer choices were also excluded from Japanese trade.

27. **B** The image of the Three Buddhist Monkeys is most commonly associated with Asia, (B); it decorates a temple in Nikko, Japan. The kinds of monkeys depicted here are not native to North America, (D), or Europe, (A), nor are they associated with Africa, (C), or South America, (E).

28. **B** Arched doorways are typical of both Gothic cathedrals (which emphasize height and light) and most mosques, making (B) the best answer. Flying buttresses, (A), and sculptures of religious figures, (D), are typical of Gothic cathedrals but not mosques. Painted geometric designs, (C), and domes, (E), are typical of mosques but not Gothic architecture.

29. **D** West Germany, a country formed during the post–World War II era, adhered to the policy—continued since the reunification of Germany—of providing comprehensive social programs, including health insurance, unemployment benefits, retirement benefits, and welfare. The country also promoted free-market trade, (A); democracy, (C); and industrial growth, (E). It joined NATO, (B), in 1955.

30. **D** In the Catholic faith, the Virgin Mary is viewed as the mother of God (in the form of Jesus Christ), who intercedes with her Son on behalf of the people of the world. Similarly, Kuan Yin, (D), is a Bodhisattva capable of hearing the problems of everyone in the world and alleviating the people's suffering. Xuanzang, (B), and Bodhidharma, (C), were both monks instrumental in transmitting Buddhism and Buddhist scriptures from India to China, while Dogen, (E), was a famous Zen master. The Maitreya Buddha, (A), is believed by most Buddhists to be the next full Buddha (after Siddharta Gautama/Shakyamuni Buddha), who will be born into this world sometime far in the future; he is a teacher-figure or savior-figure, not similar to the Virgin Mary.

31. **D** The Qing dynasty ruled China during the 1700s, during which the Chinese Empire was very powerful. The empire's wealth was built on its tributary system, according to which conquered powers turned much of their wealth over to the Chinese in homage to the empire's greatness. In the 1700s, Europeans expanded their imperial trading contacts into Asia, but the Chinese expected the Europeans to act as other lesser powers did: by paying tribute. By the late 1700s, the Qing refused Western goods altogether, making (D) the best answer. Choices (A) and (C) can be eliminated because the Chinese did not consider trade with the West an exchange of equals. Choice (B) is incorrect, because Chinese rulers were involved in setting trade policies. Choice (E) is too negative—trade wasn't a nuisance as much as it was something that needed to reflect the greatness of the empire.

32. **A**   The two philosophies that were dominant in Han China were Legalism and Confucianism, (A). The Han Emperor Liu Bang was instrumental in the ascendancy of Confucianism in Chinese society, but both ideologies were popular among large portions of the Chinese population.

33. **C**   This quotation is drawn from Oscar Romero, a leading figure in the independence movement in El Salvador in the 1960s and 1970s. He was an influential Catholic bishop who preached liberation theology, (C), the doctrine that the Church must take action against repressive governments, economic and social injustice, and human rights abuses. Christian socialism, (A), is a much broader category: it refers to belief in both socialist causes and Christianity, as well the belief that the two are related, but it is not necessarily Catholic, nor as aggressively involved in politics. Counter-Reform, (B), might be a name applied to the Catholic Counter-Reformation movement; this took place during the 17th century and was no longer relevant by Romero's time. *Pax Catholica*, (D), is a made-up term, and the Priesthood of All Believers, (E), was a doctrine of Martin Luther's regarding everyone's direct access to God (and direct responsibility for his or her own soul).

34. **B**   The statue depicted in the photograph is a marble copy of a bronze Greek statue from around the 2nd century B.C.E. The emphasis on poise and the idealization of the human body are common characteristics of classical Greek sculpture that were copied extensively by the Romans and others.

35. **D**   The quote cited comes from the Jewish historian Flavius Josephus' account of the siege of Masada, (D), where the Romans emerged victorious. Other than the mention of the Romans in the quote, another hint is the line about preferring death to slavery (many of the Jews at Masada committed suicide rather than surrender).

36. **D**   Bismarck led the movement for German unification; Cavour was a central figure in the unification of Italy. Both were active in the mid-19th century. Choice (D) makes sense: if you're going to unify your surrounding area, you probably are going to have to do it by expanding from your home base. Bismarck began in Prussia, from which he first attacked the Danish holdings Schleswig and Holstein. Cavour used Sardinia as a home base, first driving the Austrian army from the island and then focusing on capturing the mainland.

37. **B**   Bolivia was named for Simón Bolívar, its liberator, who was dead by the early 19th century. Hong Kong was still officially a British protectorate until it was returned to Chinese rule in 1993. This means that (B) must be the correct answer. India was not free of British rule until World War II, with the British recognizing Indian independence in 1947 after the formal demand for independence was made in 1942. Vietnam was liberated from French rule a very short time later than India; independence was declared in 1949, and the country was recognized in 1954, though North Vietnam had declared independence in 1945 and was recognized by the communist bloc in 1950. Regardless, (B) is the only answer choice which correctly lists Bolivia as the first liberated country and Hong Kong as the last region to be decolonized.

38.   C   The only force that had the kind of influence in India depicted in this map during 230 B.C.E. was the Mauryan Empire, (C). The other empires existed much later in Indian history: the Mughal Empire, (A), and the Delhi Sultanate, (E), were both Islamic empires, and Islam was founded in the early 7th century; the Chagatai Khanate, (B), was a part of the former domains of Genghis Khan, and so would not have been in existence before the 13th century; the Guptas, (D), ruled this territory around 230 C.E., not B.C.E.

39.   B   The sculptured headdress, facial features, and silver earrings of the figure in this carving most resemble artwork from ancient Mesoamerican civilizations, (B). The South American civilizations of the Amazon basin, (A), did not have jade to carve; the Incas are better known for architecture and geometric patterns than carving of figures dressed in this way. North American civilizations, (C), are not known for jade carving. Although the Chinese, (D), created much carved-jade art, they would not have carved a figure with this appearance, particularly this headdress style. Central Asian civilization, (E), such as those of the Mongols, likewise did not produce carved jade with resemblances to this piece.

40.   D   The first wave of Central and Southern American independence movements led to one of the most progressive forms of government common at the time, but the 19th century wasn't necessarily very progressive. Rational anarchies, (C), is incorrect, and communist republics, (E), are also a little out-of-era, while representative democracies, (B), are too progressive for the time. Absolute dictatorships, (A), describe modern totalitarian systems; the earlier absolutist systems would have been governed by kings, which leaves constitutional monarchies, (D), as the 19th-century progressive government system of choice.

41.   E   The Inca people, who lived in the Andes Mountains in what is now Peru, are famous for their majestic cities—notably Machu Picchu, which is considered one of the wonders of the ancient world.

42.   D   Sub-Saharan Africa—the lower two-thirds of the African continent—is a virtual cornucopia of cultures and faiths. This diversity has been the cause of much ethnic and religious strife throughout history. The civil war in Rwanda during the 1990s is one recent example.

43.   B   In most ancient societies, the warrior class, (B), was held to be at the top or near the top of the social hierarchy, (After all, it is generally considered wise to be careful toward people who can kill you!) In many cases, when warrior classes existed as a specialized social class, the necessary skills would have required much time to develop (which could otherwise have been spent working) and the equipment would have been very expensive, meaning that only already privileged groups such as the wealthy or the nobility could form a military class. In any event, warriors were near the top of the social hierarchy in the class systems of the ancient Indians, the Aztecs, and the medieval Europeans, to name but a few. Although farmers, (A), were considered (at least nominally) the most significant class in ancient China, there was no separate warrior class in this culture, and farmers or peasants were usually seen as being low-status people because of their poverty. Merchants, (C),

were also usually fairly high-status but did not typically have a separate social role; in some cultures (as in the Chinese class system) they were considered to be low-status because their traveling and searching after money were both nonproductive and "suspect." Hunters, (D), usually did not exist as a separate class within any formal system; by the time a society develops rigid class lines, either hunting is a minority occupation, or it is a universal one. Craftspeople, (E), were not usually as high in social rankings worldwide as warriors.

44. **A**   The *encomienda* system was the means by which the Spanish used to govern their colonies in the Americas. It involved "civilizing" projects that forced Native Americans to work on Spanish-owned plantations, much as serfs, (A). Given the high mortality rates and terrible conditions in which these laborers lived, this system was not a more humane alternative to North American slavery, (E); they were certainly not representative governments with respect for natives' rights, (B). Choice (C), is inaccurate in that an *encomienda* owner would function more as a noble than a governor and a judge; the *encomiendero* did not legally have judicial power. Technically, the holdings were not the possession of Spanish custodians, (D); they nominally still belonged to the Native Americans.

45. **B**   Of these religions, Jainism, (B), much like Buddhism, does not involve the worship of a polytheistic pantheon. In Buddhism, and to a certain extent Jainism, if the Hindu gods are regarded as existing, they are viewed as yet another type of being, and worshipping them would be somewhat akin to worshipping another person—misguided from a religious perspective. Hinduism, (A), and the Aztec, (E), religious system both involve large numbers of gods; Asatrú, (C), the modern name for a revived version of traditional Scandinavian religion, also worships a large pantheon. Taoist practitioners, (D), depending on the sect, may worship hundreds of gods just within the practitioner's own body, in addition to a very wide pantheon of other gods and spirits in the world.

46. **A**   The Safavid Empire was founded by a noble family from Azerbaijan and came to rule over an Islamic Empire in Persia and parts of Turkey. Thus, Hindi, (A), is the one language in this list that would not have been commonly spoken by at least some residents of the empire, which had no Indian territory. Azerbaijani, (B); Turkish, (C); and Persian, (E), would have been the native languages of some segments of the empire's inhabitants, and Arabic, (D), would have been used as the sacred language of the Qu'ran, if not also spoken by some of the population.

47. **C**   This map shows the three stages of the spread of Bantu languages, (C), throughout Africa, as the Bantu-speaking peoples left their original home in West Africa and spread, displacing previous African residents in central and southern Africa. The Bantu peoples would have spread Sahel farming technology, (A), but this took place prior to 1200 C.E. The map does not show European explorers' exploration routes, (B); for instance, many explorers attempted to go up the Nile to find its source. The path of Dutch settlement in Africa, (D), is not shown here: the Dutch settled in South Africa, below the end point of the arrows in this map. The Zulu Empire, (E), was an empire founded by a Bantu-speaking people of South Africa; it would have originated in the south, not ended there.

48. **D** The origins of human civilization are tightly related to the origins of agriculture: it was only through settled farming that the population surpluses needed to create the types of society we refer to as "civilization" could take place. This is not to minimize the complexity and importance of nonagricultural societies, which do develop incredibly complex social structures; but the term *civilization* has a specific meaning related to technological progress and cultural permanence that excludes groups that cannot support a sedentary population. A stable population was possible in some parts of the world because there were local crops, (D), that could be raised by people, and people happened to notice that fact. In some cases abundant natural resources, (A), permitted non-agrarian peoples to develop sedentary lifestyles, but these were very rare circumstances. Large-scale irrigation, (B), actually comes after the foundations of society; you need to have a pretty complex government to direct the construction of large infrastructural projects like irrigation. Military advances, (C), came only as a result of a large, sedentary population so that people could learn from one another's ideas and there were more people around to invent things. In any case, there would have been few slaves to capture and little to make them do before the development of agriculture. Nomadic herders, (E), following their animals may have been exposed to many environments, but this was not a primary factor in the development of the earliest human cultures.

49. **E** This quote is from Karl Marx, a social theorist/philosopher who was one of the fathers of socialism. Socialism was based on the growing disparity between the bourgeoisie (upper) class and proletariat (lower) classes of society as a result of the Industrial Revolution, (E), and the consolidation of the ownership of the forces of production, removing it from the hands of the laboring class. The Protestant, Scientific, and Copernican Revolutions were all closely tied to the Enlightenment, as was the Industrial Revolution, but none were concerned with the mode of productions and their influence on society, so eliminate (A), (B), and (D). The Glorious Revolution, (C), was a political revolution that took place in England in order to overthrow King James II due to religious concerns rather than class related social unrest; therefore, (C) is also incorrect.

50. **B** After the war, hundreds of thousands of soldiers returned home, only to find that work was scarce. Not only had the war ravaged many European economies, but during the war, the United States had developed into a world economic leader. As a result, unemployment rates exploded during the 1920s: in England, the rate neared 25 percent in 1921. The growth of the American economy resulted in diminished exports to the United States, not an increase, so eliminate (C). The Great Depression did not hit Europe until 1930, more than a decade after the end of World War I; eliminate (D). Germany was unable to pay its reparations because its economy had been decimated by the war, so (E) can be eliminated.

51. **E** The image from a tomb in Egypt is from the 13th to 11th centuries B.C.E. and depicts a grain harvest along the Nile River, so (E) is the answer. The big clue that the image is Egyptian is the presence of hieroglyphic writing.

52.　**D**　The term *ancient religions* describes native spiritual beliefs before the arrival of the dominant modern religions, including the predecessors of Hinduism in India and religious Taoism in China. Most ancient religions included beliefs in some form of spiritual transcendence, or the ability of privileged seers or wise men or women (shamans) to communicate with the spirit world on behalf of others, often through some form of trance. This makes (D) the best answer. Ancient religions were generally polytheistic, which eliminates (A). Not all early religions required sacrifice, which gets rid of (B). Such religions do not all have cosmologies that include the afterlife, which eliminates (C). Although (E) is characteristic of later religions that built mosques, churches, temples, and other structures for the purpose of worship, this is not a general characteristic of ancient religions.

53.　**C**　The passage refers to the Boxer Rebellion of 1900, (C), a nationalist Chinese uprising against foreigners (primarily European imperialists) and Chinese Christians (who were regarded as traitors for having adopted a European religion). Like many Chinese, the Boxers were angered by the abuse and exploitation of the Chinese and their resources by outsiders. The Chinese government secretly supported the rebels, although officially it condemned their guerrilla attacks. An international coalition of troops overwhelmed the Boxers within a year. The Boxer Rebellion is often seen as a stepping stone toward the eventual overthrow of the Chinese monarchy in 1911.

54.　**A**　See the explanation for question 53.

55.　**B**　Japan's rise to dominance in East Asia began during the 1894 war known as the First Sino-Japanese War, (B), in which Japan, for the first time since the start of the Qing dynasty, showed the potential to break the traditional authority of China in East Asian affairs by defeating the Chinese army in a matter of months. Although Japan won the Russo-Japanese War, (A), handily, winning itself great-power status in the bargain, that war took place ten years after the First Sino-Japanese War. The Second Sino-Japanese War, (C), was the war for control of China, which ended in Japanese defeat at the end of World War II. Japan was not a major player in World War I, (D), and lost World War II, (E), outright.

56.　**B**　The megaliths (giant stones) pictured in the photograph come from the Neolithic period, (B), of human history, about 8000–3000 B.C.E. It was during this time period that humans began to develop technologically and built stone circles such as this one (in modern-day Portugal) and the more famous one at Stonehenge in England.

57.　**A**　Ancient Roman sculpture followed the traditions of classical Greek sculpture: realistic depiction of the subject, monumental subject matter, and the use of the well-balanced *contraposto* position for the subject. Similarly, French Gothic sculptors emulated the Greeks, reintroducing naturalism to an art form that had grown highly stylized during the medieval period. Celtic sculpture is decorative and highly ornate, as is Viking carving, so eliminate (B). The sculpture in the picture clearly exhibits Western influences, allowing you to eliminate (C) and (E). Spanish Baroque sculpture, (D), was executed almost exclusively in wood; quite often, these works would be painted realistically, with great attention given to skin tones. Some were even provided with real hair, glass eyes, and clothing.

58.   **A**   The investiture controversy centered on the ceremony for the appointment of bishops (the ceremony is called investiture). During the early Middle Ages, the practice developed of allowing non-ordained royalty to participate in the investiture service. Even though this role was ceremonial —lay princes bestowed the bishop with a ring and staff, both symbols of their authority to represent Rome—it came to symbolize all efforts by royalty to bring the Church under secular control. Indeed, in many places, bishops considered themselves more beholden to the local ruler than to the Pope.

59.   **D**   Stalin, like other leaders of the Russian Revolution, understood the apparent contradiction of a Marxist communist insurgence in Russia. Marx, after all, had predicted that communism would take hold in highly industrialized nations; Marx's theory was that communism would result naturally from advanced industrialization, as it was the logical successor to capitalism. Stalin, Lenin, and Trotsky all attempted to justify the Russian Revolution within a Marxist framework. The quotation represents Stalin's effort. Karl Marx, (A), as noted above, would never have imagined a communist revolution in Russia or China. He believed that England, which in the 19th century was chock-full of oppressed workers, would be the first country to "go red." Peter the Great, (B), and Nicholas II, (C), were tsars, not communists. Dean Acheson, (E), was an important American leader during the Cold War. Although less fervently anticommunist than many of his contemporaries, he would never have justified communist revolutions, as the speaker of the quotation does.

60.   **A**   People first crossed the large expanse of the Pacific Ocean in outrigger canoes, (A), canoes that have one or two additional pylons attached to the main body, which greatly improves stability. Swimming, (B), was not the primary means whereby peoples of any era crossed the thousands of miles of ocean between the Polynesian and Micronesian islands. Caravels, (C), were a type of European ship meant for long ocean travels; two of Columbus's ships were caravels. Human settlement in Oceania predates the development of both caravels and steamships, (E), by a large margin. Although it has been demonstrated to be possible to cross the open ocean in small rafts, (D), they are not very seaworthy, and most early peoples would not have undertaken exploration without any particular destination in mind on only a raft.

61.   **D**   In the later Middle Ages and the Renaissance, one of the greatest threats perceived by most European Christians was Islamic invasion. This fear was only heightened when, in 1529, the Ottoman Empire, (D), besieged Vienna. Although the Ottomans were eventually defeated, the anxiety created in Central Europe would last for centuries. The Polish-Lithuanian Commonwealth, (A), enjoyed close relations with the Austrians during this period and would not have been likely to sack Vienna. The Hapsburg Empire, (B), was seated in Vienna; it would not have besieged its own city! The Byzantine Empire, (C), no longer existed in 1529—it had been conquered by the Ottoman Empire in 1453. The Kingdom of Granada, (E), was annexed when Ferdinand and Isabella completed the *reconquista* in 1492, so it also no longer existed by 1529.

62.   **B**   One of the many agricultural products originating in the Americas—and a nutritious and diverse source of food—is corn, or maize, which was first domesticated in Mesoamerica, although considerably later than the early crops of the Old World. Choice (B) is correct. The domestication of maize was instrumental in allowing a large enough population density for Mesoamerican cultures to develop. Barley and wheat are examples of Old World crops, while goosefoot was a spinach-like crop that grew in the Northeast. Therefore, (A), (C), and (E) can be eliminated. The llama, (D), was an animal common to Peru but not domesticated in Mesoamerica, which had no large domesticated animals at all.

63.   **A**   The Pueblo are a group of Native Americans living in the southwestern United States and in northwest Mexico since before the arrival of the Spanish. They practiced a traditional form of agriculture and lived in large, densely settled communities: the Spanish name *pueblo* comes from a Latin word meaning "village." Choice (E) is not typical of any pre-Columbian native people, nor most farming peoples generally; farms require a community to share specialized skills. Choices (B) and (D) are both typical of Great Plains peoples, while longhouses, (C), are characteristic of the Native Americans in the northeastern United States (the kind of large tree trunks needed to build a longhouse were not common in the southwest region). *Adobe*, another Spanish word, in (A) may give you an additional hint that this is the correct answer.

64.   **D**   This is a tricky question, because European colonialism in Africa, (D), did end after World War II. The question, however, asks about the *immediate* effects of the war, and the vast majority of African nations did not gain independence until the late 1950s and early 1960s. So while it may be true that World War II precipitated the end of colonialism in Africa, the events in the other answer choices are more in line with the time period in question.

65.   **D**   Eunuchs are men who have been castrated for various political or social reasons. Across cultures, eunuchs were often used to administer the royal household, as their lack of dynastic potential made them seem more trustworthy and less likely to seek power for themselves, making (D) the best answer. Eunuchs have held many different roles in different societies, but direct rule, (B), has rarely been one of them because societies in which castration is practiced have tended to be dynastic, and eunuchs have difficulty maintaining dynasties. Eunuchs did have important military leadership and public planning roles in ancient China, but this was not the norm, so eliminate (A) and (E). Choice (C) is also incorrect; eunuchs were used as harem guards in many cultures, but not all societies that had eunuchs also had harems.

66.   **B**   The term *Berber* refers to a group of historically nomadic people living in North Africa, specifically west of Egypt through to the western Mediterranean (the Maghreb). The Khoi, like the San Bushmen, are a people of South Africa who speak languages with click consonants and lived a hunter-gatherer lifestyle until only very recently, when continuing encroachment by the rest of the world has made this mode of life mostly untenable. The Khoi adopted herding from the Bantu-speaking peoples (the Zulu brought domestic cattle to South Africa during the Bantu Expansion). Islam never penetrated directly through central Africa into southern Africa, and even today the Khoi

are not traditionally Muslims; eliminate (A). Choice (C) is unlikely because European colonialism (in a sense other than the Greek and Roman expansion in the Mediterranean) did not start until several hundred years later. Agriculture, (D), is not characteristic of either people; the Khoi in particular were resistant to practicing settled agriculture, and no suitable crops would be available for their region until the 18th century anyway. Choice (E) is true of the Berbers, as they were part of the Muslim Empire, but not true of the Khoi, who had contact with very few other peoples and would have had relatively little to trade.

67. **B** The arquebus, (B), is a type of firearm that preceded the musket and rifle. It was used extensively in Europe during the 16th and 17th centuries. Although it was introduced into Japan in the 16th century, its use was banned during the Tokugawa shogunate (1603–1868). All of the other weapons listed existed in both places during this time.

68. **B** Julius Caesar fought a civil war in 50–48 B.C.E. to establish himself as the first effective emperor of Rome. Zhu Di, the third emperor of the Ming dynasty in China, came to power after a civil war with his nephew. Both were military men who usurped power by violent means. However, there was no emperor of Rome before Caesar, so he could not have been the son of the emperor, (A), (although Zhu Di was). Caesar's Gallic Wars famously expanded the borders of Rome to the Atlantic, and he did write a book about it, but Zhu Di fought the established Mongols and Vietnamese, aiming to make them dependent vassals rather than claim their territory outright. Eliminate (C) and (D). And of the two men, it was Caesar who was unpopular enough to reach the end his life under the senators' knives, so eliminate (E).

69. **B** The giant Buddha shown in the photograph was later completely destroyed by the Taliban regime of Afghanistan in an attempt to rid the country of non-Islamic influence. Explosives were required to destroy such a large stone structure, so local vandalism, (E), and improper restoration attempts, (C), do not make sense. The Buddha in the picture is about 1,500 years old and has likely survived numerous earthquakes, making (D) unlikely as well. Sri Lanka is a majority Buddhist nation, and even Sri Lankan rebel groups would not likely destroy such a sacred figure of Buddhism.

70. **C** This quotation comes from the *Analects* of Confucius. Confucius's writings appear primarily as a collection of short, metaphorical anecdotes that offer guiding principles for one's life. If you are familiar with the writings of Confucius, this is a relatively easy question, as the other answer choices don't fit very well. But if you're not as familiar with the writings of Confucius, use POE to narrow down the answer choices. You can eliminate (A), (B), and (D) because of the anecdotal style of the quotation. Ibn Rushd, (A), is considered one of the greatest Islamic philosophers, who wrote primarily on the relationships among Islam, science, and independent reasoning. The Great Code of Charlemagne, (B), was a draconian set of laws that restricted the practice of native religions in Germanic and Saxon lands under his rule. And finally, the Egyptian Book of the Dead, (D), was primarily a prayer book used in coordination with the mummification process. This leaves the Rig Veda, (E), a Hindu sacred text, as a possible answer choice. The Rig Veda is primarily a collection

of writings praising the gods, which is not evident in the quotation. Therefore, the *Analects* of Confucius, (C), is the answer.

71. **E** The Emperor Justinian, (E), commissioned the building of the monumental basilica (church) known as Hagia Sophia in what was then Constantinople (modern Istanbul) in the 530s C.E. The building was converted into a mosque after the city fell to invading Muslim armies in 1453.

72. **A** The Rosetta Stone, discovered by French troops in 1799, allowed anthropologists to decipher Egyptian hieroglyphics because its text appeared not only in hieroglyphs but also in ancient Greek—which they could read. By comparing the texts in both languages, anthropologists were able to determine the meanings of many hieroglyphs and thus begin to understand the Egyptian's ancient written language.

73. **D** The Tang dynasty, which ruled China from the 7th to the 10th centuries C.E., temporarily made Buddhism the state religion. There are two parts to this question: you are looking for (1) a religion that originated in India and (2) a nation that made the religion its official religion. The two major world religions that originated in India are Hinduism and Buddhism (Jainism has never been the official state religion of any country). Hinduism, for the most part, has not spread beyond the Indian subcontinent, which leaves Buddhism. Now you are looking for a nation that adopted Buddhism as its religion. The Mali, Safavid, and Mughal Empires were all Muslim, so (E), (B), and (C) are incorrect. This leaves the Tang dynasty and Meiji Japan as answer choices. But the Meiji era was the 19th-century period of rapid industrialization and reemphasis of traditional Japanese Shinto religion, which is out of era, particularly for the age of the spread of Buddhism. Therefore, the Tang dynasty, (D), is correct.

74. **A** The Mongols invaded Kievan Russia in the late 1230s and controlled around half of the population. Although Napoleon succeeded in invading Russia and burning Moscow, he did not conquer the entirety of Russia, and he did not control Russia at any point.

75. **A** When the Mongols invaded Russia in the 13th century, Kiev was the most powerful principality, and Moscow was an obscure trading outpost. However, with the fall of Kiev at the hands of the Tatars (another name for the group of Mongols who conquered Russia), Moscow began to grow in power thanks to the Tatars' tribute system. The Muscovite princes enriched themselves in the process of collecting tribute on behalf of their Tatar overlords. By 1480, the year the Golden Horde was driven from Russia by Ivan III, Muscovy had grown substantially as a political, military, and religious center, making (A) the best answer. The Golden Horde was not encroaching into India at this time, which eliminates (B). The Deluge, a period of significant losses by Poland to the Swedes, occurred in the 17th century, making (C) incorrect. Choice (D) is also out of era: Peter the Great ruled from 1682 to 1725. Choice (E) is the opposite of what you're looking for, as Sweden was an enemy to Russia for much of this time, culminating in the First Russo-Swedish War at the end of the 15th century.

76. **A** The *hajj*, or pilgrimage to Mecca, is one of the Five Pillars of Islam, mandated to all believers, so (A) is correct. The other Pillars are the profession of faith, ritual prayer, charity for the poor, and fasting.

77. **B** Indonesia, (B), is the world's fourth most populous country, with 230 million residents. As a Muslim-majority nation with 86 percent of the populace being Muslim, it is also the home of the world's largest Muslim population. Saudi Arabia, Iraq, and Iran all have smaller populations than Indonesia, so eliminate (A), (C), and (D). The city-state of Singapore, (E), is much smaller than Indonesia and not a Muslim-majority country (its most popular religion is Buddhism, at roughly half of all Singaporeans).

78. **A** The aqueduct pictured in the photograph comes from Portugal and dates to the early period of the Roman Empire, (A). The Romans are famous for their engineering prowess, and the aqueducts (used to transport water) could stretch anywhere from 1 to 60 miles long. Amazingly, many of these aqueducts have survived almost 2,000 years and can still be found around Europe, North Africa, and the Middle East today.

79. **D** The Navajo are a tribal group of Native Americans who lived in the Great Plains and, later on, the Southwest. The year 1500 came just after the arrival of Europeans in the Americas; the year 1800 fell during the period of European American expansion westward across North America. So this question is really asking, "How did the arrival of European settlers affect the Navajos?" As American settlers moved west, native people were either driven from their land or forced to settle permanently into lands set aside for them by the government, making (D) the best answer. Eliminate (B) and (E) because domesticated crops and farming were not widespread in most of the American plains before the Columbian Exchange. Choice (C) is too extreme. The Navajos weren't exclusively traders, and most nomadic groups are not completely peaceful; intertribal warfare is characteristic of every tribal society. For the same reason, you can eliminate (A); hunter-gatherer tribes tend to raid one another frequently.

80. **A** Arabic scholars such as al-Khwarazmi and al-Biruni are credited with developing much of the math we use today, including algebra and trigonometry. These developments took place in Baghdad in the 9th and 10th centuries C.E. The word *algebra* comes from the Arabic *al-jabr*. The Arabic scholars built on the earlier ideas of Indian philosophers, but it is primarily through the Arabs that we understand these concepts today, so eliminate (B) and (D). Choice (C) is too late—algebra and the sine law were already known by 1600. Babylonian scribes, (E), brought us the 360-degree circle and the 60-minute hour, but not algebra.

81. **E** This is a tricky question, one that requires you to pay careful attention to each word of each answer choice. Choice (E) is untrue because of the word *widespread*; before the advent of the printing press, no works of literature were available on a widespread basis. Works of ancient Greek literature were available to scholars, but scholars constituted only a tiny fraction of the population.

82. **D** The idea of removing a locally prominent person from his home base of power has appeared several times in history, both in Louis XIV's France and in Ming China, (D). Medieval priests were made bishops far from their homelands, (A), mainly because of the shortage of educated local men to fill the available bishoprics. Nobles with multiple fiefs, (B), held them for the wealth and power they provided, not to weaken their resistance to central authority. The Papacy's not being hereditary, (C), is unrelated to Louis XIV's practice. Islamic Mamluks were kidnapped and raised as private soldiers of the sultan, (E), but this was not to separate them from a local power base, but rather to prevent them from having regional loyalties that might lead to a coup.

83. **A** The British Empire took advantage of many resources India had to offer during its colonization of the subcontinent, the largest export of which was cotton, (A). The other answer choices, except for palm oil, (D), were also exports of India. To answer this question you need to know about the era in which Britain colonized India and which answer choice makes the most sense. The British started to expand their presence in India in the 18th century through the British East India Company. Which of the answer choices makes the most sense for the largest commercial export? Opium, (B), was indeed an Indian export of India, as were spices, (C), and teak, (E). But raw cotton from India fueled the British economy, which then sold finished goods back to its colonies.

84. **D** The Mamluks were a group of Muslims who were originally trained as an elite corps in the caliph's army, beginning under the Abbasid caliphate. They were slaves until they finished training, and they had often been kidnapped as children and raised in military communities. Their military might often made them able to act as a politically powerful group, including independently controlling Egypt for several hundred years. Whether or not you know this, however, you should know that in the 1200s neither the Ottoman Empire, (B), nor Turkey, (E), existed. France, (A), was never controlled by Mamluks, nor by any Muslim people, although there were several military conflicts between the French and the Mamluks. The Abbasid caliphate, (C), created the Mamluks as a group, but despite the Abbasids' troubles in the mid-1200s, the Mamluks never controlled the caliphate itself; they ruled only a portion of it.

85. **D** The Glorious Revolution was a successful effort to overthrow King James II by William of Orange due to fear over his Catholic beliefs and those of his newly issued heir. The invasion by William and his backers was relatively peaceful and was accomplished in less than a year, making (D) the best answer (although the subsequent events that resulted from the invasion and installment of William as king did not go so smoothly). While the Glorious Revolution was instigated over concerns regarding the monarch's religion, only the American Revolution was fought to gain independence from Britain, making (A) incorrect. Only the American Revolution resulted in the reclamation of power by the general public and the formation of a democratic governing body, as both England and France maintained a monarch after their initial revolutions, so (B) is not correct. As was already stated, the Glorious Revolution was fought over religious *intolerance*, making (C) an incorrect answer. And (E) is very extreme in its statement, as evidenced by the fact that the King of France eventually lost his head as a result of the French Revolution, while the rights of Catholics were severely limited after the Glorious Revolution.

86. **E** This quotation is from the Qur'an, the holy book of Muslims. The mention of God and Adam suggests the Bible, but Christianity is not one of the answer choices. Islam and Christianity spring from a shared mythology, and the Qur'an draws upon many of the stories that appear in the Christian Bible. The ancient Greeks, (A), did not have a holy book in the sense that the Muslims and Christians had the the Qur'an and the Bible, respectively. Hinduism, (B), and Buddhism, (D), do have a collection of holy texts, none of which is really considered a holy book. We also know that Islam is a monotheistic religion. In comparison, the ancient Greek religion, the ancient Babylonian religion, (C), Hinduism, and Buddhism are all polytheistic religions that are inconsistent with the use of "God" in the quotation. Therefore, (E) is the best answer.

87. **A** Each of the incorrect answers can be demonstrated through scientific measurement and observation. Choice (A), however, requires speculation regarding the use of the object. Assuming there are no descendants of the people who created this mask, there is no reliable way for an archaeologist to prove its purpose.

88. **C** Something like a caste system, or a hereditary system of class and social role, was present in many societies throughout history, but the most common association is with ancient (Brahmanic) India, (C). Tang China, (A), often segregated artisan-class city-dwellers based on their profession and would not permit them to leave their wards, but in the non-urban environment the society was much more fluid. Medieval Europe, (B), often offered little social mobility, especially for serfs, but thanks to technological progress, urban centers, and the upheaval caused by the Black Death, mobility became possible. The Aztec Empire, (D), was divided mostly into nobility and non-nobles; originally the line was not strictly hereditary. The Aztecs did not have a fully developed caste system. The Ottoman Empire, (E), did not practice a caste system.

89. **D** In East Asia, white was the color of mourning, (D), while in Europe people in mourning wore black. In East Asia, coffin burial complete with precious objects was common for the wealthy and nobility, so you can rule out (A) and (C). Confucian and popular traditions also encouraged worship of the spirits of departed ancestors of all classes, which rules out (B). However, food was a much more common offering at grave sites than flowers in 15th-century East Asia, which eliminates (E).

90. **B** The Philippines were part of Spain's colonial holdings for more than 350 years before becoming an American colony. Vietnam, (A), was a French colony from the mid-19th century to the 1950s. The French founded settlements in southern India, (C), in the late 17th and early 18th centuries. Madagascar, (D), became a French protectorate in 1885 and a full colony in 1895–1896, but gained its independence from France in 1960. Algeria, (E), was first invaded by the French in 1830 but wouldn't fall to total French control until the early 1900s. It was a part of France until it forced the French out in 1962.

91. **A** The Islamic Golden Age was the result of the stability of the Islamic empires during this period, which permitted the transmission of Greek and Roman knowledge, (A), which had been lost in Western Europe in the chaos following the fall of the Roman Empire and the decline of the

Byzantine Empire. A peaceful environment for new original progress, (B), was important, although the caliphates are better known (perhaps unfairly) for carrying on the torch of previous thinkers than for creating new realms of thought themselves. Public-sponsored research, (C), is a creature of modern life, not of this period in history. Interstate competition, (D), would require the existence of many states, which the caliphates effectively prevented by establishing such a powerful, centralized empire. Although religious permission to experiment and explore and think was essential in the development of Islamic thought during the Golden Age, religious justification for scientific and intellectual research, (E), was not the driving force behind the importance of Islamic contributions during this period.

92. E Enkidu is the companion of Gilgamesh in the Sumerian *Epic of Gilgamesh*. Hanuman is the *vanara* (a human with monkey-like traits) who accompanies Lord Rama in the latter's rescue of Sita in the Hindu epic, the *Ramayana*. Finally, Sun Wukong is the monkey companion of the monk Xuanzang in the traditional Chinese stories constituting *Journey to the West*. Choice (A) is incorrect because only Hanuman is an Indian folkloric figure. Choice (B) is incorrect because Enkidu is not a monkey. Choice (C) is incorrect because none of these figures are major Buddhist deities. Choice (D) is incorrect because not all figures are deities—only Hanuman embodies a moral ideal.

93. E This quotation by Ho Chi Minh refers to the Vietnam War, (E). The tiger in the quotation referred to Ho's North Vietnamese guerilla army against the elephant, the American military. On paper, the American military was much stronger than the North Vietnamese, thus the elephant. But the unwillingness of the North Vietnamese to give up against the Americans convinced the United States to withdraw from Vietnam. The supposed mismatch between the elephant and the tiger would not describe either World War I, World War II, or the Iran-Iraq War, in which the battles were fought between relative equals; eliminate (B), (C), and (D). The other likely answer could be the Korean War, (A), but the elephant, the United States, did not "lose" the Korean War in the same way it lost in Vietnam.

94. D The quotation cited in the question comes from the New Testament book of Acts and describes Saul of Tarsus' religious conversion. Originally a persecutor of the follower of Jesus, Saul—called Paul, (D), after this conversion—later became instrumental in spreading Christianity around the Mediterranean world. The Apostle Peter, (A), was one of the earliest followers of Jesus and the forerunner of the popes. John the Baptist, (B), was a Jewish prophet before Jesus. Pontius Pilate, (C), was the Roman leader who had a role in Jesus' trial and crucifixion. The Disciple John, (E), is traditionally viewed as the author of the Gospel of John and the Book of Revelation (both in the Christian New Testament).

95. A These three men were all philosophers, (A), from ancient Greece, ancient China, and medieval Islamic Spain, respectively. Even if you don't recognize the other names, Plato should be enough to identify that this question is asking about philosophers. Although Zhuangzi is venerated by some religious Taoists and certainly did engage in some debate, and though Averroes was also a physician, all three men have in common their philosophical contributions to the world.

HOW TO SCORE PRACTICE TEST 2

When you take the real exam, the proctors will collect your test booklet and bubble sheet and send your answer sheet to the processing center where a computer looks at the pattern of filled-in ovals on your answer sheet and gives you a score. We couldn't include even a small computer with this book, so we are providing this more primitive way of scoring your exam.

Determining Your Score

STEP 1 Using the Answer Key at the beginning of this chapter, determine how many questions you got right and how many you got wrong on the test. Remember, questions that you do not answer don't count as either right answers or wrong answers.

STEP 2 List the number of right answers (A) here.

(A) _____

STEP 3 List the number of wrong answers (B) here and divide that number by 4. (Use a calculator if you're feeling particularly lazy.)

(B) _____ ÷ 4 = _____

STEP 4 Subtract the number of wrong answers divided by 4 from the number of correct answers. Round this score to the nearest whole number. This is your raw score.

(A) _____ − (B) _____ = (C) _____

STEP 5 To determine your real score, take (C) your raw score from Step 4 above and look it up in the left column of the Score Conversion Table on the next page; the corresponding score on the right is your score on the exam.

Practice Test 2 Score Conversion Table

Raw Score	Scaled Score	Raw Score	Scaled Score	Raw Score	Scaled Score
95	800	55	680	15	440
94	800	54	670	14	430
93	800	53	670	13	430
92	800	52	660	12	420
91	800	51	660	11	420
90	800	50	650	10	410
89	800	49	640	9	400
88	800	48	640	8	400
87	800	47	630	7	390
86	800	46	630	6	390
85	800	45	620	5	380
84	800	44	610	4	370
83	800	43	610	3	370
82	800	42	600	2	360
81	800	41	600	1	360
80	800	40	590	0	350
79	800	39	580	−1	340
78	800	38	580	−2	340
77	800	37	570	−3	330
76	800	36	570	−4	330
75	800	35	560	−5	320
74	790	34	550	−6	320
73	790	33	550	−7	310
72	780	32	540	−8	300
71	770	31	540	−9	300
70	770	30	530	−10	290
69	760	29	520	−11	290
68	760	28	520	−12	280
67	750	27	510	−13	270
66	740	26	510	−14	270
65	740	25	500	−15	260
64	730	24	490	−16	260
63	730	23	490	−17	250
62	720	22	480	−18	240
61	720	21	480	−19	240
60	710	20	470	−20	230
59	700	19	460	−21	230
58	700	18	460	−22	220
57	690	17	450	−23	210
56	690	16	450	−24	210

1.

YOUR NAME: _____
(Print)   Last   First   M.I.

SIGNÆURE: _____   DATE: ___ / ___ / ___

HOMEADDRESS: _____
(Print)   Number and Street

_____
City   State   Zip Code

PHONENO.: _____
(Print)

IMPORTANT: Please fill in these boxes exactly as shown on the back cover of your test book.

2. TEST FORM

_____

6. DATE OF BIRTH

Month	Day		Year	
○ JAN				
○ FEB	⓪	⓪	⓪	⓪
○ MAR	①	①	①	①
○ APR	②	②	②	②
○ MAY	③	③	③	③
○ JUN	④	④	④	④
○ JUL	⑤	⑤	⑤	⑤
○ AUG	⑥	⑥	⑥	⑥
○ SEP	⑦	⑦	⑦	⑦
○ OCT	⑧	⑧	⑧	⑧
○ NOV	⑨	⑨	⑨	⑨
○ DEC				

3. TEST CODE

4. REGISTRATION NUMBER

7. SEX
○ MALE
○ FEMALE

The **Princeton Review**®

FORM NO. 00001-PR

5. YOUR NAME

First 4 letters of last name | FIRST INIT | MID INIT

(Columns of bubbles A through Z)

Test 1

Start with number 1 for each new section.
If a section has fewer questions than answer spaces, leave the extra answer spaces blank.

1. Ⓐ Ⓑ Ⓒ Ⓓ Ⓔ
2. Ⓐ Ⓑ Ⓒ Ⓓ Ⓔ
3. Ⓐ Ⓑ Ⓒ Ⓓ Ⓔ
4. Ⓐ Ⓑ Ⓒ Ⓓ Ⓔ
5. Ⓐ Ⓑ Ⓒ Ⓓ Ⓔ
6. Ⓐ Ⓑ Ⓒ Ⓓ Ⓔ
7. Ⓐ Ⓑ Ⓒ Ⓓ Ⓔ
8. Ⓐ Ⓑ Ⓒ Ⓓ Ⓔ
9. Ⓐ Ⓑ Ⓒ Ⓓ Ⓔ
10. Ⓐ Ⓑ Ⓒ Ⓓ Ⓔ
11. Ⓐ Ⓑ Ⓒ Ⓓ Ⓔ
12. Ⓐ Ⓑ Ⓒ Ⓓ Ⓔ
13. Ⓐ Ⓑ Ⓒ Ⓓ Ⓔ
14. Ⓐ Ⓑ Ⓒ Ⓓ Ⓔ
15. Ⓐ Ⓑ Ⓒ Ⓓ Ⓔ
16. Ⓐ Ⓑ Ⓒ Ⓓ Ⓔ
17. Ⓐ Ⓑ Ⓒ Ⓓ Ⓔ
18. Ⓐ Ⓑ Ⓒ Ⓓ Ⓔ
19. Ⓐ Ⓑ Ⓒ Ⓓ Ⓔ
20. Ⓐ Ⓑ Ⓒ Ⓓ Ⓔ
21. Ⓐ Ⓑ Ⓒ Ⓓ Ⓔ
22. Ⓐ Ⓑ Ⓒ Ⓓ Ⓔ
23. Ⓐ Ⓑ Ⓒ Ⓓ Ⓔ
24. Ⓐ Ⓑ Ⓒ Ⓓ Ⓔ
25. Ⓐ Ⓑ Ⓒ Ⓓ Ⓔ
26. Ⓐ Ⓑ Ⓒ Ⓓ Ⓔ
27. Ⓐ Ⓑ Ⓒ Ⓓ Ⓔ
28. Ⓐ Ⓑ Ⓒ Ⓓ Ⓔ
29. Ⓐ Ⓑ Ⓒ Ⓓ Ⓔ
30. Ⓐ Ⓑ Ⓒ Ⓓ Ⓔ

31. Ⓐ Ⓑ Ⓒ Ⓓ Ⓔ
32. Ⓐ Ⓑ Ⓒ Ⓓ Ⓔ
33. Ⓐ Ⓑ Ⓒ Ⓓ Ⓔ
34. Ⓐ Ⓑ Ⓒ Ⓓ Ⓔ
35. Ⓐ Ⓑ Ⓒ Ⓓ Ⓔ
36. Ⓐ Ⓑ Ⓒ Ⓓ Ⓔ
37. Ⓐ Ⓑ Ⓒ Ⓓ Ⓔ
38. Ⓐ Ⓑ Ⓒ Ⓓ Ⓔ
39. Ⓐ Ⓑ Ⓒ Ⓓ Ⓔ
40. Ⓐ Ⓑ Ⓒ Ⓓ Ⓔ
41. Ⓐ Ⓑ Ⓒ Ⓓ Ⓔ
42. Ⓐ Ⓑ Ⓒ Ⓓ Ⓔ
43. Ⓐ Ⓑ Ⓒ Ⓓ Ⓔ
44. Ⓐ Ⓑ Ⓒ Ⓓ Ⓔ
45. Ⓐ Ⓑ Ⓒ Ⓓ Ⓔ
46. Ⓐ Ⓑ Ⓒ Ⓓ Ⓔ
47. Ⓐ Ⓑ Ⓒ Ⓓ Ⓔ
48. Ⓐ Ⓑ Ⓒ Ⓓ Ⓔ
49. Ⓐ Ⓑ Ⓒ Ⓓ Ⓔ
50. Ⓐ Ⓑ Ⓒ Ⓓ Ⓔ
51. Ⓐ Ⓑ Ⓒ Ⓓ Ⓔ
52. Ⓐ Ⓑ Ⓒ Ⓓ Ⓔ
53. Ⓐ Ⓑ Ⓒ Ⓓ Ⓔ
54. Ⓐ Ⓑ Ⓒ Ⓓ Ⓔ
55. Ⓐ Ⓑ Ⓒ Ⓓ Ⓔ
56. Ⓐ Ⓑ Ⓒ Ⓓ Ⓔ
57. Ⓐ Ⓑ Ⓒ Ⓓ Ⓔ
58. Ⓐ Ⓑ Ⓒ Ⓓ Ⓔ
59. Ⓐ Ⓑ Ⓒ Ⓓ Ⓔ
60. Ⓐ Ⓑ Ⓒ Ⓓ Ⓔ

61. Ⓐ Ⓑ Ⓒ Ⓓ Ⓔ
62. Ⓐ Ⓑ Ⓒ Ⓓ Ⓔ
63. Ⓐ Ⓑ Ⓒ Ⓓ Ⓔ
64. Ⓐ Ⓑ Ⓒ Ⓓ Ⓔ
65. Ⓐ Ⓑ Ⓒ Ⓓ Ⓔ
66. Ⓐ Ⓑ Ⓒ Ⓓ Ⓔ
67. Ⓐ Ⓑ Ⓒ Ⓓ Ⓔ
68. Ⓐ Ⓑ Ⓒ Ⓓ Ⓔ
69. Ⓐ Ⓑ Ⓒ Ⓓ Ⓔ
70. Ⓐ Ⓑ Ⓒ Ⓓ Ⓔ
71. Ⓐ Ⓑ Ⓒ Ⓓ Ⓔ
72. Ⓐ Ⓑ Ⓒ Ⓓ Ⓔ
73. Ⓐ Ⓑ Ⓒ Ⓓ Ⓔ
74. Ⓐ Ⓑ Ⓒ Ⓓ Ⓔ
75. Ⓐ Ⓑ Ⓒ Ⓓ Ⓔ
76. Ⓐ Ⓑ Ⓒ Ⓓ Ⓔ
77. Ⓐ Ⓑ Ⓒ Ⓓ Ⓔ
78. Ⓐ Ⓑ Ⓒ Ⓓ Ⓔ
79. Ⓐ Ⓑ Ⓒ Ⓓ Ⓔ
80. Ⓐ Ⓑ Ⓒ Ⓓ Ⓔ
81. Ⓐ Ⓑ Ⓒ Ⓓ Ⓔ
82. Ⓐ Ⓑ Ⓒ Ⓓ Ⓔ
83. Ⓐ Ⓑ Ⓒ Ⓓ Ⓔ
84. Ⓐ Ⓑ Ⓒ Ⓓ Ⓔ
85. Ⓐ Ⓑ Ⓒ Ⓓ Ⓔ
86. Ⓐ Ⓑ Ⓒ Ⓓ Ⓔ
87. Ⓐ Ⓑ Ⓒ Ⓓ Ⓔ
88. Ⓐ Ⓑ Ⓒ Ⓓ Ⓔ
89. Ⓐ Ⓑ Ⓒ Ⓓ Ⓔ
90. Ⓐ Ⓑ Ⓒ Ⓓ Ⓔ

91. Ⓐ Ⓑ Ⓒ Ⓓ Ⓔ
92. Ⓐ Ⓑ Ⓒ Ⓓ Ⓔ
93. Ⓐ Ⓑ Ⓒ Ⓓ Ⓔ
94. Ⓐ Ⓑ Ⓒ Ⓓ Ⓔ
95. Ⓐ Ⓑ Ⓒ Ⓓ Ⓔ

Completely darken bubbles with a No. 2 pencil. If you make a mistake, be sure to erase mark completely. Erase all stray marks.

1.

YOUR NAME: _____
(Print)   Last   First   M.I.

SIGNATURE: _____   **DATE:** ___ / ___ / ___

HOMEADDRESS: _____
(Print)   Number and Street

_____
City   State   Zip Code

PHONE NO.: _____
(Print)

IMPORTANT: Please fill in these boxes exactly as shown on the back cover of your test book.

2. TEST FORM
_____

6. DATE OF BIRTH

Month	Day		Year	
○ JAN				
○ FEB	⓪	⓪	⓪	⓪
○ MAR	①	①	①	①
○ APR	②	②	②	②
○ MAY	③	③	③	③
○ JUN	④	④	④	④
○ JUL	⑤	⑤	⑤	⑤
○ AUG	⑥	⑥	⑥	⑥
○ SEP	⑦	⑦	⑦	⑦
○ OCT	⑧	⑧	⑧	⑧
○ NOV	⑨	⑨	⑨	⑨
○ DEC				

3. TEST CODE

4. REGISTRATION NUMBER

7. SEX
○ MALE
○ FEMALE

The **Princeton Review®**

FORM NO. 00001-PR

5. YOUR NAME

First 4 letters of last name				FIRST INIT	MID INIT

(Bubble columns A–Z for each letter)

Test 2

Start with number 1 for each new section.
If a section has fewer questions than answer spaces, leave the extra answer spaces blank.

1. Ⓐ Ⓑ Ⓒ Ⓓ Ⓔ
2. Ⓐ Ⓑ Ⓒ Ⓓ Ⓔ
3. Ⓐ Ⓑ Ⓒ Ⓓ Ⓔ
4. Ⓐ Ⓑ Ⓒ Ⓓ Ⓔ
5. Ⓐ Ⓑ Ⓒ Ⓓ Ⓔ
6. Ⓐ Ⓑ Ⓒ Ⓓ Ⓔ
7. Ⓐ Ⓑ Ⓒ Ⓓ Ⓔ
8. Ⓐ Ⓑ Ⓒ Ⓓ Ⓔ
9. Ⓐ Ⓑ Ⓒ Ⓓ Ⓔ
10. Ⓐ Ⓑ Ⓒ Ⓓ Ⓔ
11. Ⓐ Ⓑ Ⓒ Ⓓ Ⓔ
12. Ⓐ Ⓑ Ⓒ Ⓓ Ⓔ
13. Ⓐ Ⓑ Ⓒ Ⓓ Ⓔ
14. Ⓐ Ⓑ Ⓒ Ⓓ Ⓔ
15. Ⓐ Ⓑ Ⓒ Ⓓ Ⓔ
16. Ⓐ Ⓑ Ⓒ Ⓓ Ⓔ
17. Ⓐ Ⓑ Ⓒ Ⓓ Ⓔ
18. Ⓐ Ⓑ Ⓒ Ⓓ Ⓔ
19. Ⓐ Ⓑ Ⓒ Ⓓ Ⓔ
20. Ⓐ Ⓑ Ⓒ Ⓓ Ⓔ
21. Ⓐ Ⓑ Ⓒ Ⓓ Ⓔ
22. Ⓐ Ⓑ Ⓒ Ⓓ Ⓔ
23. Ⓐ Ⓑ Ⓒ Ⓓ Ⓔ
24. Ⓐ Ⓑ Ⓒ Ⓓ Ⓔ
25. Ⓐ Ⓑ Ⓒ Ⓓ Ⓔ
26. Ⓐ Ⓑ Ⓒ Ⓓ Ⓔ
27. Ⓐ Ⓑ Ⓒ Ⓓ Ⓔ
28. Ⓐ Ⓑ Ⓒ Ⓓ Ⓔ
29. Ⓐ Ⓑ Ⓒ Ⓓ Ⓔ
30. Ⓐ Ⓑ Ⓒ Ⓓ Ⓔ

31. Ⓐ Ⓑ Ⓒ Ⓓ Ⓔ
32. Ⓐ Ⓑ Ⓒ Ⓓ Ⓔ
33. Ⓐ Ⓑ Ⓒ Ⓓ Ⓔ
34. Ⓐ Ⓑ Ⓒ Ⓓ Ⓔ
35. Ⓐ Ⓑ Ⓒ Ⓓ Ⓔ
36. Ⓐ Ⓑ Ⓒ Ⓓ Ⓔ
37. Ⓐ Ⓑ Ⓒ Ⓓ Ⓔ
38. Ⓐ Ⓑ Ⓒ Ⓓ Ⓔ
39. Ⓐ Ⓑ Ⓒ Ⓓ Ⓔ
40. Ⓐ Ⓑ Ⓒ Ⓓ Ⓔ
41. Ⓐ Ⓑ Ⓒ Ⓓ Ⓔ
42. Ⓐ Ⓑ Ⓒ Ⓓ Ⓔ
43. Ⓐ Ⓑ Ⓒ Ⓓ Ⓔ
44. Ⓐ Ⓑ Ⓒ Ⓓ Ⓔ
45. Ⓐ Ⓑ Ⓒ Ⓓ Ⓔ
46. Ⓐ Ⓑ Ⓒ Ⓓ Ⓔ
47. Ⓐ Ⓑ Ⓒ Ⓓ Ⓔ
48. Ⓐ Ⓑ Ⓒ Ⓓ Ⓔ
49. Ⓐ Ⓑ Ⓒ Ⓓ Ⓔ
50. Ⓐ Ⓑ Ⓒ Ⓓ Ⓔ
51. Ⓐ Ⓑ Ⓒ Ⓓ Ⓔ
52. Ⓐ Ⓑ Ⓒ Ⓓ Ⓔ
53. Ⓐ Ⓑ Ⓒ Ⓓ Ⓔ
54. Ⓐ Ⓑ Ⓒ Ⓓ Ⓔ
55. Ⓐ Ⓑ Ⓒ Ⓓ Ⓔ
56. Ⓐ Ⓑ Ⓒ Ⓓ Ⓔ
57. Ⓐ Ⓑ Ⓒ Ⓓ Ⓔ
58. Ⓐ Ⓑ Ⓒ Ⓓ Ⓔ
59. Ⓐ Ⓑ Ⓒ Ⓓ Ⓔ
60. Ⓐ Ⓑ Ⓒ Ⓓ Ⓔ

61. Ⓐ Ⓑ Ⓒ Ⓓ Ⓔ
62. Ⓐ Ⓑ Ⓒ Ⓓ Ⓔ
63. Ⓐ Ⓑ Ⓒ Ⓓ Ⓔ
64. Ⓐ Ⓑ Ⓒ Ⓓ Ⓔ
65. Ⓐ Ⓑ Ⓒ Ⓓ Ⓔ
66. Ⓐ Ⓑ Ⓒ Ⓓ Ⓔ
67. Ⓐ Ⓑ Ⓒ Ⓓ Ⓔ
68. Ⓐ Ⓑ Ⓒ Ⓓ Ⓔ
69. Ⓐ Ⓑ Ⓒ Ⓓ Ⓔ
70. Ⓐ Ⓑ Ⓒ Ⓓ Ⓔ
71. Ⓐ Ⓑ Ⓒ Ⓓ Ⓔ
72. Ⓐ Ⓑ Ⓒ Ⓓ Ⓔ
73. Ⓐ Ⓑ Ⓒ Ⓓ Ⓔ
74. Ⓐ Ⓑ Ⓒ Ⓓ Ⓔ
75. Ⓐ Ⓑ Ⓒ Ⓓ Ⓔ
76. Ⓐ Ⓑ Ⓒ Ⓓ Ⓔ
77. Ⓐ Ⓑ Ⓒ Ⓓ Ⓔ
78. Ⓐ Ⓑ Ⓒ Ⓓ Ⓔ
79. Ⓐ Ⓑ Ⓒ Ⓓ Ⓔ
80. Ⓐ Ⓑ Ⓒ Ⓓ Ⓔ
81. Ⓐ Ⓑ Ⓒ Ⓓ Ⓔ
82. Ⓐ Ⓑ Ⓒ Ⓓ Ⓔ
83. Ⓐ Ⓑ Ⓒ Ⓓ Ⓔ
84. Ⓐ Ⓑ Ⓒ Ⓓ Ⓔ
85. Ⓐ Ⓑ Ⓒ Ⓓ Ⓔ
86. Ⓐ Ⓑ Ⓒ Ⓓ Ⓔ
87. Ⓐ Ⓑ Ⓒ Ⓓ Ⓔ
88. Ⓐ Ⓑ Ⓒ Ⓓ Ⓔ
89. Ⓐ Ⓑ Ⓒ Ⓓ Ⓔ
90. Ⓐ Ⓑ Ⓒ Ⓓ Ⓔ

91. Ⓐ Ⓑ Ⓒ Ⓓ Ⓔ
92. Ⓐ Ⓑ Ⓒ Ⓓ Ⓔ
93. Ⓐ Ⓑ Ⓒ Ⓓ Ⓔ
94. Ⓐ Ⓑ Ⓒ Ⓓ Ⓔ
95. Ⓐ Ⓑ Ⓒ Ⓓ Ⓔ

NOTES

NOTES

NOTES

International Offices Listing

China (Beijing)
1501 Building A,
Disanji Creative Zone,
No.66 West Section of North 4th Ring Road Beijing
Tel: +86-10-62684481/2/3
Email: tprkor01@chol.com
Website: www.tprbeijing.com

China (Shanghai)
1010 Kaixuan Road
Building B, 5/F
Changning District, Shanghai, China 200052
Sara Beattie, Owner: Email: sbeattie@sarabeattie.com
Tel: +86-21-5108-2798
Fax: +86-21-6386-1039
Website: www.princetonreviewshanghai.com

Hong Kong
5th Floor, Yardley Commercial Building
1-6 Connaught Road West, Sheung Wan, Hong Kong
(MTR Exit C)
Sara Beattie, Owner: Email: sbeattie@sarabeattie.com
Tel: +852-2507-9380
Fax: +852-2827-4630
Website: www.princetonreviewhk.com

India (Mumbai)
Score Plus Academy
Office No.15, Fifth Floor
Manek Mahal 90
Veer Nariman Road
Next to Hotel Ambassador
Churchgate, Mumbai 400020
Maharashtra, India
Ritu Kalwani: Email: director@score-plus.com
Tel: + 91 22 22846801 / 39 / 41
Website: www.score-plus.com

India (New Delhi)
South Extension
K-16, Upper Ground Floor
South Extension Part–1,
New Delhi-110049
Aradhana Mahna: aradhana@manyagroup.com
Monisha Banerjee: monisha@manyagroup.com
Ruchi Tomar: ruchi.tomar@manyagroup.com
Rishi Josan: Rishi.josan@manyagroup.com
Vishal Goswamy: vishal.goswamy@manyagroup.com
Tel: +91-11-64501603/ 4, +91-11-65028379
Website: www.manyagroup.com

Lebanon
463 Bliss Street
AlFarra Building - 2nd floor
Ras Beirut
Beirut, Lebanon
Hassan Coudsi: Email: hassan.coudsi@review.com
Tel: +961-1-367-688
Website: www.princetonreviewlebanon.com

Korea
945-25 Young Shin Building
25 Daechi-Dong, Kangnam-gu
Seoul, Korea 135-280
Yong-Hoon Lee: Email: TPRKor01@chollian.net
In-Woo Kim: Email: iwkim@tpr.co.kr
Tel: + 82-2-554-7762
Fax: +82-2-453-9466
Website: www.tpr.co.kr

Kuwait
ScorePlus Learning Center
Salmiyah Block 3, Street 2 Building 14
Post Box: 559, Zip 1306, Safat, Kuwait
Email: infokuwait@score-plus.com
Tel: +965-25-75-48-02 / 8
Fax: +965-25-75-46-02
Website: www.scorepluseducation.com

Malaysia
Sara Beattie MDC Sdn Bhd
Suites 18E & 18F
18th Floor
Gurney Tower, Persiaran Gurney
Penang, Malaysia
Email: tprkl.my@sarabeattie.com
Sara Beattie, Owner: Email: sbeattie@sarabeattie.com
Tel: +604-2104 333
Fax: +604-2104 330
Website: www.princetonreviewKL.com

Mexico
TPR México
Guanajuato No. 242 Piso 1 Interior 1
Col. Roma Norte
México D.F., C.P.06700
registro@princetonreviewmexico.com
Tel: +52-55-5255-4495
+52-55-5255-4440
+52-55-5255-4442
Website: www.princetonreviewmexico.com

Qatar
Score Plus
Office No: 1A, Al Kuwari (Damas)
Building near Merweb Hotel, Al Saad
Post Box: 2408, Doha, Qatar
Email: infoqatar@score-plus.com
Tel: +974 44 36 8580, +974 526 5032
Fax: +974 44 13 1995
Website: www.scorepluseducation.com

Taiwan
The Princeton Review Taiwan
2F, 169 Zhong Xiao East Road, Section 4
Taipei, Taiwan 10690
Lisa Bartle (Owner): lbartle@princetonreview.com.tw
Tel: +886-2-2751-1293
Fax: +886-2-2776-3201
Website: www.PrincetonReview.com.tw

Thailand
The Princeton Review Thailand
Sathorn Nakorn Tower, 28th floor
100 North Sathorn Road
Bangkok, Thailand 10500
Thavida Bijayendrayodhin (Chairman)
Email: thavida@princetonreviewthailand.com
Mitsara Bijayendrayodhin (Managing Director)
Email: mitsara@princetonreviewthailand.com
Tel: +662-636-6770
Fax: +662-636-6776
Website: www.princetonreviewthailand.com

Turkey
Yeni Sülün Sokak No. 28
Levent, Istanbul, 34330, Turkey
Nuri Ozgur: nuri@tprturkey.com
Rona Ozgur: rona@tprturkey.com
Iren Ozgur: iren@tprturkey.com
Tel: +90-212-324-4747
Fax: +90-212-324-3347
Website: www.tprturkey.com

UAE
Emirates Score Plus
Office No: 506, Fifth Floor
Sultan Business Center
Near Lamcy Plaza, 21 Oud Metha Road
Post Box: 44098, Dubai
United Arab Emirates
Hukumat Kalwani: skoreplus@gmail.com
Ritu Kalwani: director@score-plus.com
Email: info@score-plus.com
Tel: +971-4-334-0004
Fax: +971-4-334-0222
Website: www.princetonreviewuae.com

Our International Partners

The Princeton Review also runs courses with a variety of partners in Africa, Asia, Europe, and South America.

Georgia
LEAF American-Georgian Education Center
www.leaf.ge

Mongolia
English Academy of Mongolia
www.nyescm.org

Nigeria
The Know Place
www.knowplace.com.ng

Panama
Academia Interamericana de Panama
http://aip.edu.pa/

Switzerland
Institut Le Rosey
http://www.rosey.ch/

All other inquiries, please email us at
internationalsupport@review.com